SAMS
Teach
Yourself

Macromedia®
Flash® 8

in 24 Hours

Phillip Kerman

SAMS *800 East 96th Street, Indianapolis, Indiana, 46240 USA*

Sams Teach Yourself Macromedia Flash 8 in 24 Hours

International Standard Book Number: 0-672-32754-6

Library of Congress Catalog Card Number: 2004097758

Printed in the United States of America

First Printing: October 2005

08   07   06   05   4   3   2   1

Trademarks

All terms mentioned in this book that are known to be trademarks or service marks have been appropriately capitalized. Sams Publishing cannot attest to the accuracy of this information. Use of a term in this book should not be regarded as affecting the validity of any trademark or service mark.

Warning and Disclaimer

Every effort has been made to make this book as complete and as accurate as possible, but no warranty or fitness is implied. The information provided is on an "as is" basis. The author and the publisher shall have neither liability nor responsibility to any person or entity with respect to any loss or damages arising from the information contained in this book.

Bulk Sales

Sams Publishing offers excellent discounts on this book when ordered in quantity for bulk purchases or special sales. For more information, please contact

U.S. Corporate and Government Sales

1-800-382-3419

corpsales@pearsontechgroup.com

For sales outside of the U.S., please contact

International Sales

international@pearsoned.com

Acquisitions Editor
Betsy Brown

Development Editor
Damon Jordan

Managing Editor
Charlotte Clapp

Senior Project Editor
Matthew Purcell

Indexer
Ken Johnson

Proofreader
Tracy Donhardt

Technical Editor
Brandon Houston

Publishing Coordinator
Vanessa Evans

Multimedia Developer
Dan Scherf

Designer
Gary Adair

Page Layout
Bronkella Publishing

Contents at a Glance

Part IV: Putting It All Together for the Web

Part V: Appendixes

Table of Contents

Sams Teach Yourself Macromedia Flash 8 in 24 Hours

About the Author

Phillip Kerman is an independent programmer, teacher, and writer who specializes in Macromedia products. His degree in imaging and photographic technology from the Rochester Institute of Technology was earned back when "multimedia" had a different meaning than it has today. One of Phillip's internships, for example, involved programming multiple slide projector presentations with dissolves synchronized to a sound track—the multimedia of the 1980s. In 1993 he found Macromedia Authorware a natural fit for his interests and skills. After getting his start at The Human Element, Inc., he moved back to Portland, Oregon, to work on his own.

Phillip has transitioned his expertise from Authorware to Director and, now, to Flash. Over the past decade, he has had to adapt to more than 20 version upgrades—Flash 8 being the most significant of them all! In addition to retooling and building his own skills, Phillip finds teaching the biggest challenge. He has trained and made presentations around the world, in such exotic locations as Reykjavik, Iceland; Melbourne, Australia; Amsterdam, Holland; and McAlester, Oklahoma. His writing has appeared in *Macworld*, on the Macromedia DevNet website and *Developer Resource Kit* CD-ROM, and in his self-published *The Phillip Newsletter* (www.phillipkerman.com/newsletter).

Phillip is also the author of *Macromedia Flash @work, Flash MX 2004 for Rich Internet Applications,* and *ActionScripting in Flash MX* from New Riders Publishing.

Feel free to email Phillip at flash8@phillipkerman.com.

Dedication

Dedicated to my late grandfather, David A. Boehm, who inspired and supported me in addition to sharing countless books with the world. And to my wife, Diana, who listens, motivates, and challenges me, and whom I love.

Acknowledgments

Most successful feats involve the efforts of many people. This book is no exception. I'm proud of the result, but I can't take full credit. Here is my attempt to acknowledge everyone.

First, I'd like to thank the people at Sams Publishing. When Randi Roger approached me, not only did she provide the faith that I could write this book but also stressed the support I would receive from Sams Publishing. She wasn't exaggerating. The following people were professional and prompted me every step of the way: Betsy Brown, Lynn Baus, Brandon Houston, Jeff Schultz, Amy Patton, Carol Bowers, Mark Taber, Kate Small, Matt Purcell, Brandon Houston, Vanessa Evans, and Damon Jordan, who as development editor made this book flow—plus all the editors listed in the front of this book. When you look at other Sams books, you'll see many of these people acknowledged for a reason—they are great!

Macromedia is the most approachable software company I know. Without the following current and former Macromedia employees (and countless others whom I can't name), this book wouldn't be what it is (nor would Flash be the product that it is):

Jeremy Allaire, Waleed Anbar, Luke Bayes, Brad Bechtel, Matt Bendiksen, Doug Benson, Paul Betlem, Jody Bleyle, Greg Burch, Julee Burdekin, Damian Burns, Kent Carlson, Morena Carvalho, Mike Chambers, Jennifer Chan, Francis Cheng, Jeremy Clark, Henriette Cohn, Karen Cook, Jim Corbett, Kelly Cunningham, Jen deHaan, Thais Derich, Rob Dixon, Aaron Dolberg, John Dowdell, Joel Dreskin, Mike Downey, Daniel Dura, Ken Eckey, Allen Ellison, Troy Evans, Vera Fleischer, Mally Gardiner, Jonathan Gay, Craig Goodman, Peter Grandmaison, Gary Grossman, Giacomo "Peidi" Guilizzoni, Rebekah Hash, Emmy Huang, Barbara Herbert, Chris Hock, Jeff Kamerer, Forest Key, Lily Khong, San Khong, Sang Kim, Sean Kranzberg, Kit Kwan, Carol Linburn, Jared Loftus, Kevin Lynch, Sasha Magee,

Ethan Malasky, Sheila McGinn, David Mendels, Michael Montagna, Jeff Mott, Tony Mowatt, Eric Mueller, Erica Norton, Chris Nuuja, Masanori Oba, Nigel Pegg, Bill Perry, Krishna Prathab, Abdul Qabiz, Shimi Rahim, Nivesh Rajbhandari, Supriya Rao, Thomas Reilly, Erin Rosenthal, Robert Sandie, Peter Santangeli, Sharon Selden, Mark Schroeder, Werner Sharp, Mark Shepherd, Michelle Sintov, Ed Skwarecki, Tim Statler, Edwin Smith, Tracy Stampfli, Rebecca Sun, Joan Tan, Christopher Thilgen, Pradeepa Thoma, Lee Thomason, Mike Tilburg, Tinic Uro, Chris Walcott, Michael Williams, Eric J. Wittman, Matt Wobensmith, Edwin Wong, Greg Yachuk, Lisa Young, Jody Zhang, Alan Musselman, Scott Unterberg, Tomas van der Haase, Pranav Verma, Jethro Villegas, Peter Von Dem Hagen, and Suketu Vyas.

There are countless correspondents with whom I've learned a lot about Flash. Instead of naming several and inadvertently neglecting many, let me just say that participating in local user groups and online forums is a great way to expand your knowledge and build your business—they've helped me and helped this book. Of all the places I've learned about Flash, being in the classroom, teaching, has probably been the most educational for me. The students and staff of the Northwest Academy, Pacific Northwest College of Art and Portland Community College deserve special recognition.

We Want to Hear from You!

As the reader of this book, *you* are our most important critic and commentator. We value your opinion and want to know what we're doing right, what we could do better, what areas you'd like to see us publish in, and any other words of wisdom you're willing to pass our way.

You can email or write me directly to let me know what you did or didn't like about this book—as well as what we can do to make our books stronger.

Please note that I cannot help you with technical problems related to the topic of this book, and that due to the high volume of mail I receive, I might not be able to reply to every message.

When you write, please be sure to include this book's title and author as well as your name and phone or email address. I will carefully review your comments and share them with the author and editors who worked on the book.

Email: graphics@samspublishing.com

Mail: Mark Taber
         Associate Publisher
         Sams Publishing
         800 East 96th Street
         Indianapolis, IN 46240 USA

Reader Services

For more information about this book or another Sams Publishing title, visit our website at www.samspublishing.com. Type the ISBN (excluding hyphens) or the title of a book in the Search field to find the page you're looking for.

Introduction

Macromedia is not exaggerating when it says that Flash is "the professional standard for producing high-impact web experiences." You only need to visit a few sites that use Flash to understand how compelling it is. Using graphics, animation, sound, and interactivity, Flash can excite, teach, entertain, and provide practical information.

More than half a billion users already have the free Flash player (which is needed to view Flash movies). The fact that Macromedia continues to distribute this software so effectively means that the potential audience for Flash content is huge and continues to grow. Also, the fact Adobe decided to acquire Macromedia is due to Flash's enormous success.

The tools needed to create Flash movies are within your reach. After you purchase Flash, the only investment you need to make is time learning. You can even download Flash from www.macromedia.com and use it for 30 days before having to purchase it. It's exciting to watch people go from fiddling with Flash to making entertaining movies. Imagine a great musician picking up and learning an instrument in a matter of days. It really is that amazing. If you're motivated, with just a moderate time investment, you'll feel as though a powerful communication tool has been given to you.

Flash is so unique that sometimes the less experience you have, the better. If you have preconceived ideas about what Flash is or how you're supposed to use drawing tools, it might be best to try to forget everything and start fresh. This book is organized in such a way that you should start seeing successes quickly. With each task, you'll prove to yourself that you're acquiring knowledge and skills.

I don't need to give you a pep talk because you'll see for yourself. In just a few one-hour lessons, you'll be creating drawings that you may have thought you weren't capable of. After that, in a few more hours, you'll be making animations. Finally, after 24 one-hour lessons, you'll be unstoppable. I know this. I've taught Flash to hundreds of students, and invariably even those who don't have fire in their eyes at first will recognize the power Flash has given them and that they can hone their Flash skills over time. Where you take your skills is up to you, but you'll get a great foundation here.

You may not feel like a pro overnight, but you will feel that you have a powerful communication tool in your control. When you can't wait to show others your creations, you'll know you're on your way. Get ready to have some fun.

PART I

Assembling the Graphics You'll Animate in Flash

HOUR 1

Basics

What You'll Learn in This Hour:

- ▶ How easily and quickly you can draw and make an animation
- ▶ How to use Flash's workspace
- ▶ How to organize and use panels
- ▶ How the Properties panel constantly changes to show you important information
- ▶ The common file types related to Flash

The Flash environment is deceptively simple. With it, you can get started drawing and animating right away. However, Flash might not act the way you expect it to.

To make sure you get off on the right foot, it pays to first cover some basics. Although Flash is consistent with other types of software in several ways, there are many more ways in which Flash is different. Experienced users and novices alike should understand the basics covered this hour.

Panels are special tools in Flash that give you access to see and change most any setting while editing a file. The Properties panel is the most useful panel because it automatically changes as needed. For example, when you select text, the Properties panel allows you to change the font style and size.

Jump Right In

It's actually possible to learn to make a Flash animation in a matter of seconds! Although the following task doesn't cover all there is to learn, it should prove to you that it's possible to get rolling with Flash very fast.

▼ **Try It Yourself**

Make an Animation in 30 Seconds

Just to prove that it can be easy, in this task you'll make a simple animation in a matter of seconds. Follow these steps:

1. Open Flash 8 and select Flash Document from the Create New column of Flash's start page. You see a large white square in the center of your screen (it's called the *Stage*). (If the start page wasn't initially visible, simply select File, New to open the New Document dialog box, select Flash Document from the General tab, and click OK.)

2. Press the R key to turn your cursor into a Rectangle tool. When you do this, you should notice that the Rectangle tool becomes active in the Tools panel on the left.

3. On the left side of the Stage, click and drag down to the right to draw a medium-sized rectangle. This will be how your animation begins.

4. Make sure that the Timeline panel is visible; if it is not, you can press the Timeline button above the top left of your Stage or select Window, Timeline. The frames in the Timeline are numbered. Click the cell directly under Frame 20; then press F7 to insert a blank keyframe. This is where you will draw how you want the animation to appear at Frame 20 (see Figure 1.1).

FIGURE 1.1
After selecting Frame 20 in the Timeline, you insert a blank keyframe by pressing F7.

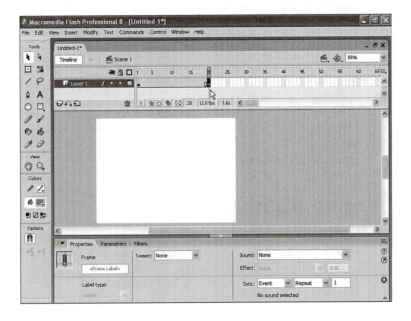

▼

5. Now press the O key to turn the cursor into an Oval tool. Click on the right side of the Stage and drag to draw a medium-sized oval.

6. Finally, return to Frame 1 (where the animation will begin) by clicking the dot underneath the 1 (for Frame 1) in the Timeline. (That dot represents a keyframe that has content—your rectangle.)

7. Make sure the Properties panel is visible; if it is not, select Window, Properties, Properties. Because the Properties panel changes based on what's selected, you should see properties for Frame 1 (because that's the last thing you clicked). If the Properties panel doesn't look like Figure 1.2, click once on the dot underneath Frame 1 in the Timeline. Finally, select Shape from the Tween drop-down menu on the Properties panel. That's it!

FIGURE 1.2
When a frame is selected, the Properties panel appears as shown here.

8. To view your animation, simply press the Enter key.

Of course you'll learn much more about making animations, but it's almost scary how easy it is to create the one in the preceding task. In a way, this is what makes Flash so challenging—you can see success quickly, but then it's easy to get carried away and neglect to learn the basics. This book concentrates on the foundational skills necessary so you can grow on your own. Don't worry—it will be fun. It's just best to get the basics first.

If you're using a Macintosh, you'll be happy to know that Flash on a Macintosh is nearly identical to the Windows version. Macintosh keyboards are different from Windows keyboards, though, so use the following legend to translate keyboard commands from Windows:

Windows Key	Macintosh Key
Ctrl	Command (the apple icon key)
Alt	Option
Right-click	control+click

For example, if you see in this book Ctrl+X, on a Macintosh you just use Command+X.

The function keys (such as F8) are the same in Windows and Macintosh. Finally, if you are on a Macintosh and have a third-party mouse that includes a right button, you should program it to invoke the control key.

Getting Your Bearings

The key to understanding Flash is always knowing where you are. You're given the power to edit everything: static graphics, animations, buttons, and more. At all times, you need to be conscious of what you're currently editing. It's easy to become disoriented about exactly what element you're working on. This section helps you get your bearings.

Let's take a quick tour of the Flash workspace:

▶ The Stage is the visual workspace. Any graphics placed in this area will be visible to the user.

▶ The Tools panel contains all the many drawing tools in Flash, including more that you can add later (by selecting Edit, Customize Tools Panel). The Flash tools are covered in depth in Hour 2, "Drawing and Painting Original Art in Flash."

▶ The Timeline contains the sequence of images that make an animation. The Timeline can also include many layers of animations. This way, certain graphics can appear above or below others, and you can have several animations playing simultaneously.

▶ Panels are "docked" next to other panels around the outside of the Stage. Alternatively, you can undock them so that they appear to float above everything else. You can also group two or more floating panels together. (On a Macintosh, the panels always float and can be grouped together; they just can't be docked to the Stage.) Basically, you can organize panels to suit your work style.

User is a general term that refers to the person watching your movie or visiting your website. Within this book, I refer to the user frequently. Occasionally, I call the user the *audience*. I've even heard the user referred to as the *witness*. It really doesn't matter which term you use—just realize that there's you (the author, creator, designer) and then there's the user (or audience, witness, or whatever term you like). As the author, you'll be able to make edits to the Flash movie, whereas the user can only watch and interact with the movie.

The Stage

The large white rectangle in the center of Flash's workspace is called the *Stage*. Text, graphics, photos—anything the user sees—goes on the Stage (see Figure 1.3).

Tools   Timeline   Panels (docked)

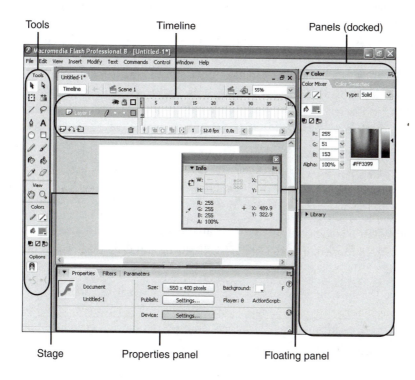

Stage   Properties panel   Floating panel

FIGURE 1.3
The Stage is the large white box in the center. All the visual components of an animation are placed on the Stage.

Think of the Stage as the canvas on which a painter paints or the frame in which a photographer composes pictures. Sometimes you'll want a graphic to begin outside the Stage and then animate onto the Stage. Off the Stage is the gray area around the outside of the white area. You can see the "off Stage" area only when the View menu shows a check mark next to Work Area. The default setting (Work Area checked) is preferable because it means that you can position graphics off the Stage. Realize, however, that any changes you make to the View menu affect only what you see. Changes here have no effect on what the user sees.

There's not too much to learn about the Stage—it's simply your visual workspace. However, two important concepts are worth covering now: Stage size and zoom level. By default, the Stage is a rectangle that is 550 pixels wide by 400 pixels tall. Later in this hour, in the "Document Properties" section, you'll see how to change the width and height of a movie. However, the specific dimensions in pixels are less important than the resulting shape of the Stage (called the *aspect ratio*). The pixel numbers are unimportant because when you deliver a Flash movie to the Web, you can specify that Flash *scale* to any pixel dimension.

Aspect ratio is the ratio of height to width. Any square or rectangular viewing area has an aspect ratio. For example, television has a 3:4 aspect ratio—that is, no matter how big a standard TV screen is, it's always three units tall and four units wide. 35mm film has an aspect ratio of 2:3 (such as a 4×6-inch print), and high-definition television (HDTV) uses a 16:9 ratio. Most computer screen resolutions have an aspect ratio of 3:4 (480×640, 600×800, and 768×1024). You can use any ratio you want in a web page; just remember that the portion of the screen you don't use will be left blank. A "wide-screen" ratio (as wide as 1:3, like film) will have a much different aesthetic effect than something with a square ratio (1:1).

To **scale** means to resize as necessary. A Flash movie retains its aspect ratio when it scales, instead of getting distorted. For example, you could specify that a Flash movie in a web page scale to 100% of the user's browser window size. You could also scale a movie with the dimensions 100×100 to 400×400.

Not only can you deliver a Flash movie in any size (because Flash scales well), but while working in Flash, you can zoom in on certain portions of the Stage to take a closer look without having any effect on the actual Stage size. The following task introduces a couple tools that are important to the Stage.

▼   **Try It Yourself**

Change Your View on the Stage

In this task, you'll explore view settings. Follow these steps:

1. Instead of working from scratch, open an existing file. Select File, Open to open the Open dialog box and find the file called ScriptableMasksPart2. fla. Adjacent to your installed version of Flash 8, go inside a folder called Samples and Tutorials, then inside a folder Samples, then to Masking, and finally into the folder called ScriptableMasksPart2.

2. Notice the Zoom control at the top right of the Stage above the Timeline (see Figure 1.4). This control provides one way to change the current view setting. Other ways include selecting View, Magnification and using the Zoom tool (the magnifier button in the Tools panel), which you'll learn about in more detail in Hour 2.

3. Change the Zoom control to 400%. Notice that everything becomes bigger. You haven't really changed anything except your view of the screen.

▼

Zoom control

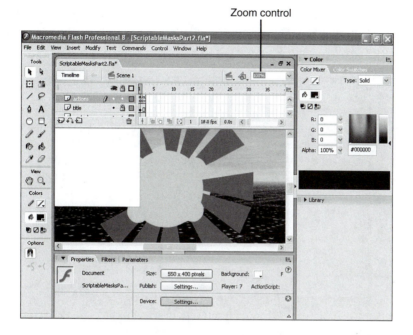

FIGURE 1.4
The Zoom control allows you to zoom in on or zoom out of the Stage. Zooming has no effect on what the audience sees.

4. Unless you have a huge monitor, you probably can't see the whole Stage. However, you can view the other parts of the Stage in one of two ways: by using the standard window scrollbars on the right and bottom or by using the Hand tool. The Hand tool is best accessed by simply holding down the spacebar. Go ahead and hold down the spacebar; then click and drag. You're *panning* to other parts of the Stage without actually moving anything. It's important to understand that the Hand tool only changes your view port onto the whole Stage. The best thing about using the spacebar to select the Hand tool is that it's "spring loaded"—that is, the Hand tool is active only while you hold down the spacebar. In Hour 2, you'll learn about other spring-loaded tools.

6. Now change the Zoom control to Show All. No matter what your screen size, Flash scales the Stage to fit your window.

7. Several interesting tools are available from the View menu, including grids, guides, and snap settings. Select View, Grid, Show Grid. Behind all the graphics onstage, you see a grid (which the user won't see), as shown in Figure 1.5. For this example, click once on the eyeball at the top left of the Timeline to temporarily hide all the graphics (so that you can more easily see the grid). You'll see next hour how the grid can help you line up graphics perfectly. Notice that after you select View, Grid, you can select Edit Grid to edit the

color and spacing of the grid. Turn off the grid now by selecting View, Grid, Show Grid (so that there's no check mark next to this menu item). Click the eyeball again to reveal the graphics.

FIGURE 1.5
Turning on the grid helps you align objects.

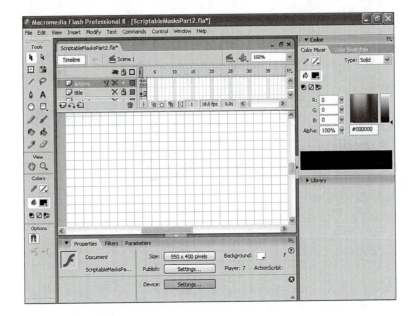

8. Guides are just like the grid in that they help you align graphics and they don't export with the movie. Guides differ from the grid in that that you drag Guides into place where you want them. First, select View Rulers (so that there's a check mark next to this item). Now you can click either ruler and drag toward the Stage to create and put into place a single guide, as shown in Figure 1.6. You make vertical guides by dragging from the left-side ruler, and you make horizontal guides by dragging from the top ruler. To remove the guides, drag them back to the ruler. As with the grid, you find the option to edit the guide settings—as well as a way to lock the guides in place—by selecting View, Guides, Edit Guides.

9. Close the file without saving.

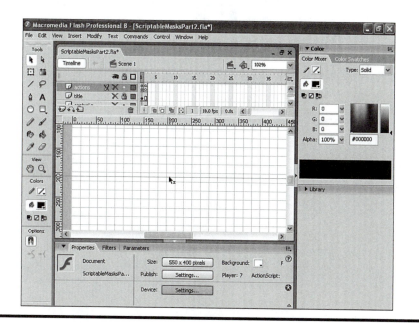

FIGURE 1.6
Guides are similar to the grid, but you can position the vertical and horizontal lines wherever you want them.

The Tools Panel

The Tools panel is the panel with which you will likely become most familiar. Any time you create or edit anything on the Stage, you need to have one tool selected from the Tools panel. On Windows, the Tools panel is dockable. The default location is docked to the left side of the Flash interface (or, on a Mac, floating on the left).

Although the Tools panel is used primarily to draw on the Stage, it's also used to edit what you've already drawn. As shown in Figure 1.7, the Tools panel is actually broken into several sections: Tools, View, Colors, and Options.

The Tools section enables you to create graphics and text (via the Line tool and the Text tool), to edit graphics (via the Eraser tool and the Paint Bucket tool), and to simply select graphics (via the Selection tool, the Subselect tool, and the Lasso tool). You'll learn about all these tools next hour. The View section lets you change your view of the Stage (as you did in the preceding task). The Colors section gives you control over the color of objects drawn. Finally, the Options section is dedicated to additional modifiers for certain tools. Depending on what tool is selected, you might not see anything in the Options section.

FIGURE 1.7
The Tools panel has tools for drawing, editing, and viewing, plus options that vary, depending on the currently selected tool.

You'll look at these tools in detail in the next few hours (in particular, Hour 2 and Hour 5, "Applied Layout Techniques"). For now, go ahead and play with these tools. If you think you lost the Tools panel, you can restore it by selecting Window, Tools.

The Timeline

You'll look at the Timeline in depth when you start animating in Hour 7, "Animation the Old-Fashioned Way." Nevertheless, you'll take a brief tour of the Timeline now. The Timeline contains the sequence of individual images that make up an animation. When the user watches your animation, he sees the images on Frame 1 followed by Frame 2, and so on. It's as if you took the actual film from a conventional movie and laid it horizontally across the screen, with the beginning on the left and the end toward the right.

Like many other windows, the Timeline can be undocked so that it floats above everything else, as shown in Figure 1.8. Docking is just one more way to organize your workspace. (I should note, however, that unlike regular panels, the Timeline— and the Tools—can't be grouped with other panels. So, in that way, they're unique.) Personally, I like the default arrangement, with the Timeline above the Stage and the Tools panel to the left. I use this arrangement for most of the figures throughout this book. Because the Timeline is a unique panel, know that you can always get it back by selecting Window, Timeline. (See the section "Organizing the Workspace," later this hour, for more details.)

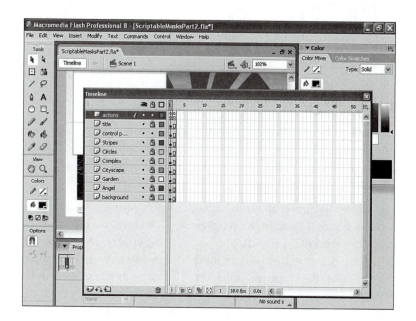

FIGURE 1.8
The Timeline (and other panels) can be picked up and moved like any floating window. This lets you customize your workspace.

When you start to create animations, the Timeline includes many visual clues to help you. For example, you can quickly see the length of an animation simply by looking at the Timeline. Also, Flash uses a few subtle icons and color codes in the Timeline; this way, you can see how the animation will play.

In addition to frames, the Timeline lets you have as many layers as you want in animations. As is the case with other drawing programs, objects drawn in one layer appear above or below objects in other layers. (You may have noticed earlier this hour that the ScriptableMasksPart2.fla file has several layers.) Each layer can contain a separate animation. This way, multiple animations can occur at the same time. By using layer names and special effects (such as masking), you can create complex animations. Figure 1.9 shows the Timeline and layers of a finished movie. You'll learn more about layers in Hour 11, "Using Layers in Animations."

FIGURE 1.9
Most anima-
tions involve
many layers.
Each layer is
independent of
the others.

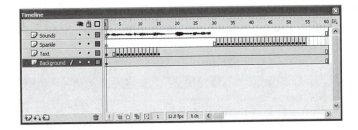

The Properties Panel

Certainly, you'll be faced with more windows in Flash than just the Stage, Tools panel, and Timeline (although these are the basic ones). This section looks at the multipurpose Properties panel (also sometimes called the *Properties Inspector*, or PI for short—though I'll call it the Properties panel throughout this book).

All panels let you view and change properties of objects. Although you can find nearly two dozen panels listed in the Window menu, you will use one panel almost all the time—the Properties panel. The Properties panel displays properties of the currently selected object so that you can make adjustments. For example, when you select a block of text, the Properties panel lets you view and change the font face and size. When you select a filled shape, you can adjust the fill color of that shape. In addition to modifying objects on stage, the Properties panel lets you modify frames in the timeline (when you select one) as well as document properties (when nothing is selected). Although you'll only look at a few variations of the Properties panel this hour, you'll eventually become familiar with all the different panels. (You can see them all listed under the Window menu.) Because there are so many panels, later this hour you'll learn ways to organize them to suit your personal workflow.

As you'll see, using panels is simple. All panels operate in the same manner. You can either keep the panel open and select an object or access the panel after you've selected an object. In either case, the panel always reflects the current settings so that you may modify or change them. For example, to change the font size of some text, you just select the text and then make a change in the Properties panel. The key is to keep the text selected while you access the Properties panel. You can also change properties of several objects at once—just select multiple objects (say several blocks of text) and make a change in the panel. (When selecting multiple objects of different types, only the shared properties are visible in the Properties panel.) You'll learn more about all this in the following tasks.

Finally, if nothing is selected, you can still make changes to the Properties panel (or any panel for that matter). Although this may seem to have no effect, you're actual-ly specifying what will happen the next time you create an object. For example, if you first select the Text tool and (before clicking on stage) you make a change to the font in the Properties panel, you'll see that font change in text you create later.

Try It Yourself ▼

Use the Properties Panel to Inspect and Change Fill Colors

In this task, you'll use the Properties panel to inspect and change fill colors. Here are the steps to follow:

1. Create a new file by selecting File, New to open the New dialog box and then selecting Flash Document and clicking OK. Make sure that the Properties panel is open. Its default location is below the Stage. If you don't see it, just select Window, Properties, Properties. Finally, ensure that the Properties panel is at full size by clicking the tiny arrow at the bottom-right corner of the panel (as shown in Figure 1.10).

Expand/Collapse arrow

FIGURE 1.10
You can click the Expand/Collapse arrow so that the Properties panel opens all the way, as shown here.

2. Take a look at the Properties panel and notice the type of information listed (Size, Publish, Background, and so on). The Properties panel is about to change.

3. Select the Brush tool by clicking once in the Tools panel; if the Tools panel is not available, you need to first select it from the Window menu. Notice that when you simply select the Brush tool, the Properties panel changes. Go ahead and paint a squiggly line on the Stage.

4. Before you draw again, select a different color from the Fill Color swatch in the Properties panel. Click the swatch and select a different color (as shown in Figure 1.11). This specifies what color you're about to paint.

5. Paint another squiggly line (in the new color) on a blank area of the Stage. Select the Selection toolby clicking the black arrow at the top left of the Tools panel or by simply pressing the V key.

6. Click once on the first squiggly line to select it. Notice that the Properties panel changes again. Additional information about the shape's coordinates

and size appear. While the shape is still selected, change the fill color by clicking the Fill Color swatch in the Properties panel and picking a new color. (By the way, the swatch with a red line through it—Stroke Color—is for shapes drawn with the Pencil tool.)

FIGURE 1.11
Before you paint again, you can select a new color.

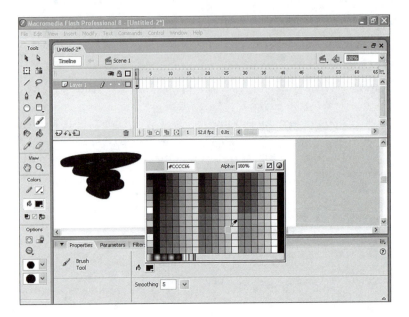

By the Way

The Coordinate System

The **coordinate system** in all multimedia tools (including Flash) refers to locations by pixels in the x (horizontal) axis and the y (vertical) axis. The top-left corner of the screen (or Stage) is considered the origin or 0x,0y. As you move to the right, the x coordinate increases; for example, 100 pixels to the right has the location 100x,0y. As you move down, the y coordinate increases; the bottom-left corner of an 800×600 screen has the location 0x,600y. Just remember that y coordinates increase as you move down (not up, as you might expect). Here's an interesting challenge: What happens if you set the location of an object to –1000x? The object is moved offscreen 1,000 pixels to the left.

---

7. Finally, make both squiggly shapes the same color. Make sure that you still have one shape selected and then click and release on the Fill Color swatch. Then (while the cursor looks like an eye-dropper) click the other squiggly shape to sample its color. This is just a quick example of how the cursor changes to tell you what will happen when you click.

The Properties panel adapts to either show you properties of whatever you've select-ed on the Stage or properties for the tool you've just selected. The following sections explore some text options to solidify this concept.

Exploring Text Options

Flash, and Flash 8 in particular, has some really powerful text options. While in a new file or the file you used in the previous task, you can select the Text tool, click the Stage, and then type a few words. When you finish typing, you can click the Selection tool. From the Properties panel, you can select a different font, change the font size, change the color, and control the text in many common ways. By the way, the Format button on the Properties panel includes additional options related to margins. Flash 8 added a new font display technology called FlashType. By modify-ing the subtle rendering settings (basically the text's thickness and its smoothing behavior) you can optimize the performance animated text or make the text as read-able as possible at different sizes and on different monitor types. You'll explore these options in depth next hour.

Organizing the Workspace

At this point, you've probably explored enough to find that your panels are scattered all over the screen. This brings up an interesting point: You're given a lot of freedom with how you organize your panels. Learning a few concepts will make organizing your workspace easier. There's docked panels, floating panels, and grouped panels. Because the changes you make stick until you change them back, select Window, Workspace Layout, Default in order that you can follow along.

On Windows, docking means panels are locked into the Flash application interface around the outside of the stage—like how, by default, the Tools are the left, Properties panel is at the bottom, and Timeline is at the top. Docked panels com-pletely fill the space between the stage and the edge of Flash's application window. The only equivalent to this on Macintosh is how the Timeline is embedded into the primary document window. In addition, you can dock panels above or below each other within a single docked area. For example, the Library panel is docked above the Color Mixer panel (by default) on the right side. The way you dock (or undock) panels is by dragging via the gripper button at the top left of a panel (see the accom-panying explanation with Figure 1.12, later).

If a panel is not docked into the interface then it's floating above it. (Select Window, Align to see an example of a panel that's floating by default.) Additionally, you can dock multiple panels above or below each other into a single floating panel. Finally, regardless of whether a panel is docked or floating, you can also group panels into single tabbed panel—which is the case (by default) for the Properties, Parameters, and Filters panels, all grouped together at the bottom. You can think of grouping as stacking the panels in the same location because you can only reveal one at a time—the others in the group are accessed via their tab. The variations might sound overly detailed but the options are simply there so you can change the layout. Each panel has its purpose and that's never affected by where you decided to put it. The idea is that you can organize panels to match your work style.

Hiding Panels

Depending on your screen size, you might find that the panels are preventing you from viewing the Stage. A simple press of the F4 key temporarily hides all the panels (except Tools and Timeline). You can press F4 again to restore them.

In addition to being able to return to the default layout, you can save your own layouts. If you find an arrangement that works well for you just select Window, Workspace Layout, Save Current. You are then prompted to name the set. The name you give the set then appears under Window, Workspace Layout.

Arranging panels can become frustrating if you don't know the basics. Because panels function unlike many computer standards, the following rundown will bring you up to speed as you follow along with Figure 1.12.

FIGURE 1.12
The anatomy of a panel.

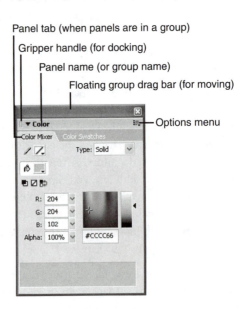

First, every panel has an options menu at the top right of the title bar. This menu provides additional options related to each particular panel.

For organizing panels, you need to realize that you can minimize or maximize any panel by clicking the Expand/Collapse arrow (or even just title bar where the panel's name appears). When panels are docked together, expanding one of the panels causes the others to move out of the way and collapsing one causes the others to fill in the extra space.

When a panel is floating (that is, not docked with others), minimizing causes it to appear as just the light blue title bar, with an extra title bar above for moving the group around.

To undock a panel, you must drag by the gripper handle (which is the vertical set of dots at the far left of the light blue title bar). You must drag the panel by this handle to undock or redock it with other panels. As you drag, you get a preview of which other panels it will snap to when you let go. You can even dock two floating panels together to make a group. The uppermost floating panel has an extra drag title bar (above the panel's light blue title bar). Dragging by *this* drag title bar moves a panel (or panel group), with no chance of it becoming docked to another. In addition, this drag title bar includes a button you can use to close the panel.

To create a new group of panels you always must use the options menu and select "Group Panel with" from which you can select one of the other panels or panel groups already present. To take a panel out of a group (or to start a new one), you use the panel's options menu and select Group Panel with New Panel Group.

It might take some time to get used to how the panels behave, but it's worth taking the time to play around. After you get it, you'll be able to quicklyorganize the panels as needed.

The Library

The Library is the best storage facility for all the media elements used in a Flash file. You'll learn to love the Library for many reasons, as discussed in further detail in Hour 4, "Using the Library for Productivity." Media placed in the Library can be used repeatedly within a file, and—regardless of how many times you use those media—it doesn't significantly add to the file size! For example, if you put a drawing of a cloud in the Library, you can then drag 100 copies of the cloud onto the Stage (making a whole sky full of clouds), but deep inside the Flash file, only one cloud exists. Using the Library is one way you can keep Flash movies small.

In practice, the Library is used in two basic ways: for editing and for maintaining (or accessing) the Library's contents. You might need to edit the contents of one Library item (called a *symbol*), and when you do, you are editing the contents of the Library. You might also need to access the Library to simply organize all the contents or to drag *instances* of the symbols into a movie. In such a case, you are maintaining the Library (as opposed to editing its contents).

A **symbol** is the name for anything—usually something visual, such as a graphic shape—you create and place in a file's Library. Although different types of symbols exist, the idea is that by creating a symbol, you're storing the graphic once in the Library. After it is in the Library, the symbol can be used several times throughout a movie without having a significant impact on file size.

An **instance** is one copy of a symbol used in a movie. Every time you drag a symbol from the Library, you create another instance. It's not a "copy" in the traditional sense of the word because there's only one master, and each instance has negligible impact on file size. Think of the original negative of a photograph as the symbol and each print as another instance. You'll see that, like photographic prints, instances can vary widely (in their sizes, for example).

The Library behaves like any other panel but because it's so important I wanted to introduce it here. You'll learn much more about the Library starting in Hour 4.

Getting Around in Flash

As mentioned earlier in this hour, an important concept in Flash is to understand where you are at all times. If you think you're in the Library, editing the contents of a symbol, for example, you better hope you are really there. It can be confusing because, although it's always possible to figure out where you are in Flash, the clues are often subtle. The following sections look at how you can determine where you are by reading the subtle clues in the interface.

The Current Layer

Although there's just one main Timeline, earlier in this hour you saw how you can have several layers within the Timeline. At this point you should open a new file and add a layer so that you can explore it; you do this by selecting Insert, Timeline, Layer. One important concept is that you can be in only one layer at a time. That is, if you draw or paste graphics, they are added to the currently active layer. The current layer is the layer with the pencil icon, as shown in Figure 1.13. You can single-click another layer to make it the active layer (notice that the pencil moves to the layer you click). The key here is to always pay attention to what layer you're current-ly editing. For example, if the current layer is locked, you won't be able to affect it at all.

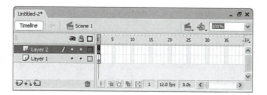

FIGURE 1.13
Not only is the current layer highlighted (in black), but it also has the pencil icon, indicating that this is the layer where anything that is drawn or pasted will go.

The Current Frame

In the Timeline, a red marker indicates which frame is currently being viewed (see Figure 1.14). This red current-frame marker can be in only one frame at a time—the frame you're currently editing. Initially you'll find that you can't move the current-frame marker past Frame 1 unless your file has more frames. You'll have plenty of opportunity to do this later; for now, just realize that the red marker indicates the current frame. If it helps, imagine a time machine. You can visit any moment in time, but you can visit only one moment at a time.

FIGURE 1.14
The red current-frame marker (on Frame 11 here) can be in only one frame at a time. It's important to realize where this current-frame marker is located at all times.

The Current Scene or Current Symbol

By far, the most difficult concept for new Flash users is that in Flash, there's more than one Timeline! A large or complicated movie can be broken into several scenes. You can think of scenes as chapters in a novel. Deep inside Flash, there's always just one long Timeline (just like a novel has one continuous story), but if you break a file into scenes, you can access the scenes individually. This is a nice feature because it means you can easily change the order or sequence of the scenes. It should be apparent that at all times you should know in which scene you're currently working. The name of the current scene is always listed above the Stage (and above the Timeline if it's docked), on what is called the *edit bar*—or what I often call the address bar. The default name is "Scene 1," and you should see this next to the icon for scenes—a movie "clapper" (see Figure 1.15).

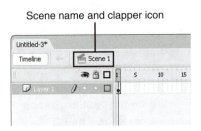

Scene name and clapper icon

FIGURE 1.15
Above the top-left corner of the Stage, you will see the name of the current scene. The clapper icon indicates that this is the name of a scene.

The edit bar often includes more information than is shown in Figure 1.15. When you learn more about the Library in Hour 4, you'll see how you can nest instances of symbols inside other symbols. When you double-click a complex object such as a symbol to edit it, everything else on the Stage dims (indicating that those other items are not editable). (This behavior of going inside one object to edit its contents also applies to grouped objects and so-called drawing objects—both of which you'll learn more about next hour.) In all cases, the best way to determine exactly what you're currently editing is to look at the edit bar. You might see "Scene 1: Group" (as shown in Figure 1.16). This means that you're in a group that is in Scene 1. Sound pretty hairy? Well, it's not really so terrible because the edit bar is very clear—you just have to remember to look there.

FIGURE 1.16
Here, the edit bar indicates that you're deeply nested inside a symbol (Wheel) that's nested inside other symbols.

Navigating Through the Interface

You've seen how the Flash interface gives you clues that tell you where you are at all times. But how did you get where you are in the first place? And how do you get out? Navigating through a Flash file is easy—and maybe that's why it's so easy to get lost. Let's look at a few ways to get around.

The edit bar contains the hierarchy of your current location, and it also provides a means of navigation. You can click the edit bar. If, for example, you're inside a symbol within Scene 1, you should see "Scene 1: *SymbolName*." If you simply click Scene 1, you are taken back to that scene (see Figure 1.17). Any time you see the edit bar, you can navigate back through the hierarchy. Remember that the edit bar provides information and that it's clickable.

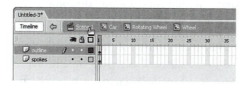

FIGURE 1.17
The edit bar provides more than just information. You can click the arrow or any name listed to jump back. Here, you can click Car to jump all the way back to the Car symbol.

Finally, you should notice two menus way off to the right of the edit bar: Edit Scene and Edit Symbol (see Figure 1.18). From these two menus, you can jump to any scene or symbol in the current movie. Of course, if you have no symbols and just one scene, using these menus won't be very interesting. However, in big files, these menus provide a quick way for you to get around. If you want, you can open one of the sample files inside the folder `Sample and Tutorials`, which is adjacent to your installed version of Flash (for example, `C:\Program Files\Macromedia\Flash 8\ Samples and Tutorials`).

Edit scene

Edit symbol

FIGURE 1.18
The Edit Scene and Edit Symbol menus are always accessible at the top right of the Stage. They provide the most reliable way to navigate to other scenes and symbols.

There are plenty more ways to get around in Flash, and you'll see them all in this book. For now, try to feel comfortable moving around and be sure to notice all the clues that Flash gives concerning where you are.

How Not To Get Lost

As a reference, here's a list of common ways to get lost and how to find your way home. This is a list based on my experience teaching new students—as well as my own experience getting lost! I'm including things here that you haven't been exposed to yet so feel free to mark this page and revisit it later.

- ▶ Edit bar. By far the most common problem is overlooking the fact the edit bar has changed to indicate you're inside a symbol or group or drawing object. I've already said to keep an eye on the edit bar. But what if it's gone? Amazing but true: You can hide and restore the edit bar via the menu Windows, Toolbars, Edit Bar. I can't imagine selecting this on purpose, but now you know how to bring the Edit Bar back.

- ▶ Changing Colors. The half-dozen or so color swatches can both determine the color you're about to draw as well as change an existing color. Remember, if you have something selected, it will change when you change the color swatch. Only when nothing is selected can you set the color for what you're about to draw. Plus (and this will become clearer next hour) there can be two colors for an object: the stroke and the fill. You'll see a pair of swatches quite often indicating these independent colors.

- ▶ Hiding docked panes. I didn't cover this yet but when a panel or group of panels is docked into the Flash interface—above or to the right of the stage—you'll see a divider line. Not only can you click and drag to relocate the divider but there's a subtle arrow button in the center of the line (shown in Figure 1.19). If you click the arrow button the entire group of docked panels is hidden. This is nice because it immediately gives you more space on the other side of the divider, plus you can quickly restore the divider by clicking again. However, it's also easy to get lost because you may not realize a bunch of panels are simply tucked away. By the way, Flash uses the same divider line and arrow button in a few other places such as the Help panel.

- ▶ Properties panel. It's important to know what sort of object you have selected. For example, if you draw a shape with the Brush tool the Properties panel will display "Shape" when you select that shape. There are other object types that you'll learn about over the next few hours—I promise you'll understand the attributes of each. People often forget the Properties panel tells you what you have selected. You may *think* something is a shape (or other type of object) but use the Properties panel to *know*.

- ▶ Info panel. The Info panel displays (and lets you edit) the size and location of any selected object. In addition, it has a grid of 9 squares with one black square—either top left or center (which you can change by clicking). This simply makes the Info panel reflect coordinates for the top left corner of the selected object or the center of that object. What's very easy to overlook, however, is the setting you make using the Info panel affects the coordinates displayed in the Properties panel's W, H, X, and Y fields. That is, you set your preference (top left or center) in the Info panel and that affects the numbers that appear in the Properties panel.

Arrow button

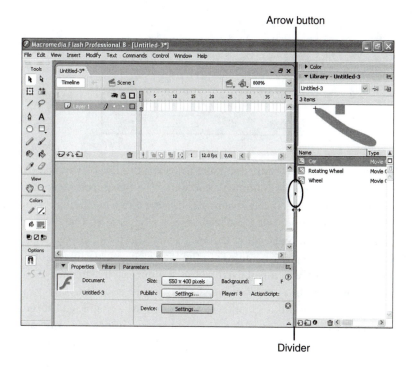

FIGURE 1.19
Dividers can resize the space between panes full of panels, and the little arrow button can quickly collapse (and hide) all the panels.

Divider

That's it for the big pitfalls. Naturally, there are many more but I'll be sure to guide you past them as they're encountered in later hours.

Document Properties

You need to specify a few far-reaching settings early in the creation of any movie. Most of these are found in the Document Properties dialog box, shown in Figure 1.20, which you access by selecting Modify, Document or double-clicking the bottom of the Timeline (where you see 12.0 fps). You should access the Document Properties dialog box now so that you can experiment with a few of its settings. (Notice that most of the same settings appear in the Properties panel if you click the Stage or otherwise deselect all objects.)

FIGURE 1.20
The Document
Properties dia-
log box provides
many global set-
tings that
should be deter-
mined at the
beginning of
every project.

First of all, you need to make sure that Ruler Units is set to Pixels. This is the standard unit of measurement in multimedia and web pages. It's important to set Ruler
Units to Pixels because this affects several other dialog boxes (including the Info
panel). Next to Background Color, you should see a white swatch that, when clicked,
allows you to change the Stage color. This isn't actually as useful as you might think
because at the time you publish a movie to the Web, you can specify any background color you want, and it will override this setting. Feel free to change
Background Color any time you want. Maybe gray will be easier on your eyes, or
black will make selecting white graphics easier. I often use a bright red background
just so it's super clear while I'm editing. Do whatever you want—not only can you
change this setting later, but it also affects only the Stage color while you're editing.

Two other Document Properties dialog box settings are important to establish early
in any project: Frame Rate and Dimensions. Frame Rate specifies the rate—that is,
how many frames per second—at which Flash *attempts* to play. I say *attempts* because
some of your users might not have a computer fast enough to keep up, so Flash just
can't display the specified number of frames in a second. Flash will not exceed the
frame rate you specify, but it could get bogged down and not keep up. Dimensions
are only important to the degree that they affect the aspect ratio of your Stage, as
discussed earlier. You need to decide up front on the shape for your Stage (sorry, it
can't be round). Do you want a wide-screen CinemaScope look, or do you want a
square Stage? You might even want a vertical rectangle if, for instance, you were
building a button bar to appear on the left side of a web page. You need to consider
this early on because the Stage shape influences how you position graphics, and
changing it later makes for a lot of repositioning.

People often confuse frame rate with speed, which is more of a visual effect.
Animators can use tricks to make something appear to speed across the screen even

while using a very low frame rate. For example, if you see a picture of a car on the left side of the screen and then a fraction of a second later, it's on the right side of the screen, that may tell your brain that the car is moving fast. However, such a trick requires only two frames—and at a frame rate of 4 fps, the second frame appears only a quarter second after the first! Frame rate—that is, how many chunks into which each second is broken—controls the visual resolution. Four frames a second may look "chunky"—each change occurs only four times a second. However, 30 fps (equivalent to the frame rate of TV) is such a fine increment that you're not likely to see the steps between discrete frames (although, of course, that's what's really happening). By the way, you can still move a car across the screen in a quarter of a second by using 60 fps—it would just involve 15 frames. You'll explore this topic in great detail in Hours 6, 7, and 21.

File Types

Clearly, the most common use for Flash is to create interactive animations for the Web. Sifting through all the different file types involved can be a little confusing. At a minimum, you need to understand three types: source (`.fla`) files, exported (`.swf`) files, and or Hypertext Markup Language (HTML; `.htm` or `.html`) files.

Source (`.fla`) Files

One of the two main file types in Flash is the source Flash movie that you save while working. It uses the file extension `.fla` (often pronounced "fla"). You can open and edit any `.fla` file, provided that you own Flash. This is your source file. With the `.fla` file, you can always restore the other file types—but nothing can restore a `.fla` file (except, maybe, doing all the work over again).

When sharing files with other workers who need to edit the source file, you share the `.fla` file. Anyone who has Flash Basic 8 or Flash Professional 8 (for either Mac or Windows) can open and edit the `.fla` file you create. However, you can't put `.fla` files into a web page for people to view—they're just files that contain your source content.

Saving as MX2004

You can actually save a `.fla` to share with a co-worker who only has Flash MX 2004. When you select File, Save As you need to select "Flash MX 2004 Document" from the "Save as type" drop-down. Flash will strip out any features your file uses that are only available in Flash 8 (and warn you too). This feature is great during the transition when people upgrade.

Exported (.swf) Files

When you're finished editing a source file and ready to distribute your creation, you simply export a .swf (pronounced "swif") Flash Player file. A .swf file can be viewed by anyone who has an Internet browser and the Flash Player plug-in. The audience can't edit the .swf—they can only watch it.

The process for creating a new .swf file is simple. You open a .fla file, select File, Export Movie, and then specify the name and file location for the .swf file in the Export Movie dialog box. Although more details are involved, the important point to understand is that exporting involves creating a new file (the .swf file), but the .fla file remains untouched. It's similar to using Save As or Save a Copy As in some other software programs. Whatever you do, you should always keep a copy of your .fla file. You can always create more .swf files from it—or make edits and then create more .swf files.

Watch
Out!

Beware of Fonts

There's one last thing you need to understand now, which applies if you work in a team environment or otherwise plan to exchange .fla files among different machines: Any .fla file you work on will open fine on any machine that has Flash installed. On a Macintosh, you might need to open Flash and then select File, Open, and on a Windows PC, you might need to make sure that the file is named with the extension .fla.

However, there's one minor catch: The font choice for any text in the .fla file must be present on the machine that is attempting to create the .swf file. It's not that you can't share a file if one person's machine is missing a particular font. Rather, that person cannot edit the text and can't create a .swf file. You can actually select a substitute font. Any time you open a .fla file that contains fonts that you don't have installed, you are given the chance to **map fonts.** That is, you can select what alternative font to use. You can easily avoid this situation by properly installing fonts on everyone's machine or by simply creating the .swf file on the appropriate machine.

HTML Files That Host the .swf File

If you have any experience creating HTML, the basic process of putting .swf files in a web page should be simple. If you have no HTML experience, it won't hurt to learn a little HTML, but you really don't have to. Remember that when you "visit" a web page, you're not really "going" anywhere. Rather, your browser software downloads a text file (with either an .htm or .html file extension). This HTML file contains not only the words you see on the web page, but additional instructions as well, including the font style and size.

In addition, the HTML file contains details about any of the pictures that are supposed to be seen on the web page—details such as the image file's name and from where it should download so that you can see it. Putting a Flash Player (.swf) file in a web page is almost as easy as putting a picture in a web page. A few other details (in addition to the filename of the .swf) can be included, such as the background color, whether you want the movie to loop, and other interesting settings that are unique to Flash.

To make this process even easier, Flash includes a feature called Publish (discussed in Hour 19, "Linking a Movie to the Web," and Hour 24, "Publishing a Creation"), which walks you through the steps of creating both the .swf file and the .html file. Every detail available can be specified in the Publish Settings dialog box (see Figure 1.21). You can specify parameters for each file format that you intend to distribute by using the tabs that appear (only the tabs for the file types you specify appear).

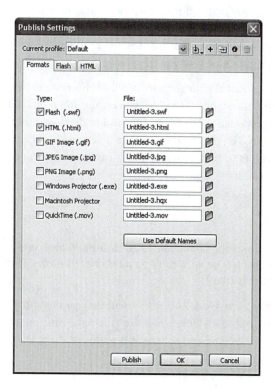

FIGURE 1.21
In the Publish Settings dialog box, you can decide what file formats you intend to distribute.

Summary

You sure covered a lot of ground this hour without actually creating any finished work. Rest assured you'll get your hands dirty next hour. Besides, the information covered this hour should be useful throughout your Flash career.

In this hour you were introduced to Flash's main workspace, including the Stage, the Timeline, and the Tools panel. You learned how to change the Stage size (through the Document Properties dialog box) and how to zoom in (by using the Zoom control). You got to see the Tools panel (which you'll use next hour to create artwork) and how the Properties panel lets you modify graphics onscreen. Although you didn't do much with the Timeline, you learned to pay close attention to clues, such as the red current-frame marker and the pencil icon, which indicate the active frame and active layer, respectively.

In this chapter you learned about other interface clues and navigation tools that help you track your current location at all times. The edit bar at the top left always tells you where you are, and the two menus at the top right let you navigate to other scenes and symbols (provided that you have some).

Finally, you learned about the file formats you'll likely create in Flash. It's important to take the time to understand all the files you create. You'll probably create many files, so it's also a good idea to keep your files and folders organized so that you can track what's going on. The old saying "Haste makes waste" is especially true when you have a million files to track. So, just take it easy, pay attention to how the Flash interface changes, and have fun.

Q&A

Q *When I hold down the spacebar (to get the Hand tool) and try moving my view over to the left or up, I can't go past the left of the Stage or the top of the Stage. Why is that?*

A Most likely the View, Work Area menu item isn't selected (that is, it doesn't have a check mark next to it). Only when this is selected can you (the author) see outside the Stage. (I recommend leaving this setting in the default, selected state.)

Q *I swear my Properties panel used to be taller. What did I do to get the "slim view"?*

A The Properties panel has a special "info area" that can be hidden via a tiny arrow button at the bottom right. You can also trigger that button by double-clicking in any blank area of the Properties panel. Just click that arrow button to restore the Properties panel's full view.

Workshop

The Workshop consists of quiz questions and answers to help you solidify your understanding of the material covered in this hour. You should try to answer the questions before checking the answers.

Quiz

1. How do you open and edit a `.swf` file?

   A. You can't, and unless you have a backup of the `.fla` file, you're pretty much out of luck.

   B. You can simply select File, Open.

   C. You can import it by selecting File, Import.

2. How can you make your animation appear to play really fast?

   A. Crank up the frame rate in the Document Properties dialog box to 120.

   B. Brick the user by employing age-old animation techniques.

   C. Suggest that users purchase the fastest computer they can afford.

3. What is the standard unit of measurement for web pages and multimedia?

   A. Inches

   B. Centimeters

   C. Pixels

Quiz Answers

1. A. Generally, you can't do anything but watch a `.swf` file. Truth be told, you can actually import a `.swf` file (as in Answer C). However, this won't work if when you exported the `.swf` file in the first place you specified Protect from Import in the Flash tab of the Publish Settings dialog box. Also, when you import a `.swf` file, just the sequence of frames is imported (no interactivity), so it's rarely very useful. In addition, there are third-party tools (such as Manitu Group's Action Script Viewer http://buraks.com/asv/) that can extract the media and scripts from a `.swf`. (You'll see more third-party tools listed in Appendix B, "Resources.") The bottom line, however, is you should always keep a backup `.fla`.

2. B. Although increasing the frame rate to 120 fps makes Flash try to play quickly, the chances of it actually playing that fast are unlikely (depending on the computer). So, although Answer A is not entirely wrong, using age-old animation tricks (which are covered in Hour 7, "Animation the Old-Fashioned Way," and Hour 22, "Advanced Animation Techniques") is the best way. Something doesn't actually have to move fast to appear to move fast.

3. C. This isn't an opinion: The standard is pixels.

HOUR 2

Drawing and Painting Original Art in Flash

What You'll Learn in This Hour:

▶ How to draw and paint in Flash
▶ The difference between lines and fills
▶ How to draw geometrically perfect shapes in Flash

Believe it or not, Flash started life as drawing software. The creators of Flash intended to make a "more natural" drawing tool. Of course, Flash has evolved to become an animation tool and, now, even a rich application development platform. Because you'll be animating images, it's convenient that you can draw these images right inside Flash.

This hour exposes you to the fundamental drawing concepts in Flash—think of it as your "basic training." There's a lot to cover, and you might find that it actually takes a little longer than one hour to complete. This lesson's length gives you ample chance to play with all the tools.

If you have little or no background creating graphics on a computer, you're in luck! Flash is so unique that the less you know, the better—just let your mind act like a sponge and soak up all the information. If you have experience with computer graphics, try to forget everything you know about drawing software and get ready to learn the "Flash way."

Graphics created in Flash are considered **vector graphics** (as opposed to *raster graphics*, which are sometimes called *bitmaps*). Unlike a bitmap, for which the computer must store information about every single pixel, a vector graphics file contains just the math to redraw the shape. Therefore, a vector circle is described with the mathematical formula for a circle. Vector files are very small (and therefore download quickly), and they scale to new sizes easily (for example, the radius for a circle can be changed). Sometimes vector graphics tend to look too "computery," containing clean lines and solid colors. Not in Flash. After you get a feel for drawing in Flash, you should understand why Macromedia has called Flash "vector clay"—it's a vector format at heart, but it can be molded naturally like clay.

Drawing on the Stage

Remember from Hour 1, "Basics," that everything your audience sees is drawn on the Stage. Sometimes, you'll want a graphic to start off the Stage and then animate into view. Drawing off the Stage requires that you have the work area selected with a check mark in the View menu. I recommend that you leave this setting checked, but you should realize that the gray area around the outside of the Stage is considered "off the Stage" and will not appear in your finished movie. The Stage is the white rectangular area.

Tools

Your drawing tools should appear, by default, on the left side of the screen, as shown in Figure 2.1. If the tools aren't visible, you can access them by selecting Window, Tools.

FIGURE 2.1
Flash's drawing toolbar might look simple, but because most tools have additional options, there's more than meets the eye.

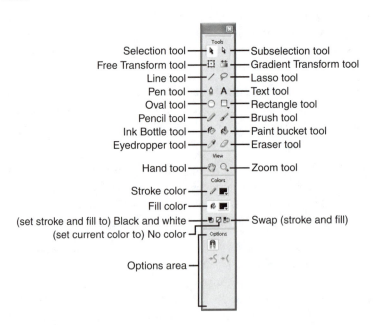

Selection tool — Subselection tool
Free Transform tool — Gradient Transform tool
Line tool — Lasso tool
Pen tool — Text tool
Oval tool — Rectangle tool
Pencil tool — Brush tool
Ink Bottle tool — Paint bucket tool
Eyedropper tool — Eraser tool

Hand tool — Zoom tool

Stroke color
Fill color
(set stroke and fill to) Black and white — Swap (stroke and fill)
(set current color to) No color

Options area

By the Way

Learning Shortcuts Without Memorizing

When you click a tool, it becomes selected. Alternatively, you can select a tool by pressing its shortcut (or quick key). You can see each tool's quick key when you roll your cursor over the tool. In the ToolTip that appears, you see both the name of the tool and a letter in parentheses. For example, when you roll over the Selection tool, you see "Selection Tool (V)." Pressing the V key selects the Selection tool. (Try it out by first clicking another tool and then pressing V.)

The following sections look at how to draw with these tools. You'll learn about all of them in this hour, although the really advanced techniques aren't covered until Hour 5, "Applied Layout Techniques." Keep in mind that whereas some tools (such as the Pencil and Brush tools) let you create artwork, others (such as the Selection and Zoom tools) simply help you modify or view your artwork. In the following sections you'll learn how to create and how to edit artwork.

Viewing and Modification Tools

Both View tools—Hand and Zoom—have no effect on artwork. You simply use them to help see your artwork. The following task walks you through a scenario in which you use both tools.

Try It Yourself ▼

Use the View Tools to Help You See

In this task you'll explore how to use both the Hand and the Zoom tools. Follow these steps:

1. Because you haven't drawn anything yet, you can use one of the sample files that ship with Flash. Open the sample file called `ScriptableMasksPart2.fla`. It's in the same Samples folder used last hour—that is, adjacent to Flash in a folder called Masking inside Samples that's inside the Samples and Tutorials folder. Select File, Open and navigate to `C:\Program Files\Macromedia\Flash 8\Samples and Tutorials\Samples\Masking\ScriptableMasksPart2\ScriptableMasksPart2.fla`.

2. You can zoom in to critically inspect or change the artwork in the file. Click to select the Zoom tool (it's the one that looks like a magnifying glass). Notice that, as with many other tools, when you select the Zoom tool, additional buttons appear in the Options section of the toolbar. You should see two more magnifying glasses appear in the Options area, as shown in Figure 2.2.

▼

FIGURE 2.2
The Zoom tool
has two
options: Enlarge
and Reduce.

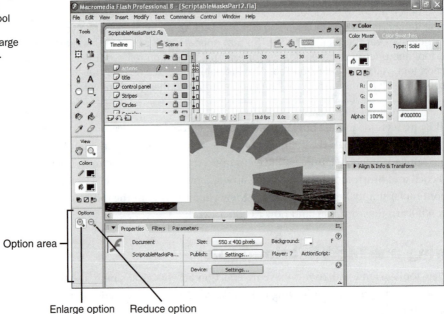

Option area ─

Enlarge option   Reduce option

3. Make sure Enlarge is selected (the option with the plus sign) and then click one of the arrow buttons displayed on the Stage. Click the same arrow a few more times, and you keep zooming in.

4. While you're close up, chances are that most of the Stage is out of view. Of course, you can use the standard scrollbars on the left and bottom to change the portion of the (now very close up) Stage. You can also do this by using the Hand tool: Select the Hand and then click and drag to change your view.

5. Now you can zoom out. Just select the Zoom tool and make sure you remember to select the Reduce option (the one with the minus sign). Click, and you zoom back out.

This task might seem pretty easy (it is), but there's more you should know. Using any View tool does not affect your file—only your perspective on it. The View menu provides some of the same functionality as the Zoom, Hand, and View tools (such as zooming in and zooming out). Similarly, none of the View menu options have a lasting impact on a file.

You used the Enlarge option of the Zoom tool by simply clicking the Stage. Another way to zoom is to click and drag. You see a rectangle as you drag, and when you let

go, that rectangle defines the viewable portion of the Stage. In the sample
ScriptableMasksPart2.fla file, for example, you can click and drag with the Zoom
tool and draw a small rectangle around the text at the top left of the stage to zoom
in on just that portion. You always see the current zoom level displayed in the drop-
down list at the top right of the Stage (above the Timeline, if it's docked), as shown
in Figure 2.3. If you click the Zoom control drop-down list, you can return to 100%.
Another quick way to return to 100% is to double-click the Zoom tool (not the
Enlarge or Reduce option, but the main Zoom tool's magnifier).

Current stage zoom level

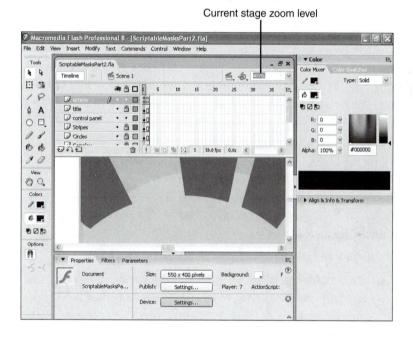

FIGURE 2.3
The exact zoom
level is always
shown at the
top right of the
Stage.

Speaking of quick techniques...both the Zoom and Hand tools have "spring-loaded"
options. That means, for example, that while you're using another tool, you can press
and hold down the spacebar to get the Hand tool. Then, when you let go of the
spacebar, Flash springs back to the tool you had. Holding down Ctrl+spacebar gives
you the Enlarge option of the Zoom tool, and holding down Ctrl+Shift+spacebar
gives you the Reduce option. These spring-loaded features provide very quick ways to
temporarily select tools without actually going to the toolbar.

Creation Tools

Although the View tools prove very useful, they can't change a file. To create artwork in Flash, you either have to add to an image, change something you've already

drawn, or remove some or all of what you've drawn. In the following sections, you'll first see how to add to your artwork. This will, naturally, give you something to change or remove later. Let's go through each tool individually and then analyze how they can all be used together.

Drawing Lines

Two tools are available for just drawing lines: the Line tool and the Pencil tool. (To be fair, the Oval and Rectangle tools draw lines, but they also draw fills at the same time, as you'll see in the "Painting Fills" section, later in this chapter.) Lines can be given a stroke color, a stroke height, and a stroke style. In addition, Flash 8 adds the ability to control the Cap (or how the line ends) and the Join (or the look of a corner where two lines meet). What's interesting is that the geometric definition of a line—the distance between two points—doesn't include mention of color, thickness, or style. It's best to think of a line this way: It's just an infinitely thin line that happens to be given a color, stroke (or thickness), and style (such as dashed, dotted, or solid). You can change any of the stroke attributes any time without affecting the underlying line.

So much for theory of lines! In the following task, you'll draw some.

▼   **Try It Yourself**

Draw and Change Lines

In this task you'll begin to draw and manipulate lines. Here are the steps:

1. Start a new file (by pressing Ctrl+N and selecting Flash Document). Lines can have different stroke attributes, so make sure the Properties panel is visible and in a convenient place first. If your Properties panel isn't present, select Window, Properties. Then you can drag the Properties panel to a blank area of the screen, as shown in Figure 2.4.

2. Select the Line tool, which draws straight lines. When your cursor is on the Stage, it changes to a crosshairs. Click and drag to create a line. You might notice a dark ring that sometimes appears while you drag. This is Flash's way of assisting you while drawing. In the case of the line, you'll find drawing perfectly horizontal and vertical lines to be quite easy when the Snap to Objects option is selected from the View menu. (Holding Shift also constrains the angle to diagonal as well.)

3. Changing any setting in the Properties panel will affect subsequent lines you draw. Select a different Stroke color in the square swatch on the Properties panel. Then change the stroke height, either by typing a number in the Stroke

▼

Height field or by clicking the arrow and dragging the slider. Set the stroke to
15. Then draw a horizontal line. For this exercise, we need a total of three
copies of this line. Use the Selection tool to select the first line, select Edit,
Copy and then choose Edit, Paste in Place then hold shift and press the down
arrow on your keyboard. Repeat this so you have three identical lines.

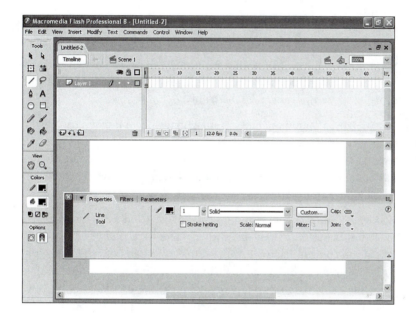

FIGURE 2.4
The Properties
panel lets you
set attributes of
the lines you
draw.

4. You can change any attribute of lines you've drawn through the Properties
   panel if you simply use the Selection tool to select the line. Select the first line
   and, from the Cap option menu in the Properties panel, select None. Select
   the second line and choose Round (the default Cap). Finally, set the last line
   and choose Square. The different Cap options are represented in an icon that
   appears on the Properties panel. I think the easiest way to really see the differences is to use the Subselection tool and click each line while holding shift.
   The skeleton of the line is shown with the two square handles at the end-
   points (as shown in Figure 2.5). (Remember to get the Selection tool back, by
   pressing V, in order to simply select the lines.) Square Cap may appear identical to None, but Square is similar to Round in that it extends both ends of the
   line by half the stroke thickness. Think of the how you could draw the Round
   cap with a compass that's pinned to the endpoint.

FIGURE 2.5
To best understand the different cap options for lines use the Subselection tool.

5. Lines have a few other interesting properties that I'll go over at the end of this task. For now, you'll see some of the options available when drawing lines. Select the Pencil tool. Notice that the Pencil tool has the option Pencil Mode. Click and hold the button that appears in the Options section to change the Pencil Mode setting, as shown in Figure 2.6.

6. The Straighten option attempts to straighten what you draw. Try drawing the letter *S*. It's likely to look jagged. Now try drawing the letter *Z*. It probably looks more like what you wanted. You'll learn to change the sensitivity later this hour, but drawing these letters should exemplify how the Straighten Pencil Mode setting works.

7. Choose the Smooth option and try drawing an *S* and a *Z*. What happens to the *S* is nice, but the *Z* has curves where there weren't any before. The Smooth option can come in handy if you find that your hand-drawn images look too jagged. Also notice that you can change the degree of smoothing in the Properties panel. This setting for Smoothing (from 0 to 10) is only visible when you have the Pencil Tool (or Paint Brush as you'll see later) *and* you have the Smooth option selected.

8. The Ink Pencil Mode setting draws *almost* exactly what you draw. Flash adjusts what you draw to reduce the file size. The simple line Flash creates takes less data to describe and results in a smaller file that's faster to download.

9. Finally, notice the Option for Object Drawing in the Tools panel when the Pencil Tool is selected. The choice between Object Drawing or not (the opposite being called Merge mode drawing) is actually quite profound. For now be sure it's deselected (so you're in Merge mode) and you'll learn much more about it later this hour in "Selecting and Transforming Objects."

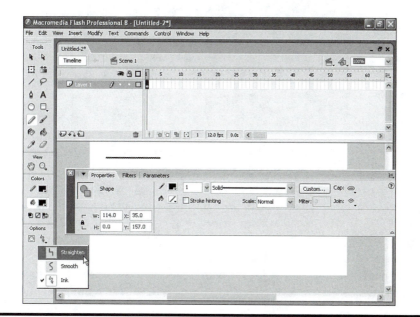

The Properties panel affects lines drawn with the Pencil tool in the same way it affects those drawn with the Line tool. One of the attributes that you haven't yet experimented with is the stroke style. The drop-down list shows you a visual representation of each style. Solid (the default) is like Hairline, but Hairline effectively sets the stroke height to the lowest number possible. You should use the other fancy stroke styles with extreme caution. This is simply because the more random-looking ones tend to add to the file size. File size issues are addressed in Hour 21, "Optimizing a Flash Site," but realize for now that you'll suffer a significant file size increase if you use some stroke styles.

If those stroke styles aren't enough notice (when a line tool is selected) the Custom button on the Properties panel provides a way for you to create your own custom stroke styles. The dialog box that appears after you click the Custom button lets you control several attributes of your own custom line styles (see Figure 2.7). These are fun, but be warned: They can significantly add to file size.

FIGURE 2.7
The Stroke Style
dialog box,
which is
accessed from
the Properties
panel, lets you
specify details
of custom
stroke styles.

The Stroke hinting feature has a very subtle effect. Namely, lines you draw will always be anchored on round pixel numbers. Flash is a sub-pixel drawing tool meaning it's possible to make a line start, end, or pivot on any coordinate—such as 103.4 pixels from the left. This is the case when Stroke hinting is not selected. At 100% zoom, such a point is rounded off to 103 but when you zoom in, one normal pixel might take up several actual pixels on the monitor. No stroke hinting is great for accuracy, but can make thin lines appear slightly blurry—because Flash is effectively rounding some points up and rounding other points down. Select Stroke hinting to ensure sharp looking lines. Just realize if you zoom way in the lines might not appear exactly where you position them.

Finally, the Scale option is the hardest feature to notice unless you know how to see it. Basically, Scale describes what sort of resizing should cause the stroke to thicken. Say you draw a rectangle which is made of both a stroke outline and a fill interior (which you'll do in "Drawing and Modifying Shapes by Using Lines and Fills"). If you enlarge (that is, "scale") the rectangle you may or may not want the stroke to also get thicker. The Scale option for Normal will cause the line to thicken in proportion to the scale where None will keep the line appearing the same thickness. Vertical and Horizontal means the thickness grows in proportion to the specified scale. For example, a line with Horizontal scale thickens only when you widen it; where making it taller has no impact on thickness. The worst part is that you won't see this effect until you put the lines inside symbol that gets scaled. You won't do that until Hour 4, "Using the Library for Productivity."

Lastly, the properties for Join and Miter will be discussed later in "Using Snap to Objects to Connect Shapes" because it only applies when you connect two lines (although it also happens when you draw a rectangle with corners).

Painting Fills

In Flash, there can be only two components to any shape you draw: lines (strokes) and fills. Some shapes are just lines (as you saw in the previous section), but some shapes are just fills (as you're about to see), and some shapes contain both (as you'll see later in this hour). Fills and lines are different. A line has no thickness—only applied stroke attributes.

A fill, on the other hand, has a left side, right side, top, and bottom. You can think of lines as the candy coating on an M&M and fills as the chocolate center (if that helps).

The two tools to create fills are the Brush tool and the Paint Bucket tool. You'll do a little experimenting with these tools in the following task.

Try It Yourself ▼

Paint Fills

In this task you'll explore the basic features and some rather advanced features of fills. Here are the steps to follow:

1. In a new file, use the Pencil tool to draw a few large circles. Be sure to first turn off Object Drawing (the option in the Tools panel when the Pencil is selected). Make at least one totally closed, one almost closed, and another obviously not closed, as shown in Figure 2.8.

2. Select the Paint Bucket tool. Notice that the Options section has two buttons: Gap Size and Lock Fill (see Figure 2.9). For now you'll explore only Gap Size; Lock Fill is covered in Hour 5, when you learn about gradients.

FIGURE 2.8
These three hand-drawn circles will be filled.

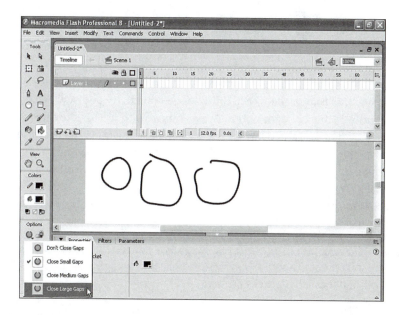

FIGURE 2.9
The Paint Bucket tool has a Gap Size option that controls the tool's tolerance.

3. If you click with the Paint Bucket tool in an empty part of the Stage, nothing happens. The Paint Bucket tool fills closed shapes with the selected fill color (the swatch next to the small paint bucket in the Colors section of the toolbox). It also changes the fill color of any fill already created. Change the Gap Size option to Close Large Gaps. Adjusting the Gap Size option should enable you to fill all your circles—even if they are not totally closed.

4. Select the Brush tool and quickly draw a line. Because you've used the Brush tool, it's really a fill (not a line), despite the fact it might look like a line.

5. Now, choose a new fill color by clicking and holding the color fill color swatch (from the Colors section of the Tools panel). Then select the Paint Bucket tool and fill the shape you just drew with the Brush tool. Not only can the Paint Bucket tool change the colors of the filled circles you've already filled, but it can also change the color of fills created with the Brush tool.

6. Now look at the Brush tool's Options area. The two drop-down lists that appear to be the same are actually quite different. The top one (Brush Size) controls the brush's tip size. On the other hand, the Brush Shape option controls the brush's tip shape. For example, you can have a calligraphy look with the angled tip, as shown in Figure 2.10. Lock Fill is covered in Hour 5, but the other option, Brush Mode, is very interesting and is covered in step 7.

FIGURE 2.10
The Brush Shape option affects the style of a drawing. Here's a calligraphy effect using the angled Brush Shape option.

7. Figure 2.11 demonstrates each Brush Mode option. Try one now. Select the Paint Inside Brush Mode option to experiment with it. Either use the closed circles you drew earlier or draw a few more circles by using the Pencil tool. Make sure you have the Brush tool selected (notice that the Brush Mode option remains where you last left it); then click and paint inside one of the circles. Try painting outside the lines. If you start painting outside the circle, the Paint Inside Brush Mode option prevents you from spilling any paint outside the shape! With Paint Inside selected, if you first click outside the shape, nothing happens.

FIGURE 2.11
The Brush tool has several Brush modes. In the Paint Selection example, I first selected the windows. The Paint Inside example worked only when I started painting inside the house graphic.

Let me recap just a few important points that are consistent for all the tools. First, certain tools have additional options that appear in the bottom section of the Tools panel. If you can't seem to find an option that you've seen before, you might have to remember for which tool it was designed. This fact shouldn't be too frustrating because any attribute you need to change after drawing is usually found in the Properties panel (which you'll learn to leave open all the time).

Another thing to notice is that sometimes the same task can be achieved a number of different ways. For example, you have seen the Zoom command in the View menu, the Zoom tool, and the Zoom setting on the Stage. And you have seen that the fill color swatch can be changed from the Tools panel, the Properties panel, and the Color Mixer panel. The fact that you can do the same task by using different methods means you can find a style that works best for you.

Drawing and Modifying Shapes by Using Lines and Fills

When you use either the Oval tool or the Rectangle tool, you create a shape by using both a line and a fill. These shapes have a fill and a stroke, with all the attributes set in the Properties panel. You can actually draw an oval or a rectangle that has no fill by changing the fill to "no color" (the red line with an arrow pointing to it, as shown in Figure 2.12).

Similarly, you can create a shape without a stroke by changing the stroke color to "no color." These tools are pretty self-explanatory. The only Rectangle tool option to take note of is the Round Rectangle Radius setting. If this setting is selected before you draw, it makes all rectangles you draw have rounded corners.

Creating ovals and rectangles is very easy. The following task walks you through a couple ways you can create and modify them.

FIGURE 2.12
When you use the Oval tool or Rectangle tool, one option for the fill color is no color (shown as a red slash).

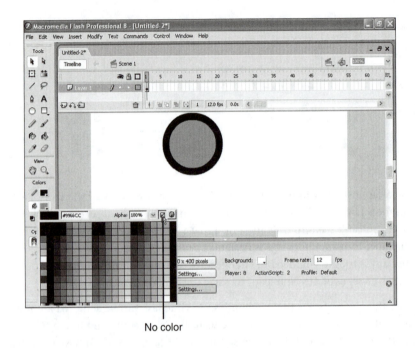

No color

▼   **Try It Yourself**

Draw and Modify Shapes

This task combines what you've learned about fills and shapes, and it shows you a couple more tricks. Follow these steps:

1. Select the Oval tool and then set the stroke height (in the Properties panel) to something significant, such as 5 or greater.

2. Select colors for both the stroke and the fill—just not the "no color" diagonal red line.

3. Draw a circle. A *circle* is just an oval that happens to have equal height and width. To draw a circle, hold down the Shift key while you draw.

4. Select the Rectangle tool, change the fill color, and draw a square (by holding down Shift while you draw). As with the Line tool and Oval tool, if Snap to Objects is selected in the View menu, the Rectangle tool will snap in certain places to form a perfect square so you don't have to hold down Shift.

▼

5. To change the fill color of the circle, select the Paint Bucket tool, pick a new fill color, and then click inside the circle you drew. The current fill color is applied to the circle's fill. The Paint Bucket tool is easy to understand—it either creates a fill or changes a fill.

6. Select the Ink Bottle tool and then pick a different stroke color. Click the edge of the circle you drew. The stroke color changes. What's really nice about this feature is that because the Ink Bottle tool affects only lines, you don't have to be particularly careful where you click because only the line portion changes.

7. The Ink Bottle tool doesn't just change the color of the stroke. When the Ink Bottle tool is selected, you can select a different height (say, 10) from the Properties panel. While you're there, pick a different stroke style. Click the circle again. You're affecting all the stroke portion's attributes.

8. Similarly to how the Paint Bucket tool can create a fill, the Ink Bottle tool can create a stroke where there wasn't one to begin with. Use the Brush tool to draw a quick shape. Then select the Ink Bottle tool and click the fill you just created. You add a stroke to the fill, effectively outlining it.

The preceding task shows that there are two fundamental components to the shapes you create—lines (or *strokes*) and fills—and each has a different set of tools. The Oval tool and Rectangle tool can create both strokes and fills at the same time. To create a new fill or affect one that's onscreen, you use the Brush tool or Paint Bucket tool. You can create lines by using the Pencil tool or the Line tool, and you can change their characteristics by using the Ink Bottle tool. I find it easiest to remember that the Ink Bottle tool draws lines because it appears in the left column of tools—under the Line and Pencil tools. The Paint Bucket tool is under the Paint Brush tool.

The Pen tool is primarily used to draw lines, but any time you use it to draw a closed shape, the shape gets filled automatically. Later in this hour you'll see how to modify drawn shapes (including removing the fill).

By simply clicking with the Pen tool, you can add sharp anchor points on straight lines. The Pen tool can also draw curves. Instead of just clicking to create a point, you can click and drag to create a curve. The direction in which you drag creates what will become a tangent to your curve. The distance you drag determines how gradual or extreme the curve will be. If that makes perfect sense, I'm surprised. You'll just have to experience it to understand. Therefore, you'll experiment with these Pen tool basics in the following task.

▼ **Try It Yourself**

Use the Pen Tool

In this task you'll use the Pen tool to draw controlled shapes. Follow these steps:

1. To begin, draw a diamond by using the Pen tool. Select the Pen tool and from the Properties panel, set the stroke thickness high (say, 20) and set the Join option to Miter. Then, toward the bottom of the Stage, click and let go (this will be the bottom of the diamond). Then, up and to the left, click once for the left corner of the diamond. Click and release for the top and right corners as well. Finally, move your cursor near the first point you created. You should see the cursor change to include a little circle, as in Figure 2.13. Later in this hour you'll learn how the cursor frequently changes to provide information. For now, know that the little circle on the Pen tool indicates that if you click it, you'll enclose the shape you started. Click to enclose the shape. It should automatically fill with the current fill color. Feel free to repeat this step by first selecting the Join option Round and the corners in the diamond will look much different.

FIGURE 2.13
The Pen tool changes to include an extra circle, indicating that a click will enclose the shape you're drawing.

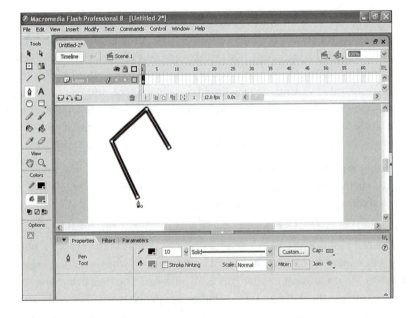

2. Next, draw a V shape by using the Pen tool. Click once for the top-left point of the V, click once for the bottom point, and then double-click for the third and final point (the top-right point). Double-clicking finishes the shape, even

if it's not enclosed; if you click again elsewhere on the Stage, you'll be starting a new shape or line. Therefore, two ways to finish what you've started with the Pen tool are to double-click and to enclose the shape (as you did in step 1). A third way is to simply select another of the drawing tools or press the Esc key.

3. Now try to create a curved line. Select the Pen tool (to make sure you're starting a new line) and then on the left side of the screen click once (and let go).

4. Now you need to lay down an anchor point on the curve you want to create. Therefore, you need to click and drag before you let go. Above and to the right of the first place you clicked, click and hold the mouse down. While holding down the mouse button, if you move the mouse to the right, you'll see that your horizontal tangent causes a curve to appear and then level off, as shown in Figure 2.14.

FIGURE 2.14
When clicking to make an anchor point, if you drag (to the right, in this case) you establish a tangent for the curve that's created.

5. Continue to hold down the mouse button while moving the mouse straight above the second point, and you should see that the shape of the curve is totally different because the tangent you're creating is different (see Figure 2.15).

FIGURE 2.15
Depending on the direction of the tangent (in this case, upward), the curve changes.

6. Finally, while still holding down the mouse button, you can increase or decrease the distance you're dragging (from the point you clicked). This affects the influence on the curve's arc. Before your hand gets tired, move the mouse to the right. Then double-click down to the right at about the same height as the first point to make an arc. Even though this curve has three points, only the middle one needs a curve to it—that is, when you create the first and last points, you didn't click and drag.

You can edit any drawn shape in the same manner in which you drew lines with the Pen tool in the preceding task. You just select a shape by using the Subselect tool (that's the white arrow at the top right of the Tools panel), and you see the same handles and anchor points as in the preceding task.

Creating Text

Now for a graphic element that involves neither line nor fill. In this section, you'll explore creating text. To create text, you simply select the Text tool, click, and start typing. If, when you first make the text, you click and drag you'll be setting the margins (otherwise, the margins adapt to what you're typing). You can modify the font, color, and style of what you've typed after you create it. Modifying your text after it's typed usually makes sense because only then will you be able to best judge how it looks.

Creating text in Flash has never been easier or more sophisticated. The following task walks you through a couple quick maneuvers.

▼   **Try It Yourself**

Create and Style Text

In this task you'll explore using text in Flash. Here are the steps:

1. Select the Text tool, click the Stage, and then type `Hello`. This "click-and-type" technique expands the margin for the block of text to the exact width of whatever you type. The circle that appears at the top-right corner of the text block indicates that the margin will automatically adjust in this way (see Figure 2.16).

FIGURE 2.16
The subtle circle in the top right corner indicates the margins will adjust to fit what you type. Once you've set the margins (by dragging any handle on the text) the circle turns to a square.

2. When you click and drag this circle (to adjust the width), it turns into a square to indicate that the margins are fixed. You can double-click the square margin control to restore the automatic margin adjustment (that is, to make it a circle again).

3. While editing the text block, you can set the margin. (Make sure the I-beam is blinking in the block; click inside the block of text, if necessary.) Grab the little circle at the top-right corner of the text block and widen or narrow the block of text. The circle margin handle changes to a square, which indicates that your margins are set and any text you paste or type into this block will

▼

wrap when it reaches this margin. Go ahead and type a couple lines of text. You should see the text wrap even though you don't press the Enter key.

Adjusting Text Margins

By the way, if you had clicked and dragged with the Text tool to the right before typing (instead of clicking and then typing), you would have created a margin in one step. You can always adjust the margins later too. There are two ways: If you're editing the actual text, you use the circle or square in the top right corner, or if you're not actually editing the contents of a text block, you can still select it using the Selection tool. In this case, you can change the margins by dragging any of the square handles in the corners.

---

4. Now that you have some text in the block and have set the margins, it's time to modify some attributes of the text. There are two ways to modify the text. First, where you're editing the contents of the text (and you can select all or some of the characters or add more). Second, you can select the entire block and pick it up and move it or just modify the attributes. (This is not the same as simply selecting all the characters while editing the block). Click the Selection tool to stop editing the text. Your text block should become selected. (If it isn't, just click it once, and a rectangle appears around it.)

5. With the block selected, observe the Properties panel to make modifications. For now, just modify the text's color, font, and font height, as shown in Figure 2.17. Any setting you make here applies to all characters in the text (because you're editing the entire block). Most of the Properties are easy to learn. There's an especially nice feature that always displays a preview of the type face when you select a different font. The preview will actually display the characters you have selected if you're editing the contents of the text block (for example, if you double-click and then select some of the characters those characters appear in the preview).

6. Change the text style of just part of your text block to bold or italic by first selecting just the characters you want to change and then selecting bold or italic. Double-clicking the text block automatically selects the Text tool. You can select the characters as you would in any word processor (just click and drag). While some text is selected, use the Properties panel's settings to change just that text. If you want to change the font, the preview includes the text you have selected. You can use this method to change the properties of individual characters within any block of text.

FIGURE 2.17
The Properties panel allows you to change text attributes such as font size and color.

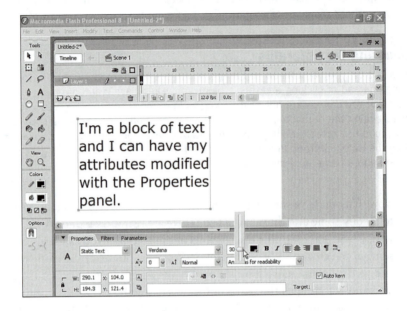

7. Select the Selection tool and then select the block of text. Using the Properties panel, change the alignment to Center Justify, as shown in Figure 2.18. Explore the other settings, which control attributes such as the margin padding and line spacing, by clicking the Format button.

FIGURE 2.18
When the block of text is selected, you can use the Properties panel > to change the alignment (to Center Justify in this case).

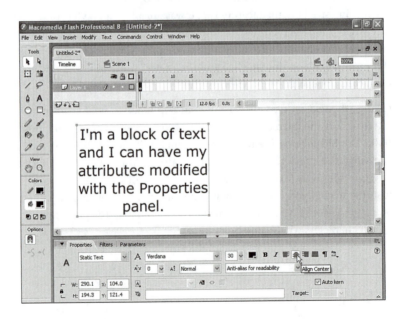

There are a few options shown in Figure 2.18 that we haven't covered yet. Specifically, the Text Type options are explored in Hour 16, "Using ActionScript for Advanced Interactivity." For now, you should always leave the Text Type drop-down in the Properties panel set to Static Text. When you do this, the text you type will never change, and your audience will see the same font you've chosen. (Dynamic is for text that needs to change while the movie runs and Input is for text you want to let the user change.) The Selectable button simply gives your users the ability to select and copy the text.

Another important option is the setting for Font rendering updated for Flash 8. This lets you control how the text *aliases* which affects how it will appear—most notably, when the text is very small. Generally, you should select the rendering option by eye—that is, simply select the option that looks best given your font, font size, and other layout conditions. For tiny text, like 8 or 10 point, Bitmap text is a good option—although you should always at least preview how Anti-alias for readability looks. The option for Use device fonts is effectively "no anti-alias" (like Bitmap text) however the user will have to have the same font installed on their machine or a substitute will be used—so it's a very risky option. There are actually two reasons to consider the Anti-alias for animation option: first, if the text is being moved for an animation it will look smoother; and second, this is the only version of anti-aliasing available when you plan to deliver your site to users with the older Flash players (more about targeting older players in Hours 19 and 24). Finally, the Custom anti-alias option (only available in Flash Professional 8) lets you fine tune the thickness and sharpness for any look you prefer.

Aliasing and Anti-aliasing

Anti-aliasing is a way of smoothing otherwise rough diagonals and curves with a blurry fuzz. If you zoom in on a diagonal line without anti-aliasing you'll see a staircase effect. Adding fuzz can make that diagonal line look better, albeit blurrier. Normally, anti-aliased text appears smoother and is much more pleasing. One problem arises when the anti-aliased text is small—it can be too blurry to read. In earlier versions of Flash the only viable solution for small text was to turn off anti-aliasing completely (which is still sometimes the best option) although now you have a variety of options. In addition, anti-aliasing affects how fast animated text can fly across the screen.

Selecting and Transforming Objects

Now that you've seen how to create lines, fills, shapes (with both lines and fills), and text, it's time to explore how to modify them. The process is simple. You select the object you want to modify by using the Selection tool and then you modify it.

Selecting exactly what you want to modify is often the most challenging part. The following section looks at some of the fundamentals, and you'll learn even more about this in Hour 5.

Object Draw Mode Versus Merge Mode

Before I can discuss selecting objects you need to understand the difference between the two ways to create objects: Merge mode and (new to Flash 8) Object draw mode. By default, and any time you *don't* have the Object Drawing option selected in the Tools panel, you're in what's called Merge mode. In merge mode, all the drawing tools create shapes. These fills and lines are all drawn on the same plane meaning that if you draw two shapes on top of each other, the one drawn second will wipe away the shape underneath. This behavior can actually be used to your advantage although it is disorienting to many at first. Appendix A goes over some such tricks.

Object Draw mode makes everything you draw a "drawing object." Unlike shapes, Drawing objects can be stacked and won't eat away at each other. Despite the fact I've taught hundreds of students how to draw in earlier versions of Flash (that only worked in merge mode) I'm pretty sure Object Draw mode is a more intuitive way to learn.

Normally, the draw mode you have selected affects what you draw. When you're in Object Draw mode, each time you click to draw line, fill, rectangle, or oval you create a new Drawing Object. Deep inside that Drawing object is a shape. You can double-click to edit the contents and you'll find a plain old shape inside. You may need to access the shape inside in order to select (and change, move, or delete) just part of the object. You'll learn much more about selecting shapes later this hour— but selecting a Drawing object means selecting the whole object. (When you're done editing the shape inside a Drawing object you double-click off the object or click the blue arrow button at the left of the address bar as shown in Figure 2.19.)

Because Drawing objects contain shapes (that won't eat away at other shapes), it shouldn't be a surprise that Flash provides a way to convert a shape or shapes into a drawing object. To convert a shape into a Drawing object, select all the shapes you want, and then choose Modify, Combine Objects, Union. Similarly, if you want the contents of a Drawing Object (that is, the shapes inside it) to reside as a shape then select the Drawing Object and choose Modify, Break Apart. Just realize those shapes will now behave like any shape and may get eaten away by other shapes on the sole plane where all shapes reside.

Edit bar

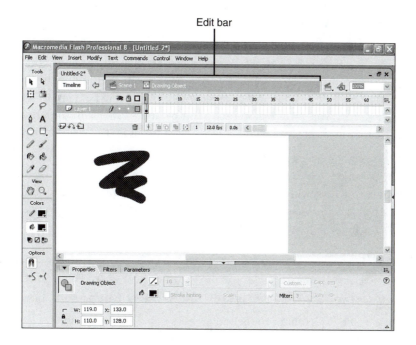

FIGURE 2.19
Use the address bar (officially, the "Edit Bar") to return to your main stage when finished editing the contents of a Drawing Object.

The whole concept of shape vs. Drawing object only applies to lines and fills. Text behaves more like a Drawing Object (though, it's really neither) because it won't eat away at other things you draw. Another tidbit to know is that you can always toggle between Object Draw mode (and not) by pressing J. Keep in mind, this only affects things you're about to draw, not things you've already drawn.

Like I said, I think Object Draw mode is more intuitive. Here's a quick review in order of importance:

▶ Realize you can only select an entire Drawing Object, not just some or portions of the shapes contained.

▶ In order to get at the shapes in a Drawing Object, double-click. Just be careful not to get lost while inside—remember to exit the object by clicking the left arrow in the address bar.

▶ The setting in the Tools panel (for Object Draw mode or not) affects new things you draw, like to convert an existing shape or shapes to a Drawing Object via Modify, Combine Objects, Union, or to turn a Drawing Object into a shape select Modify, Break Apart.

Selection Tools

The two basic selection tools are the Selection tool and the Lasso tool. The Subselect tool (the white arrow) is for selecting and editing individual anchor points (in the same way the Pen tool created them). If you're familiar with controlling shapes by using the Pen tool, this section will be familiar to you. If you're not familiar with using the Pen tool, you should master the basics before working with the Subselect tool. This section concentrates on just the Selection tool and the Lasso tool first.

The Selection tool might seem so simple that it's not worth discussing, but it's actually quite powerful. You've already used the Selection tool to select an object by clicking it once. The key to the Selection tool is that the cursor changes to tell you what will happen when you click. You can try out this tool on a couple simple shapes in the following task.

▼ **Try It Yourself**

Use the Selection Tool to Select and Modify Shapes

In this task you'll explore how the Selection tool's cursor changes to inform you what will happen when you click. Here are the steps:

1. Select the Oval tool, but before you draw, select a very thick stroke height (5 or so) in the Properties panel. Turn on Object Drawing via the Options area in the Tool panel. Draw a circle and then select the Rectangle tool, turn off Object Drawing and draw a square.

2. Select the Selection tool. Move the cursor to the middle of your square. The cursor changes to include the "move" symbol, indicating that if you were to click and drag, you would start moving this fill (see Figure 2.20).

FIGURE 2.20
The Selection tool's cursor changes when it is on top of a fill to indicate that clicking will start to move the fill.

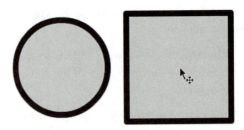

3. Click and drag. Indeed, only the fill of the square moves. Select Edit, Undo (or press Ctrl+Z) to restore the fill. Also, make sure nothing is selected by just clicking the white area of the Stage or pressing Esc.

▼

4. Position the cursor over the circle you drew. If you click and drag you'll move the entire circle because it's a Drawing Object. Its fill and stroke are contained in one object.

5. Move the cursor so that it is near the outside edge of the square. The cursor adds a curved tail, as shown in Figure 2.21. Now if you click and drag, you bend the line. Go ahead and click and drag to the left, and the line portion of the square bends. Notice that the fill bends with the line. This cursor behavior is consistent for Drawing Objects or shapes. However, because it's possible to select the square's fill and stroke independently (as it's a shape), you'll need to just click and drag—don't click and then click and drag because that selects then moves the stroke portion.

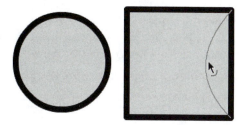

FIGURE 2.21
When the cursor is near a line, it changes to indicate that clicking will start to bend the line.

6. Make sure nothing is selected and move the cursor so that it's near another corner of the square. A corner shape is added to the cursor, which means that if you drag, you'll be moving the corner point (see Figure 2.22). Try it. It's like you're bending the line, but instead you're just moving the corner.

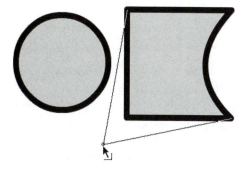

FIGURE 2.22
When the Selection tool is near a corner, it shows yet another cursor, this time indicating that you can extend the corner.

7. You've seen the cursor communicate what will happen when you click and drag. Now you can use the Selection tool to simply select something. For instance, clicking anywhere on the circle (the line or the fill) selects the entire Drawing Object. However you can select just the line portion of one side of the square by clicking it.

8. With part of the square's stroke selected, notice that the cursor adds the "move" symbol (when you're near the selected line). Click and drag now, and you can move the stroke. You can also just press Delete to remove that line portion. Do so now.

9. Deselect everything (by clicking a blank area onscreen or pressing Esc) and this time double-click on what's left of the square's stroke. When you double-click a stroke, you select the entire stroke. At this point, you could move or delete the stroke. Just leave it for now.

10. The circle was easy to select because it is a Drawing Object. Because the square is just a regular shape, if you click the fill, you select just the fill. If you click the stroke, you select just one side. If you double-click the stroke, you select only the stroke portion. However, if you double-click the fill of the square you should find that the entire square is selected. Now you can move or delete the square. In fact, you could even select Modify, Combine Objects, Union to turn the square into a Drawing Object. (Don't bother though.)

11. Another way to select the square is to *marquee* it. With the Selection tool still selected, click outside the square and drag until you you've drawn an imaginary rectangle that surrounds the square entirely. When you let go, the square becomes selected.

12. Sometimes the arrangement of other shapes onscreen makes the marquee technique difficult or impossible. Notice in 2.23 that you can't marquee just the square without selecting part of the circle. In fact, there's a preference (Edit, Preferences, General) called Contact-sensitive Selection and Lasso tools but that setting doesn't affect selecting shapes (only Drawing Objects, grouped shapes, and symbols—covered in Hour 4). To select the square in such a sticky situation as Figure 2.23, you could simply double-click the fill of the square. However, there's another tool you can use to do this: the Lasso tool.

13. Select the Lasso tool and then click and drag around a shape to select it. The Polygon Mode option for the Lasso tool makes the tool act almost like the Pen tool (though I get the feeling the Polygon Mode behaves like a string or rubber band). Select the Polygon Mode option, as shown in Figure 2.24, and click and let go. Then click and release in a new location to extend the selection. Continue to extend the selection and then double-click when you're done. (In this case, double-clicking the fill would probably be easier, but often when you're selecting several objects, you need to use this method.)

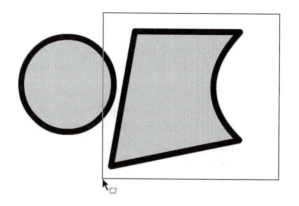

FIGURE 2.23
Sometimes using the marquee technique would select more than what you want.

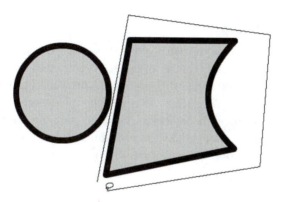

FIGURE 2.24
The Polygon Mode option for the Lasso tool lets you click for each corner of the selection you want to make.

14. Finally, you can decide to select just a portion of a shape. Suppose you want to chop off the top of the square. You can use either the Lasso tool or the marquee technique with the Selection tool to select the portion desired (see Figure 2.25). If you want to select just part of the circle you need to first double-click (to enter the drawing object) and then you can select the contained shapes as normal. Just remember to get back to your main stage by clicking the left-arrow in the address bar.

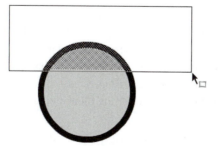

FIGURE 2.25
Using the Selection tool to marquee just part of a shape chops off the top of the circle in this case.

You use the Selection tool to employ the **marquee** technique. If you click and drag an object, it moves or bends. However, when you click the Stage where there are no objects, you see a rectangle appear while you drag (this is the marquee). You can draw that rectangle around other objects, and they will be selected when you let go. Using this marquee technique to select objects is often easier than clicking to select objects.

You'll learn how to modify what you've selected in the next section, but at this point, you have the fundamental selection techniques under your belt. More advanced techniques are discussed in Hour 5, but the best clue as to what will happen if you click is to notice the cursor change. You'll find many places in Flash where the cursor is attempting to communicate information to you. For example, you can draw a line and see the same cursor changes discussed in the preceding task.

The Dropper Tool

One of the easiest ways to modify what you've drawn is to simply change the color. For example, the Paint Bucket tool can change a fill's color, and the Ink Bottle tool can change a stroke (its color and other attributes). This works fine when you make the effort to first select the fill color, for example, and then select the Paint Bucket tool and click a fill to change it. Sometimes, however, you want one fill to match the color of another. The Dropper tool lets you sample a color from an object that is already onscreen. The cool part is that it actually samples more than just color, as you'll see in the following task.

▼   **Try It Yourself**

Select Attributes with the Dropper Tool

In this task you'll use the Dropper tool to select more attributes than simply color. Here are the steps to follow:

1. Select the Oval tool, set the stroke height to 10, and draw a circle. Change the stroke height, the stroke color, and the fill color. Then draw another circle. Finally, change both the stroke and fill color settings and draw a third circle.

2. At this point, if you wanted the second circle to have the same fill color as the first circle, you would just have to change the fill color. If you remember the color, you're in luck. However, better than relying on your memory, you can select the Dropper tool. Notice how the cursor changes to include a brush when you're over the fill of the first circle, as shown in Figure 2.26. This indicates that if you click, you'll select the fill attributes of this shape.

▼

3. With the Dropper tool, click the center of the first circle. Not only does the fill color change to the sampled fill color, but the Paint Bucket tool also becomes active. You can now fill the second circle with the color sampled by the Dropper tool.

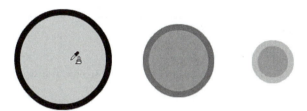

FIGURE 2.26
The Dropper tool changes its cursor to indicate that it will sample a fill when you click.

4. If you want to match the strokes on both circles, you could use the Ink Bottle tool, but you would have to set all the attributes manually. Better than that, you can use the Dropper tool to sample all the stroke's attributes in the first circle. Select the Dropper tool and move it near the stroke of the first circle. Notice that the cursor changes to include a pencil (see Figure 2.27). This indicates that you'll be sampling the stroke (or line portion) of that shape.

FIGURE 2.27
The Dropper tool changes its cursor to indicate that it will sample a stroke when you click.

5. Click to sample the stroke, and you see the stroke attributes update in the Properties panel. Also, the Ink Bottle becomes active, so you can click the second circle to change its stroke. The thing to remember is that the Dropper tool samples all attributes, not just color.

Transforming Scale, Rotation, Envelope, and Distortion

You've seen how to bend, extend, and move shapes by using the Selection tool. You've seen how to change shapes that are already onscreen by using the Ink Bottle and Paint Bucket tools. There are still more ways to modify the objects you select. The Free Transform tool is your key to even more modifications.

Basically, you just have to select an object with the Free Transform tool active. Four options appear any time you use the Free Transform tool and have an object selected. You can also find these options by selecting Modify, Transform. In the following task, you'll experiment with these options.

▼ **Try It Yourself**

Transform Drawn Objects

In this task you'll explore the four basic options for the Free Transform tool. Follow these steps:

1. Use the Rectangle tool to draw a square. Select the Free Transform tool and double-click the center of the square to select it entirely. (Interestingly, the Free Transform tool can perform many selection tasks.)

2. At this point none of the four options should be selected (see Figure 2.28). This means you're in Free Transform mode, and if you have a steady hand, it's possible to rotate, scale, or distort the shape.

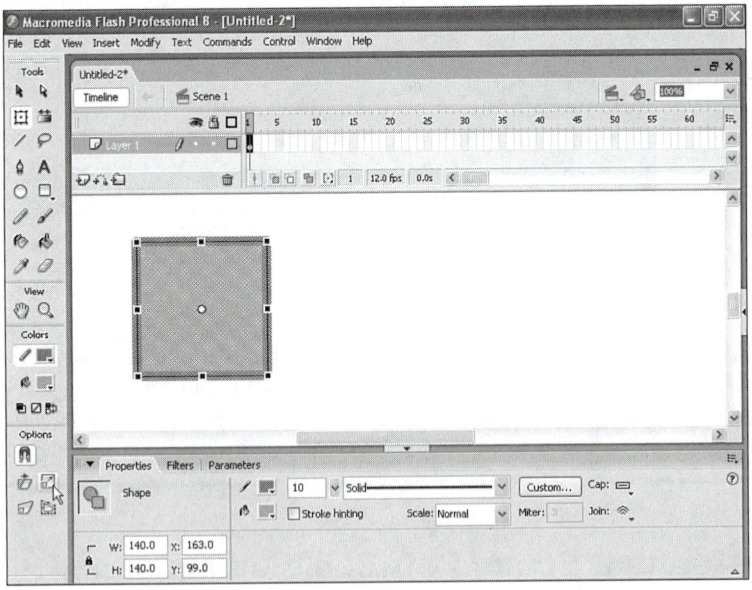

FIGURE 2.28
When an object is selected, you can choose the Free Transform tool's Scale option.

3. Explore the possibilities by rolling your cursor over the square handles at the corners and sides of the shape—but don't click yet. Depending on where you move your mouse, the cursor changes to two versions of the Scale option, as well as Rotate and Skew (as in Figure 2.29). Actually, if you hold down Ctrl, the corners make the cursor change to the Distort option.

▼

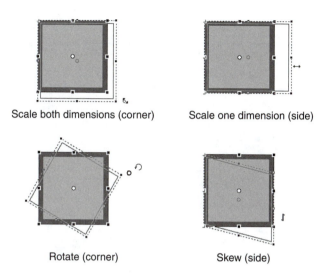

Scale both dimensions (corner)   Scale one dimension (side)

Rotate (corner)   Skew (side)

FIGURE 2.29
Depending on which handle you grab and which option is selected, you can use both Scale and Rotate to modify the shape in multiple ways.

4. Free Transform mode can be really touchy, so let's go through the options individually. The selected object shows square handles in the corners and on the sides. Notice that the cursor changes when you roll over these handles. The corner handles let you scale both width and height equally and at the same time. The side handles let you change just width or just height. Click and drag a corner handle to change the scale. Notice that this version of Scale (compared to Scale in Free Transform mode) maintains your shape's proportions (horizontally and vertically). Now drag a side handle, and you change just the width.

5. Make sure the square is still selected and choose the Rotate and Skew option. Now the corner handles rotate; side handles skew. Roll your cursor over the handles to see the cursor change.

6. Click and drag a corner handle and notice that you can rotate the square. Actually, if the default Snap to Objects option is selected (that is, if the magnet button is pressed in, as shown in Figure 2.30), the object snaps into place at 15-degree increments. (You'll learn more about this later in this hour.)

7. Select the Distort option. Drag the shape by the handles on the corners to distort. It turns out that the Selection tool can create the same effect as Distort, but only when the shape itself has a corner to grab. Without this Distort option, you would find making a distorted ellipse nearly impossible. Finally, try holding down the Shift key when you distort (by dragging a corner handle). This way, you can distort two sides evenly.

FIGURE 2.30
If Snap to Objects is turned on, when you rotate an object, it snaps to logical positions, such as 45 degrees.

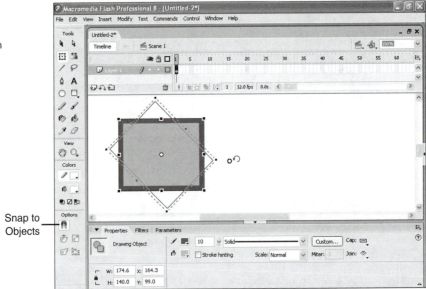

Snap to Objects

8. Finally, the wildest of transformation options—Envelope. To best understand this option, draw a new square, select the Free Transform tool, and click the Envelope option. When your shape is selected, you see many handles. Move the square handles to "influence" the shape. It's as though the shape tries to touch all the squares, even if they're pulled out to one side. The circle handles are like the tangents created when you draw by using the Pen tool. They control the rate at which a shape bends to reach the square handles.

Handles are little white squares that provide a way for you to stretch, rotate, or otherwise transform a selected object. When you select an object, it is either highlighted or appears with a box drawn around its edges. When you select the Free Transform tool's Scale or Rotate and Skew options, for example, handles are added to the selection. Different handles often have different functions, but the cursor change is your best clue as to exactly what will happen when you click.

Don't overlook the fact that you can select more than one shape or object and then transform everything that is selected in one move. Also, you can find all the tools explored in the preceding task by selecting Modify, Transform. You can find still another way to do all these things in the Transform panel. The Transform panel lets you rotate or skew any selected shape. You can also remove transformations immediately after making them by clicking the Reset button in the Transform panel (or by using the keyboard shortcut Ctrl+Shift+Z). Finally, there's a really interesting button, the Copy and Transform button, in the Transform panel. This button duplicates the selected object and applies the most recent transformation every time you click it. The result is a "spirograph" effect.

Using Snap to Objects to Connect Shapes

One of the most profound features in Flash is the way Snap to Objects helps you draw. By simply selecting View, Snapping, Snap to Objects (or clicking the magnet button in the main toolbar when the Selection or Free Transform tools are active), you can draw perfectly round circles, perfectly horizontal or vertical lines, and much more. The visual clue that Snap to Objects is helping you is the dark ring that often appears next to your cursor while you drag. When you see that ring, you know Flash is trying to help you draw.

You might already know from using other software that holding the Shift key constrains your cursor similarly to Snap to Objects. But Snap to Objects can do much more. In addition to helping you draw perfect shapes, Snap to Objects also allows you to connect two shapes. It's much more than simply making two shapes touch—they actually become bonded. In Flash, unless two shapes have been snapped together, they might look connected when they actually aren't. For example, you'll draw an arrow in the following task, but unless the arrow head is snapped to the arrow's body, it might not remain visually connected when you scale it larger. After a shape is snapped to another, it's forever connected.

Try It Yourself ▼

Use Snap to Objects to Draw Perfect Shapes and Connect Objects

This task walks you through some of the amazing ways Snap to Objects helps you draw. Here are the steps:

1. Confirm that Snap to Objects is selected in the View, Snapping menu, and then select the Rectangle tool. While you click and drag, if you're anywhere close to drawing a perfect square, you see the dark ring appear near your cursor (see Figure 2.31).

2. Select the Line tool and draw a line at a 45-degree angle elsewhere on the Stage. This time you have to hold Shift as you draw the line to constrain it to 45 degrees.

▼

FIGURE 2.31
If Snap to Objects is turned on, while you're dragging with the Rectangle tool, a dark ring appears, to help you create a perfect square.

3. Connect the top of the line to a corner of the square. To do so, select the Selection tool and make sure before you click and drag the end of the line that the cursor changes to show the corner tail. You can then click and drag to extend the line, and you see it snap to the square. Keep dragging and notice how the line can snap to a corner or a side. (There are several different logical locations on the square.) Snap the line to a corner.

4. The last step probably changed the angle of your line, so select Edit, Undo (or press Ctrl+Z) and try again. This time, single-click the line to select the whole thing; then click the end of the line and drag to move it. You should be able to snap the end of the line to the corner of the square (this time without changing any angles). The only touchy part of this step is that, when the line is selected, if you don't pick up and drag the line from the end point or the middle, you don't see the dark ring. If you don't see the dark ring, you need to let go and try picking up the line again.

5. Now draw near the diagonal line two lines that are almost parallel to it.

6. Use the Selection tool to extend (by dragging) the end points of the two lines. Extend one end to connect to another corner of the square and extend the other end to the end of the 45-degree line, as shown in Figure 2.32.

FIGURE 2.32
You can extend lines to connect end points by dragging.

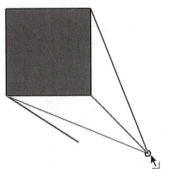

7. To prove that everything is truly snapped together, use the Selection tool to drag the corner point where all three lines merge. If everything is snapped properly, all three lines move at once and don't disconnect from the object to which they're snapped.

The preceding task gives you just a taste of how you can create perfect shapes by using Snap to Objects. Consider, for example, vertical and horizontal lines. If you select a vertical line, select it, and then pick it up from the center, you can snap it to the right end of the horizontal line. Then you can just drag the point of intersection to the right while remaining constrained to the same horizontal line (which the dark ring will help you do). A perfect arrow is created! In Appendix A, "Shapes You Can Make in Merge Drawing Mode," I show you how to create several sophisticated geometric shapes by using Snap to Objects.

Another related snap feature is called Snap Align. Snap Align creates dashed vertical and horizontal lines that appear when you're dragging an object (shown in Figure 2.33). When you select View, Snapping, you find settings to edit or disable Snap Align.

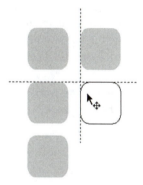

FIGURE 2.33
Snap Align helps you align objects with intuitive and subtle dashed lines.

If you select View Rulers, you can click in a ruler and drag it onto your Stage to create guides. If View, Guides, Snap to Guides is selected, you can draw objects that are lined up with and connected to the guides. The guides are just for your use—they're invisible to your audience.

Finally, if you ever find Snap to Objects or Snap to Guides distracting, remember that you can turn it off. Maybe you want to draw two lines really close, but you don't want them to snap together. In addition, you can control the sensitivity of Snap to Objects or Snap to Guides (and other ways Flash tries to improve your drawings) by selecting Edit, Preferences to open the Preferences dialog box and then selecting the Editing tab.

Summary

This long hour looked at practically every drawing tool in Flash. You have learned how to create lines, fills, combination shapes, and text. After you created some objects, you found ways to modify their color, shape, size, rotation, and location. In addition, you learned about the two drawing modes in Flash 8: Object Draw and Merge mode. You even learned how to snap two shapes together. Even if you don't think you'll be creating artwork in Flash (maybe you're working with someone else who's the "artist" for your team), you should understand two important concepts: First, the simpler the shape, the smaller the file. Second, only shapes that are snapped together are truly connected. Of course, if you're going to create the artwork, thanks to what you've learned in this hour, you now know how to use the fundamental drawing capabilities in Flash.

Q&A

Q *What's the purpose of the little white circle that appears in the center of a shape when I select the Free Transform tool? It doesn't seem to do anything.*

A That circle is the transform center point about which the shape will rotate when you rotate it. By editing the location of this circle, you can rotate an object around a point other than its visual center.

Q *Why does my Brush tool appear to be working when I click and hold, but when I release, nothing has been painted?*

A You probably have the Brush tool's Brush Mode option set to Paint Selection, in which case only fills that were previously selected are painted. Other Brush Mode options can also cause unexpected results if they were set accidentally.

Q *It looks like there are a bunch of other tools (especially those under the Options section) that we haven't looked at. Are we going to go through each one in detail?*

A Many of the rest of the tools and options are indeed covered where applicable in Hour 4. However, given the foundation this chapter has provided, you should feel comfortable exploring some of the other tools. For example, the Eraser tool has a modifier called Eraser Mode that's strikingly similar to the Brush Mode and Pencil Mode of other tools. Try to apply the knowledge you've gathered in this hour, and I bet you can figure out most of the other tools on your own.

Workshop

The Workshop consists of quiz questions and answers to help you solidify your understanding of the material covered in this hour. You should try to answer the questions before checking the answers.

Quiz

1. The quick key for the Selection tool is V, for the Pencil is Y, and for the Brush is B. Where's the best way to find the quick keys for the other tools?

    A. By looking at the front of this book where they're all listed for your reference.

    B. By going to the Macromedia website.

    C. By rolling your cursor over the tool and waiting for the answer to appear as a ToolTip.

2. Is there more than one way to set fill color?

    A. Yes. Anyplace you see a swatch, you can set fill color.

    B. Yes. There are many places where the fill color swatch appears, and setting any of them affects all the others.

    C. No. You must set the fill color from the fill swatch in the drawing toolbar (the swatch with the bucket icon).

Quiz Answers

1. C. Although Answers A and B may be true, the simplest way is to use the ToolTips. By the way, although the default is "Show tooltips," you can change this setting by selecting Edit, Preferences.

2. B. You don't need to memorize all the places where the fill swatch appears. Any fill swatch will do. Of course, you can't change the fill color by adjusting just any swatch—it must be a fill swatch, not a stroke swatch.

Exercise

Try your hand at creating perfect geometric shapes, such as a cube. Use Snap to Objects to help you. If you want to see a few examples of interesting shapes, check out Appendix A, which describes how to create some common shapes. Another idea is to try to copy a logo from a familiar brand-name product. This will force you to break down the task into geometric shapes.

HOUR 3

Importing Graphics into Flash

What You'll Learn in This Hour:

- ▶ How to import vector graphics into Flash
- ▶ How to import bitmap (raster) graphics
- ▶ Ways to avoid imported graphics
- ▶ How to optimize and maintain the best quality possible when importing

In the last two hours, you've seen how you can create sophisticated custom graphics very quickly in Flash. Despite how powerful Flash's graphic creation tools are, eventually you might want to import graphics created elsewhere. Two good reasons for this are to use photographic images or to use existing graphics (instead of re-creating them from scratch). You can certainly use these other graphics inside Flash—and that's what you're going to learn how to do in this hour.

Vector Graphics Versus Raster Graphics

Vector graphics have certain characteristics that are due to how they are stored by a computer. A vector graphics file contains the math to redraw the image onscreen. For example, a circle includes information such as the radius, the line thickness, and the color. All the graphics you create inside Flash are vector based. Vector graphics have two advantages: The file size tends to remain small (therefore, it downloads fast), and the image can be scaled to any size without any degradation of the image quality (a circle is still a circle, even if it's a large circle).

Vector graphics are great, but it's important to realize their disadvantages. Vector graphics require the user's computer to work hard to display the image (it has to do a lot of math), and vector graphics often look "computery" or antiseptic because they tend to involve geometric shapes. Both disadvantages can be overcome, but you should be aware of them.

Bitmapped graphics (also called **raster graphics**) are fundamentally different from vector graphics. A raster graphics file contains the color information for each pixel. If the image is 100 pixels by 100 pixels, that's 10,000 pixels, each of which has a color value. As a result, raster graphics are almost always relatively large files. Raster graphics also can't be scaled very effectively. They tend to get grainy, similar to a photograph that has been enlarged. An advantage of raster graphics is that they appear onscreen very quickly.

It might seem that vector graphics are obviously the better choice. However, the decision of whether to use vector graphics or raster graphics should be based on the nature of the image. If the image is geometric, with clear delineations of color, a vector graphic is a good choice. If the image is a photograph of a person or a geographic location, nothing but a bitmap will do. Selecting which format to use is pretty easy when you know the considerations of each type.

Reasons to Avoid Importing Graphics

Flash's capability to create nice vector graphics might be the best justification for this warning: Don't import graphics into Flash unless you have to! In this hour, you'll learn how to import graphics—but that doesn't mean it's always a good idea. If there's one way to make your Flash movie download or play more slowly, it's importing graphics unnecessarily. You need to find ways to avoid importing graphics.

Wanting to import graphics is a natural tendency. If you show a graphics professional who's an expert with Illustrator or FreeHand how to draw in Flash, his first question will be how to bring his Illustrator or FreeHand files into Flash. This hour you'll learn the answer.

However, if you consider why a graphics professional would ask that in the first place, you expose a problem. People can do some amazing (and complicated) things with other drawing tools. Some of the ways graphics files that get more complicated include the use of gradients, intricate text, and lots of individual objects. Using such complicated graphics in Flash causes two problems. First, Flash can't always handle all the intricacies in a complicated file, so the task becomes difficult. Second, a complicated file downloads and plays more slowly than one that isn't complicated—so why would you want such a file in a Flash movie? The number-one consideration when deciding whether to import a graphic into Flash is whether a simpler version can be re-created in Flash or whether the graphic can at least be simplified before being imported into Flash. If you ask the graphics person to re-create the image in Flash, he might say that it doesn't enable him to do what he intended. In that case, your solution lies in making the graphic simpler—not in squeezing it into Flash.

Even so, you might still need to import graphics. Maybe you have a photograph (or another raster graphic) that you want to use, or perhaps you have a simple existing vector graphic (such as a company logo) that you don't want to redraw in Flash. We'll discuss raster graphics in the section "Using Bitmaps (Also Known As Raster Graphics)," later in this hour, but first let's look at importing vector graphics.

Importing Vector Graphics

There may be times when you have an existing vector graphic that you need to include in a Flash movie. Typically, such a vector graphic is likely to be geometric— although not necessarily. Regardless of the exact form of the vector graphic, unless it's super complicated, you'll be able to import it into Flash.

Importing from a File

One way to incorporate other graphics into Flash is to import them from a file. It's as simple as selecting File, Import to open the Import dialog and then pointing to the file you want, as shown in Figure 3.1. You see several file types listed, but that doesn't mean they all work equally well. Not only are several image file formats list-ed (both raster and vector), but video and audio file formats also appear. Let's first look at the vector image formats that are available for import.

Although many file types are listed in the Import dialog box, only three vector formats are worth considering: FreeHand (.FH11 through .FH7), Illustrator (.ai), and Flash Player (.swf). Occasionally, complex data in FreeHand or Illustrator won't translate perfectly. Because of this limit, you will get the most reliable results if you first export a .swf (Flash Player) file from Illustrator or FreeHand (and then import that .swf into Flash). We'll discuss how this choice limits your ability to edit individual elements once imported later in this hour, in the section "Importing Flash Player Files."

Importing FreeHand and Illustrator Files

Flash can seamlessly import FreeHand and Illustrator source files. If you're familiar with these tools, using them is the easiest way to import vector art into Flash. It's simply a matter of selecting File, Import in Flash and then selecting a file to import. In fact, you have to decide whether you want to import to the Stage or import to a Library. We'll cover the Library in Hour 4, "Using the Library for Productivity." The last option under File, Import is Open External Library, which won't be needed until Hour 23, "Working on Large Projects and in Team Environments." For now, just select File, Import, Import to Stage and you are presented with one of the two Import dialog boxes (depending on whether you imported a FreeHand or Illustrator file) shown in Figures 3.2 and 3.3.

FIGURE 3.1
Importing
images (or
audio) is as
simple as
selecting the
file you want to
import.

Several options are available when you import Illustrator or FreeHand documents into Flash. For example, you can turn Freehand pages into keyframes or scenes. Flash just needs to know how you want to handle pages for which there is no Flash equivalent. All the options are fairly easy to interpret. (Also, you'll see the same set of options when importing Adobe Acrobat files—PDFs.)

Here are some tips to help you import drawings into Flash. First, if you use FreeHand, be sure to take advantage of FreeHand's symbols because they translate directly to Flash's symbols so that graphics can be recycled. You'll learn about symbols and Flash's Library in Hour 4. Also, each object created in FreeHand should be separated into its own layer. Although you can easily put multiple objects on one layer, you'll be able to access individual objects easier if you create multiple layers.

FIGURE 3.2
When you
import a
FreeHand file,
Flash provides
this dialog box.

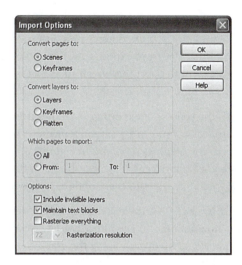

FIGURE 3.3
Illustrator's
Import Options
dialog box
includes a simi-
lar set of import
options to
FreeHand's.

There are many text effects that you can create in FreeHand and Illustrator that don't translate to Flash. For example, text attached to paths doesn't remain editable when a file is imported into Flash. Also, because only FreeHand supports strokes on text, Flash ignores this effect. Fine adjustments to font sizes and kerning are possible in FreeHand and Illustrator, but they don't work as well in Flash, so font spacing often changes slightly when a file is imported into Flash. Sometimes text automatically converts to paths (which means it isn't editable when it gets into Flash). You'll learn about converting to outlines as a solution to some text problems later in this hour, in the section "Maintaining Image Integrity." These are just some general tips. Creating the smallest, best-looking image that imports seamlessly into Flash might take some additional experimenting in either FreeHand or Illustrator.

Importing Flash Player Files

The most reliable option for importing vector graphics into Flash (besides, possibly, simply importing native FreeHand files) is to import Flash Player (.swf) files. Most graphics people don't think of .swf as an image file format, but it's certainly a standard. Of course, a .swf is not like a FreeHand file or an Illustrator file because it's not fully editable. When using newer versions of FreeHand and Illustrator (Illustrator 8 requires the free Macromedia Flash Writer plug-in), you can export your working files into the .swf format. They export amazingly well, the final files are smaller, and the image retains all the details and quality of the original.

The best process is to create a graphic in whatever program you prefer and then if that program doesn't export .swfs, open the file in a program that does (such as FreeHand, Illustrator, Fireworks, or many others found in Appendix B, "Resources").

Then simply export it as a `.swf`. You can then import the `.swf` directly into a Flash file. Even if the graphics program you use doesn't support exporting `.swf` files, you can open the file in a tool that does and export a `.swf` from there. This means that the graphics tool you select must export files in a format that is supported by the tool you use to export `.swf` files.

If you have trouble with the process of exporting `.swf` files from the graphics program and importing into Flash, you can try several remedies. First, you can investigate the export options in the graphics program. In Figure 3.4, you can see dialog boxes that appear when you export `.swf` files. You should notice some similarities between the options. Experimenting with these options is a good place to start.

In addition to exporting to `.swf` files, there are a few specific techniques you can try (covered in the section "Maintaining Image Integrity," later in this hour). Ultimately, however, the solution *sometimes* involves making the graphic simpler—that is, reducing its complexity.

Although exporting a `.swf` for Flash to import is the safest bet, it means elements such as text will not be editable inside Flash. Naturally, you could do the text layout in Flash—but that might not be ideal for your purposes. I guess the point is that `.swf` importing is the safest bet but not always the most complete option.

FIGURE 3.4
When exporting a `.swf` file from FreeHand or Illustrator, you're given one of these dialog boxes.

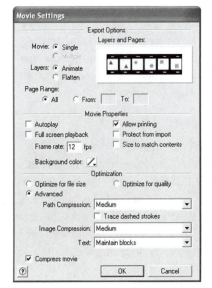

FreeHand

Illustrator

Maintaining Image Integrity

Despite how simple the export/import process may sound, it can be very frustrating when it doesn't work! I don't want to sound like a broken record, but the best way to maintain image quality is to create all your graphics inside Flash. When you must import an existing graphic or use a more advanced drawing tool, you can do several things to maintain image integrity. However, some of these tips are unnecessary when you're exporting .swf files from either Illustrator or FreeHand.

Font and text effects are usually the first things to go. Most drawing tools provide incredible font control, but Flash doesn't. (To be fair, Flash 8 added fine text controls and a much improved font display technology called FlashType covered in Hour 2.) The first consideration with text is whether the text must be editable within Flash. If you don't need to edit the text within Flash, you'll see the highest-quality results if the text is first converted to paths. You are given an option to do this automatically when exporting .swf files from FreeHand, and it doesn't affect the source FreeHand file—just the exported .swf. FreeHand's Convert to Paths feature is the same as Illustrator's Create Outlines and is equivalent to Flash's Break Apart option under the Modify menu. Of course, you'll never be able to edit the text after you use one of these options, so you should save a backup first. In addition, this can tend to increase file size. We'll look at file size issues in much greater detail in Hour 21, "Optimizing a Flash Site."

If you use gradients, you should definitely consider using the Export .swf option. Using this option helps keep the file size down and performance speed up (rather than simply retaining quality). A simple gradient, for example, can turn into a separate circle for each step. Imagine hundreds of concentric circles, each varying only slightly in color and size. You can see this effect when you pick up and move an imported graphic that has this characteristic, as in Figure 3.5. It's easy to see that such a gradient creates a larger file that plays relatively slowly—it's simply more complicated than it needs to be. When you export .swf files from Illustrator or FreeHand, the gradients are converted to Flash gradients. (In Hour 5, "Applied Layout Techniques," you'll learn how to create and edit gradients in Flash.)

FIGURE 3.5
Often an imported graphic is much bigger than it needs to be. This seemingly innocuous gradient is actually lots of individual concentric circles.

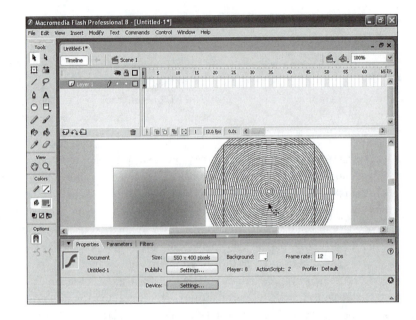

Using Bitmaps (Also Known As Raster Graphics)

In this section you'll see how bitmap (raster) graphics can be used in Flash. Raster graphics have inherently unique characteristics that can't be created inside Flash. The only warning related to using this option is to make sure you really *need* raster graphics. The following are some cases that justify the use of raster graphics:

▶ A photograph. The only time to consider using a vector alternative to a photograph is when the picture is of a very geometric object. Otherwise, photographs should be raster graphics.

▶ A series of still images extracted from frames of a short video.

▶ An image with special effects that can't be achieved by using a vector tool, such as clouds, fire, water, and other natural effects. (Of course, this is an invitation for a talented artist to re-create such an effect by using a vector tool such as Flash.)

If you're unfamiliar with the difference between vector graphics and raster graphics, learning when one choice is better than the other can take some time. The file formats `.gif`, `.jpg`, `.png`, `.bmp`, and `.pct` are all raster graphics formats. However, just because a file was saved in one of these formats doesn't mean it was done appropriately. It's the nature of the image *in* the file that matters. If all you have is a `.gif`, for example, you need to first look at its contents to judge whether it's appropriate for raster graphics. Here's an easy way to decide: If you can trace or redraw the image in the file (with Flash's drawing toolbar, for instance), you're much better off redrawing it. If it's a photograph, you would never be able to trace it (so leave it as a raster graphic). If it's a picture of a plain box, maybe you could draw it and thus take advantage of all the benefits of vector graphics without even bothering with raster graphics.

Importing Raster Graphics

Importing a raster graphic is pretty simple to do. You just select File, Import, Import to Stage, to open the Import dialog box and then point to any raster graphic that Flash supports: `.jpg`, `.png`, `.gif`, `.bmp`, or `.pct`. That's it. (In fact, Flash imports a few other esoteric formats—such as Photoshop version 2.5—but the five listed here are by far the most popular.)

However, importing not only places the graphic on the Stage but also puts a master bitmap item into the Library. If you import a raster graphic and then delete the object from the Stage, the master bitmap item will still be in the Library (which you can find by selecting Window, Library). It's called a bitmap item, and it has a little icon that looks like a picture of a tree (as shown in Figure 3.6).

After a raster graphic is imported, you need to keep it in the Library. The bitmap icon that appears in the Library provides a way to specify how the image should be exported when you create a movie for the Web. If you leave it unchanged, your raster graphics will export using the default settings. You can also specify special settings for just that image. In the following task you'll import a raster graphic and explore some of these settings.

FIGURE 3.6
After you import a raster graphic, the bitmap item will appear in your Library.

▼   **Try It Yourself**

Import a Raster Graphic

In this task you'll import a raster graphic. Here are the steps:

1. In a new file, select File, Import, Import to Stage, to open the Import dialog box and then select a `.bmp`, `.pct`, `.png`, `.jpg`, or `.gif` file. If you don't have an image handy, just visit any web page and right-click an image to select an option to save it on your desktop. Then use that image as the file to import into Flash. Note that you probably don't want to import an image saved directly from a digital camera because it's probably huge.

2. Click the graphic on the Stage and delete it. Because it's a raster graphic, it's still safely in the Library.

3. Open your Library by selecting Window, Library or by pressing Ctrl+L.

4. Click the line in your Library that has the tree icon and the name of the file you imported.

5. In the Library, select Options, Properties. (The Options menu is inside the Library window at the top right.) The Bitmap Properties dialog box shown in Figure 3.7 appears. (This dialog box might look slightly different, depending on what type of file you imported.)

▼

FIGURE 3.7
The Bitmap Properties dialog box offers control over how each bitmap item in your Library will be treated during export.

6. In the Bitmap Properties dialog box, decide what export settings to use for this graphic. (Leave this dialog box onscreen while you walk through the next section.)

Adjusting Bitmap Properties

Flash imports all kinds of raster formats but only uses JPG, GIF, or PNG in an exported movie. In addition, any raster graphic is generically called a bitmap item once inside Flash's Library. This means that no matter what file type you import, you must use the Bitmap Properties dialog box to choose between JPEG (and its compression level) and lossless GIF/PNG for exporting. You can experiment with the Bitmap Properties dialog box and click the Test button after each change to see the effects on both image quality (in the little picture at the top left) and file size (in the text information at the bottom of the dialog box). See Figure 3.8. The process involves experimentation—making adjustments and viewing the corresponding results.

Image window

FIGURE 3.8
Selecting a low
JPEG compres-
sion (10) and
clicking Test
provides a pre-
view of the
resulting image
and its file size.

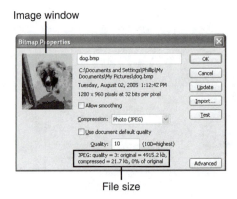

File size

JPEG compression is usually the most efficient option. Unless you import a .png or .gif, Flash sets the bitmap properties to JPEG by default. It's slightly confusing because if you import a .jpg file, Flash uses Imported JPEG Data by default, as shown in Figure 3.9. This option tells Flash to maintain the imported file's original compression (that is, don't recompress). Leaving this option selected is generally desirable because it's a bad idea to recompress.

FIGURE 3.9
Only imported
.jpg files
enable you to
use the JPEG
compression
contained in the
original file.

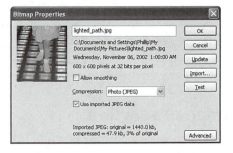

Watch
Out!

Three Ways to Use Imported Raster Graphics

There are three suitable approaches to using raster graphics in Flash. First, you can start with the highest-quality image possible (for instance, .png, .bmp, or .pct) and then experiment with Flash's JPEG compression to find the best compromise. Second, you can import a .bmp, .png, or .pct and leave the image uncompressed; this gives you the highest quality and also the largest file size. This is also the only option to maintain a .png's transparency settings. Finally, you can use image editing software—such as Fireworks—to create a .jpg file with the best compromise (of file size and quality) that can be imported into Flash. This way you can take advantage of the Selective JPG feature in Fireworks. If you use this option, you need to remember to leave the Use Imported JPEG Data option selected. If the image has already been compressed (using JPEG compression), you shouldn't allow Flash to recompress because the result would be a poor-quality image.

Importing other popular formats, such as `.bmp` and `.pct`, also causes Flash to opt for JPEG compression by default. However, the Bitmap Properties dialog box displays a different option: Use Document Default Quality, as shown in Figure 3.10. Although this looks similar to the Use Imported JPEG Data option discussed earlier, it's a different option entirely. Leaving this option selected causes Flash to use a global setting to compress the file. The global settings are made when you publish the movie. These topics are discussed in more detail in Hours 21 and 24.

You can control what compression method is used on individual imported images by simply deselecting Use Document Default Quality (or deselecting Use Imported JPEG Data for that matter—but keep in mind the earlier caution about recompression). When this option is deselected, a field appears where you can type the JPEG compression level you desire. Instead of guessing what compression level is best, you can use the Bitmap Properties dialog box to experiment. A lower number results in a smaller file but also lowers the quality. If you click Test after each change, you see a drastic difference between 100 and 1. After you make each change, you can click the Test button to review the effect on file size and quality, as shown in Figure 3.11. You should experiment until you get the best compromise of image quality and file size.

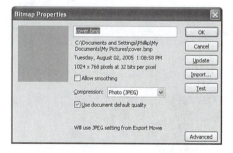

FIGURE 3.10
When you import non-`.jpg` files, you can use the global (default) quality settings for the whole Flash file.

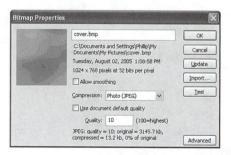

FIGURE 3.11
Setting the quality to 10 cuts this image size to less than 1/100 of its original, but the quality is visually affected.

The image portion shown in the image window at the top left of the Bitmap Properties dialog box shows exactly how the image will look when it is exported. You can zoom into this window by right-clicking and then you can pan around to get a better view.

Figure 3.12 shows the results of using several different compression levels on the same image. Notice that JPG 80 and JPG 100 are almost identical in quality, but JPG 80 has a much smaller file size.

FIGURE 3.12
The results of different compression settings on the same image shows how quality degrades and file size shrinks.

JPG 10 15KB

JPG 20 24KB

JPG 80 87KB

JPG 100 355KB

You get the ultimate quality by using the compression option Lossless (GIF/PNG). It is selected by default when you import `.png` and `.gif` files, but you can select it any other time you want to use it. When this option is selected, Flash leaves the image in its original state. This option always provides the best quality—but not without a price. File size is always highest when this option is selected. This is a suitable alternative if you're making a movie that doesn't need to download from the Web—maybe if you're just making a presentation you'll deliver on your hard drive or CD-ROM. Otherwise, you should use this option only on images that you want to retain the best quality possible. If your imported image is a `.gif` that already has a small file size, selecting Lossless is perfectly suitable. And because even 100% JPEG compression causes *some* image degradation, the Lossless option is suitable for images that are particularly important. Finally, the only way Flash supports 32-bit graphics (that is, raster images with varying degrees of transparency) is through `.png` items that you set to Lossless. That is to say, the fact that PNG is the only format that supports transparency is another perfectly legitimate reason to use PNG.

Converting a Bitmap to a Vector Graphic

Two common situations call for converting a bitmap into a vector graphic. The first is when you have a raster file that would be more suitable as a vector graphic (so you would like to take advantage of what vectors offer). The second, and more likely, time is when you want to create a special effect, such as a posterized look or an outlined effect.

In the following task you'll convert a raster graphic to a vector graphic. In Windows, you'll import the pinstripe image that is provided as a desktop pattern.

▼   **Try It Yourself**

Convert a Bitmap to a Vector

In this task you'll use Flash's Trace Bitmap feature to convert a bitmap into a vector graphic. Here are the steps:

1. In a new file, select File, Import, Import to Stage, to open the Import dialog box and point to a raster graphic that contains the most geometric shapes you can. (You can also import one I have available at www.phillipkerman.com/teachyourself.)

2. Zoom in on the graphic so that you can see what a bitmap looks like close up. It should look grainy, like the image in Figure 3.13. Obviously, this image ▼   wouldn't scale well, which is a characteristic of bitmaps.

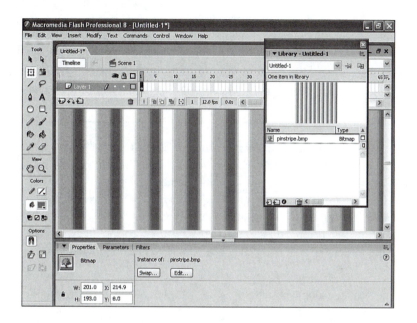

FIGURE 3.13
A bitmapped image looks grainy when you scale it or zoom in on it.

3. With the object selected, choose Modify, Bitmap, Trace Bitmap. In the Trace Bitmap dialog box that appears (as shown in Figure 3.14), enter 1 in the Color Threshold field. This indicates how close two colors must be in order to be considered the same color. Minimum Area specifies how small the smallest vector shape can be. Set this at 10. Leave Curve Fit and Corner Threshold set to Normal. (You'll see how they work in a minute.) Click OK.

FIGURE 3.14
The Trace Bitmap dialog box lets you specify how tracing will occur.

4. The graphic is now all vector shapes. The stripes on the edge might be bent, and you might see some weird artifacts on the top or bottom (which can be fixed). Even so, the graphic not only looks as good as the original, it looks better—especially if you need to scale to a larger size.

Artifacts

An **artifact** is any unwanted or obscure result of a process. For example, static on the radio is an artifact of transmission. Moire patterns in magazine pictures, color shifts on TV, raindrops on a camera lens, and typos in books are all examples of artifacts. Flash's Trace Bitmap feature sometimes leaves artifacts. JPEG compression also leaves artifacts, which are most noticeable when you set the quality to a low number.

With its nice, clear geometric shapes, the image I selected for the preceding task is particularly well suited to conversion to a vector graphic. Sometimes it's not easy for Flash to convert a graphic to a vector graphic because the image is too intricate. Other tools that are especially designed for these types of conversions, such as the Live Trace feature in Adobe's Illustrator CS2, use more sophisticated processing methods. However, before you give up on this feature, you should experiment with the settings in the Trace Bitmap dialog box. The Help button provides details about each setting.

The Trace Bitmap dialog box (refer to Figure 3.14) has several interesting options:

- ▶ **Color Threshold**—When you're tracing an image, Flash tries to lump areas of the bitmap into single shapes. The Color Threshold option specifies how different two colors can be (in RGB values) and still be considered the same. If you set this option to a high number, you will end up with fewer colors and fewer areas.

- ▶ **Minimum Area**—This option specifies the smallest area Flash will create. For a very detailed image, this number should be set rather low, unless you want a mosaic effect.

- ▶ **Curve Fit**—This option affects how closely straight and curved areas will be copied. Using the Very Smooth end of the Curve Fit scale is like having a very large pen with which to draw a shape in one quick movement. If you could use a fine pencil and as many strokes as needed, that would be like the other extreme, Pixels or Very Tight.

- ▶ **Corner Threshold**—This option determines whether corners are left alone or removed.

In addition to converting a bitmap to a vector graphic, you can "vectorize" a bitmap for an artistic effect. It just takes experimentation. Keep in mind that using Trace Bitmap sometimes results in an image that looks identical to the bitmap but with a larger file size. Consider this option only when the nature of the image is most suitable as a vector or when you want a special effect.

Figures 3.15–3.18 show several examples of bitmaps that have been converted to vectors by using different settings.

Original   Color Threshold 100 Minimum Area 100

FIGURE 3.15
This image has large, smooth vector shapes that can be filled with any color.

Original   Color Threshold 10   Color Threshold 100
                    Minimum Area 100   Minimum Area 100

FIGURE 3.16
Notice subtle differences in how the building windows are combined in the example on the right, which has a high color threshold.

FIGURE 3.17
Due to the relatively small threshold and minimum areas, this image looks posterized.

Original   Color Threshold 40 Minimum Area 40

Original

FIGURE 3.18
A large color threshold on the bottom left causes the sky to be banded.

Color Threshold 110
Minimum Area 10

Color Threshold 30
Minimum Area 10

Summary

You should create all the graphics you can right inside Flash. If this hour taught you nothing else, remember that it's always better to create graphics in Flash than to try to import them from outside.

However, there are times when you want to import graphics, such as when you have an existing graphic that would be impossible or difficult to re-create in Flash or when a graphic requires a raster file type (usually a photograph). When you're certain you want to import, there are ways to do so. If you're importing a vector graphic, you'll do best if you use a graphics tool that can export `.swf` files.

A raster graphic is pretty easy to import. Flash has options for compressing on export. Also, you can change an imported bitmap into a true vector graphic.

Q&A

Q *I'm having trouble importing images from a digital camera. I have some great shots of my cactus collection but they're so huge after I import them. How can I resize them?*

A Because multi-megapixel cameras produce originals that can be 1000s of pixels wide, you don't want to import these directly. Instead, first use an image editing program such as Fireworks to resize the image to something that will fit comfortably on a normal screen size—that is, less than 1024×768 or 800×600. By the way, taking a megapixel image and scaling it down inside Flash will not improve the sharpness. Actually, it will do the opposite, plus the filesize will be huge. Don't do that; resize (and possibly optimize) before importing!

Q *I have an original graphic as an Illustrator file, but I want to take a stab at recreating it in Flash (to see if I can make it smaller). To do this, do I have to redraw it completely from scratch or are there any tricks I can use*

A Here's a great technique that you can use to effectively trace a raster graphic. Import the graphic (even though you'll delete it when you're done). Lock the layer by clicking the dot under the padlock. Select Insert, Timeline, Layer and draw into that layer. Additionally, (before locking the layer) you can convert the graphic to a symbol (select Modify, Convert to Symbol) and then set the instance's Alpha to 50% to make it easier to trace. (Layers are covered in Hour 11 and converting to a symbol in Hour 4.)

You can also use this tracing technique to align individual objects (that need to be animated separately). The artist can deliver the complete layout as a single, full screen, graphic that you import into a locked layer.

Q *I have a photograph that must remain as a raster graphic. After I scan it into the computer and touch it up, what file format should I choose? There are so many.*

A Generally, you want to keep all your raster graphics in the highest-quality format possible before importing into Flash. One exception is when you use a tool such as Fireworks to produce an optimally compressed image (say, with varying degrees of compression using a JPEG Mask). If you use an outside program to compress the image, you should just make sure you don't recompress in Flash (simply leave the default setting Use Imported JPEG Quality). Alternatively, if you import a high-quality `.pct`, `.bmp`, or `.png`, you can compress it in Flash until you're satisfied with the compression level. JPEGs are all right, but they always have some compression that could result in artifacts. GIFs are not a good alternative because they can't have more than 256 explicit colors. Simply changing the file format of an existing image will never make a graphic better, and it will potentially make it worse. You should start with the best quality possible and then bring it down as the very last step.

Q *How do you determine how much one graphic is contributing to the final movie's file size?*

A If it's a raster graphic, you can explore the Bitmap Properties dialog box, which tells you exactly how big a graphic is. With vector graphics, determining the size is more difficult. Ultimately, you should copy the graphic into a new file and export a `.swf` of that file (by selecting File, Export). You can look at the file size. Sometimes it's not so important how much one graphic is contributing, especially if it's an important graphic. However, your concern should always be to not add to the file size unnecessarily.

Q *I've imported a raster graphic and then used Trace Bitmap to turn it into a vector graphic. The result looks fine, but the file size has grown larger than when the image was a regular bitmap. How can that be? Vectors should be smaller than bitmaps, right?*

A Not necessarily. This is a very common misunderstanding. It's possible to trace every pixel of a bitmap so that there is a tiny vector shape for each pixel. This takes more file space than the original bitmap. You can convert bitmaps into vector graphics (by using Trace Bitmap) anytime, but it really makes sense only when the nature of the image is appropriate or when you want a special effect. When Flash takes a very long time to execute the Trace Bitmap feature, it's a good indication that the file size might actually grow. (The delay occurs because the process is so complex.)

Q *I have a fairly simple graphic (as an Illustrator file) that I would like to import into Flash. It's impossible to redraw in Flash, so I have to import it, right?*

A This sounds like a contradiction to me: The file is simple, but it's impossible to draw in Flash. Make sure you're fully exploiting the potential of Flash. (Read Hour 2, "Drawing and Painting Original Art in Flash," again if necessary.) If you have to import the image, do so. Of course, you should export it from Illustrator as a `.swf` or at least try to simplify the image as much as possible.

Workshop

The Workshop consists of quiz questions and answers to help you solidify your understanding of the material covered in this hour. You should try to answer the questions before checking the answers.

Quiz

1. What's the most appropriate image file format to import into Flash?

    A. Raster.

    B. Vector.

    C. It depends on the nature or content of the image.

2. If you import a `.gif` image into Flash, what kind of compression will Flash use on the image when it exports the entire movie?

    A. It depends on the Compression setting in the Bitmap Properties dialog box.

    B. Flash always uses JPEG compression, but it's up to you to specify what quality level to use.

    C. GIFs are exported as GIFs.

3. How do you import photographs created with a digital camera?

    A. You can't, you must use conventional film.

    B. It's simple, just select File, Import.

    C. Be sure to resize the image in an outside program first, then select File, Import.

Quiz Answers

1. C. Although a vector graphic has benefits over a raster graphic, the most appropriate image file format to import into Flash depends on the graphic. Photographs usually have to stay as raster graphics.

2. A. Each image imported can have a unique compression setting that is not dependent on its original format. By default, however, imported `.gifs` get exported as `.gifs`.

3. C. Maybe I'm being mean including a question who's answer is found in the Q&A section, but be sure to read the first question in that section if you didn't get this answer right because it's important.

HOUR 4

Using the Library for Productivity

What You'll Learn in This Hour:

▶ How to create symbols
▶ How to use the Library to minimize work
▶ How to identify clues in the Flash interface to help keep your bearings
▶ How to use multiple symbol instances without increasing a movie's size

Flash's Library is so fundamental that creating a Flash movie *without* it is almost impossible. If you don't use the Library, it's fair to say that you're doing something wrong. Using the Library as much as possible is your key to productivity and efficiency. It's a key to productivity because you can have "master" versions of graphics that, with one edit, reflect the change throughout a movie. It's a key to efficiency because graphics stored in the Library—despite how many times they're used in a movie—are stored and downloaded only once.

This hour explores the Library. By far, the Library is the most important Flash feature to understand and use, so after this hour, be sure to use the Library whenever you can.

Symbols are what you put in the Library. Anything created in Flash and placed onstage (shapes, groups, other symbols, even animations) can be converted to a symbol and placed in the Library. There are three symbol types that you can choose from, and each has unique characteristics.

Item is the term used for each media element imported into your movie (and, thereby, residing in the Library). Specifically, bitmaps (as you saw in Hour 3, "Importing Graphics into Flash"), audio (as you'll see later in Hour 10, "Including Sound in Animations"), and digital video (as you'll see in Hour 18, "Using Video"), and Fonts (covered in Hour 5, "Applied Layout Techniques"). However, symbols created in Flash are surely the Library items with which you'll become most familiar.

Instance is the term given to a symbol anytime it's used outside the Library. As you'll see, there's only one master of any symbol—the one that's in the Library. However, you can drag as many instances of a master symbol out of the Library as you like. Each instance is like a copy of the original. However, as you'll see this hour, instances aren't really copies because they don't add to the file size the way extra copies would.

The Concept of the Library

The process of using the Library involves creating symbols and then using instances of those symbols throughout a movie. You always have one master version of a symbol stored in the Library. You can drag multiple instances of that symbol from the Library to any other part of the movie—even inside other symbols. This might seem like a meaningless procedure, but it has two valuable benefits. First, it means that file size remains small because only the master symbol adds to the file size, and each instance just points to the master (similarly to how a *shortcut* in Windows or an *alias* on the Macintosh points to a master file). Second, you can make a visual change to the master symbol, and that change is then reflected in each instance. This is similar to using styles in a word processing document: You make a change to the style, and each instance where you use that style reflects the change. You'll learn more about these benefits in a minute, but let's first go over the basics of how to create and use symbols.

How to Create and Use Symbols

You can use two methods to create symbols: You can either convert any selected object onstage to a symbol or make a symbol from scratch. The following task looks at the first of these methods.

▼ **Try It Yourself**

Create a Symbol by Converting Selected Objects

In this task you'll create symbols the way I prefer to—by using the Convert to Symbol feature. Follow these steps:

1. In a new file, use the Oval tool to draw a circle. Select the Selection tool and make sure the circle is entirely selected (you can double-click the center, marquee the whole thing, or do a Select All).

2. Select Modify, Convert to Symbol or press F8. Flash forces you to specify the name and default behavior for this symbol (as shown in Figure 4.1).

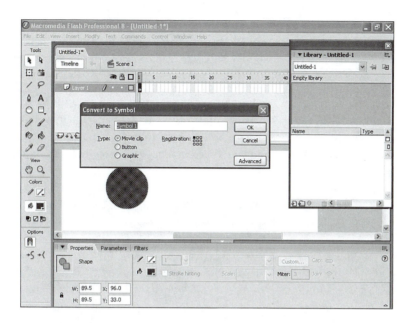

FIGURE 4.1
When you convert to a symbol, you must specify a name and behavior.

3. You should always name symbols logically. The default Symbol 1 might seem logical, but having 35 symbols all named in this manner can become unwieldy. (You'll learn more about naming symbols later in this hour, in the section "Managing the Library by Using Names, Sorting, and Folders.") Name this one Circle. We'll look at all three types of default behavior eventually, but for now just consider Movie Clip the best choice when you're not sure which behavior is best. Button is useful only when you're creating buttons, and Graphic is primarily used for synchronization applications such as lip-synching. Leave Behavior set to the default, Movie Clip, and click OK. By the way, it's possible that your Convert to Symbol dialog box is set to Advanced so that it looks much larger than the one in Figure 4.1. If this is the case, you can collapse it by clicking the Basic button (which toggles to read Advanced) because we won't be exploring the Advanced settings now.

4. Open your Library window by selecting Window, Library (or Ctrl+L), and you should notice one symbol, Circle, in the Library. When you selected Convert to Symbol, you did two things in one move: You moved the selected shape into the contents of a Library symbol and you caused the object that remained on the Stage to become an instance of the symbol. If you drag more instances from the Library window (by single-clicking and dragging the picture of the circle from the Library window onto the Stage), all those instances will be

equivalent to the instance already on the Stage. (If you double-click by accident, you see Scene 1: Circle in your edit bar, indicating that you're editing the master version of the symbol. In this case, you can simply click Scene 1 to get back to the main Stage.)

5. After you've dragged a few instances of the Circle symbol onto the Stage, it might look like you have several copies of the master, but actually you have multiple instances of the master. You're about to make a change to the master version (in the Library), and you'll see that change in each instance on the Stage.

FIGURE 4.2
The Library's options menu includes several choices, including Edit.

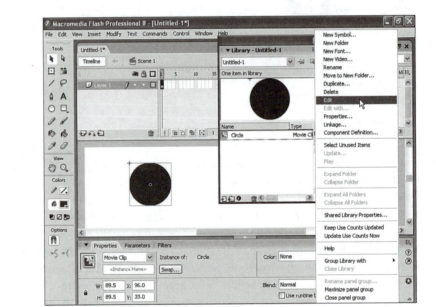

6. From the Library window, double-click picture of your Circle symbol (or select Edit from the Library's menu). It might appear that nothing has happened, but now you're inside the Circle symbol where you can edit its contents. The best indication is the edit bar, covered first in Hour 1, "Basics" (see Figure 4.3). In addition, you should see only one copy of your circle (the original) in the center of the Stage, which appears to have no borders. These clues tell you that you are currently inside the master version of the Circle symbol, about to edit it.

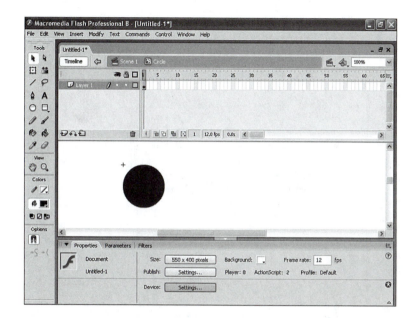

7. Now get out of the master version and reenter another way. Click Scene 1 from the edit bar, and you return to the main scene (with multiple instances of the Circle symbol). Enter the master version of the symbol by double-clicking an instance of it. You should see the edit bar change (which is always your best clue) and all the other instances dim slightly. This is similar to how you can edit the contents of a grouped shape. In this case, you're doing what's called *Edit in Place*. In any case, here is where you can edit the Circle symbol.

8. Take a "bite" out of the master graphic of the circle by using the marquee technique with the Selection tool (see Figure 4.4). If the Circle is a Drawing Object then be sure to double-click it first. This is a drastic edit—not something subtle, such as changing the color.

9. Go back to the main scene by clicking Scene 1 in the edit bar. Now all the instances of the Circle symbol have the same bite taken out of them! Any new instances of the symbol that you drag from the Library will have the same effect.

FIGURE 4.4
The edits you make to this symbol will affect each instance.

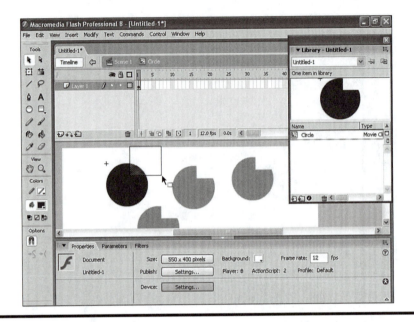

In the preceding task, you converted a selection into a symbol. This left behind, on the Stage, an instance of the symbol you created. The other way to create a symbol is to simply decide that you want a new symbol and create it, as described in the following task. Neither method is better than the other, and both give you the same result.

▼ **Try It Yourself**

Create a New Symbol from Scratch

In this task you'll make a symbol by using the New Symbol feature. Follow these steps:

1. In the file that contains the Circle symbol (or a new file), make sure nothing is selected and choose Insert, New Symbol.

2. You see nearly the same Symbol Properties dialog box that you see when you use Convert to Symbol. In this case, name the new symbol Square and set the Behavior option to Movie Clip. This time when you click OK, you are taken inside the master version of the Square symbol (which is yet to be drawn), as shown in Figure 4.5. You should see the edit bar change accordingly. Think of it this way: Convert to Symbol puts your selection in the Library (end of story), whereas New Symbol makes you name the symbol and then takes you

to the master version of that symbol so you can draw something—effectively saying, "Okay, you want a new symbol? Draw it."

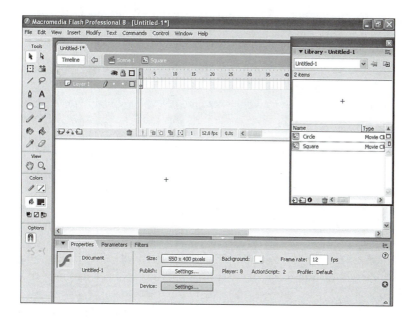

FIGURE 4.5
Selecting New Symbol takes you into a blank symbol so that you can draw its contents.

3. Now that you're in the master version of the Square symbol, you can draw the square. You'll probably want to draw it near the registration point of the symbol, indicated by the plus sign (shown in Figure 4.5). This becomes the reference point whenever you view or change the instance's location onscreen. But how do you get the square you draw in the center? Surely by now you've discovered the Paste in Place command from the Edit menu (or Ctrl+Shift+V). It lets you paste anything in the same location from which you copied it. Interesting, the standard Paste (Ctrl+V) command is really called Paste in Center which turns out to be useful here. Just select your drawn square, cut, and then immediately paste. Presto! It's centered. By habit, I quite often cut and paste everything inside my master Library symbols to get just this centering effect. (By the way, you could also use the Info panel to set the shape's transformation point to 0,0 or use the Align Panel's "To stage" option and then click both Align Horizontal Center and Align Vertical Center.)

4. When you're done creating the Square symbol, go back to the main scene by either clicking Scene 1 in the edit bar or selecting Edit Scene, Scene 1. Where's the square? Well, New Symbol just creates a symbol and keeps it safe in the Library. Drag a couple instances out on the Stage by opening the Library and then dragging as many instances of the Square symbol onto the Stage as you like.

How Symbols Help You

You might already be thinking of some ways symbols can help you, but likely there are many more you haven't even imagined. Let's go over the two fundamental advantages of storing symbols in the Library: reducing the movie's file size and minimizing your work.

Reducing File Size

Believe it or not, if you have 1 graphic in a Library symbol and 100 instances of that symbol on the Stage, your file is no larger than if you have only 1 instance. Here's how it works: The graphic, movie clip, or button in the master symbol contributes to the file size. Therefore, if the graphic is 1KB, the master symbol adds 1KB; if the master symbol is 100KB, it adds 100KB. The size depends on what's in that symbol. No matter how many times a symbol is used, however, it's only stored once. Even as you drag many instances onto the Stage, the symbol is still stored only once. A tiny bit of data is saved inside Flash that specifies how each instance is different from the others (for example, their positions), so I suppose I lied because each instance does actually add to the file size. However, it's just such a *tiny* bit of information that it's almost not worth mentioning (but I hate to lie). Imagine what would happen if it didn't work this way; a 100KB graphic used 10 times would make a movie balloon to 1MB! In reality, though, 10 instances of a 100KB symbol might make your file grow to, say, 101K (if even that much).

Symbols might seem great when you need several instances of the same shape. However, using symbols is also powerful because each instance can appear very differently from the others. So far, you've used symbols to display identical replicas of an original. The only way each instance has varied has been in its onscreen position. However, the tiny bit of extra data telling Flash where each instance is positioned onscreen can also contain how each instance is scaled or rotated differently. This way, each instance can look different. You'll learn more about this later in the hour, but for now, you should realize if you have three instances on the Stage and you have each one scaled to a different size, you haven't added to the file size in any significant way.

Minimizing Work

In addition to reducing file size, the Library can reduce the amount of work you do. For example, say you have a block of text (maybe a title) that's used in several places within a movie. If you first put the text in a symbol in the Library, each time you need that text onscreen, you can drag an instance from the Library. Later, if you want to change the text, you can edit the master version in the Library and see the change in every instance. This advantage requires only that you invest a little bit of time and planning.

Using the Library

Although you've already used the Library to do several tasks, we haven't yet taken time to really explore all the details of the Library. Let's do that now so you're sure to take full advantage of the Library's offerings.

Getting Your Bearings

Hour 1, "Basics," discusses the importance of knowing where you are at all times. In the Library, this point is especially important. Using the Library can be very confusing if you don't pay attention to subtle clues. Before you select a tool from the drawing toolbar, you should ask yourself exactly where you are and what you are doing there.

Here are a few clues to help you get your bearings in the Library:

▶ Three things: the edit bar, the edit bar, and the edit bar. The edit bar is the most important indicator and one to which you should pay attention at all times.

Moving the Edit Bar

With the timeline showing, you can hold Shift+Alt and double-click the edit bar to move it below the Timeline. You can use Shift+Alt and double-click again to move it back.

By the Way

▶ Anytime you're inside a Library symbol, you see a plus sign (usually in the center) that indicates the registration point of the symbol. More about the registration point next. Just remember that you won't see the plus sign when you're editing the contents of a regular scene.

▶ You use the registration point when controlling an instance's exact location. If a symbol is positioned at 0x and 0y (the upper left of the stage), just that registration point coincides with 0x 0y. In addition, you can use ActionScript to rotate or scale an instance and Flash will use the registration point as the axis of rotation or center from which it grows. It's confusing because, when you use the Transform tool to rotate or scale an instance, Flash uses the visual center as the center. Remember that you can always go inside and move the contents of a symbol relative to its registration point.

▶ In addition to seeing the plus sign, while editing a symbol, you never see edges to the Stage because there isn't a Stage when you're inside a symbol. When you drag instances onto the Stage, you need to place them within the Stage borders (if you want the users to see the objects). Symbols simply don't have a Stage—the point of reference of a symbol is its center (registration point).

▶ You can access the contents of a master symbol in several ways:

  ▶ First, from the Library window, you can select the symbol and then choose Edit in the Library's options menu. Alternatively, you can just double-click the symbol (double-clicking the symbol name lets you rename the symbol).

  ▶ Second, you can simply double-click any instance onscreen, and you are taken to the master symbol to edit. The difference in doing it this way as opposed to using the Library window is that while editing, you see the rest of your onscreen contents dimmed out but in position. You can also do this by right-clicking an instance and selecting Edit in Place.

  ▶ Third, you can access any symbol from the Edit Symbols menu. Recall the two buttons at the top right of the screen: The clapper button is the Edit Scene button, and the circle-square-triangle button (which looks like a graphic symbol's icon) is the Edit Symbols button (see Figure 4.6). The Edit Symbols menu provides a list of all the symbols in a movie. Also, the Edit Scene menu is an easy way to get back to a scene.

FIGURE 4.6
The Edit Symbols menu gives you quick access to all the symbols in a file.

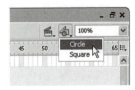

Transformation Point Versus Registration Point

I cringe to even bring this up because it sounds much worse than it is—but it's important to understand the difference between transformation and registration. Transformation is the point around which you can scale or rotate an object (while authoring) and registration is an arbitrary reference point inside a symbol. If you open the Info panel, click the center box, and then select an object, the values shown indicate the location of the transformation point. However, when you use ActionScript to move a symbol instance, the value you set for x and y affect where the registration point displays. When you use Convert to Symbol to create the symbol you choose a registration point from 9 logical positions—including the center plus any of the four sides or four corners. Plus you can always go inside the symbol and move its contents relative to its registration. You'll see the registration point as a plus (both inside the symbol and when it's selected on stage).

Any object on stage has a transformation point (shown as a white down when you select the object with the Free Transform tool). The transformation point is always the visual center *at the time the object is created* or dragged from the library. You can use the Free Transform tool to move the transformation point. In addition when you rotate or scale, the object will rotate or scale around that transformation point. For example, you could move the transformation point to the corner of a flower petal and then rotate several petal instances to make a flower.

Managing the Library by Using Names, Sorting, and Folders

The Library is so great that you'll use it all the time. As the total number of symbols in the Library grows, you'll want to develop ways to keep them organized. You can manage the Library any way you want, but this section looks at three ways in particular: naming, sorting, and using folders.

Because every symbol must have a name (and symbols are easy to rename), naming symbols consistently makes sense. How to best name symbols is subjective, but some standard practices are worth following. First, you should be clear and concise. If you have an image of a circle, you can call it Circle. There's no need to be cryptic and call it Cir. However, a name such as Red Circle with No Line might be a bit much. You should say what you have to, but nothing more. Also, you should realize that the Library can be sorted alphabetically by symbol name, so you can develop a naming strategy to plan ahead. For example, if you have several symbols all being used in a particular part of a movie, you can precede each name with the same text prefix—for example, game_. Therefore, you might have symbols named game_background, game_piece, game_scorecard, and so on. You can even use a similar method when an entire team is working on the same file. You can have each person precede symbol names with his or her initials so figuring out which symbols were created by which team members is easy. In Hour 23, "Working on Large Projects and in Team Environments," you'll learn more about such naming conventions.

As mentioned earlier in this section, the Library automatically sorts symbols alphabetically by name. If you widen the Library window, you can explore additional sorting options. (You can either resize the window by dragging a corner of it or click the Wide View button on the right side of the Library, as shown in Figure 4.7.) You should take a look at Figure 4.7 to familiarize yourself with the Library window. Note that you can sort by name, by kind (all the graphic symbols are listed separately from the button symbols, for example), by use count (meaning how many instances you've dragged from the Library), or by date modified.

The Library window has several useful features:

▶ The preview window gives you a thumbnail view and preview of any animation or audio.

▶ Column headings do more than just explain what's listed in the column. If you click a column heading, the Library is sorted by the attribute you select (Name, Kind, Use Count, Linkage, or Date Modified).

▶ You can click the tiny arrow to toggle between ascending and descending alphabetical sorting.

▶ Clicking New Symbol has the same effect as selecting Insert, New Symbol.

▶ New Folder lets you create a new folder to hold several Library items.

▶ Clicking Properties gives you access to the same Symbol Properties dialog box that you see when you create a symbol.

▶ Wide View stretches the window for you. Narrow View changes the window to a narrower view.

▶ The Pin Current Library option stops Flash's default behavior of always reflecting the library for the currently active file. By pinning the library, you can easily drag items from one file's library to another file's (because each file has its own single library).

▶ The Library's drop-down list gives you a quick way to edit another file's library without activating that file.

▶ The New Library Panel button lets you arrange library windows. For example, you might want to copy items from one library to another or you might be getting tired of jumping between two files' libraries using the list box.

▶ The Options menu provides all the options that are available. (Don't forget it's here!)

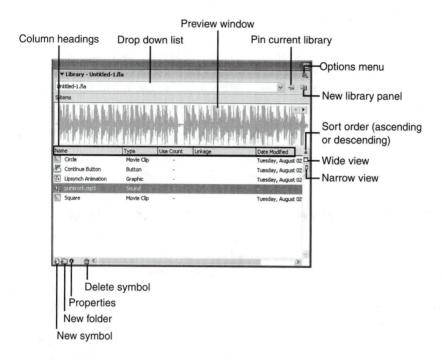

Column headings Drop down list Preview window Pin current library

Options menu
New library panel
Sort order (ascending or descending)
Wide view
Narrow view

Delete symbol
Properties
New folder
New symbol

FIGURE 4.7
Several indicators and tools are built in to the Library.

Finally, you can organize your Library by using folders. This is almost identical to using files and folders on your computer's hard drive, except that in the Library you have symbols and folders. Creating a folder is as simple as selecting New Folder in the Library's options menu or clicking the orange New Folder button at the bottom of the Library. You can name the folder immediately after you create it, or you can name it later, the same way you rename symbols (by double-clicking the name or selecting Rename from the options menu). Organizing folders is pretty intuitive, but let me mention a couple maneuvers now. You can put symbols inside folders by simply dragging a symbol's icon (which appears to the left of its name) on top of the folder. You can open a folder (to reveal its contents) by double-clicking the folder's icon. You can even put folders inside folders.

Organizing the Library isn't difficult to figure out. Most of the material just covered on the subject includes general good organization skills. If you know how to rename Library items, sort, and use folders, you'll be fine.

Using Symbols from the Library

So far, the concept of dragging a symbol from the Library to create as many instances as you want has been pretty straightforward. It's powerful but easy to use. For a simple example, imagine that you made one symbol of a cloud. You could create many instances of the cloud symbol to make a cloudy sky. But you could do much more than that. Each instance on the Stage could be different from the next. One could be large and another one could be stretched out and darkened. In the upcoming task, for example, you'll see how multiple instances of one symbol can vary in size, scale, and rotation. And later this hour you'll make a symbol that contains instances of another symbol. Such nesting means not only that you can have many instances on the Stage but that you can recycle symbols to be used in the creation of other symbols. You'll learn about this one step at a time.

Placing Instances of Symbols on the Stage

This discussion might seem like repeated material, but the concept and process are very specific. One master symbol in the Library can be dragged on the Stage as many times as you like. Each one on the Stage is called an *instance*. You'll see how each instance can vary in a minute, but first let's review a couple points. If you copy and paste an instance that is already on the Stage, you are simply creating *another* instance. Not only is this okay, but it's sometimes preferable to the alternative—simply dragging an instance from the Library—because all the properties of the instance being copied will be in the new instance. Remember that the "copy" is just another instance.

There's one other way to get an instance on the Stage (in addition to dragging it from the Library or copying one already on the Stage). Maybe you'll think I'm cheating, but as a review, consider that you can draw a plain old shape, select it, and use Convert to Symbol. This procedure puts the symbol in the Library but also leaves on the Stage an instance of the symbol. If this doesn't make sense, try repeating the task "Create a Symbol by Converting Selected Objects" from earlier in this hour.

Modifying Instances of Symbols

Believe it or not, by simply dragging two instances of the same symbol onto the Stage, you create two instances with different properties—because they vary in position. In other words, each instance is in a different location on the Stage. Each instance can be made different in other ways, too. For example, you can transform the scale of any instance on the Stage—without adding to the file size in any significant way. You can rotate each instance separately, as well. The following task explores how to vary the properties of separate instances in regard to their position, scale, and rotation.

Try It Yourself ▼

Transform the Location, Scale, and Rotation of Instances

In this task you'll transform the properties of several instances. Here are the steps:

1. In a new file, draw a rectangle and then use the Text tool to type your name. Use the Properties pane to ensure the text is Static Text. Try to position the text and resize the rectangle so that they're about the same size. Change the text color so it's legible on top of the rectangle.

2. Select everything you just drew and then choose Modify, Convert to Symbol. Name this symbol My Name. Leave the default Behavior option, Movie Clip, selected and then click OK. Onscreen you now have an instance of the My Name symbol you just created.

3. Create more instances of this symbol any way you want—either by copying and pasting the one onscreen or by dragging instances from the Library.

4. Make a change in the position of each instance on the Stage by simply moving the instance to a different location. With some of the instances, select the Free Transform tool and change their scale. (Remember from Hour 2, "Drawing and Painting Original Art in Flash," that you can scale width or height or both at the same time.) Change the rotation of other instances (remember that rotation includes skew when the Free Transform tool's Rotate and Skew option is selected and you drag the noncorner handles). You can go wild here, as in Figure 4.8, yet your file will only be as big as the master symbol. Notice, however, that only the Free Transform tool's Scale option and its Rotate and Skew option are available (you can't distort and envelop symbol instances—only Shapes and Drawing Objects).

▼

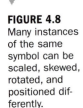

FIGURE 4.8
Many instances of the same symbol can be scaled, skewed, rotated, and positioned differently.

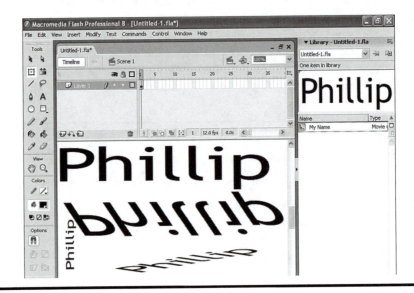

You might think that varying each instance's position, scale, and rotation provides for a lot of combinations—and it does. However, there's more. Each instance on the Stage can have a color style, a blend, plus a variety of filters applied to it. Next, we'll explore each one briefly and then, next hour, you'll see them applied in practical applications.

Using Color Styles

Color Styles include tinting the color of an instance, changing its brightness, and changing its alpha property (that is, its opacity). Similarly to how each instance can have a different location, each instance can have different color effects. To move an instance, though, you just pick it up and move it. To apply a style, you use the Properties panel.

To change an instance's color style, you simply make sure the Properties panel is visible and select the instance on the Stage. While the instance is selected, you can specify any style you want by selecting from the Color drop-down list.

Take a look at Figure 4.9 and the following list to familiarize yourself with these effects (then you can proceed to the task, which steps you through many of the subtleties of several effects):

FIGURE 4.9
The Properties panel provides several ways to change an instance.

▶ **Brightness**—This effect allows you to add black or white to the instance. It is similar to turning the lights out or turning them way up.

▶ **Tint**—This effect is similar to brightness, but instead of causing the instance to be more white (or more black), it tints the instance any color you want.

▶ **Alpha**—This effect, which is the same as opacity, lets you specify how "see through" the instance will be.

▶ **Advanced**—This effect lets you combine tint and alpha (although later this hour you'll learn a trick to figure out the eight sliders). If you don't need to both tint and change the alpha of an instance, the Advanced effect is best applied to symbols that contain raster graphics, such as a photograph.

Try It Yourself ▼

Change Color Styles on Several Instances

In this task you'll explore color styles. Here are the steps:

1. Open the file with the many instances of the My Name symbol that you created in the last task. (Redo the exercise if necessary.) Make sure you have at least four instances on the Stage.

2. Select one instance by single-clicking it. (If you double-click, you'll be taken inside the master symbol and will need to return to the main scene.) Access the Properties panel.

3. From the Color drop-down list in the Properties panel, select Brightness. The Brightness amount appears on the right of the panel, as shown in Figure 4.10. Click and hold the arrow to the right of the percentage, and you are given a slider. Adjust the slider until the percentage reaches 80%. Alternatively, you can just type the percentage 80 into the field.

FIGURE 4.10
The brightness color effect can be applied to an instance.

4. Keep the Properties panel open and select another instance. This time, select Tint from the Color drop-down list. The tint effect is pretty straightforward: You just select the *hue* with which you want to tint the instance by selecting the swatch (as in Figure 4.11). But notice the default 50% in the Tint Amount

field. If the original symbol contains several colors, the entire instance changes to the color in which you tint it. However, tinting less than 100% causes the colors to mix. For example, if the original symbol is yellow and white, tinting it 100% cyan causes everything to turn cyan. However, tinting it 50% cyan causes the white parts to become a faded cyan and the yellow parts to turn green.

5. Set the Color drop-down list of another instance on the Stage to Alpha and set the Alpha slider to 40%. Unless the selected instance is on top of something else, you're not likely to see much of a semitransparent effect. Therefore, go ahead and position the instance on the Stage to be on top of another instance. Remember that you can use Bring to Front and similar stacking controls by selecting Modify, Arrange.

FIGURE 4.11
The tint color style changes the color of an instance.

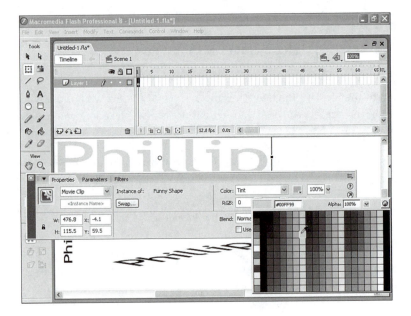

6. Finally, the Advanced setting in the Color drop-down list lets you combine alpha and tint. After you select Advanced, the Settings button gives you full control. However, figuring out the eight sliders that appear is next to impossible, so you need to use a trick to avoid using them. To learn how to use this trick, try tinting something yellow and making it semi-transparent as well. First, select an instance and choose Tint from the Color drop-down list. Then select a yellow swatch. Now, change the Color drop-down list to Advanced and click the Settings button. Notice that the pairs of numbers next to Red,

Green, and Blue have already been filled in (with something other than 0), as Figure 4.12 shows. These are based on the tint you specified earlier. Now you can select the Alpha slider at the bottom of the Settings dialog box. The trick is that by first selecting Tint, you have a nice way to choose a color. If you first select Advanced, you would have to select a color in a less intuitive manner— by using the sliders shown in Figure 4.12.

7. Go wild and bring out a bunch of instances on the Stage. Adjust the Alpha, Tint, and Brightness settings. Do anything you want. Again, note that the file is basically the same size it would be with just one instance. Also, realize that you can apply a color effect on multiple instances if you simply select more than one and then access the Properties panel. (Keep this file open for the next task, "Changing Blends on Instances.")

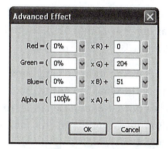

FIGURE 4.12
When you select the Advanced settings after first tinting, the sliders are initialized with the same color.

Getting More Colors

You might have noticed that when you select a tint color, the Properties panel lets you choose from only discrete swatches. It's possible to select any color. You just open the Color Mixer panel first. When you set a tint, you click (and hold) on a swatch but don't let go until you've pointed to the color you want on the Color Mixer panel. This is like the way you sample colors outside Flash—but it works within Flash, too. Also notice you can't set a clip's tint directly by using the Color Mixer panel.

By the Way

One way to describe color is by specifying the three factors: hue, saturation, and brightness. If you want to explore these factors, you can change the Color Mixer panel's option arrow from RGB (red, green, blue) to HSB (hue, saturation, brightness). **Hue** is the base color. Moving from left to right in the Flash Color Mixer panel, you see the hue change from red to yellow to green to blue and to red again (with every shade of color in between). **Brightness** is how much white is included in a color. Imagine a paint store with a bunch of hues of paint. The store could mix in white paint to create other colors. In the Flash Color Mixer panel, the brightness is shown vertically—at the top, the colors are all white and at the bottom, they're all black. Finally, **saturation** is the amount of color. For example, if you were staining a wood fence, the more stain you used, the more saturated the color would become. In Flash you vary the saturation by changing the Tint Amount slider.

Using Blends and Filters

Flash Professional 8 adds the Blend option (under Color Styles in the Properties panel) as well as the concept of Filters (a separate panel). Both features fall into the "expressive" category because they give you greater image control. But they also fit well in this Library chapter because they both apply to instances. (Here you'll learn the technical details and then in Hours 5 and 13 you'll practice more practical uses.) Blends define how overlapping instances composite (or blend with) each other. You can think of the alpha color effect as a simple type of blend because it affects how much of the objects underneath will show through. Blends, however, are much fancier, performing such effects as Invert (which looks like photographic negatives) and Darken (which shows only the darker of two colors).

Filters are like special effects filters found in imaging programs such as Adobe Photoshop—but here you apply the effects to any symbol instance. The Drop Shadow Filter, for example, is a powerful (and easy) way to make an instance appear to float off the screen. It's also interesting that filters are nondestructive, meaning they don't permanently change the symbol. This means you can apply different filters (and at varying degrees) on several instances of the same symbol—and always go back to adjust or remove the filter effect. (You can even animate filter effects, as you'll see in Part II.) In this chapter you'll see how Blends and Filters work and in the next chapter, you'll see practical ways they can be applied to your projects.

Blends

Applying a Blend is nearly identical to applying a color effect. Just select an instance and select one of the Blend options from the Properties panel, as shown in Figure 4.13.

- ▶ **Normal**—The default or no blend.

- ▶ **Layer**—Analyzes everything inside the overlay and ensures it will appear as expected. This Blend is really subtle but jumps out when you change the alpha color style on a symbol containing multiple overlapping objects. For example, if you draw an ice cream cone Movie Clip using a triangle under a circle and then set the clip's alpha to 50% you'll see through the ice cream scoop to the cone underneath—unless you also use the Layer blend. Simply put, the Layer blend makes alpha transitions accurate. Layer is also required when a nested clip is set to Alpha or Erase.

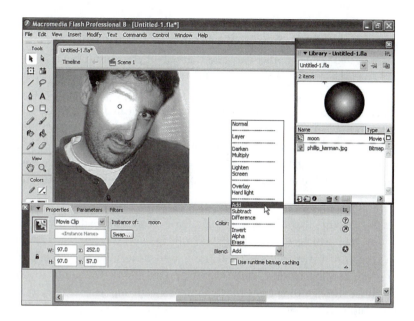

FIGURE 4.13
The Blend you select from the Properties panel affects how a symbol composites with what's underneath.

▶ **Darken**—Shows the darkest color. That is, you'll see the overlay except where the base is darker.

▶ **Multiply**—Mixes the two colors. The effect is least when base and overlay are similar colors and greatest when the base and overlay are different colors.

▶ **Lighten**—Shows the lightest color. That is, you'll see the overlay except where the base is lighter.

▶ **Screen**—Similar to Multiply, but it uses the inverse of the overlay to make a result that appears washed out.

▶ **Overlay**—Applies the Screen blend on pixels where the base is dark and applies Multiply where the base has light pixels.

▶ **Hardlight**—The exact opposite of Overlay. Hardlight applies the Screen blend on pixels where the base is light and applies Multiply where the base has dark pixels.

▶ **Add**—Adds the base and overlay, with the maximum being white.

▶ **Subtract**—Subtracts base and overlay, with the minimum being black.

▶ **Difference**—Subtracts the darker color from the lighter color regardless of whether that color came from the base or the overlay.

▶ **Invert**—Inverts the base only (makes it appear like a negative).

▶ **Alpha**—Like Erase, below, Alpha requires more than a base color and the overlaying clip on which you apply the blend. You apply the Alpha blend to a clip that's nested inside another clip, and that parent clip must have its blend set to Layer. The clip on which you set the Alpha blend should contain graphics that contain some level of transparency. The amount of transparency determines how much of the parent clip is revealed or cleared away to show through to what's underneath. That is, where the nested clip is 100% alpha (that's opaque) you'll see just the parent clip. Where the nested clip is 0% alpha you won't see the parent clip but rather see through to whatever is underneath. If you're familiar with masking, the Alpha blend lets you create a gradient alpha mask.

▶ **Erase**—Requires that the clip on which Erase blend is applied is nested inside another clip which is set to Layer. Primarily, the nested clip set to Erase will clear away its parent clip and show through to whatever is underneath. It's opposite of Alpha because where ever the nested clip is 100% alpha (opaque) you'll see through the parent to what's underneath and where the nested clip is 0% alpha you'll *only* see the parent clip.

Notice the base is just as important as the overlay—sometimes more important. Also notice that this list doesn't give you practical uses for each option. One perfectly legitimate way to use blends is by just exploring. However, you will see several practical uses in the next chapter.

Using Filters

You can apply filters to any symbol instance onstage (plus text objects). First, open the Filters panel, select an object, and then select the filter you want to apply. Take a look at Figure 4.14.

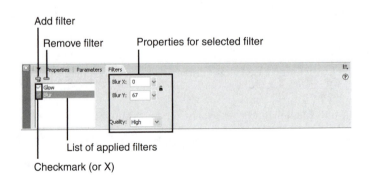

FIGURE 4.14
You can apply advanced special effects to symbol instances using the Filters panel.

To start, select an instance and then click the Add Filter button (the plus) to select a filter. The menu that appears also lets you remove, enable, or disable all filters already applied to the instance. You can individually remove filters by clicking the minus button (don't press Delete on your keyboard because you'll remove the symbol instance). You can also click the green check mark (for enabled) to temporarily disable individual filters. After you've added a filter, the properties for that filter appear on the right side of the panel. You can adjust the strength or blur of a filter, for example.

The Filters panel supports adding multiple filters to get a layer effect . For example, you can use the Adjust Color filter (say, to desaturate a color image into black and white) and then also add the Drop Shadow filter. Because multiple filters are cumulative, the order in which they're applied makes a difference. For example, if you apply a Drop Shadow and then a colored Glow, the Glow is applied to the instance as well as its Drop Shadow (and you'll see color all around the shadow). If you put a colored Glow and then a Drop Shadow, the object and its Glow are given a Drop Shadow (and the color only surrounds the instance). Because the order matters, you can click and drag to reorganize the filter order listed in the Filters panel. (The filters listed on top are applied first.)

After you've spent time setting all the properties the way you want for one or more filters, you can save the settings as a preset. Just click the Add Filter button (plus) and select Presets, Save As.

Watch
Out!

Applying Presets Removes Existing Filters

When you select on of the preset filters you've saved, it wipes away any filters already applied to an object. If you want to supplement a preset, start by applying the preset and then make adjustments or add more filters.

The properties available for each filter vary, although there are some consistencies. For example, all except the Adjust Color Filter include an option for Quality. This affects how smooth or choppy the gradations appear. Interesting, Quality affects performance but has almost no impact on file size. You'll notice the visual impact of the Quality setting most when the blur is greatest. The good news about all the filters is that you'll see their visual effects immediately, so it's worth just exploring the various options. (The Blends tend to require a little more foresight because many blends don't have any impact under certain conditions.)

Like blends, I'll just list the filters here and let you explore on your own. In the next hour, you'll get plenty of exercise applying them to real tasks:

▶ **Drop Shadow**—Creates a single-color duplicate of your instance's shape, slips it underneath your instance, and offsets the location. There are options to control the strength (really alpha), blur, angle, and offset distance. Used conservatively, the Drop Shadow can add depth to an image. Interestingly, if you simply make the shadow very blurry and the same color as your symbol instance it looks a lot like a motion blur.

▶ **Blur**—Blurs the entire content of your instance. Besides the out-of-focus look, you can blur the X or the Y more than the other to get a motion blur effect. That is, lots of Y blur makes something look like it's moving up or down.

▶ **Glow**—Makes a duplicate of your instance's shape and blurs that. It's like having a blur with a copy of your original layered on top. There are many specific reasons to use Glow, but a common one is to make text stand out when, without a glow in a contrasting color, the text is too similar to the background color.

▶ **Bevel**—Gives the instance an embossed look , almost like raised printing. The reason your instance looks raised is that the upper left is lightened (highlight) as if there's a light up to the left and the bottom right is darkened (shadow) as if that part is in the shadow of the object. Of course, you can change the highlight and shadow colors as well as the angle where the imaginary light is positioned.

▶ **Gradient Glow**—Is just like Glow except the color of the glow is a gradation. Also, you can add bands to the gradation the same way you will when you study gradients next hour.

▶ **Gradient Bevel**—Is just like Bevel except the colors for the highlight and shadow are gradated.

▶ **Adjust Color**—Works best on instances that contain a raster graphic. It's an intuitive filter for adjusting the contained color. Simply drag the Saturation slider all the way to the left (–100) to make a color photograph appear black and white.

As a summary of color styles, blends, and filters, consider the normal process you'll follow to create a graphic. Start by making symbols based on a foundation of building blocks—basically, the graphics you can import or draw in Flash. Place them on stage and then apply color styles or filters. Blends let you define how layered objects appear. When you want the same effect applied to multiple objects, you can nest symbols inside symbols, as discussed later in "Nesting Instances of Symbols Inside Symbols."

Although in Hours 2 and 3 you learned lots of ways to either create or import graphics, the color styles, blends, and filters shown previously give you ways to create even more advanced effects. Plus, compared to importing raster graphics with the same visual effect, applying effects to instances in this manner is much more bandwidth friendly. You're already being efficient by storing graphics in the Library, but because all these effects are applied at runtime, they are almost always smaller than raster alternatives. Of course, they're also better because you can make edits right inside Flash. I should note that even though such runtime effects don't add much to file size, they do tend to reduce your movie's performance by making it play slower. Don't worry, though, because the impact is not an issue unless you overdo it—plus, you'll learn ways to optimize performance in Hour 21, "Optimizing a Flash Site."

How Each Instance Behaves Differently

You've already seen how each instance on the Stage can be uniquely positioned, scaled, rotated, and colored. There's one more way in which instances can be different from one another: They can behave differently. Remember the Behavior option for creating a symbol? You have to decide among Graphic, Button, and Movie Clip. So far, I've suggested just using Movie Clip, which is the default. Later, we'll look much more closely at the Button and Movie Clip options (see Hour 14, "Making Buttons for the User to Click," and Hour 12, "Animating Using Movie Clip and Graphic Symbols"). For now, we'll discuss how the Behavior option relates to instances on the Stage.

When you create a symbol, you must select a behavior. Later on you'll learn about the differences between the behaviors, but for now they're not terribly important because you can change the behavior. From the Library window, you can change any symbol's behavior via Properties, which you access by clicking the little blue i button, by selecting the Library's options menu, or by right-clicking the item and selecting Properties. The Symbol Properties dialog box reappears; it's almost identical to the dialog box you use when you create a symbol in the first place as shown in Figure 4.15. Think of this setting as the default behavior. Any instance dragged out of the Library while the symbol is, say, set to Graphic starts out as a graphic. Changing the master symbol to another default behavior has no effect on instances already spawned, only new ones you drag onto the stage.

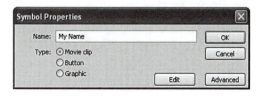

FIGURE 4.15
The Symbol Properties dialog box lets you change the default behavior for a symbol.

Not only does a master symbol have a default behavior, but each instance onscreen also has its own behavior. You can use the Properties panel to see and change the behavior of any instance or instances already on the Stage. For example, you can use the Properties panel to see that the instances used in the last two tasks have the Movie Clip behavior. That's because the master symbol was a Movie Clip at the time the instance was placed on stage. You can change the behavior of any onscreen instance by simply selecting it and changing the Behavior drop-down list in the Properties panel. Later you'll be deliberate in your choice of behavior—just realize you can always change the symbol's default behavior or the behavior of any instance.

Nesting Instances of Symbols Inside Symbols

You can drag a symbol from the Library and create an instance anytime. You can even use instances of one symbol to create other symbols! This means you could draw a bunch of houses (as shown in Figure 4.16) with just one line. Sure, there's a House symbol, but that was drawn with several instances of another symbol, Box, and a few instances of a symbol called Line. Actually, the Box symbol was created with four instances of the Line symbol. This case shows an excessive use of hierarchy, but it proves a point: Instances of symbols can be used to create other symbols. In the next task you'll see how to perform such nesting.

FIGURE 4.16
The house, duplicated and modified, was created with several instances of a Line symbol.

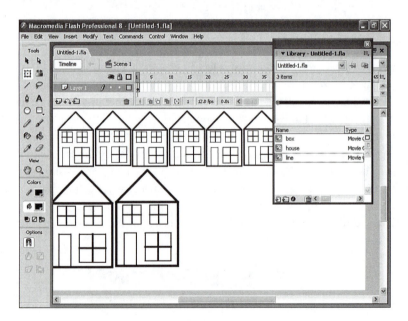

Try It Yourself ▼

Make a Symbol by Using Instances of Another Symbol

In this task you'll nest symbols inside each other. Here are the steps:

1. In a new file set the background color to something other than white. Select Modify, Document and select pale red from the Background Color swatch. Then use the Oval tool to draw a circle and fill it with gray.

2. Select the entire circle and then choose Modify, Convert to Symbol. Name the symbol Circle and click OK.

3. Next, make an eyeball from two instances of Circle. One way you could do this is to create a new symbol and then, while inside the master Eyeball symbol, drag out instances of Circle. Instead, you should do it another way, which might be more confusing at first, but I think it'll be easier. There are two ways to get stuff in the Library: either create a new symbol or convert something you select to a symbol. In this case, you should use the Convert to Symbol method. To make the Eyeball symbol, notice that you already have one instance (Circle) on the Stage. Copy and paste this on the Stage (or drag another instance from the Library). Change the Brightness color style of one instance to –100%; by using the Properties panel, select Brightness from the Color drop-down list and set it to –100%. Make sure the other instance is set to 100%. It might help at this point to change your movie background color to any color except black or the default white; to do this, deselect everything and use the Properties panel to change the background color to gray. This will help you see the all-white instance of Circle.

4. Arrange the two instances so that the black one is on top, scaled smaller, and set near the edge of the white instance, as shown in Figure 4.17. (If necessary, you can use Modify, Arrange to change the stacking order.)

5. Select both instances and then choose Modify, Convert to Symbol or press F8. This takes what's selected—a couple of instances—and puts them in the Library. Name this symbol Eyeball and click OK.

6. Left behind, on the Stage, is an instance of the Eyeball symbol that you just created. If it's really big, scale it down a bit and then copy and paste it to make two instances that are exactly the same size. Rotate one instance of Eyeball if you want.

7. Drag an instance of Circle onto the Stage. Because it'll start out on top, send it to the back by selecting Modify, Arrange, Send to Back. Scale it large enough to be the face for the two Eyeball instances. Change the Tint color effect of this instance of Circle to bright yellow.

▼

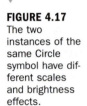

FIGURE 4.17
The two instances of the same Circle symbol have different scales and brightness effects.

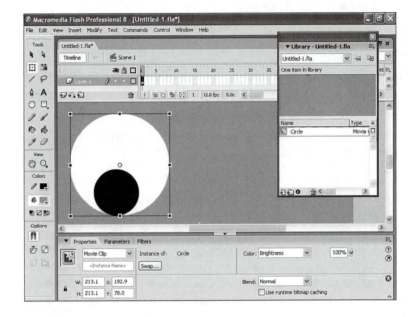

8. Now you'll make the entire face a symbol. First, though, select the Brush tool, confirm you're in Object Drawing mode, pick a fill color different than the fact, then draw a smile on the face.

9. When your symbol looks like the one shown in Figure 4.18, select everything, choose Modify, Convert to Symbol, name the symbol Face, and click OK. You now have a Face symbol that can be used over and over again throughout a movie. It's nothing more than recycled circles plus a smile. By the way, there's no need to put the smile in the Library by itself (unless you needed to use it independently with other faces) because it's really in your movie only once—inside the master version of the Face symbol. I should note that you're welcome to go inside and make edits to any element you want. For example, you can double-click the Face instance on stage, select one of the Eye instances, and change its rotation or add a Drop Shadow. Keep your bearings by paying attention to the edit bar.

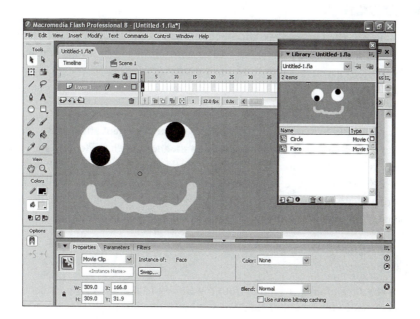

FIGURE 4.18
The Face symbol was created with multiple instances of the same clip.

Overnesting

There comes a point where too much hierarchy affects file size negatively. In the case of the house in Figure 4.15, all I had was one line recycled many times. Earlier I said that Flash stores the original data in the Library, plus information concerning how each instance varies. Usually the original data is the big portion and instance information is insignificant. However, if you take the instance information to an extreme, it can actually work against you. To prove this point, suppose you make a one-pixel dot, put it in the Library, and then use it millions of times to create all kinds of graphics—and then you tint each pixel instance individually. The extra data for those millions of instances would indeed outweigh the dot in the Library. It's a balance. You should combine convenience with efficiency. In the case of the house, I found that by creating the box from scratch (not with four instances of the Line symbol), I cut my exported movie size in half!

Watch Out!

Summary

There's more to the Library than you might expect. In this hour, you have learned the basics of managing the Library as well as some of the ramifications of using the Library. You can get shapes into the Library either by selecting New Symbol or by selecting Convert to Symbol. Remember that converting to a symbol leaves behind an instance of the symbol you just created.

When you have some symbols in the Library, you can use them anywhere in a movie. Instances of symbols don't significantly add to the file size. Plus, each instance can be modified in terms of position, rotation, scale, tint, brightness, alpha, and blend plus all the filters. Therefore, you can recycle but change a single graphic. In this hour you also learned that you can use instances of symbols in the creation of other symbols. As you begin to understand the hierarchy of symbols, you'll be unstoppable.

Q&A

Q *When I try to drag a symbol from my Library to the Stage, my cursor changes to the international "No" symbol. It used to work. Why doesn't it now?*

A You can drag symbols from the Library onto the Stage provided that you have an open layer into which to drop them. Your problem is occurring because the current layer (with a pencil in it) is locked, the current layer is invisible, or the red current-frame marker is in an interpolated frame (as discussed in Hour 8, "Using Motion Tweens to Animate," and Hour 9, "Using Shape Tweens to Morph"). You'll learn more about layers in Hour 11, "Using Layers in Animations."

Q *Libraries seem like they can save a lot of time and keep movie sizes down. Is there any way to use these benefits among several files?*

A As a matter of fact, Flash has a powerful feature called Shared Libraries. You'll create and use shared libraries in Hour 23, "Working on Large Projects and in Team Environments."

Q *I set the blend of an instance to Invert and expected to see a negative version of that symbol. It just made my symbol black. How do I get that inverse look?*

A Remember that blends almost always require both the overlaying instance (that has the blend applied) as well as the objects (shapes, drawing objects, or other symbols) that are underneath. To see the inverse of an instance's contents, create a solid shape (say, a rectangle the same dimensions as the instance you want to invert) and put it underneath the instance with the blend applied. (You can play around with the color of that shape for different effects.) Alternatively, put the instance's blend back to Normal, covert the shape to a symbol, and apply a blend to that solid instance. Make sure the solid is on top of your original instance.

Q *I want to create a clock with a minute hand and second hand. None of the 9 registration point options (when first converting the shape to a symbol) were appropriate, so I went into the master symbol but I can't move that registration point. How do I move it?*

A You can't. But, you can instead select the entire contents of your symbol and move it relative to the registration point.

Q *Okay, I moved the contents so the registration point aligns with the exact axis of rotation but when I rotate the instance on stage it's still using the center point. I know for a fact this used to work in my dad's version of Flash back when I was younger. What gives?*

A You need to edit the transformation point. That's the white circle that appears when you use the Free Transform tool and select the symbol instance. If the transform point seems to be in an odd location, remember that it's always the visual center—at the time the object was created. If you've gone and edited the contents of the master symbol it could get all out of whack. Not to worry, you can always edit it by hand.

Workshop

The Workshop consists of quiz questions and answers to help you solidify your understanding of the material covered in this hour. You should try to answer the questions before checking the answers.

Quiz

1. If you don't see a symbol that you know you've created listed in the Library window, what is the likely cause?

   A. You have an outdated version of Flash and should get the upgrade.

   B. You're either not looking at the Library window for the current file or the symbol is hiding in a folder.

   C. You forgot to name the symbol; therefore, it isn't listed.

2. Which of the following are clues that you are currently editing the master version of a particular symbol?

   A. The edit bar contains the symbol's name, and a big plus sign appears in the middle of the screen.

   B. The Properties panel is grayed out.

   C. The symbol is highlighted in the Library window.

3. Should you consider using another color style setting instead of alpha when you simply want an instance to be faded back?

   A. No, nothing beats alpha.

   B. Yes, you should never use alpha.

   C. If the instance is not on top of anything else, then, yes, you should consider using brightness or tint instead.

Quiz Answers

1. B. A Library from another file can fool you, and putting symbols in folders can effectively hide them from your view. The drop-down list in the Library lets you view the library for any other currently open Flash file. Consider, too, that Answer C can't be correct because every symbol must have a name.

2. A. The edit bar is the main clue that you're in the Library. By all means, don't let the Library window fool you—answer C is way wrong.

3. C. If the alpha color effect is used, it's only effective (and therefore worthwhile) when it's on top of something that can show through it. Brightness and tint can be used to get the same effect, and both perform better than alpha on slower machines.

HOUR 5

Applied Layout Techniques

What You'll Learn in This Hour:

- ▶ How to create custom color swatches and gradients
- ▶ Practical ways to use blends and filters
- ▶ Additional tricks for creating perfectly aligned graphics

You've spent the last few hours acquiring basic drawing and graphic-importing skills. This hour, you're going to concentrate on gaining fine control of the features involved with these skills.

On the one hand, this chapter could be called "Advanced Drawing" but the techniques you'll learn have just as much to do with accurately presenting graphics with the right color and alignment as it does with creating graphics from scratch. In fact, I'm probably more authorized to discuss how to present graphics because I'm usually the one assembling the graphics—not the one creating them. Everything you learn in this hour should help you create perfect layouts (which is a much different matter than the subjective topic of creating nice looking graphics).

Controlling Color

Choosing colors in Flash is a matter of personal choice. You can use any color or color combination you want. In the following sections you'll learn how to create and save color swatches to easily create customized color palettes for movies. This will help you ensure a color theme is maintained throughout a Flash Movie or an entire site. You'll also see how to create and control gradients.

Creating Solid and Gradient Swatches

In Hour 2, "Drawing and Painting Original Art in Flash," anytime you wanted to color a line or fill, you selected the swatch of your choice from the Fill Color or Stroke controls in the Tools panel or Properties panel. Clicking the fill color exposes all the swatches that are currently available. By default, only 216 "web-safe" colors are available. If your computer's display can show only 256 colors (that is, "8 bit"), it is recommended that you use only colors within the web-safe selection of 216 colors. The remaining 40 colors are used in the browser's buttons and menus for different platforms and may not display as expected. Most likely, your users will not be limited to 256 colors, so this topic might be best for a history book. You can create any color you want.

Creating a custom color swatch involves two basic steps: using the Color Mixer panel to pick a color and then saving it as a swatch. This process is easy, but it's still worth stepping through carefully the first time. In the following task, you'll create a custom color by using both the Color Mixer panel and the Swatches panel.

▼   **Try It Yourself**

Create a Custom Color and Swatch

In this task you'll look at several ways to create colors and then save them as swatches for use later. Here are the steps to follow:

1. Make sure both the Color Mixer panel and the Swatches panel are visible.

2. In the Color Mixer panel, click the color picker, shown in Figure 5.1, and drag as you move through all the colors. Although this choice of colors isn't infinite, there are many more than 216 variations.

3. You should notice as you move through the color picker that the numbers in the RGB fields (for red, green, and blue) change. Colors are mixed from 256 shades of the colors red, green, and blue, with numeric values 0 to 255. These numeric values can be particularly useful. For example, a company that wants its logo colors to remain consistent can provide specific RGB values.

4. Another way to select a color is to sample it from somewhere else, even from outside Flash. For example, to use the exact shade of blue used on the Sams website, point your web browser to www.samspublishing.com and resize the Flash application so that you can see both at the same time.

5. In the Mixer panel or Tools panel, click and hold the fill color. As you drag, move to the website in the background (see Figure 5.2). The current fill color changes to exactly the same color when you let go.

▼

Color picker

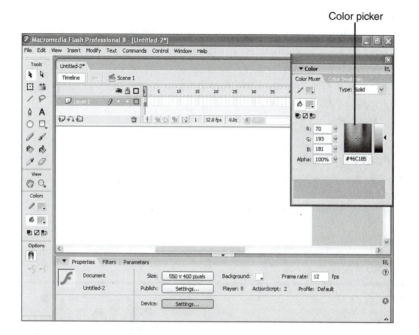

FIGURE 5.1
Selecting a color from the Color Mixer panel requires that you click the color picker square.

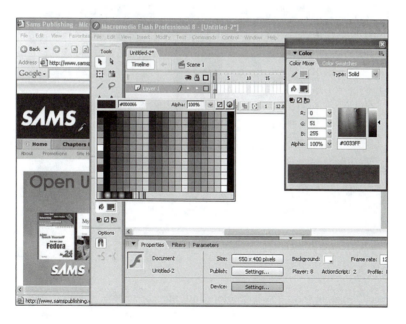

FIGURE 5.2
Sampling a color from outside Flash is possible. On the left side of the screen, a web page is positioned for sampling.

6. Now that you've created a new color, you could use it immediately by selecting the Brush tool and trying it out. Instead of trying it now, save it as a
swatch so you can easily select it later, without using the Color Mixer panel. In
the Color Mixer panel's options menu select Add Swatch . This adds the current color to the bottom of the Swatches panel. Another way to add a swatch
is by enlarging the Swatches panel and then clicking underneath all the existing swatches.

By the
Way

The Panel Options Menu

Remember that each panel has a subtle options menu available at the top right of
its title bar.

7. Scroll to the last color in the Swatches panel to find the new color. You can
also find the color anytime you click to select a color for your fill color or
stroke color (see Figure 5.3).

FIGURE 5.3
After a swatch
is added, it
appears almost
everywhere—as
a fill color, a
stroke color,
and a text color.

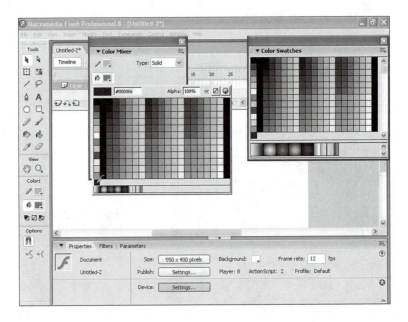

You've seen a couple ways to select colors and one way to save a swatch. Even though
we added a swatch for a custom color selected from the Web, it's also convenient to
save any color—even one for which there is already a swatch. For example, if you're
using the same orange color repeatedly, you don't have to remember it's the one in
the 18th column and 7th row of the Color Swatches panel. Just save a swatch and it

will be one of the few swatches in the last row. I often create a whole row of black swatches (21 across) just so I can easily see where my custom swatches begin.

In the preceding task you sampled a color and added it to the swatches. You can also enter the exact RGB if you know it. Alternatively, you can use HSB (for hue, saturation, brightness) if you change the setting in the color Mixer panel's options menu. Also, the Hex value always appears under the color picker. In addition, that same editable Hex field appears in the color swatches that pop up next to the fill color or stroke color (in the Tools panel or Properties panel).

Finally, notice that for any color setting, there's an option for the percentage of alpha. The lower this percentage, the more transparent the color will be. This is convenient; however recall from Hour 4 that you can also simply apply the Alpha color effect on a symbol instance. That's not the same thing unless the symbol is all one color. But I'm pointing this out because the exact appearance of a color changes when you modify the alpha. If the color is in your client's corporate logo, you probably don't want to change its alpha.

Color Systems

By the Way

There are several ways to describe color. Your monitor has three color guns that project red, green, and blue, respectively. Using RGB to describe a color tells each gun how much of its color to project. With 256 shades of color for each gun (0–255), practically any color can be created by mixing the three guns (16.7 million colors or so). Even though RGB may be the most intuitive color system, other systems exist that are not better or worse. Consider that the range of 0–255 used in RGB means nine characters are necessary (three for each color because the number 255 has three digits).

The Hex system was developed to describe RGB by using only six characters. Hex uses only six characters by extending the base 10 numbering system (which has only 10 characters, 0–9) to a base 16 system (0–9 plus A, B, C, D, E, and F). The result is that red, green, and blue each get two characters. For example, FF0000 is pure red (the highest value for red, FF, and no green or blue). Magenta is FF00FF (a mix of red and blue). In Flash you'll see two designations of a value that is presented in Hex: the prefix 0x, as in 0xFF000, and the more standard prefix #, as in #FF0000. HTML also uses the Hex system to describe colors.

Still another system HSB uses the three factors Hue (think angle in a color wheel), Saturation (how much chroma the color has or how rich it is), and Brightness (or how much white—as if you're adding white to a paint color).

There's no difference in the resulting color when you use any system: RGB, Hex, or HSB. For example, in the previous example, the blue I sampled had 0,0,102 (when expressed in RGB) which is identical to saying #000066 in Hex. It's almost like the difference between English and Spanish: You can say "red" or "rojo," and the result is the same. I find Flash's Color Mixer panel a nice way to get a feel for the differences. You can select a color, use the options menu to change the setting from RGB to HSB, and then view the results.

Even though the process you just learned for creating swatches is time-consuming at first, it can really help you down the line. For instance, although swatches are saved only with the current Flash file, after you've taken the time to create custom swatches, you can save them as a Flash Color Set file. From the Swatches panel's options menu, you select Save Colors. The file that you save can be used with other files or by other team members. To load colors that have been saved this way, you select Replace Colors from the Swatches panel's options menu. (Notice that the feature is called Replace, not Add—so it will replace any custom colors you've already created.)

No doubt you've noticed that the fill color can be a gradient. You'll see both radial and linear gradients in the default color swatches any time you click to specify the fill color. In the following task, you'll learn how to create your own custom gradient.

▼ Try It Yourself

Create a Custom Gradient

In this task you'll create a custom gradient. This task requires that the Mixer is fully expanded and that the Swatches panel is present. Follow these steps:

1. Expand the Color Mixer panel and arrange the Swatches panel so that the two panels are not docked to each other. (If they're grouped together, just use the options menu in the Color Mixer and select "Group Color Mixer with, New panel group.") Click the bucket icon in the Color Mixer Panel in order to define a gradient for the fill portion. (You can actually set a gradient for both the fill and the stroke separately.)

2. Select Linear from the Type drop-down list. Notice that the Color Mixer panel changes in several ways. A sample gradient appears in the color picker area; two little triangle arrows appear at each end of the gradient sample (which you'll see lets you edit the color at either end); and the Overflow drop-down menu appears from which you can set the gradient to appear once (called "extend"), "reflect" (meaning it goes from the first color to last color then back to the first, and so on), or "repeat" (meaning it goes from the first color to the last then first to last again, and so on). (See Figure 5.4.)

3. Either arrow (indicating the end of a gradient range) can be edited. The one with a black triangle indicates that it's the one being edited currently. Click the one on the left, and the pointer head changes to black. Now edit this starting color by clicking to select a color of your choice in the Color Mixer panel's color picker, as shown in Figure 5.5. Be sure to move the brightness slider, or your color may remain black.

▼

4. Select Radial Gradient from the Fill Style drop-down list, and you see the Color Mixer panel change again—but only in that the gradient sample is oval.

5. Click the pointer on the right side of the gradient and then select a bright blue color. Remember that simply clicking in the color picker only selects a hue; you probably need to raise the brightness (by clicking in the white-to-black vertical gradient). You should now have a radial blend that goes from yellow to blue.

Extend

Reflect

Repeat

FIGURE 5.4
Gradient overflow options are shown visually in the drop-down menu in the Color Mixer panel.

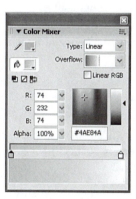

FIGURE 5.5
With the left side of the gradient selected, you can use the Color Mixer panel to change the color.

6. To add more colors to the gradient, click underneath the gradient definition bar in the Color Mixer panel (the short wide sample gradient). New pointers appear, and you can move them and edit their colors. To remove a color, drag the pointer down (not left or right).

7. To save this gradient in your Swatches panel, either select Add Swatch in the Color Mixer panel's options menu or just click in the Swatches panel to the right of the gradients that are already saved.

Now that you have a custom gradient, you'll learn how it can be used in a movie.

Using and Transforming Gradients

Whether you use the default gradients or create your own (as you did in the previous task), there's more to using gradients than simply selecting one of your choice for the fill or stroke colors. The Gradient Transform tool gives you some powerful ways to edit the precise look of your gradients.

It's interesting that the Gradient Transform tool does nothing but edit gradients already applied to a fill or stroke on stage—that is, it doesn't create anything. If you select the Gradient Transform tool, then select an existing gradient, you're given handles that let you adjust the attributes of a gradation. You can adjust the falloff rate, center point, rotation, and (in the case of radial gradients) the shape and focal point. Also, when you create fills that use a gradation—such as when you use the Bucket tool—you have an option called Lock Fill. While Lock Fill is selected all the shapes you fill are part of the same gradient. If that gradient goes from black to white, the transition is spread out through all the objects. If Lock Fill is not selected, each shape repeats a single gradient from black to white. In the following task you'll practice using the Gradient Transform Tool and the Lock Fill option.

▼   **Try It Yourself**

Transform Attributes of Gradients Used in a Movie

In this task you'll explore using the Lock Fill option and the Gradient Transform tool to gain full control of gradients. Follow these steps:

1. Select the Rectangle tool, make sure Object Drawing is deselected in the options area, select a solid fill color, and draw two squares close together. Deselect everything by pressing Esc.

2. Select the Paint Bucket tool and a radial gradient from the fill color swatch (the white-to-black default is fine).

3. Make sure the Lock Fill option is not selected, as shown in Figure 5.6. Click once in each square to fill it with the radial fill. Both squares have the entire radial effect—from white to black. This is the normal mode. Notice that the radial gradient centers around where you clicked. Continue to click in different locations within each square to see how the center of the gradient appears where you click.

4. Click once near the edge of a square that borders the other square. Click Lock Fill. Now the last fill you made will define the start of all subsequent fills because Lock Fill has been turned on. (Although it's not required, I encounter fewer problems if I first fill one shape and then turn on Lock Fill before continuing.)

▼

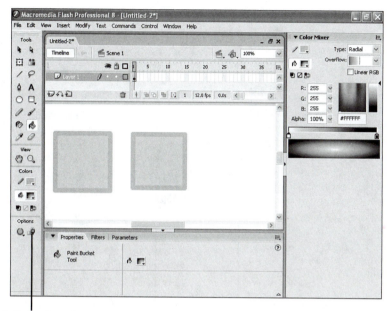

FIGURE 5.6
Lock Fill is not selected.

Lock fill deselected

5. Click the other square, and you should notice that the gradient continues from where it started in the first square—that's the effect of Lock Fill. Also, if you click the first square again, the center point of the gradient remains locked.

6. Now select the Gradient Transform tool to edit the fills you've made. With this tool selected, you can edit only fills that are already on the Stage.

7. Click the fill of one of the squares, and several handles appear, as shown in Figure 5.7. You can now move the gradient's center. The handles on the edge let you change the shape of the radial gradient, the falloff rate, focal point, and the rotation.

8. You'll probably find these handles to be very intuitive, but you should experiment with them a little bit. Click and drag the Move handle to change the center point of the fill. (Notice that in Figure 5.8 there are six handles that all change your cursor.)

FIGURE 5.7
You can use the Gradient Transform tool on this gradient, which spans multiple shapes because Lock Fill was selected.

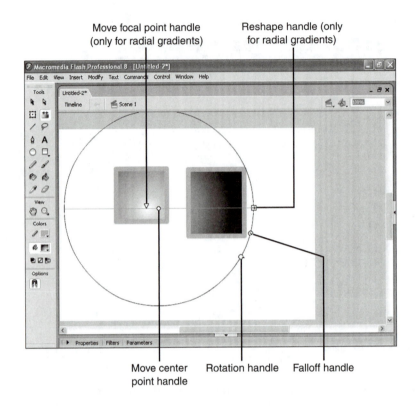

Move focal point handle
(only for radial gradients)

Reshape handle (only for radial gradients)

Move center point handle

Rotation handle

Falloff handle

FIGURE 5.8
The different features of the Gradient Transform tool have different cursors.

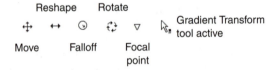

Reshape   Rotate

Move   Falloff   Focal point

Gradient Transform tool active

9. Click and drag the Reshape handle to make the gradient an ellipse rather than a perfect circle. Notice in Figure 5.8 that the Reshape cursor is similar to the cursor you see when you scale an object.

10. The Focal Point handle lets you change the symmetry of the radial gradient. The effect is similar to the Reshape handle, however the Focal Point identifies the hot spot within the entire shape. You can think of the Focal Point handle adjusting how oblong the gradient should appear.

11. Use the Falloff handle to change the rate at which the gradient changes from white to black. A custom Falloff cursor is shown in Figure 5.8.

12. Adjust the rotation of the reshaped gradient. You see the same Rotation cursor that is shown with the traditional rotation tool in Figure 5.8. Realize that with radial gradients, you have to reshape the fill before the rotation handle will provide any results.

You might think that we've spent an inordinate amount of time with gradations. However, it's really a quite powerful effect—sort of the poor-man's 3D. Figures 5.9 and 5.10 show two simple examples (including a pseudo-sphere) that I created using gradients.

FIGURE 5.9
A simple filled circle becomes a sphere when you tweak a radial gradient.

FIGURE 5.10
A subtle gradient (with Overflow set to reflect) adds a subtle touch to this picture frame.

Setting Text

Back in hour 2 you learned the basics of placing text in your movies. Here you'll learn additional details to ensure text appears exactly as you intend—especially when that text changes at runtime or includes special effects. Plus, I have a few incidental tricks to help make text appear exactly how you intend.

Static Text Layout

Any time you need text that's going to be locked down you should use the Static Text option (from the Text Type drop down in the Properties panel). When I say "locked down" I mean the text doesn't need to change at runtime. For example, if you want to display the time or a different message every day the user visits, you need to use Dynamic Text. If you want a field into which the user can type his name, you must use Input Text. That is, both Dynamic and Input can change at runtime; Input is changeable by the user. In other cases the text is locked down, so use Static text.

We'll get to Dynamic and Input text in a minute, but for now let me point out the ways to control static text. One of the main benefits of Static text is that the user doesn't need the font you use. However, you will need the fonts at the time you generate the `.swf`. This is important when working on a team when your colleague sends you a `.fla` that uses a font you don't have installed. You can make changes to any part of the file, except the text. And, as long as you send the file back to be published, everything should work just fine. When you open a `.fla` that contains fonts you don't have installed, Flash displays the "Missing Font Warning" dialog shown in Figure 5.11. Unless you want to globally substitute a particular font (that is, if you're planning to create the `.swf` on a machine that does have the missing fonts), simply select "Use Default."

FIGURE 5.11
Select "Use Default" on the Missing Font Warning dialog and you can send a `.fla` back to a teammate to publish with the necessary fonts.

Using Find and Replace to Replace Fonts

Incidentally, you may want to globally replace every instance where you used a particular font. (And you don't like the idea of removing the font from your system, relaunching Flash, and using the Choose Substitute option in the Missing Font Warning.) You can use Flash's advanced Find-and-Replace panel. Just press Ctrl+F and what looks like a standard dialog appears. However, you can do fancy stuff such as limit your search to a particular font (from the second drop down, select Font then select the font you're looking for in the third drop down). It's pretty sweet. If you accidentally set one block of text to 12 point instead of 11 you can find it immediately using this tool.

There are a few more points I want to share about using Static text. First, be conscious of the Selectable option (in the Properties panel when a text block is selected) and only enable selectable text when it makes sense. That is, users probably don't need to select things like headlines or text that appears only briefly during an animation. I see a lot of cases where it looks like a mistake when text is selectable as well as cases where I want to select the text but can't.

I have another tip for making any color text look good on any background. Sometimes you'll notice, on a foreign film, they'll use white subtitles. That works great on a dark background but the same white is impossible to read on a white background. If you want to ensure text will stand out on any color background you can use the Glow Filter that's included in Flash Professional 8. For example, if your text is light, you can create a Glow in a dark color as shown in Figure 5.12. Just set the blur factors to something low, like 2. Interestingly, the low quality setting makes the text stand out more (the blur isn't as smooth, but that makes the text sharper).

FIGURE 5.12
The Glow Filter or Drop Shadow Filter can add the needed contrast to make light text stand out on a light background.

We're going to move on to Dynamic and Input text which are really everything Static text is plus more. That is, the tricks I showed for Static text apply to Dynamic and Input text. (The only exception is the way Flash automatically includes font outlines for Static text.)

Embedding Fonts for Dynamic Text

I've explained that Dynamic and Input text can change at runtime. Obviously, the user can change Input text by simply typing. But to see how to write the instructions to change Dynamic Text at runtime, you'll have to wait until Hours 15 and 16 before learning how to use ActionScript. Fonts become an issue with Dynamic or Input text when you consider the fact Flash doesn't know all the characters it needs to include when publishing a .swf (the way it does with Static text). When the movie runs on your user's machine Flash will find a substitute for any missing fonts. (This only happens with Static text if you select "Use device fonts" from the font rendering drop down in the Properties panel.) Because the exact characters appearing in a Dynamic or Input text field can change Flash, by default, embeds no fonts. So, this is a problem only when the end user doesn't have the particular font installed.

There are ways to reduce or prevent Flash from having to find a substitute font—which is always different and often worse than your preferred font. You can select one of the Device Fonts listed at the top of the font drop down list: _sans, _serif, or _typewriter. These not only have little to no impact on file size, they force the Flash player to find a working substitute on the user's system, respectively: Arial (or Helvetica), Times, or Courier. The disadvantages of this approach are, one, it's not 100% foolproof (because a user could have removed the font—though this is pretty unlikely because they're such common fonts) and two, you're limited to only three very basic fonts!

To ensure a font used in your Dynamic or Input text appears to the user exactly as it does on your machine (where that font is installed) you need to embed the necessary characters. I say "necessary characters" because you shouldn't embed more than you need as every added character adds to the file size. For example, if you're using Dynamic text to display a digital clock you only need the numerals 0 through 9 plus : and A,M,P (for AM or PM). The way you select the characters to embed press the Embed button in the Properties panel which is only available with Dynamic or Input text that uses a font other than one of the three device fonts listed earlier. The Character Embedding dialog, shown in Figure 5.13, lets you select groups of glyphs (what I'd call characters). For example, you can embed just the uppercase alphabet (A through Z). Here's a huge tip: don't click the "All" option. If you want to include "all" characters you probably just need to select the Basic Latin choice (that's the same as upper and lower case, numerals, and all punctuation). Often you won't need all 52 punctuation marks. For the digital clock I mentioned you can select Numerals in the list above and then type AMP: into the "Include these characters" (which can be read "also include these characters" because they get added to the groups you've selected above).

There are other reasons why you may need to embed font characters. Embedding is also required when you want to:

▶ Rotate the text (or put text inside a Movie Clip that is rotated)

▶ Mask part or all of the text

▶ Use Filters on the text

You've already seen how to use the Transform tool to rotate objects. If that object is a block of Dynamic or Input text or a symbol instance which itself contains Dynamic or Input text, you'll need to embed the characters. In Hour 11 you'll see how a mask layer lets you hide and reveal parts of objects in other layers. Odd shaped masks won't work on Dynamic or Input text unless you embed the characters. Finally, if you plan on applying Filters to Dynamic or Input text (with Flash Professional 8), you need to embed the font.

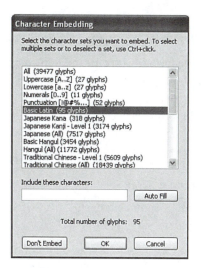

FIGURE 5.13
You can selectively embed specific characters (glyphs) to ensure users will see text with a font installed on your machine.

If you're getting the feeling that it's just easier to always embed fonts when using Dynamic or Input text, I suppose that's true—however, don't embed unless you have to! It always adds significantly to the final file size for your .swf (around 50K per font). Also, remember when you do need to embed, only embed the characters you're using.

Applied Examples Using Color Styles, Blends, and Filters

After you learned how to create symbols in the Library last hour, you learned about Color Styles, Blends, and Filters because they only work on instances of symbols. In this section you'll learn a variety of practical uses for these. I can't cover every combination because, besides the fact there are so many, the idea behind having so many options available is for you to explore and use for your own expressiveness.

Using Color Styles

There's not a whole lot to say about the Color Styles. The most common effects are tinting or changing the alpha of a clip. Compared to Blends and Filters, Color Styles may seem rudimentary. However, they're fairly powerful—and besides—they're all that's available in Flash Basic 8.

The first "effect" I'll show is really more of a trick: how to tint and set the alpha on a clip. That is, you can select either Tint or Alpha from the Color Style drop down menu (but not both). In order to set both in an intuitive manner, select Tint and then select the base color you want to use. Next, select Advanced and then press the

Settings button where you can set the Alpha percentage. When the advanced settings dialog appears it will match the tint you previously set.

Here's a real effect, drop shadow. However, let me warn you that you can do this much more effectively and easily using the Drop Shadow Filter if you have Flash Professional 8. You can also use the following technique if you want a drop shadow to appear for users with the Flash Player 7.

▼   **Try It Yourself**

Simple Drop Shadow on Text

You can use this trick for any symbol, but in this task I walk you through adding a shadow to text. Here are the steps.

1. Create a text block in very large font—say, 22 point. Leave the text black. Make sure the text is Static. Select the text object and convert it to a Movie Clip symbol (press F8) and name it `Title`.

2. Select the instance of Title now on stage and copy. Then select Edit, Paste in Place (Ctrl+Shift+V). With the duplicate instance selected, use the Properties panel and select Alpha from the Color Styles. Set the percentage down to about 40% or so (you can change it later).

3. Because the semi-transparent duplicate is both on top of and aligned exactly with the original, do the following to move it to the back. Select Modify, Arrange, Send to Back. Then nudge the shadow down to the right by pressing the down arrow 3 times and the right arrow 3 times. That's it!

▲

Why did we put the text inside a Movie Clip first? Check it out: if you want to edit the wording on your text you can simply go inside the symbol and edit the contents. The change is propagated to each instance on stage. Incidentally, you can do this poor-man's drop shadow with any symbol regardless of whether it contains text.

Practical Uses for Blends

The key to understanding the Flash Professional 8 feature Blends is to remember there are usually two players: the overlaying instance (the one with a blend applied to it) and all the objects underneath (which gets composited with the overlay). Also, realize you can nest the blends by applying a blend on one symbol instance residing inside another instance. You should also feel free to explore the different blends. When you find one that works well for a particular effect be sure to take time to study why it worked. That is, it doesn't do you any good to simply memorize the technical effect for each blend if you can't use them in a practical manner.

Perhaps the most powerful blend is Layer. When a Movie Clip instance on which you want to apply an alpha contains multiple overlapping objects, Layer is a life-saver. For example, I created a Flower Movie Clip (shown in Figure 5.14) by repeated-ly duplicating an instance of just the petal and rotating it. (In fact, I set the registra-tion point to the corner of the petal then used the Transform panel by typing in 30 degrees and pressing the "Copy and apply transform" button 12 times.) When I applied the Alpha Color Style on the flower instance, the portions of contained petals that were overlapping had a different alpha amount (as shown on the left of Figure 5.14). I simply left the alpha setting as is, and changed the Blend to Layer and it came out as expected.

FIGURE 5.14
The overlapping petals inside a flower clip with an alpha Color Style has an unexpected look (left) but improves when the Blend is also set to Layer (right).

Another useful Blend is Hard Light (as well as the similar Overlay). The basic orienta-tion is to apply the Hard Light or Overlay blend to a clip containing a gradient. This effect is nice because you can add a highlight or sheen that doesn't permanently change an imported raster graphic. (After all, you could create the same effect using Photoshop before you import an image but that wouldn't be editable once inside Flash.) In addition, when you learn how to animate starting in Hour 7, you can ani-mate the highlight making an otherwise static image almost come to life.

Try It Yourself ▼

Use the Hard Light or Overlay Blend to Add a Highlight

1. Import a photograph, say, of a sports car. Select the Rectangle tool and ensure Object Drawing is turned on. Draw a filled rectangle the same size and loca-tion as the photograph.

2. Open the Mixer Panel and then select the rectangle. Make sure the Fill color is active in the Mixer panel and then select Radial from the Type drop-down. Now edit the gradient so that it starts at white (probably already set) and ends at a 0% alpha gray. Just click the ending triangle on the right and then select a gray color. Then, set the alpha to 0.

▼

3. Use the Gradient Transform tool to change the center point and falloff of the gradient. I made the falloff very sharp and positioned the center on top of the car headlight.

4. The highlight looks pretty bad because it goes from white to gray and finally to clear. Wouldn't it be cool if the white would stay but the gray blended into the car's color? That's what Hard Light (or Overlay) can do. Select the drawn rectangle and convert it to a Movie Clip (press F8). Select the newly created instance and use the Properties panel to choose Hard Light from the Blend drop down. You can see what Overlay looks like—it should be more subtle so the highlight will include more of the car's color.

This technique works best when you keep the effect subtle. By the way, there's a similar technique to make a ribbon-like sheen. Instead of the radial gradient, make a multi-step gradient (or one that repeats). It's probably best for something like the picture frame shown earlier in Figure 5.10—not necessarily a car however.

The highlight effect just shown is much more interesting when you add a little bit of motion—that is, when you animate it. The following "practical" use for the Invert blend really requires animation for you to see anything. But, it's still worth looking at now.

Basically, you can get a lot of mileage by applying the Invert blend to a black rectangle (the same size as the stage) covering your entire stage. To see the effect, draw a bunch of shapes on to the stage. Then, make sure Object Drawing is turned on when you draw a black filled rectangle the same size as the stage. Convert the rectangle to a Movie Clip and set the Blend to Invert. Then, to simulate how the effect can be animated, select the clip and then alternate between cut (Ctrl+X) and undo (Ctrl+Z). So just imagine that a ball animates across the screen and when it hits a window this inverted blinking happens. It's pretty effective despite the simplicity.

There are so many more practical and gratuitous situations for the Blends. Hopefully this section has given you a couple starter effects that you can expand upon.

Practical Uses for Filters

A lot of the Flash Professional 8's Filters are effective on their own. For example, just add a Drop Shadow filter to a clip and it immediately appears to float over the stage. I've got one simple and one advanced example to give you a taste for using Filters for practical situations.

You might laugh when you see how easy you can use Filters to desaturate a photograph so it looks black and white. (But, then again, if you ever tried this in earlier versions of Flash you'll be blown away!) One sentence task: Import a photograph, convert it to a Movie Clip symbol, use the Filters panel to select Adjust Color, then move the Saturation slider all the way to the left (-100). It's easy, too, to make a photo look old-fashioned with a sepia-tone effect. Just bump up the Saturation a little and use the Hue slider to pick a yellow tinge.

If the desaturation trick was too easy, the following effect is more involved. Basically, it's a combination of a few things you've already done this hour: old-school drop shadow and the Hard Light Blend, all on top of the Bevel Filter. Basically, it adds some realism to the plastic-looking effect you get with a plain Bevel Filter.

Try It Yourself ▼

Combining Techniques to Improve the Bevel Filter

There's a definite trend to make icons have a soft 3D plastic looking character. Even the Flash application icon has this look. It's easy to create by combining a few features.

1. Use the Rectangle tool to draw a square filled with a solid dark pale red color (I used #AC6560) and no stroke. Select the Free Transform tool then click the Distort option. To distort it so it looks like it's facing the left, hold shift and drag the top right corner handle up. Then select the Rotate and Skew option and rotate it clockwise just a few degrees so it looks like Figure 5.15.

FIGURE 5.15
This unassuming distorted rectangle will become quite sophisticated after we're done with it.

2. Select the distorted rectangle and convert it to a Movie Clip and name it Rectangle Middle. From the Filters panel, select Bevel. Crank up the Blur to 18; the strength to 150%. Leave the highlight color white but change the shadow color to the same color as the rectangle's fill (or a tad darker). Click the Shadow color chip and then the eye dropper cursor will let you select the rectangle you drew. Step back and see how nice the bevel looks. There's nothing wrong with it but it looks like a computer drew it.

3. To add more character we'll use two techniques you've already learned about. First, let's add a subtle highlight using the Overlay blend on a duplicate of the rectangle. Copy the instance of Rectangle Middle and copy it. Select Edit, Paste in Place, then select Modify, Break Apart. Without deselecting, convert this shape to a Movie Clip (press F8) and name it Rectangle Top.

▼

4. Double-click to enter the `Rectangle Top` symbol. Change the fill color to a radial gradient in the same manner you did in the task "Use the Hard Light or Overlay Blend to add a Highlight." This time, make the gradient go from a bright red to a very dark red, almost black. Position the hot portion of this gradient near the top left of the rectangle. But, this time, make the falloff more gradual so that the gradient covers the entire shape as Figure 5.16 shows.

FIGURE 5.16
The gradual falloff for this gradient will add some dimension when you use it with the Overlay blend.

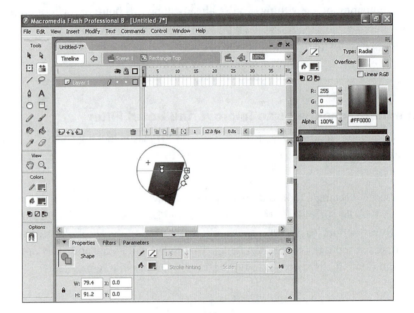

5. Go back up to your main scene and select the Rectangle Top instance (not containing a gradient). Change its Blend to Overlay.

6. It should look pretty good, but a drop shadow will add the final touch. You're welcome to try the Drop Shadow filter (on the `Rectangle Middle` instance) but you'll get more control over the shape and location of the shadow if you make another instance. Open the Library and drag another instance of `Rectangle Middle` onto the stage. Using the Filters panel, select Drop Shadow. Set the Blur to 16 and the strength to 50%. Then, click Hide object. Now, rotate and skew the instance to make it look the shape a shadow might actually look. You will probably need to reposition it so the bottom left corner of the shadow aligns with the bottom left corner of the two other instances already on stage. I find it easiest to adjust the shape and location while it's on top of the other instances, but when you're done select Modify, Arrange, Send to Back. Figure 5.17 shows the finished layout.

Rectangle Top (with Overlay blend)

Rectangle Middle (with Bevel filter)

Rectangle Middle
(skewed and Drop Shadow filter with
Hide Object option)

Finished

FIGURE 5.17
To produce the
finished look on
the right, there
are three pieces
shown separate-
ly on the left.

Summary

You've acquired a lot of skills in these first five hours. Refining those skills and
applying them to whatever challenges you encounter is just a matter of practice. Of
course, becoming a great artist involves more than technique—you have to learn to
see.

In this hour, you created and used swatches and custom gradients. You also got plenty of practice using the Gradient Transform tool.

Perhaps the most valuable aspect of this Hour was how some of the later tasks had
very practical and specific applications. It's relatively easy to learn all the tools but
much harder to apply the tools. The applications for Color Effects, Blends, and
Filters are so great that I can't cover it all here, but you got a good start this hour.

Q&A

Q *I turned on the Lock Fill option of the Paint Bucket tool, but when I fill a
shape with a gradient, I just see a solid color. What's going on?*

A If you think you're looking at a solid, it's possible that you're just seeing one
end of the gradation. The best way to use the Lock Fill feature is to first fill a
shape with Lock Fill turned off and then turn it on and continue to fill other
shapes. Otherwise, what often happens is that the gradient's Fill Transform
handles are set so that the falloff is extremely large. If this happens, you can
try setting the Stage zoom level to 25% and selecting the Fill Transform tool.
You might then see the handles for the gradation way off the Stage.

Q *What is the best color specification system to use: RGB, HSB, or Hex?*

A Whichever one you prefer. No one system is better than the other. For every
color onscreen, there's a corresponding color value in any of the systems. If
your client provides its trademark colors in RGB, you should use RGB. If someone provides you with the hexadecimal values for color, you should use that
system. The three systems are practically the same.

Workshop

The Workshop consists of quiz questions and answers to help you solidify your understanding of the material covered in this hour. You should try to answer the questions before checking the answers.

Quiz

1. Why would you ever embed a font in a Dynamic Text field if it adds to the file size?

   A. Users will only see Times New Roman if you don't.

   B. You can't color Dynamic text unless the font is embedded.

   C. It's the only way to ensure the font will appear correctly when the user doesn't have the same font installed.

2. When you create a gradient swatch, which panel(s) do you use?

   A. The Swatch panel and the Gradient panel

   B. The Properties panel

   C. The Color Mixer panel

3. Because Flash Basic doesn't include Filters or Blends it's pretty much impossible to use for graphics?

   A. True.

   B. No, you can still do some stuff—just not as advanced.

   C. No, Filters and Blends only apply to Raster graphics so you're fine if you don't plan on using those.

Quiz Answers

1. C. First, you should only be using Dynamic or Input text if you need to. When you do, and you're not 100% certain users will have the same font installed, then you should embed characters. And, then, only the characters you really need.

2. C. The Color Mixer panel is where you create and edit a custom gradient. Note that there is no Gradient panel, so Answer A is definitely incorrect.

3. B. Personally, I find the difference between Flash Basic 8 and Flash Professional 8 particularly notable that I definitely only recommend Flash Professional 8. However, you can still be effective in Flash Basic 8.

PART II

Animating in Flash

Understanding Animation

▶ The fundamentals of animation

▶ The common terms of animation

▶ How to use the basic Flash features related to animation

▶ The common misconceptions of animation (and how to overcome them)

There's nothing like animation. It can inspire, educate, and entertain. It's memorable, too; no doubt when you hear the name *Disney*, images pop into your head immediately. You are on the verge of gaining the power to communicate with animation. Before we jump into animation, there are several concepts worth studying first. This hour discusses animation in general and as applied to Flash to ensure that you understand exactly where you're headed. If your goal is clear, acquiring and applying the technical animation skills discussed in the next several hours will be easier.

How Animation Works

Animation is made from individual images. Regardless of how motion is created in an animation, an animation is still a collection of fixed images. Suppose you see a car drive by. You see the car throughout the entire time it's within sight, but you are likely to blink. Your brain covers up the fact that you missed part of the action. When you watch a movie or television, the screen is blinking very fast—sometimes it shows an image, and other times it's black. The fact that the black moments are so short makes you *think* you're watching full motion.

The image projected onto the retina of your eyes remains even after the light stops. If you close your eyes, the last thing you saw remains imprinted for just an instant, and then it fades. This **persistence of vision** is why you don't notice the blank spots between frames of a movie, assuming that they are short enough.

Elements of Animation

Now that you know a little bit about how animation works, we can discuss how it applies to Flash. As discussed in the following sections, several general animation terms have specific meanings in Flash. You need to understand both the general meanings and how the terms apply to Flash.

Frames and Frame Rate

As mentioned earlier in this hour, animation is a series of still images. Each image is called a *frame*. In movies, frames are the individual pictures on the film itself. In Flash, frames are the little rectangular cells in the Timeline. They're numbered at the top of the Timeline, and every fifth frame is gray; the rest of the frames are white with a gray outline. The Timeline displays all the frames, but normally you can look at the contents of one frame at a time. (Later you'll use the Onion Skin option to view multiple frames.) The red current-frame marker can be in only one place at a time—the frame you're currently viewing. You don't draw into a frame on the Timeline—you draw onto the Stage. The current-frame marker indicates the frame whose contents are currently onscreen. Figure 6.1 shows the Timeline in its initial state. Until this movie's duration is extended, you can't move the red current-frame marker past 1, and only Frame 1 is enclosed by a solid white box with a hollow circle.

By default, a Timeline is initially one frame long. The current-frame marker is unmovable at that point because it can be placed only in a frame of an animation, and so far the animation has only one frame. Let's look at an animation that has more frames, but instead of building an animation, you can download a sample from my website: www.phillipkerman.com/teachyourself/sourcefiles.

Download and open the `keyframing.fla` file so you can follow along. Now you can click in the numbered area of the Timeline on Frame 15. The current-frame marker moves to where you click; be sure to click in the numbered area toward the top of the Timeline—not in the cells (see Figure 6.2).

This example illustrates a few important concepts. First, if you click and drag the current-frame marker in the number area above the frames all the way from Frame 1 to Frame 60, you see a quick preview of the animation. This technique is called *scrubbing*. The preview you're given is dependent on how fast you scrub. Naturally, the *frame rate* is locked when the user watches an animation. If you select Control, Play or just press Enter, you see this animation play at its correct *frame rate*. To stop, you press Enter again. You should also notice the status area near the bottom left of the Timeline. The three numbers are the current frame number, the frame rate, and the current time elapsed (see Figure 6.3).

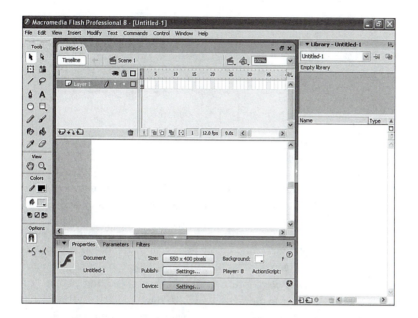

FIGURE 6.1
The Timeline, with its many cells, is initially only one frame long.

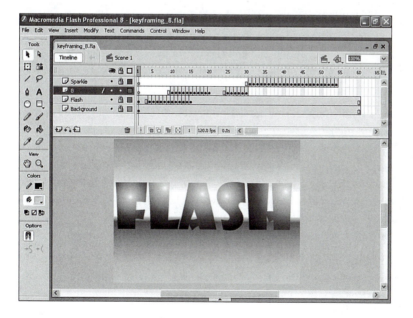

FIGURE 6.2
A 60-frame Timeline is shown, with the red current-frame marker on Frame 15. You can move the current-frame marker to any frame within the 60 frames by dragging in the numbered area.

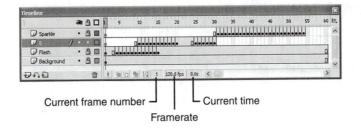

Current frame number ┘   └ Current time

Framerate

Scrub is a term that is used in all kinds of animation software. It's a technique for previewing an animation. You simply grab the red current-frame marker and drag it back and forth (through all the frames of the animation). You move your mouse in a scrubbing motion—hence the name.

Frame rate is the rate at which frames are played back for the user, measured in frames per second (fps). A frame rate of 30 fps means that 30 frames will be displayed every second. It is easy to confuse frame rate with speed, but they're not necessarily the same. If an entire animation uses 10 frames at 10 fps, it might look identical to the same movement using 20 frames if the frame rate is set to 20 fps. Both of these animations take 1 second to finish.

Speed isn't the reason you pick one rate over another. The issue is the capability of the user's machine. The frame rate you specify should really be called "maximum frame rate." Your movie will never exceed this rate, but on a slow computer, it might play more slowly.

The current frame number (on the left) indicates the location of the red current-frame marker. It changes while you're playing or scrubbing, reflecting that you can be in only one frame at a time. The frame rate (the middle number) normally indicates the frame rate for the movie that you last specified (by selecting Modify, Document and making a selection in the Document Properties dialog box). However, the number shown can be reduced if after you play the movie, Flash estimates that it can't actually keep up with the "requested" frame rate. It's not entirely accurate, but it does provide a good estimate.

Let's change the frame rate to something very high and see what happens. With the keyframing.fla sample file open, you can access the Document Properties dialog box by selecting Modify, Document. (You can also open this dialog box by pressing Ctrl+J, by double-clicking the frame rate number on the Timeline, or through the Properties panel, when nothing is selected, by pressing the button to the right of Size.) Change the frame rate to 120. Press Enter to play the movie and notice that as the red current-frame marker moves through the Timeline, the frame rate changes to show how fast Flash is actually playing. It wants to go 120 fps, but it may not be able to keep up. Now the status shows a more realistic frame rate, one that your computer can maintain. In reality, however, the frame rate shown here is not particularly accurate because it shows only how fast Flash plays during authoring—not in the actual exported movie. If you were to export this movie and play it in a browser, it would likely play slightly faster because the Flash authoring environment is not part of the picture.

Current time (the third number) indicates how long it takes to reach the frame you're viewing from the start of the movie. For example, how long it takes an animation to play 50 frames depends on the frame rate. At 24 fps, it should take about 2 seconds. At 12 fps, it should take about 4 seconds. The duration of the movie is based on the frame rate.

Frame Rate Versus the Number of Frames

The numbers in the status area are very important. When you design an animation, you should pick a frame rate and stick to it. When you change the frame rate, you're changing it for the entire movie. For example, say I have an animation of a character walking, running, jumping, and sitting still for a few seconds. If the portion where he's walking is too slow and I try to speed it up by increasing the frame rate, that portion might look better. But then the character will run extra fast, his sitting time will go by more quickly—everything will be faster! It's best to leave the frame rate alone and find another way to increase the speed.

There are ways to change the *effective speed*. Suppose you have an animation of an airplane moving across the sky. You need to decide the effective speed of the airplane according to the size of the airplane and how much sky you're showing. If you move the airplane all the way across the screen in 36 frames, you can't determine whether that's the right speed unless you consider the frame rate. At 12 fps, the airplane takes 3 seconds to move across the sky.

Effective speed is how fast something seems to move. **Actual speed**, in comparison, is absolute and can be measured. If an animation uses 12 frames (at 12 fps), the elapsed time of 1 second is the animation's actual speed. The viewer's psychological impression determines effective speed. Therefore, you can use illusions to increase or decrease an animation's effective speed. If a lot of action and changes occur in those 12 frames, it's effectively fast. If only one slight change occurs, the effective speed is slow.

If an airplane in the sky travels completely through my view in 3 seconds, the airplane is probably pretty close to me. If the plane is at 20,000 feet, it would take about 15 seconds (or longer) to move across the sky. If 3 seconds is too fast for the airplane in an animation, you can make it appear slower by slowing down the frame rate or by increasing the number of frames used in the Timeline. If you slow the frame rate to 2 fps, it will take 18 seconds for 36 frames, but the animation will be very jumpy (plus you're changing the rest of the animation). If you extend the animation to take 240 frames, the airplane takes 20 seconds to complete the motion. You'll learn how to do these things in the next few hours, but for now, it's only important to understand the difference between frame rate and total frames.

Frame Rates of Different Types of Animation

To put the animation you're about to embark upon into perspective, let's compare some traditional animation media. In a motion picture, the frame rate at which the images appear is 24 fps. Even at this relatively slow rate, you don't notice the moments when the screen is black. Television plays at 30 fps.

In computer animation, the screen doesn't blink between frames, but you do have a choice about what frame rate to use. Technically, the user's monitor will flicker as much or as little as she has it set to flicker, but in any case, it will be much faster than an animation's frame rate. In computer animation, frame rate affects how frequently the onscreen graphic changes or, conversely, how long it pauses before advancing to the next frame. In practice, if you go much below Flash's default setting of 12 fps, your user will start to notice jumpiness, and if it's much higher than 36 fps, it may not perform well on all machines. Remember that traditional movies use 24 fps and look quite smooth.

It might seem that you should always crank up the frame rate as high as you can, which would address the problem of jumpiness. However, it's not that easy. First of all, more frames can mean that your movie has a bigger file size. Also, it often requires a computer that can display images quickly. If your user's machine can't keep up, it slows down the animation and makes it not only jumpy but slow.

Finally, creative animation techniques enable you to fool the user in ways other than relying on persistence of vision and a fast frame rate. You'll see examples in Hour 7, "Animation the Old-Fashioned Way," when you create an animation that uses only three frames. In Hour 22, "Advanced Animation Techniques," you'll learn about even more techniques. For now, just remember that frame rate is important, but it isn't everything.

Keyframes and Blank Keyframes

A keyframe is simply a frame in which you establish exactly what should appear on the Stage at a particular point. A keyframe might include an image, or it might be blank. A blank keyframe is still a keyframe; it's just one in which nothing appears on the Stage.

In traditional film animation, every frame is a keyframe—that is, something new appears onscreen with each frame. In Flash you can make every frame a keyframe, but you can also take some shortcuts. If the first keyframe occurs on Frame 1 and the next keyframe doesn't occur until Frame 10, there won't be any changes onscreen during Frames 2–9. The keyframe in Frame 1 establishes what will appear in Frame 1, and it doesn't change until the keyframe in Frame 10, which establishes what appears then. This is totally appropriate for something that doesn't need to change every fraction of a second. When you create a keyframe, it's as if you're telling Flash, "Put this stuff on the Stage and keep it here until you reach the next keyframe." The next keyframe says the same thing: "Now, put this new stuff on the Stage." You have two things to decide when you create keyframes: when you want them to occur (in the Timeline) and what you want to appear onscreen at those moments.

Establishing a keyframe is simply a matter of clicking the cell in the Timeline exactly where you want a keyframe to occur. After you click a single cell in the Timeline, select Insert, Timeline, Keyframe (or, better yet, press F6). A couple things happen when you do this. Flash places a keyframe in that frame (indicated by either a solid or hollow circle), and it copies the Stage content from the previous keyframe. If at the previous keyframe you have nothing on the Stage, a blank keyframe is inserted. If at the previous keyframe you have something drawn on the Stage, that shape or symbol instance is copied onto the State at the new keyframe. This can be convenient because a keyframe gives you a chance to specify both when you want an onscreen change to occur and what the onscreen contents should change to. Often you want just a small change. Creating a keyframe enables you to start with a copy of the previous keyframe's content instead of redrawing it from scratch.

Whatever you draw in a keyframe continues to be displayed until the Timeline arrives at the next keyframe (blank or otherwise). If keyframes are placed one after another, the screen changes with every frame. If the frame rate is 10 fps, you see 10 keyframes in 1 second.

However, keyframes don't have to occur one after another. If you insert keyframes at alternating frames, changes appear five times per second (still at 10 fps). For any frames between keyframes, you see the content of the previous keyframe, either an image or a blank screen. Say you want a box to appear onscreen and remain still for 1 second before it moves. In one keyframe you draw a box, and then 10 frames later (1 second at 10 fps) you insert a new keyframe in which you can move the box to a new location.

▼

Try It Yourself

Analyze a Finished Animation

In this task you'll view a sample animation and make some edits so you can better understand keyframes. Follow these steps:

1. Download the file keyframing.fla from my website: www.phillipkerman. com/teachyourself/sourcefiles. In Flash, open this file and then press Enter to watch the animation (see Figure 6.4).

FIGURE 6.4
This Timeline has many clues about what kind of animation is taking place.

2. Notice that there are separate named layers: Sparkle, 8, Flash, and Background. (We'll look at each separately.) You might need to resize the height of the Timeline to see all the layers (as illustrated in Figure 6.5). (Hour 11, "Using Layers in Animations," covers layers much more extensively.)

3. The Background layer appears initially in Frame 1 and remains unchanged onscreen for the duration of the animation. Notice that there's a keyframe in Frame 1, followed by many regular frames. It's possible to extend or reduce the duration of any of the background layers by first holding Ctrl and then moving the box at Frame 60 (but don't do this yet). Figure 6.6 shows a close-up of the Timeline.

▼

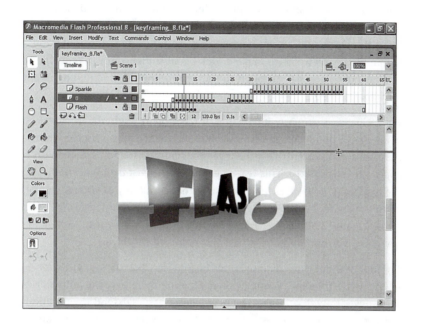

FIGURE 6.5
You can resize the height of the Timeline to see all the layers.

4. Scrub Frames 31 through 60 by dragging the current-frame marker in the numbered area of the Timeline. Notice the animation of Sparkle. In the Sparkle layer, notice a keyframe in each frame from 31 to 54. Onscreen, a different drawing of the Sparkle appears for each frame. Scrub past Frame 54, and the Sparkle is gone. That's because in the Sparkle layer, there are no frames after 54.

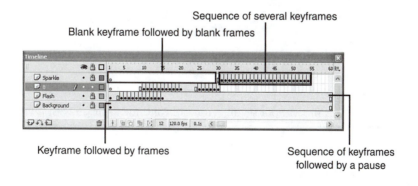

Sequence of several keyframes

Blank keyframe followed by blank frames

Keyframe followed by frames

Sequence of keyframes followed by a pause

FIGURE 6.6
Here's a close-up of the Timeline.

▼

5. The layer called Flash is more interesting. In Frame 1 the word *Flash* appears, but there isn't another keyframe until Frame 4, where the word changes. Then, in Frames 4 through 15, a different keyframe for every frame contains a modified image of the word (to make it look like it spins). You can press the comma and period keys to step through this animation (because scrubbing might be too abrupt).

6. The "8" layer is similarly interesting. It has a blank keyframe in Frame 1 (shown by a hollow circle). It's not so much that the 8 is offscreen at the start—it doesn't exist (that's the idea of a blank keyframe). The 8 doesn't appear until Frame 10. This is where you see the first (solid) keyframe. When the 8 appears, it changes in every frame that contains a keyframe. Actually, it pauses at Frame 20—there isn't another keyframe in that layer until Frame 25. Finally, Frame 30 is the last frame for this layer. Not only is it the last keyframe, but no frames exist past this point (in this layer).

7. Try adding frames after Frame 30 in the 8 layer. Click the cell at Frame 60 and select Insert, Timeline, Frame or press F5. When you play the animation now, the 8 never fully disappears. The new regular frames extend the duration of the contents at the keyframe in Frame 30. One way to remove the frames following the keyframe in Frame 30 is to hold down the Ctrl key and drag the box (indicating the end of a span) that is now at the end of the Sparkle layer to the left (see Figure 6.7). (Note that you don't need to hold Ctrl if you've previously selected Edit, Preferences and clicked the Span Based Section option.)

FIGURE 6.7
After you add frames to the end of a layer, you can reduce the duration if you hold Ctrl and drag the box to the left.

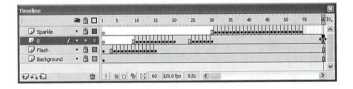

8. Close this file without saving. (You can continue to tinker with it later.)

The practical example in the preceding task is a great chance to see keyframes, blank keyframes, and regular frames in a working file. (By the way, I created this file to exemplify specific points. When you learn more you'll probably find ways to improve it.)

Tweening

You can put whatever you want in keyframes. The space between two keyframes effectively "holds" the onscreen contents from the first keyframe. Alternatively, you can tell Flash to interpolate the change in a process called *tweening*. For example, suppose that in one keyframe there is an airplane on the left of the stage. The next keyframe shows the airplane on the right side of the stage. Flash can calculate how to move the first image to the second.

Tweening is the process of interpolating two keyframes. Tweening smoothes out a big change by breaking it into little steps. If a circle at the bottom of the screen jumps to the top of the screen 1 second later (at 10 fps), the change appears abrupt. If the two frames are tweened, you see the circle move a little bit (about 1/10 of the total distance) 10 times. The coarse movement is smoothed out with small changes in the in-between frames. Flash calculates these tweened or interpolated frames so you don't have to do all the work.

The Meaning of Tweening

By the Way

The word **tweening** is from the word between, and it is used in conventional animation, as well as in Flash. If you look at the credits on any full-length animated feature film, you're likely to see the names of both the principal artists and the tweeners. The principal artists draw the keyframes, and the tweeners fill in the blanks between them. Similarly, in Flash you draw the keyframes, and Flash creates the frames in between.

Just so you can see what it looks like, check out the tweened frames in Figure 6.8. Tweening really is as simple as drawing two frames and making Flash tween the difference. You'll learn more about tweening during Hours 8, "Using Motion Tweens to Animate," and 9, "Using Shape Tweens to Morph." For now, you just need to realize that Flash will help you by doing some of the tedious work.

FIGURE 6.8
When you have two keyframes separated by several frames, you can tell Flash how to get from one to the next.

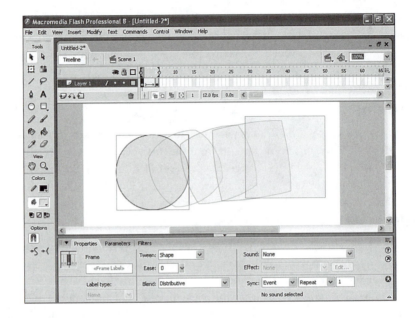

Summary

Although you didn't actually create any animations this hour, you did take a good look at animation. The concepts discussed in this hour, however, prepare you for the next few hours. In this hour you learned about familiar media such as television and film, including how persistence of vision gives the illusion of animation work.

As a part of this discussion, you learned several important terms, including frame rate, keyframes, and tweening. Frame rate is how fast Flash attempts to display the contents of each frame in sequence. Keyframes are where you establish what will be on the Stage at a particular time. Finally, tweening is Flash's way of filling the spaces between keyframes. These three concepts (and many more) will become almost second nature as you practice during the next three hours.

Q&A

Q *What is the best frame rate to use?*

A There's really no right answer. If there were a rule, it would be to use the lowest frame rate possible. This means fewer total frames, which in turn means a slightly smaller file. More importantly, it means that low-end computers are likely to play back the animation at the intended rate. In addition, it can mean less animating as there are fewer frames to animate. The only downside is that you have to be very creative to create animations that use only a few frames to communicate an idea or a movement.

Q *My monitor's refresh rate is 75Hz, meaning it blinks 75 times per second. However, I can crank the Flash movie's frame rate all the way to 120 fps. What would be the value of doing that?*

A Nothing, really. First of all, you'll likely find that if you set the frame rate to 120 fps, Flash won't keep up. If you're playing only a frame or two, it can actually go much faster than 36 fps. But even if Flash could display 120 fps (on a fast computer), it won't play that fast for the vast majority of the audience. Generally, going much over 36 fps is simply asking for trouble.

Q *It was really helpful deconstructing that keyframing.fla file. Can you add some more files like that?*

A Sure. In fact, at the site (www.phillipkerman.com/teachyourself/sourcefiles) you'll find several other files that appear later in the book.

Q *I've set my document properties to 24 fps, but the display on the bottom of the Timeline changed to 18.2 fps. How do I change it back?*

A First of all, this is a sign that your movie can't play at 24 fps. The 18.2 indicates that the last time you played the movie, it could reach only that frame rate. The frame rate set in the document properties has not changed. If you really want to change the display number, you need to access the document properties again (by double-clicking the 18.2) and click OK. Keep in mind that just because you set the frame rate to 24 fps doesn't mean Flash will play that fast. It will try, but it might not succeed.

Workshop

The Workshop consists of quiz questions and answers to help you solidify your understanding of the material covered in this hour. You should try to answer the questions before checking the answers.

Quiz

1. What is the visual effect of a movie that has a keyframe in every frame?

   A. It appears very smooth.

   B. It appears jumpy.

   C. It might have no visual effect.

2. If you set the frame rate to 2 fps, what is the visual result?

   A. The animation looks jumpy.

   B. You see the blank (black) pauses between frames.

   C. You can see subliminal messages between the frames.

3. If a document's properties are set to a frame rate of 60 fps, how long will it take to reach Frame 90?

   A. 1.5 seconds exactly

   B. 1.5 seconds or more

   C. None of the above

Quiz Answers

1. C. Many factors besides how frequently keyframes appear affect how an animation looks. First, the nature of the content has more impact than how many keyframes you have. You could have very similar or very different content onscreen for each keyframe. Also, frame rate affects how an animation appears.

2. A. A frame rate of 2 fps is slow enough for you to notice the still frames, but the visual effect is jumpiness. (In fact if the contents of each frame is the same you won't see any changes.) The pauses between frames are just that—pauses—not black frames.

3. B. It's very unlikely that your computer can actually display 60 fps if the animation is particularly complex. It will probably take longer than 1.5 seconds to display all 90 frames. If your computer *could* keep up with the frame rate of 60 fps, it would take slightly less than 1.5 seconds because it has to travel only 59 frames from Frame 1.

HOUR 7

Animation the Old-Fashioned Way

What You'll Learn in This Hour:

▶ How to make a frame-by-frame animation

▶ How to use the Onion Skin tools for assistance

▶ Some tricks that can make you more efficient when animating frame-by-frame

It's finally time to animate! You've assembled the graphics that will be animated, and in Hour 6, "Understanding Animation," you learned about the basic components of an animation (frames, keyframes, frame rate, and tweening). Now you're ready to create your own animation.

Instead of starting with the two ways Flash can tween for you, you're going to begin by animating each step in an animation the old-fashioned way: frame-by-frame. You'll learn about shape and motion tweening in the next two hours (Hours 8, "Using Motion Tweens to Animate," and 9, "Using Shape Tweens to Morph").

Understanding the Brute-Force Animation Technique

If you've ever made a flip-book, you already know how to make a frame-by-frame animation. Each page in a flip-book contains a slightly different image so that when you fan through all the pages, the image is animated. That's basically what you're going to do in this hour. However, instead of drawing something different on each page of a book, you'll be drawing a different image in each keyframe of the Flash Timeline. Whether you draw each image on a page of the book or in a Flash keyframe, I call this the *brute-force technique* because it's manual and very involved.

In this hour you will learn about features and techniques of Flash that make the animation process easier. However, frame-by-frame animation isn't a "feature" of Flash; it's a technique that you implement by using Flash's features. I mention this because I doubt you'll find "frame-by-frame" anywhere in the Flash manual or help files.

Enough talk! In the following task you'll make a quick animation, and then we can discuss what you've built.

▼ **Try It Yourself**

Make a Frame-by-Frame Animation

In this task you'll make an animation of a stick man taking a walk. Follow these steps:

1. Draw a stick man by using only lines (no fills) and make sure everything is snapped together, as in Figure 7.1.

FIGURE 7.1
In this stick man drawn with lines, lines are used because they are easier to modify than shape fills.

2. Single-click just to the right of the keyframe dot in Layer 1—that is, click in the second cell of Layer 1.

3. Select Insert, Timeline, Keyframe or press F6 to insert a keyframe in Frame 2 with a copy of the stick man graphic.

4. To make a slight change to the stick man in Frame 2, first make sure that you are editing Frame 2. You should see the red current-frame marker in Frame 2. If it's not there, click in Frame 2 of the Timeline.

5. Bend one leg of the stick man slightly and change the end point of the arm so it looks like it's swinging (as in Figure 7.2).

FIGURE 7.2
In the second keyframe, you bend the stick man's leg in preparation for taking a step.

6. If you want to preview what you have so far, use the scrub technique. Grab the red current-frame marker and drag it back and forth. Okay, there's not much yet, but you can see the stick man beginning to take a step.

7. To create the third frame, click in Layer 1 right after Frame 2 and select Insert, Timeline, Keyframe to copy the contents of Frame 2 into the new keyframe in Frame 3.

8. Make a slight change to the stick man—bend the leg more and swing the arm more.

9. Continue to insert keyframes, one at a time. Make an edit to each new frame to keep the arms and legs moving, and then select Insert, Timeline, Keyframe again.

Previewing an Animation Using Test Movie

There are three ways to watch an entire animation: scrubbing, playing, and testing. Scrubbing the red current-frame marker is a good way to preview as you work. The only problem with scrubbing is that the speed isn't consistent—it is only as smooth as you scrub. To play an animation, you select Control, Play or use the Play option on the Controller toolbar or press Enter. However, as you'll see later (when creating buttons the user can click, special effects layers such as masks, and animating using movie clips), playing a movie doesn't always show you *exactly* what your viewers will see, so I strongly recommend that you avoid previewing by using Play. The best way to view an animation is by selecting Control, Test Movie.

Test Movie exports a `.swf` file into the folder where your file is saved, names this file the same as your file but with a `.swf` extension, and then launches the Flash Player program so that you can view the results. You'll see how this works when you first save your source `.fla` file into a new, empty folder. After you use Test Movie, the folder will contain an additional `.swf` file.

Test Movie Versus Publishing

Selecting File, Publish or File, Publish Preview is equivalent to testing the movie. In addition to generating a `.swf`, it just creates the `.html` page to host it and (in the case of Publish Preview) immediately lets you view the results in the browser. I suppose this is even more accurate than test movie because you see the movie in the final format—but test movie is quicker and only good while you're working.

`.swf` Files

As you recall from Hour 1, "Basics," a **`.swf` file** (pronounced "swif") is an exported Flash file. This is the kind of file you put in web pages. It differs from the source Flash (`.fla`) file in that it is not editable. The critical concept is that a source file is a `.fla` file, and that's the file you need to keep. You can always export again to create a `.swf` (from a `.fla`), but you can't get an editable `.fla` from a `.swf`.

You might have noticed that when you're testing a movie, the menus change. That's because you're actually running Flash Player, which is a different program than Flash. Also, the movie loops by default, which is something you'll learn about later, when you publish a movie to the Web (in Hours 19, "Linking a Movie to the Web," and 24, "Publishing a Creation").

Editing One Keyframe at a Time

The concept behind the frame-by-frame animation technique is simple. You just put a keyframe on each frame. An entirely different image appears on each frame—sometimes drastically different, sometimes only slightly different. The beauty is that you can put anything you want in one keyframe because it doesn't matter what's in the other keyframes.

Although frame-by-frame animation is a simple concept, it can be a lot of work. Imagine conventional animation, in which an artist must draw each frame even when only a slight change is necessary. It's detailed, meticulous work and, unfortunately, it's not really any easier in Flash, although Flash provides functions such as Undo that help. You need to realize that this technique is for situations that require it—such as when you're working with something that has lots of details, such as an animation of someone walking (which, actually, is one of the hardest things to animate because we all know what it *should* look like). No other Flash animation technique gives you this level of control to change each frame.

Changing the Frame View Setting

Just because frame-by-frame animation is a lot of work doesn't mean you can't use a little help. One way to make the process a little easier is by changing the Frame View setting. In Figure 7.3 you can see the Frame View drop-down menu. If you select Preview, each keyframe in the Timeline is displayed as it appears on the Stage. Figure 7.4 shows the stick man animation with Frame View set to Preview. Preview lets you see all the frames of the animation without actually stepping through them. The Preview in Context setting draws the preview in the correct proportions (including blank whitespace), so the stick man would likely appear smaller.

The Frame View settings don't actually change an animation. For example, if you set Frame View to Large, it just makes the Timeline take up more space within Flash; the user will never notice the difference. Also, you can change the Frame View setting any time and change it back without changing the file.

Using the Onion Skin Tools

Probably the greatest helpers for frame-by-frame animations are Flash's Onion Skin tools. The onion skin technique was originally developed for conventional animation. When an artist draws each frame by hand, she needs a way to judge how much change in the image is necessary from one frame to the next. She draws a frame on tracing paper (which has the translucency of onion skin) that is placed on top of the previous frame. That way, she can see through to the previous frame and draw the next image accordingly.

FIGURE 7.3
The Frame View drop-down menu is available to change the size and character of the Timeline. You can make each frame larger or include a visual preview of the contents of the Stage in each frame.

FIGURE 7.4
The stick man animation is shown with Frame View set to Preview so that an image of the onscreen contents appears in each frame of the Timeline.

In Flash, the Onion Skin tools have the same effect, but of course you don't use real onion skin. Flash's Onion Skin feature allows you to edit one keyframe while viewing as many frames before or after the current frame as you want.

To begin working with the Onion Skin tools, open the stick man animation file and click the leftmost Onion Skin button at the bottom of the Timeline (see Figure 7.5). Select Large by clicking the Frame View drop-down menu that is just to the right of the Timeline's frame numbers. With Onion Skin turned on, you can place the red current-frame marker on any frame you want and edit that frame, and then you see a dim view of the other frames in the animation. Which frames appear depends on where you position the Start Onion Skin and End Onion Skin markers. These markers can be difficult to grab when you try to move them; I often find myself accidentally grabbing the current-frame marker. It's easiest to grab the markers when Frame View is set to Large.

FIGURE 7.5
When Onion Skin is turned on (via the leftmost button), you can see the contents of adjacent frames.

You would probably turn on Onion Skin while creating an animation (instead of after it's done). To practice, in the following task you'll try creating the stick man animation again—this time with the help of Onion Skin.

Try It Yourself ▼

Use Onion Skin to Help Create an Animation

In this task you'll use the Onion Skin feature to ensure natural motion in the way a stick man walks. Here are the steps:

1. Start a new file and set Frame View to Large.

▼

▼

2. Turn on Onion Skin. Notice that the Start and End Onion Skin markers (see Figure 7.6) cannot be moved beyond the beginning or end of the animation (because it's only one frame long at this point).

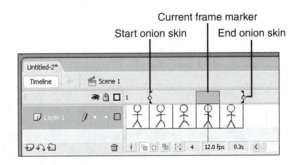

FIGURE 7.6
The Onion Skin markers indicate how many frames are included in the Onion Skin view.

3. Draw a stick man similar to the way you did in the previous task (using only lines).

4. In Frame 2, select Insert, Timeline, Keyframe or press F6 to copy what was in the previous frame and paste it into the new keyframe.

5. While editing Frame 2 (the red current-frame marker should be in Frame 2), drag the end of one leg of the stick man to move it to a different angle. This time, the position of the leg from Frame 1 is visible (though dimly), even though you can only edit the contents of Frame 2.

6. In Frame 3, insert another keyframe. When you move the leg, you can judge how much to move it, based on the position of the leg in Frame 2.

7. Continue to insert keyframes, one at a time. Make an edit to each new frame and then select Insert, Timeline, Keyframe again.

8. When you have several frames, experiment with changing both the Start and End Onion Skin markers. By default, the markers are set to Onion 2, meaning you can see two frames ahead and two behind. I rarely use the End Onion Skin marker at all—I just position it at the current-frame marker. I would rather see where I've been than where I'm headed. You can move the markers to several preset positions from the Modify Onion Markers drop-down menu (the rightmost Onion Skin button, pictured in Figure 7.7).

▼

Modify onion markers drop-down menu

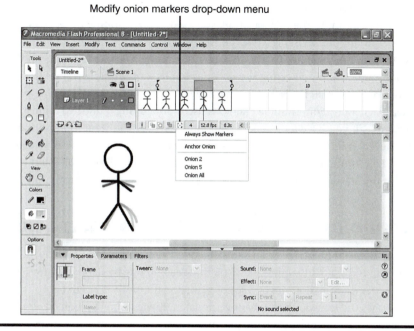

FIGURE 7.7
The Modify Onion Markers drop-down menu has several preset options.

▶ **Always Show Markers**—This option leaves a faint version of the markers visible in the Timeline even after you turn off Onion Skin.

▶ **Anchor Onion**—This option locks the two markers where they are, no matter where the red current-frame marker is.

▶ **Onion 2**—This option sets the markers to two frames ahead and two frames behind.

▶ **Onion 5**—This option sets the markers to five frames ahead and five frames behind.

▶ **Onion All**—This option moves the Start Onion Skin Marker to Frame 1 and the End Onion Skin Marker to your last frame.

Before we finish with Onion Skin, let's look at two remaining features: Onion Skin Outlines and Edit Multiple Frames. You can choose either Onion Skin or Onion Skin Outlines, but not both. Onion Skin Outlines displays the other frames within the Onion markers as outlines instead of as dim images. Outlines can be helpful when the dim view makes images difficult to distinguish.

Edit Multiple Frames is quite interesting because you don't commonly use it to produce an animation. In the previous task, you used onion skinning to see the contents of surrounding keyframes, but you were editing only one frame at a time—the current frame. You could move the stick man's leg close to the faded image in the previous frame without affecting the previous frame. Edit Multiple Frames lets you edit the contents of all the frames within the Start Onion Skin and End Onion Skin markers. Generally, Edit Multiple Frames is useful for editing a finished animation. For example, if you have a finished animation for which you want to move the contents of every frame, Edit Multiple Frames is invaluable. In this situation, you just turn on Edit Multiple Frames, select Modify Onion Markers, Onion All, select everything on the Stage (or press Ctrl+A), and move everything anywhere you want.

Enhancing a Frame-by-Frame Animation

Frame-by-frame animation can be a ton of work. Even with helpers such as the Onion Skin tools, it still requires that you draw each frame by hand. But just because frame-by-frame animation *can* be a lot of work doesn't mean it has to be. For animation that has the same look as a feature animated movie, frame-by-frame animation is required, and it involves skill and patience. However, by using a few tricks, you can pull off the same effects with a fraction of the work.

The following sections look at a few tricks that are especially suited to frame-by-frame animation. You'll learn even more in Hour 22, "Advanced Animation Techniques."

Incorporating Pauses

There's no rule that says you *must* put a keyframe in every frame. If your frame rate is left at the default 12 frames per second (fps) then it only makes sense to make every frame a keyframe if you need the image to change 12 times per second. This might be unnecessary, and it becomes a lot of work when you consider the total number of frames you must draw. What if you don't always want the images to change every 1/12 second? Incorporating pauses is the answer—and it's very easy.

In the previous examples you inserted a keyframe in every frame, one after another. Remember that a keyframe is where you tell Flash that something new is appearing on the Stage. In addition, a keyframe says "this image should appear now, and it should remain until a new keyframe comes." To incorporate a pause, you just follow a keyframe with a non-keyframe frame. If you want a 1-second pause (and you're running at 12 fps), you just follow your keyframe with 12 frames.

There are two ways to create pauses, either as you're making an animation or after you've made one. To incorporate a pause while creating an animation, you either insert a keyframe (by pressing F6) or insert frames (by pressing F5 or selecting Insert, Timeline, Frame) farther down the Timeline than the next frame. Figure 7.8 shows five keyframes in a row, but then a pause appears. That pause was created by first clicking the cell in Frame 11 and selecting Insert, Timeline, Keyframe.

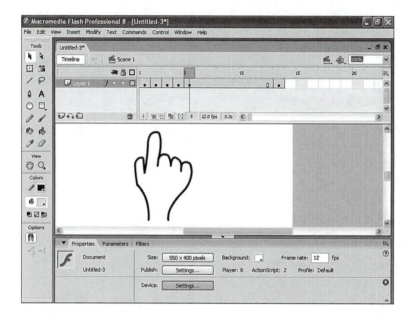

FIGURE 7.8
This frame-by-frame animation pauses after Frame 5 because there isn't a keyframe until Frame 11. Therefore, nothing changes on the Stage between Frames 5 and 11.

Creating a pause is slightly different when you want to edit an animation you've already created. To insert a pause (or increase one that already exists), you click the keyframe you want to pause and select Insert, Frame (F5). This effectively pushes out everything that appears later in the Timeline.

In a practical sense, pauses can enhance an animation. A pause can become a visual element of an animation. Suppose the stick man walks all the way across the Stage, and you want him to walk back. In this case, you might want to include a pause when he's about to turn around. In Hour 22, you'll see how pauses can cause the audience to anticipate that a change is about to happen, which makes people pay closer attention.

Implying Motion

Two frames are all you really need for an animation. Suppose that the stick man begins on the left side of the Stage in Frame 1. The next frame is a keyframe, and he's all the way over on the right side. Show this "animation" to enough people, and you'll find some who swear that they actually saw him move across the screen. In the real world, there's no way to get from one place to another without traveling through all points between, but in animation, you don't have to draw every step.

To prove the two-frame theory, you can make a simple animation of the stick man kicking a soccer ball. Draw a stick man in Frame 1 with a ball near his foot. In Frame 10, insert a keyframe and move the ball off to the right. Extend the stick man's leg so that it looks like he just kicked the ball. It's pretty amazing, but it looks convincing. If you add just one more keyframe at Frame 4 and move the stick man's leg back a tad (as if he's about to kick), the animation looks great! Stick man stands (pause), he winds up (pause), and he kicks. Imagine how much more work it would take to draw all 10 frames.

FIGURE 7.9
With just three keyframes, you can make an effective animation that implies more motion than is actually occurring.

Although a long frame-by-frame animation might take a long time to produce, you'll see that there are many tricks to save you time. For example, after you create an animation of the stick man taking one complete stride, you can make that sequence repeat (by copying and pasting frames or—better yet—using a movie clip, as you'll learn in Hour 12, "Animating Using Movie Clip and Graphic Symbols"). Although this isn't as simple as a two-frame animation, it means you don't have to create every frame by hand.

Creating implied motion is a great skill. In a way, you're trying to fool the audience, but it's more than that. Unnecessary animation adds extra work and can actually detract from your core message. It's hard enough to tell a story with animation; the last thing you need is a distracting animation that's superfluous.

Summary

This hour covers frame-by-frame animation, which is a technique, not a Flash feature. This hour is more than just an exercise in how to animate the hard way. In later hours, you'll learn ways that are easier—although not always better. During this hour you had a chance to look at several fundamental concepts. You learned how keyframes can be used to specify when an image is to change, and you experimented with the Onion Skin animation helpers. Also, you learned how to use pauses and blank frames to imply motion and to stop motion. As your learned about these techniques and tools, you made your first animation!

Q&A

Q *When would you insert keyframes one frame at a time rather than insert several by using Modify, Frames, Convert to Keyframes (or Convert to Blank Keyframes) for an entire span?*

A When you want to make a successive adjustments to each keyframe, it makes sense to draw the first frame, insert a keyframe, and then adjust the new frame before inserting a third frame. This process is effective because each time you insert a keyframe, Flash copies the contents of the previous keyframe. Inserting one keyframe at a time ensures that each keyframe is the same as the previous one, so that you need to make only a slight change before continuing. When you intend to draw an entirely new image into each keyframe, you should consider inserting blank keyframes (either one at a time or by selecting Modify, Timeline, Convert to Blank Keyframes). That way, each new keyframe starts with no contents.

Q *What's the difference between inserting a keyframe and then deleting the contents on the Stage and simply inserting a blank keyframe?*

A There is no difference; the result of either operation is a blank keyframe (indicated by a hollow circle in the cell of the Timeline). Inserting a regular keyframe and deleting the contents is the easier of the two techniques to learn because you don't have to think about blank keyframes. All you have are keyframes, and some just don't have any contents.

Q *Is frame-by-frame the best type of animation?*

A No. It's the most appropriate when you want each frame to appear differently from the next, but it takes the most work, too. In the coming hours, you'll see that other techniques are often easier and much more efficient.

Workshop

The Workshop consists of quiz questions and answers to help you solidify your understanding of the material covered in this hour. You should try to answer the questions before checking the answers.

Quiz

1. If you draw an image on the Stage in a keyframe, how long does that image remain on the Stage?

    A. Just during the one frame in which you drew the image

    B. Until another keyframe that contains a different image is encountered

    C. For the entire Timeline

2. How many frames are necessary to create an animation?

    A. One

    B. Two or more

    C. No fewer than three

3. In what part of this book do you actually get to animate?

    A. In the next 2 hours.

    B. In the last 2 hours.

    C. Here! You've been creating animations all hour!

Quiz Answers

1. B. Think of using a keyframe as you telling Flash to put an image on the Stage now and leave it there until notified otherwise (by another keyframe).

2. B. Although a feature-length movie may have 24 different images each second, you can imply motion very effectively with just 2 frames.

3. C. Frame-by-frame animation *is* animation. The other types of animation you're going to learn about are those in which Flash takes care of the frames between keyframes that you create. If nothing else, you should now understand keyframes clearly.

Exercise

Here's a great exercise that will let you experience an entirely different way of creating. Unlike the stick man exercises (where you created each new keyframe based on the previous keyframe), this time you'll draw an entirely new graphic into each keyframe.

Draw a bird flying. First select Frames 1 to 100 and use Modify, Timeline, Convert to Blank Keyframes. Turn on Onion Skin so you can view just the previous two frames. Start on Frame 1 and draw the bird (just use the Brush to draw a curved V shape). Press the period (.) key, which is the Next Frame quick key—and, using the Onion Skin tools as a guide, draw another V that moves across the screen. You can go pretty quickly: next frame, V, next frame, V.... If you want the bird to move fast, increase the space between the current V and the previous one. This exercise is good for experimenting with different types of motion.

Using Motion Tweens to Animate

What You'll Learn in This Hour:

▶ How to create a motion tween
▶ The basic properties of a motion tween
▶ How to use the Ease In and Ease Out effects
▶ How to use tricks to make your motion tweens look natural and realistic

Creating an animation frame-by-frame (as you did in Hour 7, "Animation the Old-Fashioned Way") can be a lot of work because you have to draw every frame yourself. With *tweening*, Flash fills in the blank frames between two keyframes. Flash has two types of tweening: motion tweening and shape tweening. This hour we'll cover motion tweening. Motion tweening animates clip properties such as location, scale, rotation, tint, alpha, as well as filters applied with Flash Professional 8. Shape tweening morphs one shape into another.

Creating a Motion Tween

A basic motion tween is very easy to produce. Let's create one in the following task, and then we can analyze it.

▼

Try It Yourself

Create a Basic Motion Tween

In this task you'll make a circle animate across the screen by using the Motion Tween feature:

1. In a new file, draw a circle on the Stage.

2. Select the entire circle and choose Modify, Convert to Symbol (or press F8). Name it Circle, leave the behavior set to the default Movie Clip, and click OK.

3. Click Frame 30 in the Timeline and select Insert, Timeline, Keyframe (or press F6).

4. Click on the keyframe in Frame 1; the red current-frame marker moves to Frame 1. Position the circle where you want it to appear at the beginning—in this case, to the left side of the Stage.

5. Click in the last keyframe (Frame 30) and notice that the red current-frame marker moves to Frame 30. Position the circle on the right side of the Stage.

6. Try scrubbing. The animation looks pretty abrupt. The circle stays on the left side for 29 frames and then jumps to the right side. To make the movement smoother, you can use tweening to have Flash take care of the in-between frames.

7. Set tweening in the beginning keyframe, in this case the first keyframe (in Frame 1). Select the keyframe in Frame 1 and then observe the Properties panel. When a frame is selected, the Properties panel contains a Tween drop-down list.

8. Select Motion from the Tween drop-down list. Leave all the default settings, as shown in Figure 8.1.

   That's it! Notice in Figure 8.2 that Flash has drawn an arrow with a blue background to represent the interpolated frames—those between two keyframes.

9. Select Control, Test Movie (or press Ctrl+Enter) to see what happens.

▲

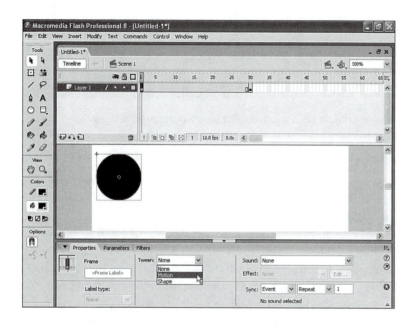

FIGURE 8.1
The Properties
panel opens,
with the first
keyframe
selected.

Interpolated frames

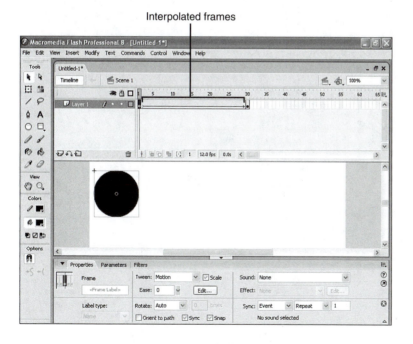

FIGURE 8.2
The Timeline
includes an
arrow on a blue
background to
indicate that
Flash is tween-
ing these
frames.

Following the Rules of a Motion Tween

The previous task worked because the instructions carefully followed the rules of a motion tween:

▶ You can't have multiple objects in keyframes.

▶ The one object you do have must be an instance of a symbol.

Flash is very unforgiving when you don't follow these rules.

The good news is that Flash gives you several hints when you don't follow the rules for a motion tween. Sometimes you'll see an exclamation point button on the Properties panel (when you select the first frame of a tween that breaks one of these rules). When you click the exclamation point button, the message "Motion tweening will not occur on layers with ungrouped shapes or on layers with more than one group or symbol" appears. In other words, this message is saying, "You didn't follow the two rules." You don't even have to press a button to know something is wrong—the exclamation point is enough. In addition to this warning appearing, the resulting Timeline will often look different. A dashed line will appear as another indication that you broke the rule (see Figure 8.3).

FIGURE 8.3
If you don't follow the rules for a motion tween, Flash warns that something is wrong.

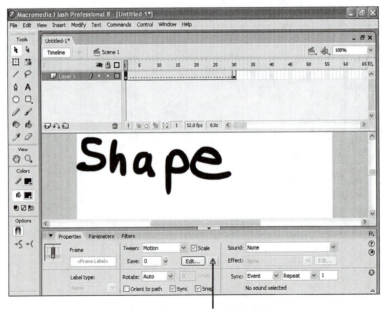

Exclamation point button

Motion Tweens and Groups

You probably noticed when you pressed the exclamation point button that the warning implies that you can motion tween either a symbol or a group. Unfortunately, Flash gives you a break here, but I would still recommend that you follow the rule that you only motion tween instances of symbols. If you have a grouped shape in the first keyframe and then you insert a keyframe later in the Timeline, you can use motion tweening with no apparent harm. However, Flash turns your grouped shape into a symbol, calls it Tween 1, and pretends nothing happened. It's as if Flash does the thinking for you. Personally, I would rather be in control and create symbols intentionally when I'm about to do a motion tween. Also, if you have a single drawing object in the two keyframes, Motion Tween works! But your file will be twice as big as it needs to be because you have two copies of that drawing object instead of a single symbol (that's used twice) in the Library.

Motion Tweening Techniques and Tips

You should feel proud of the circle you moved across the screen in the preceding task. Actually, Flash did the work—you just established the two keyframes. As you're about to see, Flash can tween any two keyframes, no matter how different they are from one another. Plus, there are some ways to make the process even easier for you.

Tweening More Than Position

Recall from Hour 4, "Using the Library for Productivity," that you learned that each instance on the Stage can be different from all the others, even if you just have one master symbol in the Library. Instances can be positioned in different locations, scaled to different sizes, rotated differently, have their color effects set differently, and have special effects filters applied. In Flash Basic 8, there are seven ways in which instances can be varied: position, scale, rotation, skew (which is a type of rotation), brightness, tint, and alpha. Flash Professional 8 adds filters. Flash can tween changes in all these properties.

Let's try to tween more than just an instance's position. The following task is just an exercise to practice tweening—it's not supposed to be subtle. We'll address the smoothness in the "Fine-Tuning a Motion Tween" section, later in this hour.

▼   **Try It Yourself**

Tween Position, Scale, Rotation, and Color

In this task you'll explore other tweening properties:

1. In a new file, use the Text tool to create a text block that contains your name. Don't worry about the exact size, but make it big enough to see clearly.

2. Using the Selection tool, select the text block (not the text itself). Then select Modify, Convert to Symbol (or press F8) and name the symbol My Name. Click OK.

3. Click Frame 30 in the Timeline and insert a keyframe (by selecting Insert, Timeline, Keyframe or pressing F6).

4. Click on the keyframe in Frame 1 (the red current-frame marker moves to Frame 1) and position your name in the bottom-left corner. This is the initial position of the text.

5. While the first keyframe is selected, choose Motion from the Tween drop-down list in the Properties panel.

6. Click on the keyframe in Frame 30 so you can edit the end position. Select the Free Transform tool (or press Q) and use Scale to scale the text large enough to occupy the entire Stage. You might need to position it closer to the center.

7. Scrub to get an idea of how the tween looks. From this point forward, remember that you'll only be able to edit the properties for the instance in either the beginning or ending keyframe, not between—that's where Flash is responsible for the tweening.

8. Move the red current-frame marker to Frame 30 and modify the color effect on the instance of the My Name movie clip. To do this, select the instance My Name and from the Properties panel select Tint in the Color Styles drop-down list, as shown in Figure 8.4. Pick a bright color and set the percentage to 100%. Scrub for a quick preview.

9. Go to Frame 1 and use the Free Transform tool to stretch your name really tall. (You might need to adjust the position.)

10. While still in Frame 1, use the rotate option to rotate your name counterclockwise just a few degrees, as shown in Figure 8.5. Do a little skewing, too. When the Rotate option for the Transform tool is selected, the corner handles rotate and the middle handles skew.

▼

FIGURE 8.4
The Tint color style is applied to the instance in Frame 30.

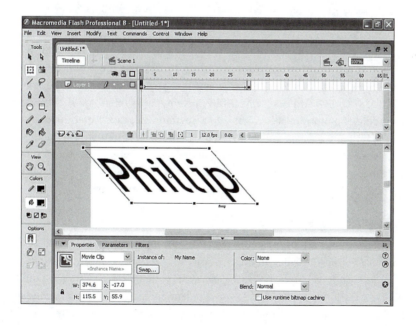

FIGURE 8.5
You can change any property of the instance in Frame 1, and Flash will tween accordingly.

11. Check out your animation by scrubbing or testing the movie. You created two very different keyframes, and Flash figured out how to animate from one to the other.

Did you Know?

> ### A Motion Tween Shortcut
>
> Because you'll likely use motion tweens a lot, there's a great shortcut to know. Just right-click your starting keyframe (on a Macintosh, use Control+click), and then select the option Create Motion Tween from the list that pops up.

Beware of Flash's Territory

You are responsible for establishing keyframes. When you choose to tween, Flash is responsible for the frames between your keyframes. Consider this to be "no-man's-land," although Flash calls these frames *interpolated frames*. If you edit anything you see on the Stage while the red current-frame marker is between two keyframes, you'll insert a keyframe automatically (perhaps without even knowing it).

To illustrate, suppose you have two keyframes and no tweening. Remember that keyframes establish when something should be on the Stage and where it will remain until another keyframe comes along. If you position the red current-frame marker anywhere in the middle and grab the object onscreen, you'll be editing the contents of the previous keyframe and thus influencing every frame from the first keyframe to the next. (You'll see a visual clue of this when you click an object on the Stage: The span in the Timeline that the first keyframe influences will turn black.)

Messing with no-man's-land is different when you have a motion tween already established. If you position the red current-frame marker in the middle of a motion tween (as in Figure 8.6), it won't be apparent that you can even select the symbol on the Stage. If you click and drag it, you can move it. However, if you move a symbol in the middle of a motion tween, you add a keyframe. Flash is forfeiting control of that frame to you by giving you a keyframe. Adding a keyframe in the middle of a motion tween is sometimes useful, as you'll see later this hour. Just realize that you're taking away Flash's control of a frame when you insert a keyframe (either by using Insert Keyframe or by grabbing the symbol and moving it).

Knowing Where You Are

It's important to pay attention to the red current-frame marker as you edit keyframes for a motion tween. Consider any of the tasks you've done so far this hour. If you want the motion to go from the left to the right, your starting keyframe should have the symbol positioned on the left. If you accidentally leave the current-frame marker on the end frame and then move the symbol to the left, you're actually editing the end keyframe, and the object will move to the left—not to the right. Always be sure the red current-frame marker is in the right place before you edit the contents on the Stage (see Figure 8.7).

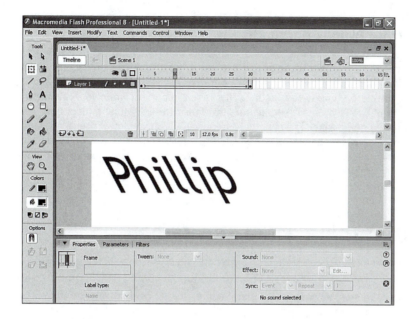

FIGURE 8.6
The red current-
frame marker is
positioned over
the interpolated
frames of the
tween.

FIGURE 8.7
The red current-
frame marker
indicates the
frame in which
you are current-
ly editing.

Sticking to a Pattern

Hopefully you're beginning to see a pattern. To summarize, here's the basic pattern we've used so far:

1. Motion tween will tween only one object, and that object is a symbol. Make that object a symbol before creating the ending keyframe, or else the new keyframe will contain a shape or drawing object, not a symbol.

2. After you've created your beginning and ending keyframes containing one instance each, you can adjust the position, scale, rotation, skew, brightness, tint, and alpha of either the beginning or end keyframe.

3. Keep an eye on the current-frame marker in your Timeline to be sure it's located in the keyframe you want to edit.

You'll refine your technique over time, but you should follow these basic steps during your entire Flash career.

Did you Know?

Setting Tweens Automatically

In the tasks so far, you set up two keyframes and then returned to the first one to set tweening. Another variation can be handy. Specifically, when you set the tweening in one keyframe and then add a keyframe, the second keyframe will automatically have the same tween setting. This is not important when your animation has a total of two keyframes (because a keyframe's tween setting affects how it will get to the next frame, of which there is none). When you know you need more keyframes, this technique is useful. Just remember that the last keyframe will have an unnecessary tween setting. That's no problem unless, later upon adding more keyframes, you find tweens you didn't expect.

Fine-Tuning a Motion Tween

Making a motion tween is pretty easy when you know how. Making it look good is another matter. There are a few basic techniques for fine-tuning a motion tween that will make the results more natural and believable. Although we'll see even more techniques later (in Hour 22, "Advanced Animation Techniques"), the following sections cover concepts that specifically apply to motion tweens.

Using Multiple Keyframes

Every motion tween involves just two keyframes. In the first, you tell Flash how to tween to the next keyframe. But suppose you want a symbol to move up and then back down. In this case, you need three keyframes: one in the initial location, another in the upper location, and a third in the end location. However, in this case you have only two tweens: one going up from the first keyframe to the second keyframe, and one going down from the second keyframe to the third keyframe. The process will be easier if you can sort things out this simply.

Often, you want the end of a motion tween to correspond exactly with the beginning (like a yo-yo moving down and then back to where it started). In the following task you can try this.

▼   **Try It Yourself**

Make an Animation Finish Where It Starts

In this task you'll make a circle return to exactly where it began (so that it loops seamlessly):

▼
    1. In a new file, draw a circle.

2. Select the circle and convert it to a symbol (by selecting Modify, Convert to Symbol or pressing F8). Call it Yo-Yo, leave the behavior set to the default Movie Clip, and click OK.

3. Position the yo-yo in its starting position, near the top of the screen.

4. Click Frame 20 in the Timeline and insert a keyframe (by selecting Insert, Timeline, Keyframe or pressing F6).

5. Before you move anything, click Frame 10 in the Timeline and insert another keyframe. At this point you should have three identical keyframes.

6. Make sure the red current-frame marker is on Frame 10 and move the yo-yo down to the bottom of the Stage. (Clicking the keyframe in Frame 10 to add the keyframe not only moves the current-frame marker but also selects all the contents of this frame that are on the Stage.)

7. Set motion tweening for Frame 1 (which specifies how to tween to Frame 10) and for Frame 10 (which specifies how to tween to Frame 20). To do this, you can use the right-click method if you want. To set tweening for two keyframes (Frames 1 and 10) at the same time, click the keyframe in Frame 1, hold Shift, and then click the keyframe in Frame 10. Then access the Properties panel and set tweening for both keyframes (see Figure 8.8). Select Motion.

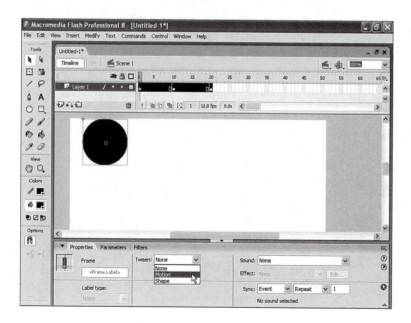

FIGURE 8.8
The Properties panel affects every keyframe selected.

> **8.** Select Control, Test Movie (or press Ctrl+Enter). Save the animation. (You'll add to it in a minute.)

Step back and consider what you did in the preceding task. You made sure the first and last keyframes were identical before editing the middle keyframe. It's very common in animation to establish the ending keyframes first before editing the initial frames. You did it here so that the first and last keyframes contained the yo-yo in the same position; in Hour 22 there's a whole section dedicated to this technique of starting with the end point.

By the way, it might not hurt to remind you that Motion Tweens affect all the properties that vary between the instances in two keyframes—not just position. You may think that with a name like "motion" tween it would only make things move.

Using Ease In and Ease Out

The only problem with letting the computer (or Flash) do tweening for you is that the result looks like a computer did it—it's almost too perfect. For example, the yo-yo from the preceding task moves down at the same rate as it moves up, instead of going faster on the way down and slower on the way up.

Flash has a way to address the fact that some kinds of motion accelerate while others decelerate: It's called *easing*. Because every tween is between only two keyframes, you only have to think of two keyframes at a time. *Ease in* (think "ease into animation") means that the motion starts off slow and speeds up at the end. *Ease out* is the opposite—the object starts by going fast and then slows down at the end of its motion.

You can see the effects of easing by opening the yo-yo animation you just created. Click the first keyframe and from the Properties panel set the Ease slider to –100 (by moving the slider down). Notice that the word "In" appears to the right of the slider. This causes the animation to start off slowly and then accelerate at the end (Figure 8.9 shows how the Properties panel looks). When you select Control, Test Movie, you'll see that the trip down should look pretty good.

FIGURE 8.9
The Ease setting in the Properties panel of a keyframe can affect acceleration or deceleration.

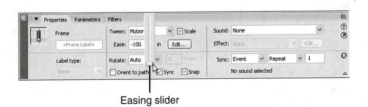

Easing slider

For the second tween (between Frames 10 and 20), you want to ease out as it reaches the peak, so select the keyframe in Frame 10 and from the Properties panel set Ease to 100 (by moving the slider up). Then select Control, Test Movie again. The result is that the yo-yo slows down before it reaches the top, making it look more natural. You'll find other ways to make your animation believable, and this quick experiment should spark some ideas.

Custom Easing

Ease In and Ease Out are great; however, you can apply only one setting per tween (between two keyframes). That is, say you want an animation to ease in at the beginning and then ease out at the end. In the past you'd have had to add more keyframes, but in Flash 8 there's a custom easing option where you can fine-tune the easing behavior.

Let's take a quick tour of the Custom Easing dialog box and then use it in a task. Select a keyframe, use the Properties panel to add a Motion Tween if you don't already have one, and then click the Edit button adjacent to the Ease slider. The Custom Ease In / Ease Out dialog box appears like Figure 8.10.

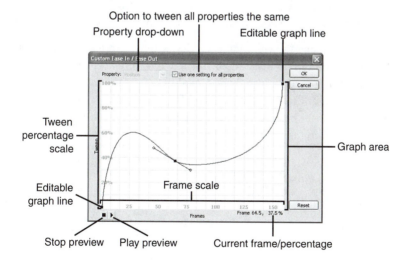

Option to tween all properties the same
Property drop-down
Editable graph line
Tween percentage scale
Graph area
Editable graph line
Frame scale
Stop preview
Play preview
Current frame/percentage

FIGURE 8.10
You can fine-tune your tween's easing with the Custom Easing dialog box.

Here's a quick tour of the key features of the Custom Easing dialog box:

▶ The graph area displays a line to show how much of the tween has completed (0%–100% on the vertical scale) over time (that is, the number of frames between the two keyframes shown on the horizontal scale). A tween with no easing is a straight 45° line going from 0% in the first frame to 100% at the last frame. You can see some finished examples of custom tweening in Figure 8.13 later in this hour.

▶ You can click right on the graph line to control. These control points include Bézier handles (like the Pen tool) to modify the exact shape of the graph. You're initially given a control point at the beginning and end of the tween. You can make a tween ease in and out with just these two points (as you'll do in the next task). Add more control points only when you need the easing behavior to change in the middle of a tween.

▶ By default, one graph applies to all properties that are changing within the tween. That is, if you uncheck the Use One Setting for All Properties option, you can make a separate graph for each property listed in the Property drop-down list. You select a property (say, Position) and then make a graph for how the changing position (in the tween) will ease. Then you select another property (say, Scale) and control how the changing scale will ease. Remember that a difference in any property (position, scale, rotation, color effect, and filters) will animate during the tween. Here you're just controlling how quickly it reaches 100% of those changes.

▶ The Play preview button is helpful because you can make lots of adjustments without closing the dialog box and returning to it.

▶ Your cursor changes to communicate what will happen if you click. There are five things you can do while modifying a graph: add a control point, select a control point, move a control point, modify the graph shape before or after a control point, or deselect all control points. The cursor for each is shown in Figure 8.11. Note that you can remove control points by simply selecting one and then pressing Delete.

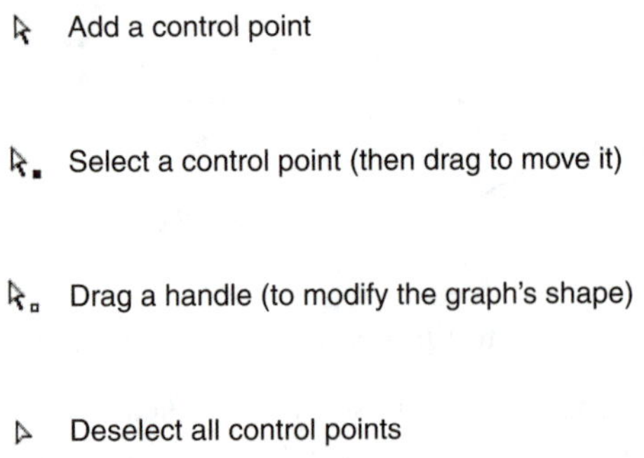

FIGURE 8.11
The cursor changes to tell you how you'll modify a graph.

Add a control point

Select a control point (then drag to move it)

Drag a handle (to modify the graph's shape)

Deselect all control points

The Custom Easing dialog box makes the most sense after you give it a try. The next task explores a couple of typical uses for custom easing: easing in and easing out in the same animation.

Try It Yourself ▼

Make an Animation Ease In and Ease Out

In this task you'll see how to combine Ease In and Ease Out in a single motion:

1. In a new file, draw any shape and make it a symbol. Place the symbol somewhere on the left side of the Stage.

2. Click Frame 50 in the Timeline and insert a keyframe (by selecting Insert, Timeline, Keyframe or pressing F6).

3. While the red current-frame marker is in Frame 50, move the instance of the symbol to the right side of the Stage.

4. Go back to the keyframe in Frame 1 and create a motion tween (by right-clicking and selecting Create Motion Tween).

5. Test the movie (by selecting Control, Test Movie) and remember how it looks.

6. Now we'll use custom easing. Click the keyframe in frame 1 and click the Edit button adjacent to the Easing slider.

7. Interestingly, we won't actually add any control points—there is already one at the beginning and one at the end. Select the first control point by clicking right on the black box at the bottom left of the graph. Grab the handle (it should appear on the graph line) and drag it down to the base of the graph and about 3/4 of the way across (that is, nearly to the bottom-right corner).

8. Select the control point at the end (upper right) and then drag the handle up to the top and over to the left about 3/4 of the way to the left (almost to the upper-left corner). Your graph should look like Figure 8.12. Test the movie and watch how it behaves.

▲

Notice that, as time passes at the beginning, the graph is mainly horizontal—meaning it's not completing much of its tween. Then, in the middle it's nearly a vertical line, meaning it is doing most of its tween. Finally, it slows back down as it approaches the end. You can click anywhere between the two keyframes and press F5 many times to insert more frames. Also, you can crank up the frame rate to something like 50fps. Both of these edits should make the tween more obvious. I produced the following graphs in Figure 8.13 to show a few typical easing behaviors. See whether you can previsualize the animation's behavior and then read the description of each.

FIGURE 8.12
This S-curve graph makes a single tween that eases in and eases out.

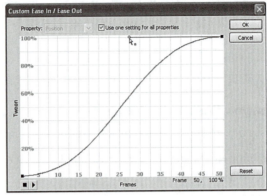

FIGURE 8.13
Compare this variety of custom easing graphs.

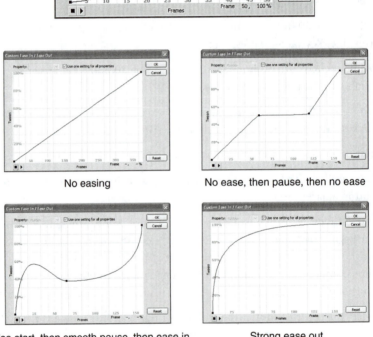

No easing   No ease, then pause, then no ease

False start, then smooth pause, then ease in   Strong ease out

Rotating in a Motion Tween

If you manually rotate a symbol in one keyframe, Flash tweens the rotation appropriately. In addition, in a motion tween you can tell Flash to rotate a symbol a specific number of rotations. For example, you can use this option to make an animation of a wheel rotating. In the Properties panel when a keyframe set to motion tweening is selected, you can set the Rotate drop-down list to CW (for clockwise) or CCW (for counterclockwise), as in Figure 8.14. One rotation is usually plenty; any more will just cause the increments of rotation between frames to be greater. Also, notice that the default setting for Rotate is Automatic, meaning that Flash will tween rotation if you manually rotate the symbol in either keyframe. The None setting will leave a manually rotated symbol in its rotated position during the entire tween. Because perfectly round symbols are not interesting when rotated, if you want to try rotating the yo-yo, consider drawing a graphic off-center inside the master version of the yo-yo symbol.

Avoid Gratuitous Effects

There is such a thing as too much of a good thing, and gratuitous animation is a fine example. There's no harm in playing with all the bells and whistles available in Flash. In fact, I encourage it while you learn. Just realize that to effectively communicate an idea or tell a story (which, after all, is what animation really is for), you should refrain from superfluous animation, which can ultimately detract from your message. For every effect you want to add, ask yourself: "Does this help clarify my message or not?"

FIGURE 8.14
By using the Properties panel while selecting a keyframe with motion tweening, you can make Flash rotate an exact number of turns, either clockwise or counterclockwise.

Summary

Congratulations! You've learned the fundamental skills of motion tweening. It's fun making Flash do all the work, especially after last hour's frame-by-frame animations. Look back at what you learned this hour, and you'll see that it is pretty simple: Just set two keyframes, specify how you want Flash to tween, and you have a motion tween! Although it is simple, when you add easing, rotating, and all the ways you can modify a symbol instance (scale, rotation, skew, position, color effect, and filter), you have numerous possibilities.

Just because the tasks this hour were fairly simple doesn't mean the motion tween is for simple effects. Actually, you should always consider motion tween before you choose shape tweening (covered next hour). Although some situations require a shape tween, motion tweens are always more efficient, and—when used creatively—can be very effective and natural looking.

Finally, I don't want to end on a sour note, but I do want to remind you of some of the points discussed last hour. Specifically, a few strategically placed keyframes (presented frame-by-frame) can often be just as effective as—or even more effective than—a computer-generated tween. The best animators think in keyframes. It's fine to employ Flash to come in and tween certain segments, but it's a skeleton of well-placed keyframes that makes a good animation.

Q&A

Q *When I insert a keyframe, Flash automatically creates a motion tween from the previous keyframe to my newly inserted one. Why is this happening?*

A When you insert a keyframe, Flash copies the previous keyframe (the contents and the frame settings). If the previous keyframe has been set to tween, the new keyframe will have the same setting.

Q *Why can't I motion tween more than one symbol?*

A You can have multiple shapes inside the symbol you're tweening. But the rule is that you can use only one symbol per layer. You'll see in Hour 11, "Using Layers in Animations," that you need to separate each tweening symbol into its own layer.

Q *When I use the Rotate setting in my keyframe, my symbol always rotates around the visual center, despite the registration point I chose when I created the symbol. How do I rotate around something other than the visual center?*

A The symbol rotates around the transform center point. Use the Transform tool to modify the axis of rotation for the instance. For more about this, review Hour 4.

Q *Why doesn't my motion tween follow a smooth path?*

A Motion tweening can tween more than just position. When tweening position, Flash moves directly from one keyframe to the next, finding the shortest path between two points. Wouldn't it be cool if you could draw a curve and tell Flash to follow the path you drew? You can. This is called a Motion Guide layer, and it's covered in Hour 11.

Q *I'm trying to use the Custom Easing dialog box to make my animation go past the end of its motion—say, 120% of its tween. How can I do that?*

A You can't do it with just two keyframes. You can insert a new keyframe somewhere before the ending and place your instance in a location past the destination. Also, although it might not be appropriate for your case, be sure to consider doing this in a frame-by-frame animation. Quite often just a few strategically placed keyframes are more effective than a tween. Finally, you'll learn more about this technique—called overkill—in Hour 22.

Workshop

The Workshop consists of quiz questions and answers to help you solidify your understanding of the material covered in this hour. You should try to answer the questions before checking the answers.

Quiz

1. According to the suggested process of creating a motion tween, what should you always do before inserting keyframes?

    A. Save the file and take a deep breath because Flash might crash.

    B. Ensure that the object in the first keyframe is an instance of a symbol.

    C. Use the Properties panel to tint the instance in the first keyframe.

2. When you want to edit the position of a symbol instance in a particular keyframe, what must you first ensure?

    A. That the red current-frame marker is in the frame you want to edit

    B. That you concentrate on the frame that you intend to edit and then move the instance

    C. That the symbol isn't red

3. A motion tween requires two keyframes. When establishing that you want a tween between those two keyframes, exactly where do you make your tween settings?

   A. In the Properties panel, when the symbol instance in Keyframe 1 is selected

   B. In the Properties panel, when the second keyframe is selected

   C. In the Properties panel, when the first keyframe is selected

Quiz Answers

1. B. Saving is always a good idea, but it's not really necessary. You want to make sure the first keyframe contains a symbol because it will be copied into the new keyframe and you need symbols in both keyframes for a motion tween.

2. A. As surprising as it sounds, people often try option B (also known as the E.S.P. method). This issue falls under a general suggestion I call "know where you are." If you want to edit Frame 1, you need to make sure the red current-frame marker is in Frame 1.

3. C. You always establish how Flash is to tween from one keyframe to the next by accessing the Properties panel for the *first keyframe*.

Exercises

Most of the motion tweens you implemented in this hour tweened only position. Try these exercises that use motion tween on other properties, such as scale and color effect:

1. Create a bouncing ball that squashes a little bit before bouncing back when it hits the ground. You'll need five keyframes: In addition to the first keyframe with the ball up high, you'll need a keyframe for when the ball reaches the ground and another keyframe for when the ball's in a squashed position. Use onion skinning to line up the bottom of the squashed ball with the bottom of the unsquashed ball. You need a keyframe in the down position but not squashed, and you need a keyframe at the end that corresponds to the initial position. Try using easing where you think it helps.

2. Make a simple tween in which text tweens from entirely transparent to its normal opaque (non-alpha) state. Consider other ways to achieve this besides using the Alpha effect. Be sure to make a symbol from text before you add keyframes.

HOUR 9

Using Shape Tweens to Morph

What You'll Learn in This Hour:

▶ How to make shape tweens
▶ What alternatives to shape tweening are available
▶ How to apply shape hints for more control

There are several ways to keep a Flash movie small and running swiftly. Recycling symbols from the Library and using motion tweening are two of the best ways. Unfortunately, the shape tween, as you're about to learn, is one of the least efficient features in Flash because it causes file size will grow. However, shape tweening is pretty cool looking! There's no other way to get the "morph" effect in Flash. So when appropriate, it's perfectly acceptable to use shape tweens.

A **morph** is a kind of animation that naturally changes one shape to another. *Morph* is a general term, but it's the closest common term that describes how Flash's shape tween works.

Making a Shape Tween

Shape tweens are fun because they look really cool and they're easy to create. Compared to motion tweens, they look more dynamic because every attribute—including the shape—animates. Basically, all you do is draw one or more shapes or Drawing Objects in two keyframes and set the tweening in the first keyframe to Shape. Let's create one in the following task, and then we can analyze it.

▼   **Try It Yourself**

Make a Simple Shape Tween

In this task you'll make a simple animation using shape tweening:

1. In a new file, draw a circle on the Stage. (Don't group anything and don't convert anything to a symbol.)

2. Insert a keyframe in Frame 30 (by clicking in the Timeline at Frame 30 and pressing F6 or selecting Insert, Timeline, Keyframe). This will be the end of the tween, and it will match the beginning.

3. Insert a keyframe in Frame 15. While the red current-frame marker is on Frame 15, put a little dimple into the circle: Use the Selection tool to first deselect the circle (click off the circle), and then bring the pointer close to the edge until the cursor changes to a curved-tail pointer. Click and drag toward the center of the circle to reshape it, as shown in Figure 9.1.

FIGURE 9.1
You bend the edge of the circle in one of the keyframes. Flash will do the tweening.

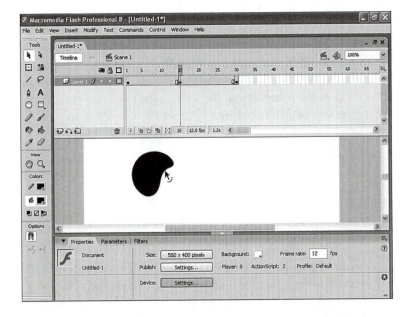

4. Set shape tweening for the two spans. To do this, click Frame 1, hold Shift, and then Click Frame 15. In the Properties panel, select Shape from the Tween drop-down list.

▲   5. Select Control, Test Movie (or press Ctrl+Enter) to see what happens.

Following the Rules of a Shape Tween

Flash is unforgiving when you don't follow its rules. Luckily, the rules for a shape tween are very simple: no groups and no symbols. That's it! Remember these two things, and shape tweens will be easy.

Turning Text into a Shape

Recall from Hour 2, "Drawing and Painting Original Art in Flash," that text acts as if it is grouped or a Drawing Object from the beginning. This means that you can't use text in a shape tween unless you first break it apart (by selecting Modify, Break Apart). If text contains more than one character, you have to break apart twice—once to break the text into individual characters and another time to turn it into individual shapes. Remember, too, that after text becomes a shape, it's no longer editable!

Watch Out!

Techniques and Tips

Just because the rules for a shape tween are simple doesn't mean that creating a good-looking shape tween is easy. There are several techniques to make the process easier and the results better.

Keep It Simple

If you ignore all other tips, keeping it simple is one you really should heed. There are very few rules for a shape tween—as long as you don't group anything or use symbols, it will work. However, when you have a million different shapes tweening to a million other shapes, the results will look random. The two symptoms that you aren't keeping it simple are unexpected results and the "checkerboard" effect you're about to see.

For example, consider these unexpected results. You imagined your name morphing gradually into a circle shape, but despite breaking apart the text, you got a garbled mess. Or you got the checkerboard effect in the tweened areas (as in Figure 9.2). These are signs that you're likely creating something too complicated for Flash. Actually, Flash is interpolating the in-between frames very accurately, but it can be very difficult to go from one extreme such as your name to something as simple as a circle. Flash will get you from here to there, but the trip might look pretty messy.

FIGURE 9.2
The checker-
board effect is
the common
result of an
overly complex
shape tween.

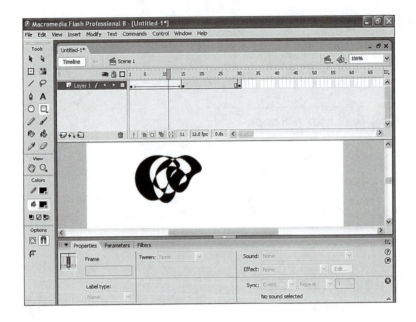

The solution is to keep it simple. Do just one thing at a time. For example, try to tween just one letter of your name into a circle. In Hour 11, "Using Layers in Animations," you'll see that it's easy to do several tweens simultaneously (in separate layers). You'll also see later this hour that you can help Flash by using a feature called Shape Hints. However, the simpler the animation is, the better. You'll find that a simple animation will be easier to create and more like what you expect, and it will also probably result in a more effective movie—if not also a smaller file.

Don't Mix Lines and Fills

It's best to avoid tweening between shapes that don't have the same combination of fills and lines because the results are unpredictable. Tweening a straight line into a bent line usually works fine. But if you try to tween from a line to a filled shape, you might get unpredictable results. As an analogy, consider bending a wire. You could also start with clay and reshape it. But if you had to turn a wire into the shape of clay, it would be difficult or impossible. This analogy is similar to Flash tweening lines and fills. Flash can tween lines; Flash can tween fills; it can even tween a fill with a line. Flash has difficulty, however, when one keyframe has a line and the other has a fill or when one keyframe has both line and fill and the other only has one. Flash does what it can to interpolate the in-between frames when you mix them, but eventually something has to give; Flash can't perform miracles.

To avoid these problems, convert the lines to fills by using Modify, Shape, Convert Lines to Fills. Better yet, keep things simple by drawing in both keyframes of a tween just lines, just fills, or both.

Stay Out of Flash's Territory

When Flash is tweening a span of frames, it colors the tweened frames in the Timeline either blue (for motion tweening) or green (for shape tweening). These *interpolated* frames are what I call Flash's territory (see Figure 9.3). Generally, you should stay out of this area. For one thing, you can only draw into keyframes, so you can't draw into this territory. Also, in shape tweens, you can't even select objects when the red current-frame marker is in this territory. (However, you saw in Hour 8, "Using Motion Tweens to Animate," that with motion tweens you can actually grab and move symbols in interpolated frames, which adds keyframes.)

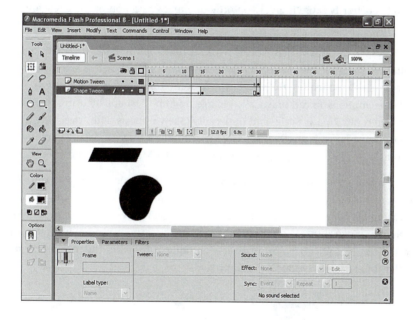

FIGURE 9.3
The interpolated frames (where Flash is responsible for doing the tweening) are green for a shape tween and blue for a motion tween.

You can't do any harm to interpolated frames of shape tweens, but trying to edit them can be very frustrating. You can't draw into them, and you can't select objects. The best way to think of these frames is that they are Flash's territory—not yours. You are responsible for the keyframes, and Flash is responsible for the tweening.

Know When a Motion Tween Will Suffice

It's easy to fall in love with the shape tween. There's nothing like it. Feel free to use it when necessary. However, because shape tweens are inherently less efficient and harder to produce than motion tweens (the file sizes are larger and play more slowly), you should always choose motion tweening when you can. If you can get the same effect with either, you should always opt for motion tweening.

Let's say you have a shape you want to tween from a blue circle to a red square. Only a shape tween will suffice because the actual shape is changing. However, if you just want to tween a blue circle into a red circle, you're much better off doing it as a motion tween. Draw a circle, convert it to a symbol, insert a keyframe later in the Timeline, use the Properties panel to set Color Effect to tint the circle instance in the second keyframe, and set Tween to Motion when you select the first keyframe. To do the same animation as a shape tween, you would draw a circle (don't convert it to a symbol), insert a keyframe later in the Timeline, fill the circle in the second keyframe with a new color (perhaps using the Bucket tool), and set shape tweening in the first keyframe. The result of each operation is the same, but the motion tween method is better because it gives you only one master version of the circle and therefore a smaller file size.

Sometimes it's obvious which type of tween is more appropriate. If something's just moving or changing color, a motion tween is appropriate, whereas significant changes to a shape require the shape tween. Sometimes, however, it's not so obvious. For example, you can drastically change a symbol's shape by using the Free Transform tool's Rotate, Scale, and (especially) Skew options. Plus, tweening the properties of a Filter (using Motion Tween) can have a huge impact. Figure 9.4 shows how drastically different the beginning and end of a Motion Tween can be.

Although you should definitely lean toward motion tweening when you can, don't forget the keyframe techniques you learned in Hour 7, "Animation the Old-Fashioned Way." A few strategically designed keyframes can often be more effective than a drawn-out tween (of either type). You'll learn even more ways to trick the user in Hour 22, "Advanced Animation Techniques." It's what the user thinks she sees that matters—not what she actually sees.

FIGURE 9.4
Before choosing Shape tween consider distorting a Movie Clips and using Motion Tween. Each original clip (left) appears in a much different form on the right (the last flower uses the Glow filter). All these examples are "Motion tweenable."

Refining and Fine-tuning a Shape Tween

Shape tweens don't always come out the way you expect. The tips we just covered are really more like rules and cautions. Even if you heed all the warnings, you still might have shape tweening results that are anything but what you expect. Flash has a feature especially for shape tweening that helps you tell Flash what you really want. It's called the Shape Hint feature, and it can make the difference between a shape tween that looks like a mess and one that looks like what you had in mind.

Using Shape Hints

A shape hint gives you a way to tell Flash exactly how to map one point in the beginning shape to another point at the end of the shape tween. You'll want to use shape hints when Flash doesn't create a shape tween that matches what you had in mind.

Points inside a shape are **mapped** during any tween. The term *map* refers to how one point in the starting shape corresponds to a specific point in the ending shape. Consider how every point on a printed map corresponds to a real location. A point on the map can be mapped to a real location. When Flash motion tweens a box from small to large, one corner of the small box is mapped to the same corner in the large box. Every point is mapped. Mapping points in a shape tween is more complex, so there's a feature called Shape Hints that lets you control how Flash maps individual points. In the following task you'll step through how to use shape hints.

Try It Yourself ▼

Use Shape Hints for a Better Shape Tween

In this task you'll use the Shape Hints feature to create a more controlled shape tween:

1. In a new file, select the Rectangle tool and ensure Object Drawing in the options portion of the Tools is turned off. Draw a perfect square by using the Rectangle tool (just hold Shift while you drag).

2. In Frame 25 of the Timeline, insert a keyframe (by clicking in the Timeline at Frame 25 and then pressing F6 or selecting Insert, Timeline, Keyframe).

3. Change the shape in Frame 25 to a triangle. There are many ways to do this, including starting from scratch and using the Onion Skin tools to help line up the triangle with the square. You should make the triangle as similar as possible to the square by following the next steps.

▼

4. In Frame 25, draw a vertical line that doesn't touch the square.

5. Select the Selection tool (make sure Snap to Objects is turned on under View, Options), click once on the line to select it, and click and hold in the center of the line. (Make sure you have the solid circle, indicating that you've grabbed the center; if you don't, try grabbing the line again.) Now drag the line so it snaps in the center of the horizontal top of the square (as in Figure 9.5).

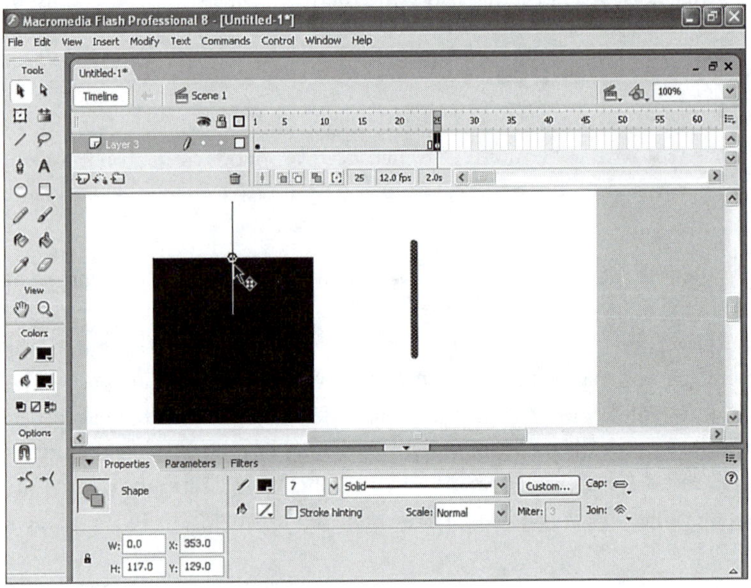

FIGURE 9.5
Dragging a vertical line while Snap to Objects is turned on lets you perfectly position the line at the center of the square.

6. Click off the line and grab the top-left corner of the square. Drag it until it snaps to this bisecting line. Do the same for the top-right corner of the square.

7. Select and delete the excess portions of the vertical line.

8. Select the first keyframe and use the Properties panel to set Tween to Shape. Scrub, and you see that the results are probably not what you expected. Now is your chance to use the Shape Hints feature.

9. Under the View menu, ensure that Show Shape Hints has a checkmark (select it if not).

10. Place the red current-frame marker in Frame 1 and select Modify, Shape, Add Shape Hint (or press Ctrl+Shift+H).

11. Notice a little red circle with the letter *a* (a shape hint). Temporarily move the red current-frame marker to Frame 25 and notice that there's also an *a* shape hint in this frame.

12. Make sure you're back in Frame 1 and that Snap to Objects is turned on (by selecting View, Snapping, Snap to Objects). Use the Selection tool to drag the shape hint so that it snaps to the top-left corner of the square. (Notice in Figure 9.6 that it's still red, indicating that you haven't really mapped this point to an end point yet.)

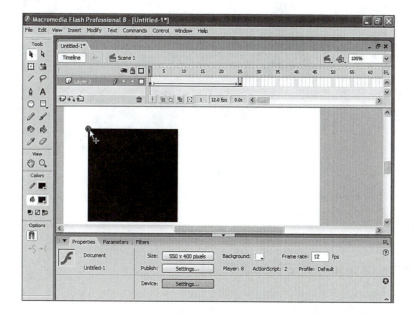

FIGURE 9.6
Although you've added a shape hint in the first keyframe and even attached it to the shape, it's still colored red because you haven't added a shape hint for the ending keyframe.

13. Go to Frame 25 and position Shape Hint *a* so that it snaps to the middle of the left side of the triangle. Notice that the shape hint turns green, indicating that it's been mapped. Also, when you return to Frame 1, the shape hint is colored yellow to indicate that it's been mapped.

14. Scrub to see the results so far. If it looks good, you don't need to add any more shape hints. (For this exercise, however, it will likely not look very good.)

15. In Frame 1, add another shape hint (by pressing Ctrl+Shift+H), and the new hint is automatically given the name *b*. Position it in the top-right corner of the square.

In Frame 25, map Shape Hint b to snap to the middle of the right side of the triangle (similarly to how Shape Hint a was mapped). See Figure 9.7.

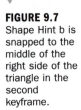

FIGURE 9.7
Shape Hint b is snapped to the middle of the right side of the triangle in the second keyframe.

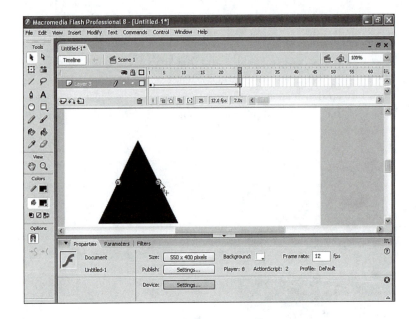

17. At this point, the results should be much better than before you added any hints. Use Test Movie to see.

Understanding Shape Hints

The time-consuming part of the preceding task was creating the triangle to match the square perfectly (and that should have been a review). Adding the shape hints was fairly simple. Granted, I told you where to place the hints. However, figuring out logical positions for shape hints is usually pretty easy. Think of it this way: You're telling Flash "this point in the starting shape goes with that point in the ending shape."

You should notice that after you add one shape hint, you can see how the point under the hint in the first keyframe hurries to the corresponding point (under the hint) in the end keyframe. Carefully watch the points while you slowly scrub.

Less Is More

Don't use more Shape Hints than necessary. Don't add 10 shape hints to the first frame and then map them all. Rather, add one shape hint and map it, and then evaluate the results; one might be enough. Feel free to continue adding shape hints all day long, but realize that sometimes less work is necessary. There's no reason to add more hints than you really need.

A few more details about shape hints are worth understanding:

▶ You can't add shape hints unless you are currently in the first keyframe of a span with shape tweening already set. In other words, you have to have a shape tween already and be in the first frame in order to add a shape hint.

▶ You can use the menu selection View, Show Shape Hints to make the shape hints you have invisible (but they will still be used).

▶ Shape hints are recognized only after they've been mapped—that is, snapped to a point on the shape in both the first keyframe and the last keyframe. They change color after they are mapped. This means you still have to snap both the start and end hint, even if their default positions seem acceptable as is.

▶ You can remove one hint at a time by right-clicking (or using Control+click on a Macintosh). In addition, you can remove them all by selecting Modify, Shape, Remove All Hints.

▶ Shape hints can be used only with a pair of keyframes! Just as tweening occurs between only two keyframes at a time, a shape hint works between only two keyframes at a time. However, shape hints can't be used from one keyframe to a second and then to a third. In the previous task, you might want to add a third keyframe where the shape turns into a square again. If you want to use shape hints from one keyframe to another and then a third, you must have four keyframes. Use a shape hint from the first to the second and then use another from the third to the fourth (see Figure 9.8).

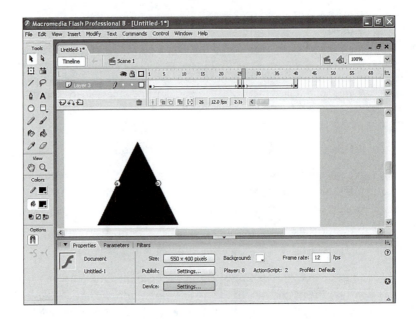

Summary

Now that you understand shape tweens, you know both ways Flash can do tweening for you (shape and motion). You learned this hour that a shape tween is fundamentally unique in that it allows you to morph shapes. The only rules with shape tweens are that you can't have grouped shapes and you can't have symbols. This makes shape tweens easy to create, but some techniques are necessary to ensure that the results come out as expected.

You can use shape hints to help Flash figure out what you have in mind. Adding shape hints is a little touchy, but you just need to be very specific.

I have two parting tips as you create more and more animations on your own:

▶ Although shape and motion tweens can help you create an animation, sometimes the most effective animation is the most subtle. That means sometimes the best solution is frame-by-frame animation, such as what you did in Hour 7.

▶ Don't be satisfied with serendipitous results. Sometimes mistakes are cool looking, but try to persist in making Flash do exactly what you have in mind. Resist the temptation to accept something that's only *close* to what you want. If you take the time, you can create anything.

Q&A

Q *What causes the dotted line to appear in the green interpolated frames of my shape tween?*

A You either did something that contradicts the rules of a shape tween (that you have no groups and no symbols), or you don't have two keyframes. Remember that a tween is between two keyframes. You should check to make sure you have two keyframes and that in each you have no groups and no symbols.

Q *My animation is acting funny. Shapes appear only in my keyframes, never in the interpolated frames. I know I did everything according to the rules because I'm not getting the dotted line. What's wrong?*

A Just because the dotted line isn't present doesn't mean you're doing everything correctly. For example, if you have some shapes in the start and the end of your tween, all will appear fine. However, if in either keyframe you have a group, text (which is like a group until it's broken apart), or a symbol, all these objects will disappear during the tween. The only time you see the dotted line is when *all* the objects onscreen are groups or symbols.

Q *When I click in the green interpolated frames (Flash's territory), I can set the Properties panel Tween setting. I thought this area was under Flash's control. Why am I given access to it?*

A You're actually accessing the previous keyframe's properties. Remember that the span after one keyframe (before the next one) is controlled by that first keyframe. Any non-keyframes after a keyframe are under the influence of the first keyframe. With tweening, it's the same: Interpolated frames get drawn by Flash, but the previous keyframe controls exactly how the tweening will act. One keyframe controls its frame and all subsequent frames until the next keyframe. The good news is that the Properties panel gives you access to frame properties of keyframes without having to be really careful where you click. Just be aware of which keyframe you're accessing.

Workshop

The Workshop consists of quiz questions and answers to help you solidify your understanding of the material covered in this hour. You should try to answer the questions before checking the answers.

Quiz

1. What is the ideal number of shape hints to use for a good shape tween?

    A. 10 because we have 10 fingers and 10 toes

    B. No more than 5

    C. No more than necessary

2. Which type of tween will result in a smaller file: Shape or Motion?

    A. A shape tween will result in a smaller file.

    B. A motion tween will result in a smaller file.

    C. It depends on how many colors are used in the file.

3. How can you use text in a shape tween?

    A. Text cannot be used in a shape tween.

    B. Make sure the text is broken apart.

    C. Make sure the text isn't grouped or in the Library.

Quiz Answers

1. C. There's just no reason to use more shape hints than absolutely necessary. Each time you add a shape hint, check to see whether the results are satisfactory.

2. B. It's safe to say that motion tweens, by definition, will result in smaller files. This is important because some effects can be achieved by using either a shape tween or a motion tween, but you should always opt for motion tweens when you can.

3. B. In fact all the answers are true, but Answer B is best. Text acts as if it's grouped from the start. All you have to do is use Modify, Break Apart twice.

Exercise

You can spend a lot of time playing with shape tweens. Here is an exercise that will sharpen your skills: Create a shape tween from one letter to a similar shape, such as from the letter A to a triangle or the letter C to a circle. Remember that you'll have to break apart the text. Use shape hints to make it look the way you want. (Tip: If you want to try your whole name—just do one letter at a time.)

HOUR 10

Including Sound in Animations

What You'll Learn in This Hour:

▶ How to import and use sounds in keyframes
▶ Audio concepts such as sample rate, frequency, and compression
▶ How to apply tricks to minimize sound's impact on file size

Sound really makes a movie come alive, but the power of audio is subtle. People often don't even notice or remember the sounds you use. But create a movie without sound (or with bad sounds), and the audience notices right away. The effect of audio is often subconscious, and that's what makes it so powerful.

Regardless of why sound is useful, it's very important to use audio effectively because it's invariably the largest portion of an exported movie's file size (with the exception of video—half of which is audio anyway). There's no reason to allow the audio to add more size than it has to. Unfortunately, there's no "Make the Audio Come Out Good" button. The choice between good audio and a small file size is more of a battle than a balancing act. It's simply a matter of understanding the technology, and that's the goal of this hour.

Importing Sounds

Flash has great support for audio but no internal way to record or create sounds. You need to find an existing sound, have one provided for you, or use sound software to record or create your own. This simply means that in Flash, you can import sounds but you can't create them.

Two basic steps are involved in getting audio into a Flash movie. First, you need to import the sound. Then, you need to decide where and how to use it. This is similar to importing raster graphics (as you did in Hour 3, "Importing Graphics into Flash"). When you import a sound, it's stored in the Library like an imported bitmap. The sound appears in the Library where you can access all the sound's individual properties (just like bitmap items).

> ### Digging Up Sounds or Making Your Own
>
> There are many sources for existing audio, such as clip media CDs. You might find, however, that rather than search existing sources, it's often easier to hire a professional musician or narrator to provide exactly what you need. This is also true for customized graphics or photographs versus clip art. Although in the short term hiring someone to create sound or art for you might mean a much bigger investment, it's often worth it. Consider that you're likely to get the perfect match for your message compared to something you find that's just "close enough" (but not quite right either). Also, you have direct contact with the artist, so you can resolve copyright issues at the start. Finally, by customizing your audio or graphics (and purchasing exclusive rights to its use), you won't risk another company using your art. Several potential problems arise when multiple parties use the same image or sound. Some other company's product or message could reflect poorly on yours, its website could be more popular than yours (making you look like a follower), or an image could become overused, making everyone's use look unoriginal and cliché.

Supported Formats

Flash can import digital audio in the following file formats:

- ▶ MP3

- ▶ WAV

- ▶ AIF (also called AIFF)

- ▶ AU

The only catch is that unless you have a newer version of QuickTime installed, when running Windows, you can't import AIF or AU, and on a Macintosh, you can't import WAV. Just download and install the free QuickTime player software from www.apple.com, however, and you'll be able to import audio in any of these four formats.

People often want to know which format is best. In general, it doesn't matter. You should simply start with the best quality sound possible. Between AIF and WAV, there's no inherent quality difference. A high-quality AIF file is the same as a high-quality WAV file. The AU format is nearly always compressed at a low quality, so you can all but forget that format. MP3 files always have some compression, so ultimately those files are not best. However, when MP3s are compressed very little, their quality remains high. Plus, the MP3 might have been optimally compressed (and, as you'll see in this hour, Flash won't recompress it). There are two valid reasons to use MP3s:

▶ Your only source is an MP3 file.

▶ You believe the MP3 file you have has already been optimally compressed.

MP3s don't get any worse after you bring them into Flash, but they certainly can't get any better. What's more, some MP3s aren't very good to begin with. I recommend avoiding MP3s as source files unless they're all you have or you're totally satisfied with their current quality.

You'll learn more about digital audio later this hour, in the section "Digital Audio Fundamentals." For now, it's enough to know that just four sound formats can be imported into Flash. What about songs on audio CDs? CD audio tracks aren't in WAV, AIF, AU, or MP3 format, so you can't use them directly. Luckily, however, most sound-editing software—and Apple's excellent free product iTunes—provides the ability to extract music from a CD and save it in WAV or AIF format. Of course, you should realize that significant copyright concerns arise when you use audio from a published CD. Plus, many CDs and digital music files you download incorporate Digital Rights Management (DRM) technology that makes them difficult or impossible to copy. (Alas, some such CDs won't even play in your CD player.)

It turns out you can usually use sound in your animation without necessarily worrying about all these details, as you'll see in the next task.

Try It Yourself ▼

Import a Sound

The process of importing sounds into Flash is very simple. Follow these steps:

1. In a new file, select File, Import, Import to Library and then select an audio file to import. (In Windows, you'll likely find a few WAV files in the folder `C:\Windows\Media` or `My Documents\My Music`, or you can just search for `*.wav` and `*.mp3`; Macintosh users can use Find for Files of Type: Sound.) You can filter the files shown in the Import dialog box by setting the Files of Type drop-down list to All Sound Formats, as shown in 10.1.

2. After you select an audio file and click OK in the Import dialog box, you probably won't see (or hear) anything different. However, the sound has been

▼

imported and now resides in the Library. Just open the Library window (by pressing Ctrl+Lto see it. Now that the movie contains the sound file, you can use the sound.

FIGURE 10.1
When importing audio (or any media type, for that matter), you can filter the types of files listed to include just sound formats.

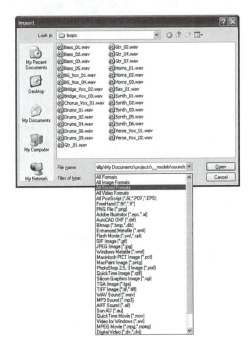

3. Although we're not covering how to "use" sounds in depth until the next section, it's very easy. Let's do it now. There are two basic ways to use the sound in a keyframe. One way is to drag the sound from the Library window onto the Stage. However, this method requires an available editable frame (both an unlocked layer marked as editable with pencil and the current-frame marker in a non-tweened frame). The other method requires you to select a keyframe (by clicking under 1 in the Timeline) and then in the Properties panel select the sound you imported from the drop-down list (as shown in Figure 10.2). This list will display all the sounds previously imported into the movie.

4. Test the movie, and you should hear the sound. (Of course, your computer speakers and sound card must be functioning.)

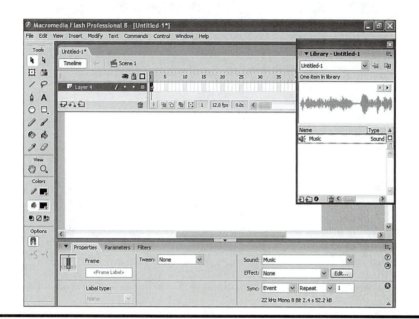

FIGURE 10.2
The imported sound appears in both the Library and the Properties panel (when a keyframe is selected).

Using Sounds

Now that you've imported sounds into a movie, you can explore how to make them play at the correct times. There's really only one place you can use sounds in Flash: in keyframes. (An exception is adding sounds dynamically by using the Sound object in the ActionScript language for which I'll provide the starter code after this hour's summary.) If you want a sound to play whenever the user places his or her cursor over a button, you still need to place the sound in a keyframe—it's just a keyframe in the button. Attaching sounds to a button is rather more complex, and we'll cover it in depth in Hour 14, "Making Buttons for the User to Click."

Now that you understand sounds go in keyframes, you need a way to put them there. When you select a keyframe, the Properties panel provides a way to control what sounds play when you reach the selected keyframe. Flash provides other clues for you to "see" where sounds have been placed. For example, if your Timeline is long enough, you'll see a waveform (a picture of a sound) for the sounds being used (as shown in Figure 10.3).

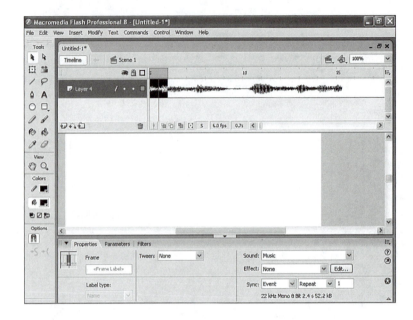

However, using the Properties panel is the best way to see which sounds have been
added to which keyframes. But just like any other panel, the Properties panel displays only the sound used in the *selected* keyframe. Misreading this panel is very easy
because it changes when you deselect keyframes. Figure 10.4 looks almost identical
to Figure 10.3. However, in Figure 10.4, the Properties panel shows that no sound is
being used. When you look closely at the Timeline, you see that there's a waveform
displayed but no keyframe selected. Therefore, it's necessary to look at the Properties
panel *after* you've selected a particular keyframe.

Sync Settings

When you have the Properties panel reflecting sound for the intended keyframe, you
can decide exactly how the sound should play. The most fundamental choice you
need to make is the Sync setting. This controls exactly how a particular instance of
the sound will play—or, more specifically, the priority of the sound compared to the
visual elements in the animation. Before you try out the Sync settings, see the following list and Figure 10.5 for an explanation of each:

▶ **Event**—Should be your default choice, especially for sound effects and other
"incidental" sounds. When Event is chosen, sounds will start to play when the
keyframe is reached and keep playing until the sound is done. Event sounds
might not coincide with visual elements the same way on everyone's machine.
Sounds don't play more slowly or quickly (that would make them sound

funny), but a machine with slower graphics performance might take longer to display visual elements. Suppose you have a 1-second sound set to Event and your frame rate is 12 fps. You would expect that during the sound, 12 frames would be displayed, but a slow machine might display only 6 fps during that 1 second. In either case, the sound will finish 1 second later, as you would expect, but exactly how many frames will have been displayed can vary.

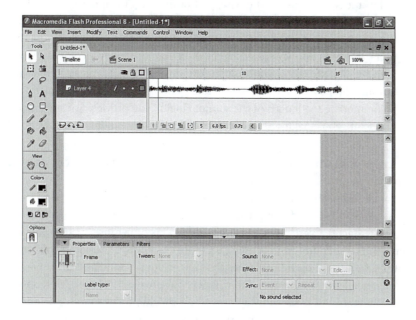

FIGURE 10.4
The Properties panel can be confusing. It only displays (or lets you specify) sounds when a keyframe is currently selected. Here, the keyframe isn't currently selected, so the Properties panel displays nothing.

▶ **Start**—This setting is almost the same as Event, except that multiple instances of the same sound are prevented. With Event, a sound can be layered on top of itself, similar to singing a "round." Start, on the other hand, plays a sound if it's not already playing.

▶ **Stop**—This setting is kind of weird—it's for when you want a specified sound to stop playing. For example, say you import a sound called "background music" and make it start playing in the first keyframe of one layer. Then you import another sound, "narration," and make it start playing in the first keyframe of another layer. Then, in frame 10, you place another keyframe with the same sound (background music) set to Stop, just that sound will stop. Both sounds start at the beginning, but on frame 10 the background music stops and the narration continues to play. This is a bit strange because normally you use the Properties panel to specify the sound you want to play where here you specify the sound you want *not* to play. Think of Stop as "stop this sound if it's playing."

▶ **Stream**—This setting causes the sound to remain perfectly synchronized with the Timeline. Because, again, you can't have sounds playing slowly if the user's machine can't draw frames quickly enough, this setting forces Flash to skip frames to keep up. Stream sounds start playing when the keyframe is reached and continue to play as long as there is space in the Timeline. In other words, if your sound is 3 seconds long and you're playing at 12 fps, the Timeline has to be at least 36 frames; otherwise, part of the sound will never be reached. (You can compare the Stream setting to a Graphic Symbol's behavior.) The benefit of the Stream setting is that the synchronization will always be the same. If in this case you place a graphic in Frame 12, it will coincide perfectly with the first second of your sound. Just remember that when you're using Stream, you have to ensure that there are enough frames in the Timeline to accommodate the length of the sound. Finally, you preview Stream sounds as you scrub, thus making the process of synchronizing audio to images possible.

The decision as to which Sync setting to use isn't terribly difficult. Event should be used for any short incidental sounds—such as *rollover sounds*. Actually, I suggest Event for all sounds that don't require critical synchronization. Background music that just plays and loops doesn't need to be synchronized. Therefore, you should use Event for it. Start is a perfectly good alternative to Event because it's the same but prevents the same sound from layering on itself. For example, suppose you have a row of five buttons. If each button has the same rollover sound and the user quickly moves across all five, an Event sound will play once for each button. If the sounds are short enough, this is probably appropriate. However, if the sounds are quite long, they will become discordant. If you use the Start Sync setting, only one instance of the sound will play at a time, regardless of how fast the user moves his or her mouse. Event can be a better choice than Start when a little bit of overlap is okay. Conversely, say you want to hear a "smack" sound effect every time a ball bounces on the ground. If you choose Event, you'll hear a smack for each bounce, even if the ball bounces a second time before the first sound finishes. In any event, Start and Event are good for the majority of sounds you'll play.

FIGURE 10.5
For each instance of a sound, you must select a Sync setting (via the Properties panel).

Rollover is when the user places his or her cursor over a button, so a **rollover sound** is a sound that plays when the user rolls over a button. You'll learn about rollover effects for buttons in Hour 14.

The Stop Sync setting is very powerful. It gives you a way to stop specific sounds. Using this method can be a little tricky because it stops only one sound per keyframe. When you learn about behaviors (in Hour 15, "Using ActionScript and Behaviors to Create Nonlinear Movies"), you'll learn that you can insert the Stop All Sounds behavior to stop all sounds at once. Depending on the situation, this might be appropriate. If you're giving the user the ability to get several sounds going at once, you'll want to learn about Stop All Sounds. However, suppose you have one sound playing in the background, and when a tween starts, you want a special sound effect to play (and keep playing) until the tween ends. You can put the background sound in an early keyframe and then, in the first keyframe of the tween, place the sound effect and set its Sync setting to Event or Start. In the last frame of the tween, you can put the same sound effect but with the Stop Sync setting. This way, the sound effect will stop at the end of the tween, but the background sound will continue.

Finally, Stream is good for one thing: synchronizing graphics with sound. This is especially useful for character animation in which you want a character's lips to synchronize with its voice. When trying to synchronize sounds with images, you can use the scrub technique, and if you use Stream sounds, you can hear the sound as you scrub. Because Stream sounds effectively lock themselves to the Timeline, you probably don't want to change the movie's frame rate. For example, a 3-second sound will take 36 frames at 12 fps. If you do some work and then change the frame rate to 24 fps, the same 3-second sound spans 72 frames! Flash automatically spreads the Stream sound out so that it takes 3 seconds when you change the frame rate, but Flash doesn't change your graphics, which now play in 1.5 seconds. See Figure 10.6 for a before-and-after example of changing the frame rate after an animation is built.

In spite of this issue, you should stick with a frame rate (which, really, isn't anything new—it comes up even if you don't use sounds). Stream sounds remain pretty appealing. However, you should realize that on slower-performing machines, frames will be skipped to make sure a stream sound stays synchronized. It's often more important that every frame of your animation appears even if it means the sounds may drift out of synchronization. My point is that you should use Stream only when the synchronization is critical (and you don't mind dropping frames). Otherwise, use Event or Start.

FIGURE 10.6
Here, the same animation and sound are shown with frame rates of 18 fps (top) and 6 fps (bottom). Notice that keyframes and tweening are not affected, but the sound uses less of the timeline when the timeline is only advancing at 6 fps. The short silence at the start of this sound means users won't hear anything until a few frames of the animation have played.

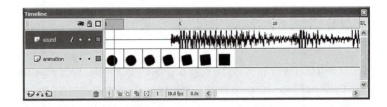

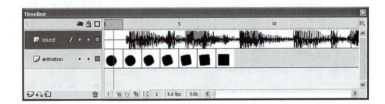

Effect Settings

The Properties panel provides some pretty fancy effects you can apply to the volume of a selected sound. In the drop-down list next to Effect are effects such as Fade In and Fade Out as well as Fade from Left to Right and Fade from Right to Left. In order to understand and customize these settings further, you can either select Custom from the list or click the Edit button on the Properties panel to access the Edit Envelope dialog box, which is shown in Figure 10.7.

FIGURE 10.7
You can position the Sounds Common Library next to the Library for the keyframing sample file in order to transfer sounds.

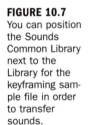

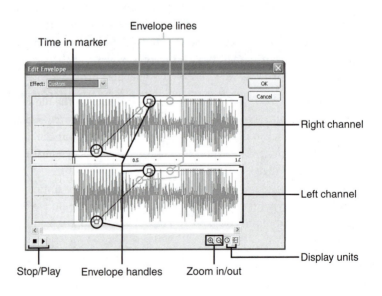

Here are additional details for the Effect settings:

▶ **Left Channel/Right Channel**—This option displays different wave forms if your original sound was stereo. Even if you use only mono sounds, you'll still get the left and right channels so that you can still create panning effects. In the case of mono, the same sounds will come out of each speaker—you'll just be able to modify the volume of each.

▶ **Envelope lines**—These indicate the volume level at any particular time in the sound. When the line is at the top, the sound plays at full 100% volume. (Some audio tools are different because they use the middle to indicate 100% and anything higher to indicate amplified or boosted sound, but this is not the case in Flash.) If the envelope line is getting higher as you move to the right, the volume will increase.

▶ **Envelope handles**—These are like keyframes within sound. If you want the envelope lines (indicating volume) to change direction, you need to insert a handle. All you need to do is click anywhere on a line, and a handle will be inserted. No matter which channel you click, a matching handle is placed in the other channel. A handle in one channel must match the moment in time (left to right) of the handle in the other channel. However, the volume (height) can vary between the two.

▶ **Time In marker**—This marker lets you establish the starting point of a sound. You're effectively trimming the extra sound (or silence) at the beginning of the sound file. You're not telling the sound to start any later, but the sound you hear will begin wherever the Time In marker is placed.

▶ **Time Out marker**—This marker lets you trim extra sound off the end of a sound file. Often you'll have a moment of silence at the end of a sound file, and even if you don't hear anything, it still adds to the file size. You can get rid of it by moving the Time Out marker to the left. You won't actually destroy the source sound in your Library, but when you export the movie, the unused portions of the sound won't be used (so your file stays small).

▶ **Stop/Play**—This option lets you preview all the settings you've made. This is important because although the waveform can let you "see" a sound, you ultimately want to judge the effect of a sound with your ears.

▶ **Zoom In/Out**—This option lets you zoom out so the entire sound fits in the current window or zoom in for a close up to control precisely how you place the Time In/Out markers or envelope handles.

▶ **Display Units (Time or Frames)**—This option simply changes the units displayed (in the center portion) from time units (seconds) to frame units. Time is not as useful as Frames when you want to match sound to a particular frame (where something visual occurs). If the display shows a peak in the music at 1 second, you have to use frame rate to calculate exactly which frame that translates to. With the display set to Frames, Flash does the calculations for you.

Panning is an effect that makes sound seem to move from left to right or right to left. It's simply a trick in which the volume for one channel (left or right) is increased while the volume for the other channel is decreased. When combined with a graphic moving in the same direction, this technique can be very effective. Imagine, for example, a car moving across the screen at the same time the audio pans in the same direction.

Despite all the details in the Edit Envelope dialog box, you really only have two basic ways to use it: You can either use a preset effect or make your own. Actually, you can start with a preset (such as Fade In) and then make modifications to it, essentially making a custom effect based on a preset. Use the effects in any way you think appropriate. Listen to the effect after each change by clicking the Play button. Nothing you do here will affect the master sound in your Library. You can actually use the same sound several times throughout a movie, with different effects in each instance.

One of the most important things to remember is that the Time In and Time Out markers can save file size. Only the sounds and portions of sounds actually used will be exported when you publish a movie. Unused sounds in the Library and portions trimmed from the beginning or end of a sound will not be exported. Trimming a few seconds off the end of a sound can mean many seconds (even minutes) saved in download time for your users. Also, changing the volume of a sound has no impact on file size, so setting the envelope lines to the lowest level makes no sense.

Loop Settings

The Properties panel has an option to either let you specify how many times a sound repeats or have the sound loop forever.

Some sounds loop better than others. Basically, a sound that loops well ends the same way it starts. There's an art to making sounds loop. Although importing a large song and using the Time In and Time Out markers to establish a nice looping sound is possible, it isn't easy. More likely, you'll have to find a sound already prepared by an audio engineer. A professionally prepared sound can loop so seamlessly that you can listen to it and not even notice it's looping; it will just sound like it's endless.

You'll get to explore looping sounds as well as other effects in the next task.

Try It Yourself ▼

Add Sounds and Sound Effects to an Animation

In this task you'll add sounds to a sample movie. Follow these steps:

1. Download the file keyframing.fla from my website (www.phillipkerman.com/teachyourself/sourcefiles). In Flash, open this file and then press Enter to watch the animation.

2. Open the Library for the keyframing.fla file by selecting Window, Library (or pressing Ctrl+L).

3. Now these sounds will be available to your file, but you need to put them into keyframes. First you need to make a new layer just for the sounds by selecting Insert, Timeline, Layer. (Don't worry if Flash puts the new layer under all others—it doesn't really matter where it appears.) Name this layer Background Music. (You'll learn more about layers next hour.)

4. Select the first frame of the Background Music layer and look at the Properties panel. From the Sound drop-down list, select Visor Hum Loop. To make this sound loop continuously, change the drop-down list from Repeat to Loop (see Figure 10.8).

5. Select Control, Test Movie. The sound loops nicely, and it adds a bit of drama to the movie. In the following steps, add some incidental sound effects.

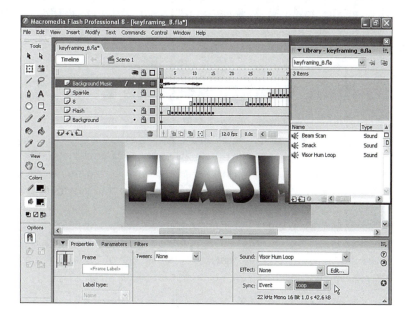

FIGURE 10.8
Flash can loop a sound indefinitely with the Loop setting.

6. Select Insert, Timeline, Layer and name the layer Sound Effects. You're going to insert a sound effect right when the "8" is rotated to the left, which happens at frame 14. In Frame 14 of Sound Effects, select Insert, Timeline, Keyframe (or press F6).

7. Select the keyframe you just inserted and from the Properties panel select Smack from the Sound drop-down list. Just leave the default settings (Event Sync and Repeat 1) because you don't want this sound to loop.

8. Select Control, Test Movie. The Smack effect is good, but the hum keeps humming throughout the whole movie.

9. To stop the hum, select Frame 30 of the Background Music layer and select Insert, Keyframe (or press F6). Make sure you're selecting just this keyframe, and then use the Properties panel to insert the Visor Hum Loop again, but this time select the Stop Sync setting to cause any instances of this sound to stop. (You can use Test Movie again to see and hear the results.)

10. Finally, add a sound effect for when the pink sparkle animates. At Frame 30 of the Sound Effects layer, select Insert, Keyframe (or press F6), select just this keyframe, and then insert the Beam Scan sound. Use Test Movie, and it should be measurably better than the silent version. (By the way, these sounds only add about 3KB to the total file size!) One thing you can try is to remove the excess silence at the start of the Beam Scan sound. Just select Frame 30 in the Sound Effects layer and press Edit on the Properties panel. Then you can cut sound off the beginning by dragging the Time In marker in the Edit Envelope dialog box (refer to Figure 10.8).

Controlling Quality and File Size

Now that you know how to incorporate sound in a movie, it's time to talk about optimizing it for export. A direct relationship exists between quality and file size. If you want the best-quality sound, the file size will grow. Conversely, small file size means lower sound quality. This is just a fact. You ultimately need to make a decision about how to balance this tradeoff. Is a high-quality sound important enough to make your audience sit through an extended download time? Is a speedy download worth the sacrifice in quality? You should be very deliberate in your decision-making process to end up with the best compromise possible. While exploring this topic further, we'll first cover some digital audio fundamentals, and then you'll learn how to apply this knowledge to Flash's compression settings.

Digital Audio Fundamentals

Earlier this hour I suggested there were two sensible ways to use audio in Flash. You can start by either importing as high-quality audio file as possible (.wav or .aif) and let Flash compress it when you publish or importing an MP3 which, by definition, is already compressed.

If you take the route of importing high-quality sounds, you'll want to know a few basics about .wav and .aif sounds. The two primary factors that affect the file size are sampling rate (that is, how many pieces of sound are saved per second) and bit depth (or how much detail is saved in each of those samples). CDs have 44,100 samples per second (often expressed as 44K) and 16-bit depth (meaning 65,536 "shades" of sound). So, a 44K/16-bit audio file is very good. If you listen to an 8-bit sound file, it will have a much lower dynamic range (from high to low). The quality loss when you listen to files with a lower frequency rate (for example, 22K, 11K, or lower) are not quite as obvious, but they tend to sound hollow. It's worth mentioning that a longer sound will be bigger and stereo sounds are twice the size of mono.

The Mystery of the Deep Voice

Digital audio tape (DAT) uses 48K/16-bit audio. On several occassions a professional audio person will supply audio in this format, and it's a problem in Flash. The sign that you've imported 48K audio is apparent when you play back the movie. The sounds are slowed down so that they sound an octave deeper. They're actually playing slower (44,100 samples per second instead of 48,000). Flash tops out at 44,100—so you'll need to resample using an audio editor before you import into Flash.

By the Way

If you want to start with MP3s, there is really just one factor: bit rate. A 1 second MP3 file that's 256 kilobits (Kb) has a bit rate of 256 kilobits per second (Kbps). MP3s can have bit rates up to 320Kbps. In fact, it's possible to have a variable bit rate MP3 (VBR instead of CBR for constant bit rate). The reason a variable bit rate is useful is that the portions of the sound with more detail use a higher bit rate (up to 320Kb), while other places in the sound might not need as much depth. A VBR MP3 often sounds better than an equivalent-sized CBR MP3 because there's more detail where it's needed. So, in fact, the average bit rate is more important than simply the bit rate. This discussion leaves out exactly how your audio compression tool applies the MP3 algorithm. The software cuts out details from the sound where your ear is least likely to notice. In the end, it's basically magic because you're left with a small sound file that sounds almost as good as the original.

Bringing this back to the world of Flash, realize the easiest way to approach audio is to bring in an uncompressed audio file and let Flash apply MP3 compression upon publishing the .swf. That is, you can bring in a .wav and Flash will internally convert it to an MP3. Flash's MP3 compression is not VBR so it's possible to create a better sounding MP3 outside of Flash. If you import an MP3 Flash won't recompress it (unless you override the default settings). In the next section you'll see exactly how to control Flash's export settings. This brief overview of digital audio should give you enough information to analyze your source audio files before you import them into Flash.

Export Settings

All this theory is interesting, but how do you apply it to your sounds? You have two places in Flash where you can specify quality and compression settings: the Sound Properties dialog box, which is unique to each imported sound, and the Flash tab of the Publish Settings dialog box. The Sound Properties dialog box affects settings that are unique to the individual sound and the Publish Settings dialog box affects all sounds globally.

Global Publish Settings

To set the default sound format for every sound in a Flash movie, you select File, Publish Settings. Make sure that under the Formats tab you've checked Flash (.swf), and then click the Flash tab (see Figure 10.9). You see two different sound settings in this dialog box: Audio Stream and Audio Event. Audio Stream affects sound instances that use the Stream Sync setting, whereas Audio Event affects sounds that use the Event or Start Sync setting. (The Audio Stream setting also affects the audio from videos you've import, as you'll learn in Hour 18, "Using Video.") If you click the Set button, you can see all the options available, as shown in Figure 10.10.

There's a Set button next to both Stream and Event so you can set the compression for sounds used each way separately. There are five choices for sound compression. With the exception of when you use Raw (which is really no compression), you need to specify additional options for the compression you choose. For example, you can't just say "compress using MP3"—you have to specify how much MP3 compression. Because each option has its own unique characteristics, let's look at each in detail:

▶ **Disable**—This option is pretty simple: It tells Flash not to export any sounds. When you select Disable from the drop-down list, there are no other options to set.

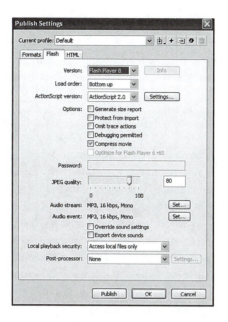

FIGURE 10.9
The Flash tab of the Publish Settings dialog box provides a way to set the default sound settings globally for an entire file.

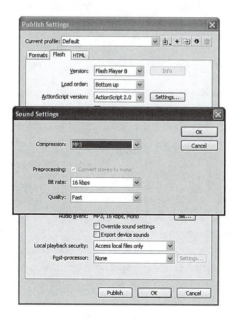

FIGURE 10.10
You can set the type of compression for all sounds in a movie in the Publish Settings dialog box.

▶ **ADPCM**—This option is almost the same as Raw (below), except that you can optionally choose a different sample rate than your original sound (usually to lower the sample rate because increasing it just makes the file bigger without improving the sound). You can also convert stereo to mono. ADPCM compression is coarse and never sounds as good as an MP3 compression. The only reason to use this option rather than MP3 is when you have to deliver a movie to Flash Player 3.

▶ **MP3**—This option provides great compression. When exporting, always use the Quality setting Best because it won't affect the file size but will improve quality. The bit rate is simply how much data per second you're letting the MP3 file take. The higher the number, the better. In theory, a bit rate of 56Kbps will be maintainable on a 56Kbps modem, although reality is sometimes different from theory because other factors can slow the download performance. We'll explore more issues related to downloading in Hour 21, "Optimizing a Flash Site." You really just have to test this and keep lowering the bit rate until just before the sound becomes unacceptable. You can judge the result by testing the movie or, as you'll see in the next section, "Individual Export Settings," you can test each sound individually.

▶ **Speech Compression**—This setting is optimized for the human voice. In practice, however, you should always compare the quality/file size effects of speech compression to MP3 because the best choice varies case-by-case.

▶ **Raw**—This option leaves your sounds intact, although you do need to specify a sample rate (frequency rate Raw is useful while you're testing because you won't have to sit through the time Flash takes to compress your sounds every time you use Test Movie. Just remember to set it back later, or your files will be huge.

You've just learned how to set the default sound settings for both Stream and Event sounds from the Publish Settings dialog box. It's important to understand that the default publish setting affects only uncompressed (that is, non-MP3) sounds you've imported. You'll see in the next section how to set sound settings for each imported sound individually. Imported uncompressed sounds (`.aif` and `.wav`) will, by default, use the settings you make in the Publish settings. Imported compressed sounds (MP3) don't recompress and therefore don't follow the Publish settings. One exception is when you select the Override Sound Settings check box (in the Publish settings). Checking this box causes the settings you apply here to be imposed on *all* sounds in the movie, regardless of their individual export settings. Override Sound Settings can be useful when you want to publish a single copy for a special purpose.

Say you want a copy to demonstrate from your hard drive—download time isn't an issue, so you could make all the sounds play at their highest quality (Raw).

Individual Export Settings

In addition to a movie's globally specified sound settings, each sound item in the Library can have its own individual settings, which apply to every instance of that sound. Just double-click a sound in the Library (or select Options, Properties), and you see the Sound Properties dialog box, as shown in Figure 10.11.

This dialog box is similar to the Bitmap Properties dialog box you studied in Hour 3. In the same way that individual imported bitmaps can have their own sets of compression settings, so, too, can imported audio. The choice of settings is identical to the settings in the Publish Settings dialog box. However, in this dialog box, for each change you make, you're given details of the effect on file size and quality. Down at the bottom of the dialog box you can see how much the file compresses for each change. If you click the Test button, not only does Flash perform the compression you specified, but the sound starts playing and you can hear how it sounds. (This is similar to the Test button for bitmaps, although with bitmaps you judge the visual effect.) This gives you all the information you need to decide what settings to use. You can listen to the sound while assessing the effect on file size.

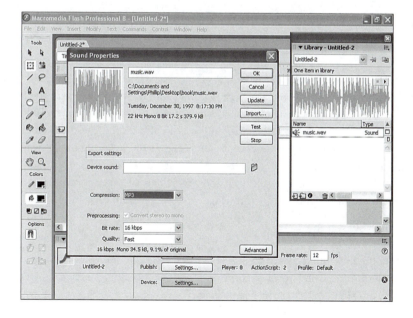

FIGURE 10.11
The Sound Properties dialog box provides individual control of exactly how a sound will be exported, regardless of the default publish settings.

Let me translate a couple options you'll see depending on what sounds you import. When you import a noncompressed format (.aif or .wav), you'll see the Default option, meaning Flash uses whatever settings you specify in the Publish Settings dialog box. If you import an MP3 (already compressed), you'll see the Use Imported MP3 Quality check box. This means "don't recompress." You can uncheck this option, but only do so if you're in a fix. That is, it's better to go back and make another MP3 from the original sound than to recompress inside Flash.

The Sound Properties dialog box also gives you the same ability to replace sounds as you have for replacing bitmaps. For instance, if you've edited a sound in a sound editor and you want to import the replacement sound, just click the Update button. (If the file has moved, you are asked to point to the new location.) In addition, if you want to replace a sound (without taking the trouble of reassigning every keyframe where you've already used the sound), just click Import and select the new file when prompted.

Tricks for Efficiency

Obviously, the best way to reduce file size in respect to audio is to avoid using audio. Although this might sound facetious, it's worth consideration. You should force yourself to consider each sound you use, and if it's not adding something to your file, it's most certainly distracting because it's adding to the file size (and that's a distraction during download). Gratuitous sound effects are worse than gratuitous visual effects because sounds add more significantly to the file size. Just be extra critical when asking yourself whether a particular sound is really necessary.

After you've decided that a sound is, indeed, necessary, you still have ways to reduce the sound's impact on the file size. The best way is to trim any silence at the beginning or end of the audio. Silence still adds to the file size. Ideally, you should do this before importing the audio into Flash, but you can also do it for each instance through the Edit Envelope dialog box (refer to Figure 10.7). Another great way to reduce file size is to use a short looping sound instead of a long linear sound. Of course, there's a possibility of selecting a loop that can become monotonous, but you might be surprised how much mileage you can get from one simple loop. Sprinkle a few incidental Event sounds that are independent of the loop, and the effect can often sound very interesting.

Probably the most subjective question is "Which level of compression is appropriate?" Determining which level of compression is appropriate is really a subjective decision, but that doesn't mean I can't make a few suggestions. First of all, there's a common misconception that audio containing voice can withstand the most compression, whereas music can't. This is just plain false! A better generalization would be to say that sounds of natural items (acoustic instruments and voices, for example) are best kept at a high quality, whereas sounds of synthetic items (such as a distorted electric guitar and synthesized keyboards) will likely be perfectly acceptable at a lower quality. This is true because any sound on the computer is fake—you're trying to make the user believe the sound is one thing or another when, in fact, it's just electronic data. When you attempt to simulate something natural, such as a voice or an acoustic instrument, your audience has a good recollection of what that sound is supposed to sound like, and they'll notice if it doesn't sound right. On the other hand, sounds from an electric guitar, for example, can be distorted and still sound perfect. (Heavy metal connoisseurs may disagree, but you get the idea.) Ultimately, you'll still need to test each compression setting to hear how it sounds, but just remember that it's easier to notice that something's wrong when a natural sound gets distorted.

One other fact: If everything else is kept equal, a mono sound will appear "cleaner" than a stereo sound. This doesn't mean that you shouldn't use stereo. Instead, simply realize that in order to maintain quality in a stereo sound, you usually can't compress as much (and add to this the fact that stereo sounds are twice as big as mono sounds). Therefore, just be absolutely sure you *need* stereo sound (and remember you can still pan the left and right channels without a stereo sound).

Summary

Flash supports audio elegantly. Including audio in a movie is a simple process of importing the sound and then deciding in which keyframe you want the audio to play. Many options are available on *how* the audio plays—for example, whether it plays and finishes naturally (the Event Sync setting) or whether you want it to lock itself to the Timeline so images remain synchronized no matter what (the Stream Sync setting). You can also use sophisticated envelope controls for each instance of a sound used.

Because the effect on file size is the biggest "cost" of using audio, Flash provides a variety of compression technologies and settings to individually or globally specify the kind of compression to use. I'm sure you'll find MP3 or Speech to be the best quality, when considering file size, for almost any sound you want to use, but other alternatives do exist. If nothing else, I hope this hour has made you more deliberate and restrained about adding audio to your movies. Don't get me wrong—the power of audio is great. Just try not to abuse this power; your slow-connection users will thank you.

Q&A

Q *I placed a long-running sound in the first frame of my movie. However, when I test the movie, the sound only plays for the first few seconds and then repeats. Why?*

A You've probably set the Sync setting for the keyframe (on the Properties panel) to Stream and haven't extended the Timeline long enough. If your sound is 10 seconds long and you're playing at 12 fps with Stream selected, you're going to want to make sure 120 frames are available in the layer of the Timeline in which you placed the sound. An Event sound doesn't have this restriction (although it also doesn't have the same synchronization behavior). Also, looping may be caused simply because your movie loops when you test it. While you're testing a movie, you can disable looping by selecting Control, Loop.

Q *I put a sound in the first frame of my movie, but when I click Play, I don't hear anything. I verified that my speakers are plugged in and that my computer sound level is cranked. What else could it be?*

A I wish I could say that you must use Test Movie because otherwise the sound won't work. Of course, Test Movie is always the best option for visualizing exactly what your users will see and hear. However, even Play should let you preview the sound. You might check two things: First, Mute Sounds under the Control menu should be unchecked, and the envelope settings for the sound instance should not be two horizontal lines at the lowest sound level. Second, you might check the original sound that you imported to make sure it's not just silence.

Q *I imported and placed in a keyframe a song I ripped from my band's CD; now every time I test the movie my computer hangs for a long time. Is there any way to speed this up?*

A Selecting short punk rock songs is one way. Seriously, just go into the Publish settings, select Raw for both Stream and Event, and remember to select Override Sound Settings. Now it won't perform the compression (the thing that takes forever) every time you publish. Just remember to change it back later before you're ready to publish for real.

Q *I imported an MP3 file that was only 61KB, but when I export the movie, it becomes 900KB. I'm sure my graphics aren't that big because when I remove the sound, the file goes down to 5KB. What could possibly be wrong?*

A Most likely you're resampling the sound (as Raw) and Flash is converting the sound into the size it would be as an uncompressed sound. Check the Publish Settings dialog box in Flash and confirm that you don't have Override Sound Settings selected. Then inspect the Sound Properties dialog box for the Library item of your imported sound and confirm that the MP3 settings match the original attributes of your file (shown near where the date and file location are displayed).

Q *Where is that starter ActionScript code for playing an external MP3 file that you promised?*

A Put an MP3 file (named in this case music.mp3) adjacent to your .swf (and remember to upload it when you post it on the Web); then put this code in the frame where you want the sound to start playing:

```
my_sound = new Sound();
my_sound.loadSound("music.mp3", true);
```

That's it. The true option says "start playing this sound as soon as you can— don't wait for it all to download first."

Workshop

The Workshop consists of quiz questions and answers to help you solidify your understanding of the material covered in this hour. You should try to answer the questions before checking the answers.

Quiz

1. Which is a better-quality audio format to use for original files—AIF or WAV?

   A. AIF, because it was developed for the Macintosh

   B. WAV, because it was developed more recently

   C. Neither, because they can both be the same quality

2. Where do you place sounds in order to hear them in the final movie?

   A. In the Library, in symbols, or in keyframes

   B. In keyframes (no matter where they are)

   C. In the sound layer

3. After importing a few sounds, you have to wait longer every time you use Test Movie. What is causing this phenomenon, and what can you do to fix it?

   A. You forgot to select Fast Export when importing the sounds, so you need to reimport and pick that option.

   B. You can only hear the sounds when you select Control, Play. Don't use Test Movie if you have sounds.

   C. Sounds can take a long time to compress. Temporarily change the Publish Settings dialog box settings to Raw and select Override Sound Settings to save time during development.

Quiz Answers

1. C. There's nothing inherently better about AIF or WAV—either can be high quality or low quality.

2. B. Sounds are placed into keyframes, either via the Properties panel (when a keyframe is selected) or by dragging the sound right onto the Stage from the Library.

3. C. This tip is a bit esoteric but will no doubt save you a lot of time. Just remember to go back to your normal Publish Settings dialog box settings when you're ready to deliver.

HOUR 11

Using Layers in Animations

What You'll Learn in This Hour:

▶ How to control animation by using layers
▶ How to change layer properties for sophisticated effects
▶ How to incorporate Guide, Motion Guide, and Mask layers

The most interesting thing about layers in Flash is the fact that most people think they're for visual layering. This is understandable because almost every graphics editing tool has layers for just this purpose: to layer graphics on top of or below other graphics. Despite the fact that layers in Flash have the same effect, that's not their real value. Rather, each layer is a concurrent Timeline where an animation can play. This hour you'll learn how layers primarily help you animate and, to a lesser degree, let you control visual layering.

How Layers Work

If you're familiar with Photoshop, Fireworks, or almost any other graphics editing tool, you are already familiar with using layers as a visual tool to control stacking order. In Flash, layers provide the same visual effect. But you have already learned that graphics can be stacked if they're Drawing Objects, grouped, or turned into symbols—so why do we need layers?

The True Purpose of Layers

In Flash, multiple layers are really multiple Timelines—and that's their value. The images contained in layers are stacked above or below other layers, but their primary purpose is to provide you with separate Timelines in which you can control animations independently.

You might recall from Hour 8, "Using Motion Tweens to Animate," that the rule for motion tweens is that you can animate only one thing per layer (and that *thing* has to be an instance of a symbol). Suppose you want two circles, with one appearing to race past the other. It's simple; just use two layers. In the following task you'll try something simple to get started with layers.

▼ **Try It Yourself**

Use Two Layers to Animate Two Circles

In this task you'll make two circles move across the screen. One will appear to move faster than the other.

1. In a new file, draw a circle, select it, and convert it to a symbol (by pressing F8). Name it Circle, leave the behavior set to the default Movie Clip, and click OK.

2. With the instance of Circle on the Stage, do a motion tween. To keep things from getting too complicated, name this layer Fast (indicating that the circle in this layer will move fast). To name the layer, click once in the Timeline so that it has the focus and then double-click on just the name of the layer (initially Layer 1) and type a new name.

By the Way

Focus Indicating Active

Focus applies to all kinds of computer buttons and fields generally. For example, when you fill in an online form, only one field has focus at a time. That is, if you start typing, you'll be typing into whichever field currently has focus. When you tab through a form, the focus moves from one field to the next.

In Flash, several buttons and fields also reflect focus. Even the Timeline can have focus (indicated by a subtle highlight on the name of the selected layer). When you click the stage, the timeline loses focus (indicated by the selected layer's highlight turning gray). Quite often, it might not be entirely clear which window, panel, or button has the focus, but you should be conscious of which does.

3. Because the Timeline has only one frame so far, position the instance of Circle on the left side of the Stage. Then click the cell in Frame 31 of the Fast layer. Select Insert, Timeline, Keyframe (or press F6).

4. Make sure that the red current-frame marker is on Frame 31 and move the circle all the way to the right side of the Stage.

5. To make a motion tween, either right-click (use Control+click on a Macintosh) on the first keyframe and select Create Motion Tween or select the first keyframe and from the Properties panel select Motion from the Tween drop-down list. (Most of this is a review of Hour 8.)

▼

6. Create a new layer by either selecting Insert, Timeline, Layer or clicking the Insert Layer button at the bottom left of the Timeline (see Figure 11.1). Name this new layer Slow, the same way you named the other layer Fast (in step 2).

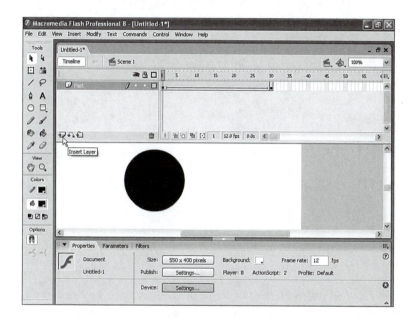

FIGURE 11.1
Using the Insert Layer button at the bottom left of the Timeline is a quick way to insert a new layer (just like selecting Insert, Timeline, Layer).

From this point forward, you need to be conscious of the layer in which you are currently editing (that is, you need to know where you are). You can only be "in" one layer at a time, which is indicated by the pencil icon in the layer (see Figure 11.2).

7. Next you'll copy an instance of Circle from the Fast layer and paste it in the Slow layer. To do this click an instance of Circle (to select it) and copy it (by pressing Ctrl+C). By clicking an object on the Stage from the Fast layer, you cause that layer to become active. Before you paste, make sure you make Slow the active layer by clicking the word Slow and then pasting. Position the copy of Circle you just pasted on the left side of the Stage, but do not cover the other one.

8. To keep things straight, tint the instance of Circle in the Slow layer. Select it and in the Properties panel, select Tint from the Color Styles drop-down list and then select a color that is different from the color of the other circle.

9. In Frame 31 of the Slow layer, select Insert, Keyframe. Move the instance of Circle in Frame 31 over to the right side of the Stage (but not as far to the right as you moved the circle in the Fast layer).

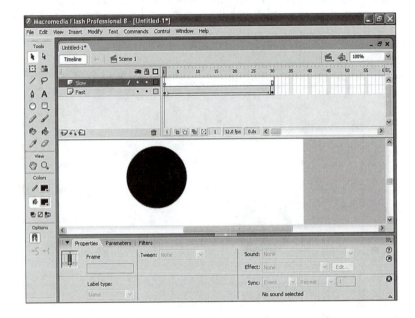

10. Set a motion tween for the first frame of the Slow layer. Test the movie, and you see two circles moving across the screen—two things animating at once!

11. Save this file because you'll use it in the next task.

The discussion so far this hour shouldn't suggest that layers are to be avoided. Just the opposite: You should feel free to use as many layers as you need, even if only for visual layering. Although a Flash file with hundreds of layers might be harder to edit, all those layers are combined upon export (not unlike what happens with Photoshop's Flatten Image command). Although layers can be useful for organization and stacking purposes, they're absolutely *necessary* for animation effects.

Layer Properties That Help You Edit

You've already seen how the pencil icon indicates which layer is currently being edited. Other icons in the Timeline indicate layer properties that can be modified. Check out Figure 11.3 for a quick overview of these properties, and then we'll discuss each in detail. (By the way, most of the buttons and features listed have ToolTips.)

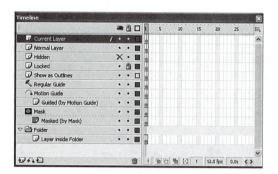

FIGURE 11.3
There are several layer types and properties.

Figure 11.3 shows almost every variation of layer property. Here's a quick introduction to each one:

▶ **Layer Name**—This property lets you give any layer any name you like. You'll stay organized better if you take advantage of this feature and name layers logically.

▶ **Show/Hide Layer**—This property allows you to hide the contents of any individual layer temporarily by clicking the dot beneath the eye. If you click the Eye button on top, you hide or show all layers. Remember that this affects only what is seen while editing because exporting a .swf sets all the layers to Show. Compare this to Guide layers (below) which don't appear in your .swf.

▶ **Lock/Unlock Layer**—This property lets you individually lock or unlock layers selectively (or all at once). We'll revisit the previous task and you'll see how useful locking layers can be.

▶ **Show Layer as Outlines**—This property lets you view the contents of a layer as outlines, almost like making the layer contents invisible but not as extreme. Similarly to Show/Hide, this setting affects only how the layer appears to you (the author). The outline color can be changed through the Layer Properties dialog box (available if you double-click the Layer Outlines button or the Layer Type icon, such as the Page Curl on the far left). In addition, if you use Edit, Preferences to open the Preferences dialog box, select the General tab, and select the Highlight color setting Use Layer Color, then the clips selected in this layer will highlight in the same color.

▶ **Normal Layer**—This layer type is the plain page icon with a curl in the bottom-right corner. This is the default type of layer.

▶ **Guide Layer (regular)**—This layer type is a special layer into which you can draw anything you want (usually shapes, to help align graphics or notes to other team members). Everything contained in a Guide layer is excluded from export when you create a `.swf`, so it won't show up in your final file, nor will it add to file size

▶ **Motion Guide Layer**—This layer type acts like a Regular Guide (they're both guides, after all); however, a Motion Guide layer contains a line to which you associate a motion tween, which is in a Guided layer (see below). This is how you make a motion tween follow a path.

▶ **Guided Layers**—This layer type is available only if the adjacent layer above it is set to Motion Guide. In the Guided layer, you can create a motion tween that follows the path drawn in the Motion Guide layer.

▶ **Mask Layers**—This layer type lets you place any shape or Movie Clip symbol that will define the visible (and nonvisible) portion of the layer below it, which is set to Masked. Just like a mask you put on your face, in a Mask layer you draw where you want holes in the mask.

▶ **Masked Layers**—This layer type is available only when the layer directly above is set to Mask. The contents of a Masked layer will be invisible except in areas where objects are placed in the Mask layer. You won't see this effect until you test the movie or lock both the Mask and Masked layers.

▶ **Folders and Layer Folders**—These settings are very different from the other layer properties because you can't have any content in them. However, after you make a layer folder, you can nest other layers (and even other layer folders) inside it. And, when you make a Folder layer visible or invisible, all the contained layers follow suit.

Some of the icons indicating layer properties (in Figure 11.3) are easy to access, whereas others involve several steps. We'll look at Guide and Mask layer types later this hour. In the following task, you'll begin to work with the easy ones: Show/Hide, Lock/Unlock, Show as Outlines, and Layer Folders.

▼ **Try It Yourself**

Experiment with Hiding and Outlining Layers

In this task you'll explore the visual layer properties:

1. Open the file you created in the previous task and scrub a little to recall how it plays.

2. How do you know which circle is in which layer? If the circles intersect the same area, you'll see one in front of the other. Move the current-frame marker to Frame 1. By just looking, you can't really tell which one is which. You could

read the layer name that you wrote—but Fast and Slow aren't very clear and, besides, you could have made a mistake. The fact that the layers contain instances of the same symbol makes it even more difficult to tell. To figure it out, temporarily change the Show/Hide option for one layer at a time. Try clicking the eye at the top of the Timeline. Notice that this hides every layer. Click the eye again, and the layers will all be shown again. To hide just one layer, click the dot under the eye in the layer of your choice. Click the dot in the Fast layer. Not only do you see a red _ over the dot (when it's hidden), but everything on the Stage from that layer is hidden (just temporarily). By process of elimination, you can figure out which layer is which by making one invisible.

3. Make all the layers visible again, and you can determine which circle is which another way—by using outlines. Click the square button on the top of the Timeline (see Figure 11.4) to Show All Layers as Outlines. This should make the contents on the Stage appear in outline form. Hopefully, they appear in different colors so that you can tell them apart.

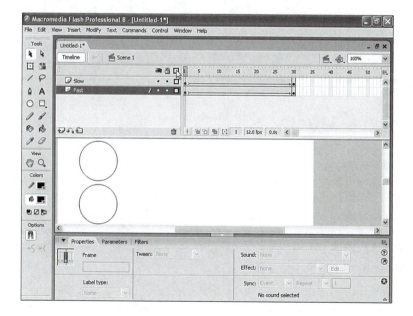

FIGURE 11.4
The contents of layers can be viewed in outline form.

4. If both layers are showing up in the same color, just double-click the Show Layer as Outlines box for one layer. If you click the button once, it toggles between the Outline and Normal views. When you double-click, you're taken to the Layer Properties dialog box, which is similar to that shown in Figure 11.5. Alternatively, you can single-click a layer (to make it active) and then

select Modify, Layer. We'll cover this dialog box more later, but for now, select a different color from the Outline Color swatch and then click OK. The outlines in that layer should have a different color now.

FIGURE 11.5
All layer settings
are shown in
the Layer
Properties dia-
log box (which
is accessible by
selecting
Modify, Layer or
by double-
clicking the
Page Curl icon
or the Show
Outlines icon).

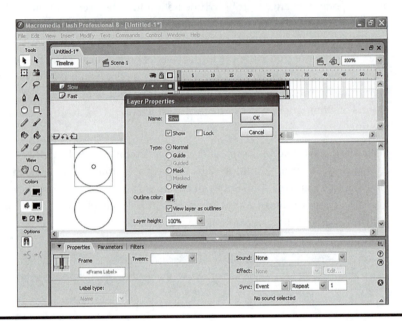

Managing Layers

On the surface, layer folders are a pretty straightforward feature. Remember that you can nest layers inside of folders. Although layer folders probably don't warrant an entire task, let me point out a couple hidden benefits. Besides just collapsing the Timeline, a folder can be hidden just like a layer can. When you hide or show a layer folder, you automatically hide or show all the nested layers. If hiding layers is a good feature, hiding layer folders is a great one. You can also lock or unlock layer folders. In practice these two subtle features may have greater value than layer folders themselves.

Another way to manage a ton of layers is to select the Short option from the Timeline Properties menu as shown in Figure 11.6. This will shorten your timeline by about 30%.

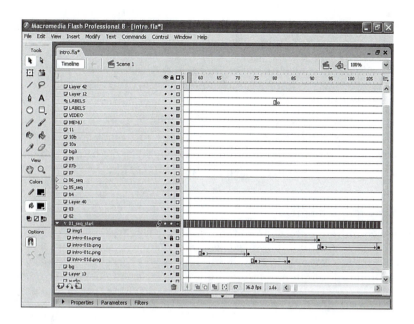

FIGURE 11.6
The timeline's short option squeezes more layers into a smaller space.

Using Layer Properties for Visual Effect

The four remaining layer types (Guide, Motion Guide, Mask, and Masked) are very powerful. Unlike the layer properties covered so far this hour, these four will have a lasting visual impact on your user. That is, they affect the final .swf. Using these layer properties is more involved than simply clicking an icon in the Timeline. However, when you see what they can do, you'll understand why it's worth the additional effort.

Guide Layers

Guide layers become invisible when you export a movie. (I said we would be covering layer properties that have lasting effects, and the first one we look at is something that becomes invisible.) Guides are very useful and if you use them correctly, they can have a huge impact on what your audience sees, even though they won't be exported with the movie.

Why would you want something you draw to be excluded from export? There are two primary reasons. One reason to use Guide layers is for registration purposes. Into a Guide layer, you can draw lines or shapes to which other objects can snap for consistent positioning. Maybe you want a title to appear in several sections of a movie. If you draw a horizontal line into a Guide layer, all the titles can be snapped to that line. But when the movie is exported, no one will see that line.

Another reason to use Guide layers is that you might have lots of visual content that you keep on the Stage for personal reference or notes to others in your group. If it's all in a Guide layer, you'll see it only while authoring. Similarly, you might have a layer of an animation that you decide at the last minute to remove. Instead of actually removing the entire layer, you can just change it to a Guide layer. It will still be there as a backup if you change your mind later, but otherwise no one will see it. You'll create a guide layer just for alignment in the next task.

Perfect Registration

Registration refers to alignment. In commercial printing, registration is critical because each ink color is printed separately. Registration marks are used to line up all the plates precisely. In multimedia, registration serves much the same purpose. For example, if you're looking at several pages of text, if they're all registered the same, you won't see text jumping all over the screen between pages.

▼

Try It Yourself

Use a Guide Layer to Define the Off-Limits Area

Suppose you're building a presentation that includes onscreen text and a graphic frame that provides borders. You would like to position the text onscreen without overlapping the borders. A shape in a Guide layer can serve to define the areas that are safe for text. Just follow these steps:

1. In a new file, select the Rectangle tool and turn off Object Drawing. Draw a filled box the size of the Stage. (You can use the Info panel to make it the exact size.) Then use the Pencil tool (with the Pencil Mode set to Smooth) to draw an enclosed irregular box within the box you just drew. Select the center shape with the Selection tool and delete, as shown in Figure 11.7. (You can certainly do this maneuver with Object Drawing enabled. Draw the filled rectangle; draw the outline; fill the outline; then select both objects and choose Modify, Combine Objects, Punch.) Select the entire (now cutout) shape and convert it to a symbol (called Frame Shape). Name this layer Registration. This will become the Guide layer.

▼

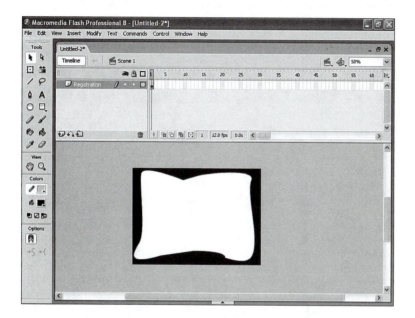

FIGURE 11.7
The Registration layer will become the Guide layer.

2. Select Insert, Timeline, Layer and name the new layer Interface. On this layer, a copy of the Frame Shape will tween into place late in the Timeline (which will better demonstrate the need for Guide layers). First, select the instance of Frame Shape on the Registration layer and copy. Then go to Frame 25 of the Interface layer and select Insert, Timeline, Keyframe (or press F6). Verify that the current layer is Interface (if it is not, click the layer name) and then select Edit, Paste in Place (or press Ctrl+Shift+V) on Frame 25.

3. Click Frame 35 of the Interface layer and select Insert, Timeline, Keyframe (or press F6). Move the current-frame marker to Frame 25 and scale the instance of Frame Shape much larger so that you can't actually see the borders onscreen (as in Figure 11.8). Finally, set motion tweening in the Properties panel when Frame 25 is selected. Scrub to see that the Frame Shape won't appear until Frame 25, when it tweens from outside the Stage.

4. Click in Frame 35 of the Registration layer. Select Insert, Timeline, Frame (or press F5) to make this layer last as long as the Interface layer. Click the Layer Outline button for the Registration layer (so that only this layer shows as an outline). Scrub from the beginning of the movie to the end. Notice that the outlined Registration layer gives a clear idea where Frame Shape will eventually appear, so that you can avoid placing text in that area. However, if you select Control, Test Movie, you'll see that the Registration layer is visible the entire time. Until you change this layer to a Guide layer, it will export with the rest of the movie.

FIGURE 11.8
The first place Frame Shape appears is in Frame 25. Here you scale it larger than the Stage so it will appear to tween from outside.

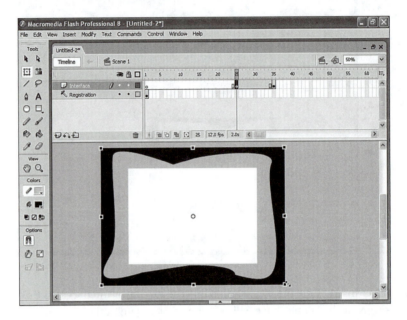

5. To make the Registration layer a Guide layer, access the Layer Properties dialog box by either double-clicking the Page Curl icon to the left of the layer name or (with the layer selected) selecting Modify, Timeline, Layer Properties. In the Layer Properties dialog box (refer to Figure 11.5), select the Guide radio button, the Lock check box, and the View Layer as Outlines check box; then click OK.

6. Insert a new layer (by selecting Insert, Timeline, Layer) and name this layer Text. Verify that all the layers are set to Normal except Registration, which should be set to Guide. (If they're not, access each layer's properties individually and set them appropriately.)

7. In Frame 1 of the Text layer, create a block of text with a large font size, such as 40. Type as much text as you can, being careful not to exceed the borders shown in the outline in the Registration layer (see Figure 11.9).

8. Test the movie. You might want to turn off Loop from the Control menu while it's playing.

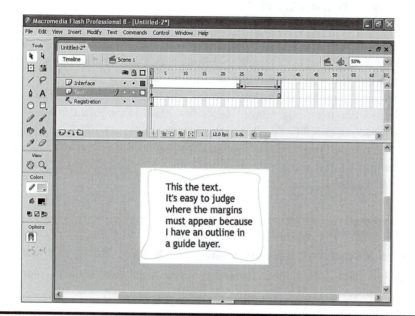

FIGURE 11.9
Using the outlined shape in the Guide layer, you can place the text precisely so that it doesn't interfere with the borders.

In the previous task, you created a Guide layer that defined a safe area onscreen for the Frame Shape symbol that hadn't arrived onscreen yet. You might have other shapes that don't appear unless certain conditions are met. For example, if you have buttons that in their Over state expand with large graphics or include a drop-down effect, you might not want other elements on the Stage to be placed where they will be covered up by the button. You could copy the shape of the button when fully expanded and paste it in the Registration layer. If you want to leave reminder notes to other team members or to yourself, you could enter them in a Guide layer as well. The idea is that you can put anything you want into a Guide layer, and it won't export with the movie.

Using a Guide layer for registration, as you just experimented with, is nice because you can use any shape, group, or symbol in the Guide layer. Another feature, called Guides (under the View menu), is confusingly similar: Vertical and horizontal lines are dragged from the rulers on any side of the Stage (View, Rulers must be selected from the menu)—as you did in Hour 2, "Drawing and Painting Original Art in Flash." Using the Guides feature becomes almost identical to using lines in a Guide layer (provided that you've left the default Snap to Guides setting in the View, Snapping menu).

Motion Guide Layers

Guide Layers are pretty useful, but Motion Guide layers are much more exciting! A Motion Guide layer is actually a regular Guide layer that happens to have an adjacent layer (below it) set to Guided. The exciting part is that a motion tween in the Guided layer will follow any path drawn in the Motion Guide layer. That means you can draw an S-shaped line in a Motion Guide, and then the Guided layer can include a motion tween that follows the shape. Similar to a regular Guide layer, a Motion Guide layer will be invisible to the user. The thing to remember with Motion Guide layers is that two layers are involved: the Motion Guide layer and the Guided layer. In the next task you'll make a ball in a Guide layer bounce along a line drawn in the Motion Guide layer.

▼   **Try It Yourself**

Create a Bouncing Ball Animation by Using a Motion Guide

In this task you'll use a Motion Guide layer to produce a classic bouncing ball animation:

1. In a new file, draw a bouncing line (using the Pencil or Pen tool). This will become the path the ball will follow (see Figure 11.10). It might actually work best if you just draw straight lines and then bend them and snap them together. Regardless of how you draw it, just make sure it's one continuous line that doesn't overlap at all. It doesn't have to be perfect looking because this is only going to be a guide (and thus, invisible). Make sure the line is a Shape (by breaking it apart if it's a Drawing Object).

2. Double-click the Page Curl icon to access the Layer Properties dialog box (or select Modify, Timeline, Layer).

3. Name the layer Path, lock it (so you don't mess it up), and change its type to Guide. (Notice that there's no Motion Guide option here.)

4. Insert a new layer by clicking the Insert Layer button at the bottom left of the Timeline or by selecting Insert, Layer. Name this new layer Ball.

5. Most likely the inserted Ball layer will appear above the Path layer. You're going to make this new layer a Guided layer (meaning that it can follow the drawing in the Path layer). Before you can make a layer a Guided layer, it must be directly below the layer that is set to Guide. You can change the layer stacking by dragging layers around. Go ahead and drag the Ball layer down (so it's just below Path).

▼

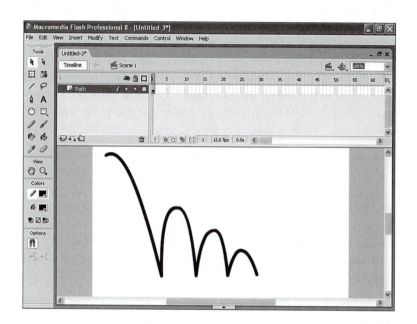

FIGURE 11.10
A pretty simple
drawn line will
be used as a
motion guide
(for a tween to
follow).

Notice that not only does this change the layer order, but it also causes the
Ball layer to be Guided. You can see this because Path now has a slightly different icon (the arch), Ball is indented, and a dashed line separates the two, as
shown in Figure 11.11. This is what you want, but you might not be so lucky
to have everything fall into place like this (depending on exactly how you
drag around the layers). In addition, when moving layers around, you might
not want Flash to change all the layer properties for you. If that's the case, perform an Undo so that you're back to where just the Path layer is a regular
Guide layer (with the cross icon) and the Ball layer is above it. You're going to
do the same thing again the hard way so that you know how it works.

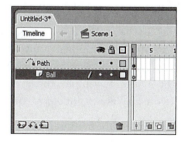

FIGURE 11.11
The Motion
Guide layer
(Path) has a
special icon, and
the Guided layer
(Ball) is indent-
ed. A dashed
line separates
the two layers,
indicating that
they're related.

6. Drag the Path layer above the Ball layer. Nothing changes except the layer order. You can't just change the Path Guide layer to a Motion Guide layer (which is what you want in the end). Instead, you can make the Ball layer a Guided layer (now that it's directly under a Guide layer). Access the layer properties for the Ball layer (by double-clicking the Page Curl icon or, with the layer selected, choosing Modify, Timeline, Layer Properties). Notice that the type Guided is available. Only when the layer just above this layer is a Guide layer do you see this option. Click Guided and then click OK.

7. Now you're going to create the animation and snap it to the guide. Into Frame 1 of the Ball layer, draw a circle and make it a symbol (called Picture of Ball). Now, in the Ball layer, click in Frame 50 and insert a keyframe (by pressing F6). Notice that the Path layer doesn't live this long. In the Path layer, click in Frame 50 and insert a frame (not a keyframe) by pressing F5. Go back to Frame 1 of the Ball layer and create a motion tween (by right-clicking the first keyframe in this layer or selecting the frame and picking Motion from the Tween drop-down list in the Properties panel).

8. Finally, you need to make the ball actually follow the path. This is easiest if you first lock the Guide layer because you're going to snap Picture of Ball to the path, but you don't want to edit the path. Lock the Guide layer by clicking the dot under the padlock in the Path layer. At this point you should find that the Picture of Ball can't be dragged anywhere but onto the line drawn in the Path layer (and you don't disturb the line as it's locked). In Frame 1, make sure Picture of Ball is at the start of the path. Go to Frame 50 and snap the center of the Picture of Ball instance to the end of the path drawn in the Path layer. Test the movie. The ball should follow the path.

What took all the time in the preceding task was learning about changing layer properties and learning some mechanics of how they need to be ordered. All you do is draw a path, make it a Guide layer, make a new layer that's a Guided layer, do a motion tween, and snap the instance in each keyframe to the drawn path. (Sounds pretty easy when I say it like that but, really, that's all you did.)

One little detail that people seem to forget: When you snap a symbol instance to the guide, you must snap the center of the symbol (which is editable by using the Free Transform tool). If you set the motion tween plus the layer types to Guide and Guided first, Flash won't let you snap any point *other* than the center.

Let's quickly explore one other option for motion guides. When you select a keyframe with a motion tween, the Properties panel shows the option Orient to Path. The effect of this option is that the instance being tweened will rotate toward the direction it's traveling. You can see the effect of this option best when the symbol isn't perfectly round. We can change Picture of Ball temporarily to see this effect. From the Library window, you can access the master version of Picture of Ball. In the master version, just draw another little circle next to the circle (don't let it touch because you want to be able to remove it later). Back in your main scene, you can look at the Properties panel for the first frame of the Ball layer; to do this, you make sure that you're in the scene, select the first keyframe, and then bring up the Properties panel. Select the option Orient to Path and then view the results by clicking Play. Turn off Orient to Path (in the first keyframe) to see the difference.

In the previous bouncing ball task, I purposely had you step in every possible pitfall so that you could learn how to recover. However, it happens to be much easier with the Add Guide Layer button. If you've already drawn a ball, you can click the Add Guide Layer button (see Figure 11.12) to automatically add a new layer, make that layer a Guide layer, and make the current layer a Guided layer. This button attempts to do several steps in one move, but it can be difficult to use.

FIGURE 11.12
The Add Motion Guide button just to the right of the Insert Layer button does several things with one click.

Mask Layers

While Guide layers are useful and Motion Guide layers are exciting, Mask layers are both! Masking is really a different feature entirely. Mask Layers is similar to Guides and Motion Guides only in that it's a layer property, and you need at least two layers: one for the Mask layer and one for the Masked layer (similar to Guide and Guided). The graphical contents of the Mask layer determine which parts of the Masked layer will show through. It's as if you're drawing the holes to see through in the Mask layer.

The basic orientation of the Mask and Masked layers is similar to the Motion Guide/Guided layer arrangement. For masking, you first specify one layer's Type property as Mask. Then, you'll find the Masked setting available when you access the layer properties for a layer directly below the Mask layer. However, you won't actually see the masking effect unless you test the movie or lock all the layers involved. It will all make more sense when you create a spotlight mask in the next task.

▼ **Try It Yourself**

Use Masking to Create a Spotlight Effect

In this task you'll create a spotlight effect that appears to light up a skyline of buildings:

1. Create the spotlight and its motion. To do so, in a new file, draw a filled circle and convert it into a Movie Clip symbol called Spot.

2. Name the layer in which the Spot instance resides Spot Motion.

3. Insert keyframes in Frames 10, 20, and 30. In Frame 10, move Spot to a new location, and move it again for Frame 20. Frame 30 should match Frame 1.

4. Set up motion tweening in Frames 1 to 10, 10 to 20, and 20 to 30, either with the right-click method or from the Properties panel.

5. Change the Spot Motion layer's Type property to Mask. Double-click the Page Curl icon for this layer to access the Layer Properties dialog box.

6. Notice that the Page Curl icon changes to the Mask icon (see Figure 11.13). Lock the Spot Motion layer so that you don't accidentally change it.

7. Insert a layer below the Spot Motion layer and change its type to Masked. Click the Add Layer button (at the bottom left of the Timeline). The new Layer might appear above the Spot Motion layer; that's fine. Name the new layer Skyline.

FIGURE 11.13
The Mask layer (Spot Motion) no longer has the Page Curl icon; after you change its type to Mask, the icon looks different.

8. In order for Skyline to be a Masked layer, it must be below the other layer, so click and drag down the Skyline layer. If you get lucky, the Skyline layer will automatically change to Masked (and you'll see an icon like the one shown in Figure 11.14). However, it's easy to do by hand, too. If you must, access Skyline's Layer Properties dialog box and change the type to Masked (which will be available only if the next layer above it is already set to Mask). The result should resemble Figure 11.14.

▼

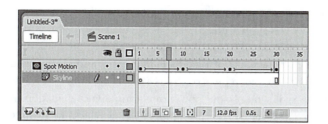

FIGURE 11.14
The Masked layer Skyline has a special icon; it's indented, and a dashed line separates it from the Mask layer above.

9. In the Skyline layer, draw lots of boxes in different colors to resemble a city skyline. You will see the mask effect only if you test the movie or lock all the layers.

10. Change the background color of the movie to black (by selecting Modify, Document or clicking the Stage and using the Properties panel).

    As interesting as this looks, there's something missing. This is the way a spotlight would look in space, where there's no atmosphere. The black background is too dark. You need to make another layer with a dim version of the skyline to make this more believable.

11. Select all the boxes you drew in Skyline (you need to make sure that just this layer is unlocked to select it). You can easily select everything in that layer by clicking the keyframe in Skyline layer. With everything selected, convert the shapes into a Movie Clip symbol called Building Graphic.

12. To put another instance of Building Graphic into a new layer, create a new layer (by clicking the Add Layer button) and name it Dim Skyline.

13. Analyze the Type property of each layer (which is easy to see by its icon). Chances are that the Dim Skyline layer is also a Masked layer. One Mask layer can have several Masked layers. Set Dim Skyline to Normal, but only after you move it down below Skyline. If Skyline is no longer directly under the shadow of Spot Motion, it will also revert to Normal. Drag the Dim Skyline layer down below Skyline, and then set the Type property for Dim Skyline to Normal.

14. Copy the instance of Building Graphic and paste it in place (by pressing Ctrl+Shift+V) into the Dim Skyline layer. Hide all layers except Dim Skyline (so you're sure which one you're affecting). Then, with the instance of Building Graphic in the Dim Skyline layer selected, access the Properties panel. Set the Color Style to Brightness and set the slider to –40%.

    Looks great, eh? You didn't need to create this Dim Skyline layer to learn about masking, but it's a nice touch.

You can do some sophisticated stuff with masking. For example, you could edit the master version of Spot and maybe cut out part of the fill (by using the Lasso tool). The Masked layer will show through only where there's something in the Mask layer. Unfortunately, this is an all-or-nothing situation. That is, the mask is either on or off. You can pull off the effect of a graduated mask by putting the graduation in the Masked layer (because it won't work in the Mask layer). Another idea is to make a duplicate of the Spot symbol—but one with a transparency gradation fill. Then you can make a separate layer where this duplicate follows the same path as the spot.

The preceding task was a case of moving the mask. Quite often, however, you'll find situations in which the Mask layer should remain still and the Masked layer is the one to move. Suppose you're building an animation of someone sitting inside a train, and you want the effect of mountains and clouds passing by the window. If you had a wide picture of mountains and clouds, you could easily do a motion tween to make it pass by. Without masking, you would have to cover up the left side and the right side (surrounding each window) with graphics of the inside of the train. These carefully sliced covers would need to be in a higher layer (to cover up the picture), and it would be more work than it needed to be. With masking, all you need is a Mask layer with the exact shape of the windows and a Masked layer containing the tween of your wide picture. This is a case of the masked part moving and the mask staying still. Just realize that any time you want to cut out part of another image, you can do it without really cutting anything. Masking has amazing potential for visual effects.

While Masking is still very useful, Flash Professional 8 added a feature that can be used in a similar manner: the Blend feature (that you first saw in Hour 4). Where two layers are involved for masking, blends require at least two symbol instances (layered but not necessarily in separate layers). Compare the Erase blend to a traditional layer mask. It just so happens the Erase blend (and the Alpha blend) is more complex because you actually need three symbol instances. In fact, the instance on which you set the Erase blend must be nested inside another symbol. In Hour 4 I detailed each blend as well as introduced nesting (which comes up again next hour). For comparison to Mask layers, here's how you can do the previous spotlight effect using blends:

Place an instance of the bright buildings on stage. Create a new symbol *inside of which* you nest two clips: one instance of the buildings (dimmed via its brightness color effect) and—on another layer—an instance of the spotlight clip. Call this symbol "spot animation." Set the instance of the spotlight to the Erase blend. Use a Motion tween to animate the spotlight inside the "spot animation" clip. Then, place the "spot animation" in the main timeline on top of the bright buildings. Finally, set the "spot animation" instance to have the Layer blend. Figure 11.15 shows the layout of both how you did it in the preceding task (top) and how you can do it with blends (bottom)

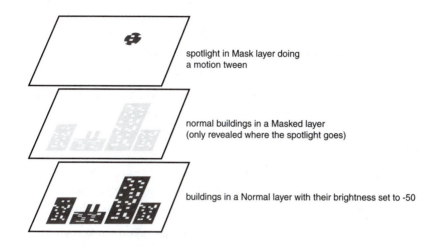

spotlight in Mask layer doing a motion tween

normal buildings in a Masked layer (only revealed where the spotlight goes)

buildings in a Normal layer with their brightness set to -50

FIGURE 11.15
You can create the same spotlight effect using either Mask layers (top) or using the Erase blend (bottom).

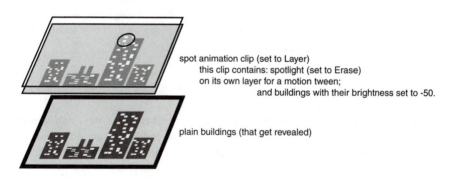

spot animation clip (set to Layer)
this clip contains: spotlight (set to Erase)
on its own layer for a motion tween;
and buildings with their brightness set to -50.

plain buildings (that get revealed)

On the surface, this is no easier or better than using mask layers. It should come out looking the same as the preceding task. However, what's really cool is how you can make the spotlight use the Alpha blend instead of Erase. Then, fill the spotlight with a gradient that goes from 0% alpha to 100%. This will produce a spotlight that has soft edges. If you're already comfortable with Photoshop blends, you can probably work out this sort of effect in your head. If not, try to learn masks first. In Hour 13, "Creating Special Effects," you'll see additional effects like these. In addition, you can find other practical examples using Blends in Hour 5, "Applied Layout Techniques."

Summary

We covered a lot of material for something that appears to be a simple interface component—layers. It's hard to say that layers aren't primarily for visual stacking because that's exactly how they work. Remember that Drawing Objects and groups (or, better yet, putting objects in the Library) also lets you stack them (within one layer). However, creating separate layers is sometimes more convenient.

Layers are useful for more than creating the layering effect, however. The number-one rule of motion tweens is that only one object (an instance of a symbol) be tweened per layer. If you want more things to animate, you have to put each one in its own layer.

This hour we discussed layer properties, how entire layers can be hidden or locked at will, and how the Show Layer as Outlines feature provides a way to view the contents of any layer as an outline. Those properties are accessible right in the Timeline.

The Guide Layer property excludes an entire layer from export but keeps it in the source Flash file for any purpose, including registration. Motion Guide layers let us pair up the Guide layer with a motion tween (in the lower layer) to follow a drawn path. Finally, Mask layers (paired with a Masked layer) give us a way to hide all portions (except those we indicate) of another layer.

Q&A

Q *I have one layer set to Mask and another to Masked. When I add a new layer, it automatically becomes Masked. However, if I change the new layer to Normal, it causes my old Masked layer to become Normal, too. What gives?*

A Masking involves two layers: one Mask and one Masked. They must be directly adjacent, with the Mask layer on top of the Masked layer. If the new layer you added is between the two, changing it to Normal will require the old Masked layer to be Normal, too. You have to get that new layer out of the shadow of the mask before you change it to Normal. Often you can't even drag the layer down (it just stays in the shadow of the Mask layer unless you drag down and to the left). You should be able to drag it up above the Mask layer, and it will change to Normal; then you'll likely be able to move it back down (below the Masked layer) with success. However you must maneuver it, just realize that both the Mask/Masked and Motion Guide/Guided features require at least two adjacent layers.

Q *I created an elaborate Motion Guide and have the guided layer successfully following that guide. But why doesn't my animation look good?*

A A Motion Guide certainly doesn't ensure a good looking animation. In fact, in many ways it can become a crutch. I actually recommend avoiding Motion Guides except when appropriate. If you step back and really think about the visual message you're trying to communicate you might find just a few carefully placed keyframes will make a more compelling animation.

Q *I used three instances of the same symbol in my Mask layer but only the first one I placed is behaving like a mask, the other two are being ignored. Why?*

A I can't say exactly why but I do know that you need to break apart symbol instances (or Drawing Object shapes) when you have more than one in your Mask layer.

Q *I made a Guide layer and then I made a 40-frame motion tween. I was careful to set the layer's properties so there's a Motion Guide layer above my Guided layer. However, when I try to attach the contents of Frame 40 in the Guided layer to the Guide layer, the Guide layer is missing. Why?*

A It is likely that the duration of the Guide layer is less than 40 frames (it's probably just 1 frame). All you need to do is extend that layer by selecting Insert, Timeline Frame or pressing F5. Don't use Insert, Timeline Keyframe (or press F6) because that would be necessary only if something is changing visually in that layer—and you probably just want the Guide layer to remain static.

Workshop

The Workshop consists of quiz questions and answers to help you solidify your understanding of the material covered in this hour. You should try to answer the questions before checking the answers.

Quiz

1. How can you draw into a Mask layer and see the effect of the mask on the Masked layer at the same time?

   A. You can't.

   B. You need to use red fill.

   C. You need to lock both layers.

2. How many layers can be masked by setting one layer to Mask?

    A. One. Each Masked layer must have its own Mask layer.

    B. As many as you want.

    C. None. It's the other way around; one Masked layer can have lots of Mask layers below it.

3. What is the one situation in which being efficient (such as using the Library) is not especially important?

    A. Nowhere in Flash. You should always be efficient.

    B. In Guide layers—because they don't export with the movie.

    C. In layers you hid—because they're hidden.

Quiz Answers

1. A. I love trick questions. In fact, you can lock both layers and see the effect, but you can't draw into a locked layer (while it's locked anyway). Don't worry if I tricked you; this quiz is just supposed to teach.

2. B. One Mask layer can shadow as many Masked layers as you want. It actually appears to happen outside your control sometimes when you're adding layers. Masked layers have a special icon, and the layer name is indented.

3. B. I suppose you should always be efficient, but Guide layers aren't exported with the movie, so they won't hurt the user in any way. Also remember that hiding a layer only hides it while you're authoring (just use Test Movie to see this).

Exercises

1. Create a Mask layer that contains filled window shapes, and in the Masked layer place a large image (imported or created in Flash) of the sky and some clouds. Motion tween the image to create the effect that the sky is passing by (in the windows). Remember that each window will likely need to be a plain shape (not a symbol), because they're in a Mask layer.

2. Make a motion guide in the shape of a circle. Suppose you want an object to follow a circle during its motion tween. An enclosed circle for a Motion Guide layer won't work. However, in the Guide layer, you can create an outline of a circle and then cut out a very small segment. Snap the object in the Guided layer to the start of the circle, and in another keyframe, snap the object to the other end of the circle. Try this. Depending on the total number of frames, you might find that the segment you delete can be bigger than you'd think.

HOUR 12

Animating Using Movie Clip and Graphic Symbols

What You'll Learn in This Hour:

▶ How to make and use nested clips
▶ That a movie clip is a symbol with its own independent Timeline
▶ How Movie Clip symbols are fundamentally different from Graphic symbols
▶ That movie clips are addressable

When you see what Movie Clip symbols can do, you'll be blown away. Inside a movie clip, you can create an animation and then animate an instance of that clip. This means, for example, that you can create a rotating wheel clip and then animate the rotating wheel so that it not only rotates but moves across the screen as well. Symbols, as a general concept, should not be new to you. You learned quite a bit about them in Hour 4, "Using the Library for Productivity." Probably the biggest benefit of symbols is that, while you keep one master version in the Library, you can use as many instances of the symbol as you like throughout a movie, with no significant impact on file size. You should also recall from Hour 8, "Using Motion Tweens to Animate," that the object you tween must be an instance of a symbol. I'm sure you've also noticed that any time you create a symbol, Flash asks whether the symbol should have the symbol behavior Movie Clip, Button, or Graphic. Next hour you'll learn all about buttons, but this hour you'll learn as much as you can about animating with Movie Clip and Graphic symbols.

This hour doesn't try to summarize all the uses for movie clips because there is so much to say that I couldn't cover everything. The primary goal of this hour is for you to understand movie clips and how they compare to plain old Graphic symbols.

Movie Clip Symbol Behavior

Some people wrongly think that Graphic symbols are only for when the symbol contains a single frame and Movie Clip symbols are only for when you have multiple frames. The differences go much deeper than that. The best approach is to simply always use Movie Clips unless you have a reason to use Graphic symbols (which you'll learn this hour). The first thing to learn is that both Movie Clips and Graphic symbols can contain one or more frames. However, only Movie Clips will automatically loop regardless of where you place instances of that clip.

Here's an example of how Movie Clips will automatically loop: Say you make a Movie Clip of a wheel (a circle with lines for spokes). You can then use an instance of your Wheel symbol inside another Movie Clip called Rotating Wheel—where the Wheel symbol rotates. Then you can create another movie clip that serves as the Car (which includes two instances of the Rotating Wheel symbol). Because the Rotating Wheel is a Movie Clip, the wheels will rotate whether you put them on stage or inside the Car. Finally, the Car symbol can be animated across the screen, and both wheels will rotate the whole time. Don't worry if this is confusing; you'll do a task next to make it clear. Just remember, you can use movie clips even when you don't need multiple frames.

Creating Nested Movie Clips

Making a movie clip is like making any symbol. In the following task, you'll first create an animation inside a movie clip. Then, when you tween an instance of the clip, it will tween as well as animate. Specifically, you'll make a wheel and then use an instance of that wheel to create a rotating wheel. Finally, you'll use two rotating wheels to create a car symbol. You'll animate the car (and see its wheels rotating, too).

▼ **Try It Yourself**

Use a Movie Clip to Make a Rotating Wheel

In this task you'll nest a clip of a wheel inside a clip that will become an animating wheel that you can use anywhere you want:

1. Draw a circle with a few lines crossing it. Don't make it perfectly symmetrical— that way you'll be able to see it rotate, as in Figure 12.1. Select the entire shape and then select Modify, Convert to Symbol (or press F8). Name the symbol Wheel, choose the default Movie Clip behavior type, and then click OK. You're going to make a movie clip of the wheel spinning next, but you need an instance of the plain wheel first; remember that you can't motion tween anything except symbol instances.

▼

FIGURE 12.1
This Wheel symbol will be easy to notice when it's rotating.

2. Select the onscreen instance of the Wheel symbol and convert it to a symbol. Select Modify, Convert to Symbol (or press F8), name it Rotating Wheel, make sure you leave Movie Clip set as the behavior, and then click OK. I know you already had a symbol, but consider what converting to a symbol does: It takes what's selected (the instance of Wheel) and puts it into the Library. In step 1 you put a shape in the Library. In this step you took an instance of Wheel and put it in the Rotating Wheel symbol.

3. Go inside the master version of Rotating Wheel by simply double-clicking the instance onscreen. In the edit bar you should see Scene 1: Rotating Wheel. If you now single-click to select the instance (inside Rotating Wheel) you should see "Instance of: Wheel" in the Properties panel (as shown in Figure 12.2). This means that Rotating Wheel contains an instance of Wheel.

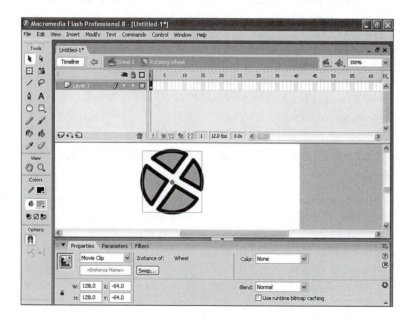

FIGURE 12.2
The Properties panel displays a selected symbol's original name.

4. While inside Rotating Wheel, we'll do a simple motion tween of the Wheel instance. To do this, click in Frame 20 and insert a keyframe (by pressing F6). Select the first keyframe and from the Properties panel select Tween Motion, Rotate CW 1 Time.

5. Go back up to the scene. You should see an instance of Rotating Wheel, although now it has a 20-frame rotation you can't see. Use Test Movie to ensure that it rotates.

6. Create another instance of Rotating Wheel by either copying and pasting the instance onscreen or by dragging another instance from the Library. Position the two Rotating Wheel instances side-by-side and then use the Brush tool to draw the car body. Select everything and convert it to a symbol called Car (leave it with the Movie Clip behavior).

7. Insert a keyframe at Frame 30 (in the main Timeline) and then with Frame 1 selected, set the Properties panel to Tween Using Motion. Move the instance of Car in either Frame 1 or Frame 30, and you should be able to see the car move when you scrub (just like any other motion tween). To see the wheels rotate, test the movie. Scrubbing only previews the animation across the Timeline in the current movie clip, not any nested movie clips. (Only Graphic symbols preview when you scrub.)

If you aren't familiar with nesting symbols, the preceding task might have been a little confusing. (Review Hour 4 if necessary.) In the preceding task you worked from the specific to the general. You made a Wheel symbol, and you made a Rotating Wheel symbol that contained Wheel because you needed a symbol *inside* Rotating Wheel to do a motion tween. Then you used two instances of Rotating Wheel in the creation of the Car symbol.

Comparing Movie Clip Symbols to Graphic Symbols

It makes no difference whether your master symbol is a graphic or a movie clip. The symbol behavior affects only the default symbol behavior for instances dragged straight from the Library. What matters is the symbol behavior of the instance on the Stage. If you drag a movie clip from the library, it will start with the Movie Clip behavior, but you can change it (for a given instance) to Graphic by using the Properties panel, as shown in Figure 12.3. It's the instance's behavior that matters.

Graphic instances that contain multiple frames have a few unique options. The Properties panel changes to include a few extra options. When you select a symbol with the Graphic behavior, the Properties panel lets you specify which frame (within the symbol) will appear first. In addition, other options from the drop-down list provide a choice between Loop, Play Once, and Single Frame. By combining these settings, you can vary exactly how an instance with the Graphic behavior appears.

Suppose you have two instances of Rotating Wheel that use 20 frames for one rotation. You could use both instances as graphics and set both to Loop, but on one, you could set the first frame to 10. The two wheels would both rotate continuously, but they would be offset by 180 degrees.

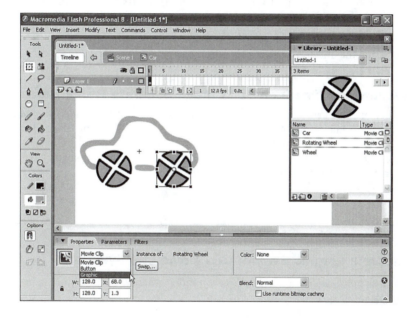

FIGURE 12.3
An instance on the Stage (regardless of the master symbol's default behavior) can have any behavior you select from the Properties panel.

If you compare the options in the Properties panel when a movie clip is selected (compared to a graphic), you'll notice only one seemingly minor field for Instance Name. It really isn't minor at all, as you'll see in the section "Addressable Movie Clip Instances," later in this hour, and again in Hour 15, "Using ActionScript and Behaviors to Create Nonlinear Movies." For now, just realize that you can name movie clip instances individually in the Properties panel.

If the only difference was a few settings in the Properties panel, you could do exercises with Loop, Play Once, and Single Frame, and that would be the end of it. However, Graphic symbols differ in another major way. Multiframe Graphic symbols (even when set to Loop) are synchronized and need to match the duration of the Timeline in which you place them. For example, a 10-frame Graphic symbol placed in Frame 1 of a Timeline will display Frame 1 in Frame 1, Frame 2 in Frame 2, and so on. If you place this Graphic symbol in a Timeline that's only 5 frames long, the instance of the symbol will display Frame 5 when it gets to Frame 5, but it will go no further. It's locked to the Timeline where it's used. (If it helps, you can compare the Graphic behavior to sounds set to Stream, which you learned about in Hour 10, "Including Sound in Animations.")

Movie Clip instances are independent of the timeline where they're used. They always play all their frames and loop. Think of a movie clip as marching to the beat of its own drummer. A 10-frame movie clip doesn't care if it's placed in a 10 frame timeline, 100 frames, or just 1 frame. It plays all its frames when it can, like Rotating Wheel used in creating the Car in this hour's first task. (Movie Clip behavior is like sounds with the Sync setting Event.) The next task will drive home the differences between graphic and movie clip instances.

By the Way

Independent Timelines Don't Mean Separate Frame Rates

Just because a movie clip has an independent Timeline doesn't mean you can change the frame rate. "Marching to the beat of its own drummer" doesn't mean you can have independent frame rates. You get one frame rate for an entire movie. There are some advanced tricks to simulate frame rate changes, but the fact remains that there's only one frame rate per movie.

▼ **Try It Yourself**

Compare a Graphic Symbol to a Movie Clip Symbol

In this task you'll see how movie clips loop independently of the Timeline in which they reside:

1. In a new file, select Insert, New Symbol (or press Ctrl+F8), name the new symbol Numbers, select Movie Clip for the behavior, and then click OK. (Notice that this takes you inside the master version of Numbers.)

2. In Frame 1 of Numbers, use the Text tool and type 1 near the center of the screen. Insert a keyframe in Frame 2 and change the onscreen number to 2. Continue inserting keyframes and changing the contents to match the frame number all the way to Frame 10.

3. Get back to the main scene (make sure you're not still in Numbers) and drag an instance of Numbers onto the Stage from the Library. Select Control, Test Movie (or press Ctrl+Enter)—remember, using Test Movie is the only way to see movie clip animation. All 10 numbers appear in sequence, even though you used only 1 frame of the main Timeline.

▼

4. Back in the scene, insert a frame (not a keyframe) in Frame 5 (click Frame 5 and then select Insert, Timeline, Frame or press F5), which really just extends the life of this Timeline. Use Test Movie again, and you should see no change.

5. Drag another instance of the Numbers movie clip onto the Stage. Select just this instance and change the instance behavior to Graphic by accessing the Properties panel. With the instance still selected, make sure the Options drop-down list is set to Loop. Now test the movie again.

6. The result is that only Frames 1 through 5 of the graphic instance are displayed while the movie clip continues to run. (If the movie is playing too fast, try a lower frame rate.) Back in the Timeline, try scrubbing back and forth in the main scene. Although the Graphic symbol shows only the first 5 frames (it has only 5 frames to live), it also gives you a good preview while scrubbing.

7. While you're testing the movie, select Control, Stop. This stops the red current-frame marker from advancing, but notice that the movie clip keeps right on playing. The graphic is locked to the Timeline into which it's placed, whereas the movie clip plays independently.

There are a few additional points to notice in the preceding task. First, movie clips always loop. (There's no "play once" option. In Hour 15 you'll learn how to write a script that says "Stop at the last frame.") But because of this, movie clips are sometimes extra work. Also, it might seem like a drag that only Graphic symbols are previewed when you scrub, but there's good reason for this. Graphics are previewed because they're locked to the Timeline, and therefore Flash knows exactly how they'll play. Movie clips play at their own rate (and can be started or stopped any time through scripting). Therefore, Flash has no idea exactly how they'll play and can't give you a preview. If nothing else, just remember to always use Test Movie if you want to see what the user will see.

When to Use Movie Clips

Generally, you should use movie clips for everything you can, even if it's just a static (single-frame) graphic. However, there are some reasons to use Graphic symbols instead.

Multiframe Graphic symbols are appropriate any time you really need to preview while you're working. The fact that movie clips don't preview when you're scrubbing can be a real hassle. For example, if you're synchronizing lip movements in a character, you probably want to use multiframe Graphic symbols. Also, a movie clip's automatic looping means that if you don't want it to loop, you need to do more work—you need to put a script into the last frame to make it stop. Also, specifying a first frame by using multiframe Graphic symbols is so easy that it's hard to resist this feature. Using scripting in movie clips to do this is more complicated and slightly more work (though also—ultimately—more powerful, too).

Although the Graphic symbols lock themselves to the Timeline (making synchronization easier), there are difficulties to overcome as well. A common problem arises when the number of frames in the symbol doesn't match (or evenly divide into) the number of frames where you place it. For instance, if you use Graphic symbols for Rotating Wheel in this hour's first task, you have to make sure the Car symbol has exactly 20 frames in order for the wheels to fully rotate. If the car has 1 frame, the wheels won't spin. If the car has 10 frames, you'll see half the rotation, and then it will repeat. A movie clip, in contrast, will continue to play, regardless of how many frames it is given. If your nested animation has a different number of frames than your Timeline, you should either use movie clips or make sure the Graphic symbols have the appropriate number of frames. Using movie clips is usually much easier because they're more flexible than graphics.

This discussion shouldn't distract from the main reason to use symbols (either movie clips or graphics), which is that you want to create a motion tween. You can use motion tweening only on an instance of a symbol. If the symbol you're tweening happens to have multiple frames, so be it. By nesting clips inside clips, you can create very complicated effects that would be very difficult to create by hand in one Timeline. So although either a graphic or a movie clip qualifies (as a symbol instance) for motion tweening, the difference is that a movie clip animates on its own time, and it doesn't matter how much space you provide in the Timeline where it is used.

Subtleties of Movie Clips

We've already discussed the biggest difference between Movie Clip symbols and Graphic symbols—a movie clip's Timeline is independent. Obviously, there's more. Movie clips are addressable, in that you can use ActionScript to direct messages to individual instances of a movie clip, such as a Stop command. Also, Movie Clip instances download in a different manner than Graphic instances.

Addressable Movie Clip Instances

Remember that the Properties panel provides a place to name a movie clip instance (see Figure 12.4). What's the point of naming an instance if the symbol already has a name in the Library? It provides a way to give each instance on the Stage a unique name. Only then can you address individual movie clips. Think about how you address a person. You first say his name, and then you tell him what you want. If you want him to stop, you say, "Joe, stop." This is the concept of addressing, which we'll talk about more in Hour 15.

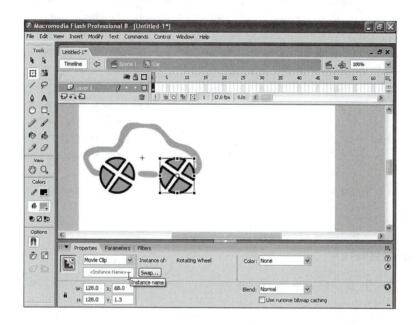

FIGURE 12.4
The Properties panel, when set to Movie Clip, gives you a way to name a particular instance on the Stage.

Do you recall how the movie clip kept animating even when you stopped the Timeline in the last task? Stopping the Timeline is like yelling "Stop!" into a crowd. Simply saying "stop" isn't enough. You have to say, "Hey, Movie Clip 1, you stop." But you can't talk to an individual instance unless that instance has a name. As you'll soon see, you can do much more than tell movie clips to stop.

Instance Names Versus Symbol Names

By the Way

Don't confuse the master name for a symbol in the Library with the instance name for just one instance on the Stage. Every item in the Library must have a unique name, but symbols in the Library exist just once. You can drag as many instances of a symbol as you need to use throughout a movie. Any instance set to Movie Clip can be given its own instance name, regardless of the properties of the master in the Library. If the instance name is unique (that is, different from any other instances), you can address it directly. People often think that because the master in the Library has a name, the instance does, too. The truth is that an instance has no default name (and you'll see gray text reading "**<Instance Name>**" in the Properties panel).

Effects on Download Order

All this trash talk about graphics shouldn't scare you off. Besides being totally appropriate for scrubbing, they also have a nice effect on downloads. Specifically, Graphic symbols only need to download one frame at a time—and therefore exhibit a better streaming effect than Movie Clip symbols. That is, a movie that uses Graphic symbols (or even no symbols) can begin to play before it's entirely downloaded. In the case of a frame containing a movie clip, all nested frames need to download before Flash will proceed to the next frame. If Flash reaches a frame that contains a ton of Movie Clip instances which in turn include lots of nested frames, you'll experience a pause. Even though the later frames in nested clips may not be needed right away, Flash needs to be prepared for a script that immediately jumps to the last frame. This isn't a super-critical point because Flash files tend to be very small, and there are other ways to optimize a movie (many of which are discussed in Hour 21). I just thought it would be worth mentioning at this point how Graphic symbols stream better.

Summary

This hour didn't contain a lot of new material. You already knew two big concepts: how nesting of symbols works and how symbols can be used for both motion tweens and efficiency. When doing motion tweens, maybe you tried to make a symbol a multiframe symbol. Now you should understand that you can do that and there are options about whether the multiframe symbol you're tweening is behaving like a movie clip or a graphic.

You can't scrub when using movie clips—or at least you won't see them animate until you run Test Movie. This is another reason to avoid using movie clips when you really need the capability to scrub—such as for lip synching. Finally, the fact that only movie clips can be given an instance name will prove, in the long run, to be the most significant attribute of movie clips.

Q&A

Q *I did the Car with Rotating Wheel task, but when I first made the Rotating Wheel symbol, I forgot to specify the default symbol behavior as Movie Clip. I went back to the Library to rectify this error, but it still doesn't work (the wheels don't rotate). Why not?*

A Changing the symbol properties of the item in the Library affects only any new instances you drag from the Library, which will have the properties of the master in the Library. However, instances already in a movie will have the same behavior they started with. Your instances of the Rotating Wheel symbol are behaving like graphics. Go to where they're used (inside the Car symbol) and, with the Properties panel open, select each instance. Then change the Symbol Behavior setting from Graphic to Movie Clip.

Q *I can't find the Loop Once option on the Properties panel when I have a movie clip selected. I swear I've seen it before. Where is it?*

A You could have seen Loop Once in the Properties panel, but not when a movie clip was selected. Only instances behaving as graphics have this option—which is a good reason to use Graphic symbols. Of course, when you become accomplished with ActionScript, you'll find ways to achieve the same effect when using a movie clip—although it still might take more work than simply using the option available to instances of graphics.

Q *In this book I keep reading the phrase "instances behaving as graphics." Why don't you just say "Graphic symbols"?*

A There's a difference. The master symbol has one default symbol behavior, which you can change by clicking the Library's options menu and selecting Properties. However, each instance on the Stage can be changed to something different from the master that spawned it. An instance always starts the same as its master. But not only can each instance be changed (to behave like any type); changing the master has no effect on instances already on the Stage.

Workshop

The Workshop consists of quiz questions and answers to help you solidify your understanding of the material covered in this hour. You should try to answer the questions before checking the answers.

Quiz

1. How many frames can you use inside a Graphic symbol? How many inside a Movie Clip symbol?

   A. You can use one frame for a Graphic symbol and as many as you want for a Movie Clip symbol.

   B. You can use as many as you want for either.

   C. It doesn't matter how many frames you use in the master symbol; it only matters whether the instance behaves like a graphic, which can have one frame, or a movie clip, which can have as many frames as you want.

2. What happens if you name two symbols in the Library the same? What about naming two movie clip instances the same?

   A. You can't do either.

   B. You can't name two symbols the same unless you separate them by using Library folders, but there's no problem naming two instances the same.

   C. You can name two symbols or two instances the same, but it's a bad idea because Flash might lose one.

3. Although movie clips are recommended over graphics, when should you use Graphic symbols?

   A. You should always avoid them always.

   B. Graphic symbols enable you to synchronize Graphics to the Timeline and sometimes even make the file play faster.

   C. Graphic symbols are easier on the eyes because they're antialiased.

Quiz Answers

1. B. You can use as many frames as you want in the creation of movie clips or graphics. Depending on where you use graphics, though, you might need to concern yourself with the number of frames the instances are given to live.

2. B. Although there's no problem naming multiple instances the same, it might become a problem when you try addressing just one, such as when George Foreman addresses one of his many sons named George, Jr. But there's certainly no rule against it.

3. B. Some people actually agree with Answer A (graphic instances should be avoided), but for truly varied applications, using movie clips to simulate Graphic symbols can be problematic. Plus, who cares how big the file becomes if you're not delivering it to the Web? Finally, if something saves you a *ton* of time in production, it could be worth the cost of slightly larger file sizes—especially if the cost doesn't turn out to be terribly significant.

Exercises

In the first edition of this book, the following exercises produced a fair number of frustrated readers emailing me (which, by the way, you should feel free to do). They're tricky exercises but worth going through. To make things a bit easier, I've uploaded source files for both of these (and many others) to www.phillipkerman. com/teachyourself/sourcefiles.

1. Despite all the negative talk about Graphic symbols, this activity practically requires them.

   Create an animation of a steam engine train. First, make a Graphic symbol of just the stack. Then go inside the stack symbol to animate the smoke stack, possibly by using a shape that starts out as a rectangle. Use shape tweens to Frame 5, where the stack is bulging, Frame 6 where it's extra tall and expels smoke, and Frames 7 through 10, where it's normal again.

   Use the stack symbol in the creation of the train itself. (Be sure to give the train exactly the same number of frames as the stack.) Bring the train into the main Timeline and motion tween it across the screen. By scrubbing, you'll be able to judge where the clouds of smoke appear.

   In another layer, add symbol instances of clouds, which will appear and stay in the same location as they motion tween to 0% alpha. Try this by using Graphic symbols for everything.

2. Create an animation of a Ferris wheel. First, make the passenger car a movie clip so that you can animate it. Make a Graphic symbol called One Rotation and inside it create circular motion guide to motion tween the passenger car one full rotation in about 28 frames.

   Now place 10 instances of One Rotation inside a 36-frame movie clip named Ferris Wheel. For each instance of One Rotation, access the Properties panel and specify the first frame for each. Start one on Frame 1, the next on Frame 4, the third on Frame 7, and so on. In the end, you'll have 10 cars rotating in the same manner but starting at different locations.

Creating Special Effects

What You'll Learn in This Hour:

▶ How to paint with bitmaps
▶ Special effects you can apply to text that's converted to shapes
▶ Practical uses for Flash Professional 8's filters
▶ Advanced masking special effects.

This is the last hour in the animation part of the book (not that you won't do any more animation but you'll get into more interactive and web features). As such you'll get a chance to take the knowledge gathered over the last few hours and apply it to practical exercises. This hour is comparable to Hour 5, "Applied Layout Techniques," where you combined the graphics creation skills acquired in the first part. Here you'll create animations using frame-by-frame animation, tweens, sounds, and layers. This hour should both be fun and serve as an affirmation of how far you've come in the first half of the book.

Very few new details about Flash will come up this Hour. Instead, the exercises concentrate on specific effects you'll likely need to communicate to the audience. Arguably, some of the tasks this hour border on cliché or gratuitous. That's okay. It's fine to study—even copy—what others have done while you're learning. It's not likely you'll use these exact effects on a real project, but you'll certainly apply the techniques.

Effects with Shapes

We'll start with a few relatively simple features of Shapes and then work up to more advanced techniques. I say "shapes" but these work with Drawing Objects as well. The point is, you can't do the following tricks with Text blocks, grouped objects, or symbol instances. You can go inside a symbol and use these techniques on any shapes contained. This section is almost like a defense for shapes which, after all my praise for symbols serves as a good balance.

Painting with Bitmaps

You've already seen how to create and modify gradients. You can also use—as the fill or stroke color—an imported bitmap (really any raster graphic is fine). The way you create and modify a bitmap color is comparable to gradients: you use the Color Mixer to select the image and you use the Gradient Transform tool to modify it. It's really easy and pretty cool, even if it's not terribly practical.

▼   **Try It Yourself**

Use an Imported Bitmap as a Fill Color in a Hall of Mirrors

After you start painting with a bitmap you'll experiment with some special effects.

1. In a new file, open the Color Mixer panel and make sure the Fill Color swatch is selected (click it). From the Type drop-down menu, select Bitmap. Because this is a new file you'll be faced with the standard Import dialog. So, select any raster graphic you have on your computer. (If you already have a bitmap in your library, selecting Bitmap from the Type drop down menu displays a set of "swatches" each with a preview of the imported bitmap.)

2. Select the Rectangle tool and set the stroke to "no stroke" (the diagonal red line). Draw a square on stage. The fill should contain your, now imported, raster graphic.

3. Select the Gradient Transform tool and click the fill of your square. You can modify the size and location of the bitmap fill. Notice the bitmap repeats when it's smaller than the rectangle. Interestingly, the Gradient Transform has additional handles to change just the width or height as well as the skew of the fill—options that don't apply to Linear Gradients. Let the cursor change help you figure out the modification type for each handle.

4. So the bitmap fill is pretty cool, what about something more practical? Here's just one: an easy hall of mirrors. Use the Gradient Transform to set the contained image as big or bigger than the square—that is, make sure the image doesn't repeat.

5. Select the rectangle and open the Transform panel. Type 80 into both the width and height fields then repeatedly press the "Copy and apply transform" button near the bottom right of the Transform panel. The result should look like Figure 13.1.

▼

6. Often I find it's best to use the Gradient Transform tool to make some final tweaks on the location of the fill of the smallest rectangle. For example, I moved the eyes in the photo so that they were visible. The mirror effect still looks good.

Using a bitmap as your fill or stroke color can be a bit cheesy. I'm sure you can restrain the urge to be too garish. With that warning in hand, let me tell you it's possible to tween a shape whose bitmap fill changes over time. That is, make one keyframe containing a shape with a bitmap fill, then in a second keyframe use the Gradient Transform to tweak the bitmap fill. Then do a Shape tween from the first frame to the second. The thing to remember is that you need to use Shape tween (not Motion).

Breaking Apart Text

Text is much like a Drawing Object in that it won't eat away other shapes in the same location (the way shapes drawn in merge mode do). If you select a text block and choose Modify, Break Apart the first time it breaks the text into a separate block for each character. The second time (or if the text block is only one character long) Modify, Break Apart turns the text into shapes. Why is this useful? Well, if you want to animate each character of the text independently, you'll need to make symbols out of each character. Plus, if you want to change the shape or fill with a gradient—even mixed color—then the text must be a shape. You can experience both effects in the following two tasks.

▼   **Try It Yourself**

Animate a Block of Text, One Character at a Time

1. In a new file select the Text tool, pick a very large font size—like 60—click the stage, and type DROP.

2. Select the Selection tool and single click the entire block of text. Position the text where you want the animation to end—for example at the bottom of the stage. Choose Modify, Break Apart (or press Ctrl+B). Each letter is a separate block of text now.

3. With all the letters selected, choose Modify, Timeline, Distribute to Layers. Delete the layer with nothing in it by clicking "Layer 1" and then clicking the trashcan icon in the timeline.

4. Before we animate these letters they each need to be a Movie Clip instance. Click once to select the D and select Modify, Convert to Symbol (F8), name it "D" and make sure it's a Movie Clip. Do the same for the other letters (but name them appropriately).

Did you *Know?*

> ### Repeating Symbols
>
> If you repeat this task with a word containing duplicate characters (say the two Os in ZOOM) you probably realize you shouldn't make two symbols based on the letter O. But as a way to ensure the second O lines up perfectly, do this: when you get to the second O, go ahead and make another symbol—maybe call it temporary O. Then, select the instance on stage (that's in place) and click the Swap button in the Properties panel. Swap it with the first O. Then delete the temporary O in the library. This way everything lines up and you didn't need to drag or eyeball anything.

5. Because the letter instances are perfectly in place the way we want them to *end*, let's not mess them up. We'll duplicate these keyframes later in the timeline however. First, click once in each layer at frame 50 and insert a frame (F5). Then in the D layer, click frame 10 and insert a keyframe (F6). In the R layer, insert a keyframe in frame 15. In the O layer, insert a keyframe in frame 20. In the P layer, insert a keyframe in frame 25.

6. Return to frame 1 by clicking above the 1 in the timeline. Click on the D and hold shift then drag up so the letter appears above the stage. Do the same for the other letters. Finally, click the keyframe in frame 1 of the D layer and select Motion tween from the Properties panel (or right click and select Create Motion Tween). Do the same for the first keyframe in the other layers.

7. Test the movie. You're welcome to modify the timing and make other tweeks.

▲

Turning Text into a Shape

Text blocks are like but not exactly the same as Drawing Objects, symbol instances, and groups. Of course you can put text in any of the above object types but it's not necessary because text won't get eaten away the way a plain shape will (when two shapes overlap). However, there are several reasons why you may want to turn text into a shape. As a shape you can distort the text in any manner you want. In addition you can fill it with gradient or mixed colors. For that matter, you can add a stroke to the text if it's a shape. Alas, once you convert text to a shape you can never edit the characters again—they're shapes not text. So, understand in this section you'll learn special effects for text that's locked down and won't likely change.

The way you convert text to a shape is easy. Select Modify, Break apart twice. The first time you Break Apart it will break a text block into individual text blocks that are one character each. Once the text is a shape you can do any sort of shape maneuver: use the Free Transform tool's Distort and Envelop options; apply a stroke and remove the fill; change the stroke or fill to a gradient or bitmap; or just stretch and reshape using the Selection or Subselection tools. The next task lets you play with all these options.

Try It Yourself ▼

Convert Text to a Shape for Special Effects

1. In a new file select the Text tool and pick a large and very bold graphic font and type a word on the stage. Use the Selection tool to select the block (not the contained characters as you would with the text tool) and then select Modify, Break Apart. Without clicking (which would deselect) select Modify, Break Apart again. Now all the letters are shapes.

2. Use the selection tool to stretch and bend the characters. Don't distort things so much that you can't read the word, but realize you can reshape any way you want. I find it interesting to modify the shape for the particular word at hand. For example, in Figure 13.2 I made the facing "p" and "a" almost mirror each other and the "c" fits into the adjacent "a" like a jigsaw puzzle. I adjusted the letter spacing too.

3. Before we go wild filling this shape, let's make a dramatic shadow. Select all the shapes and choose Modify, Group. This will make the shapes safe from erasing the shadow. Copy the group and paste it. Position the duplicate out of the way of the original. With the duplicate selected choose Modify, Transform, Flip Vertical. Then select Modify, Ungroup. ▼

FIGURE 13.2
You can go wild reshaping text once it has been converted to a shape.

4. Use the Free Transform tool and first select all shadow characters. Use the Distort option and hold shift while you drag the bottom right corner out to make the shadow get bigger the way it might appear when the sun is low. See Figure 13.3.

FIGURE 13.3
A dramatic shadow only takes a little bit of tweaking with the Free Transform tool.

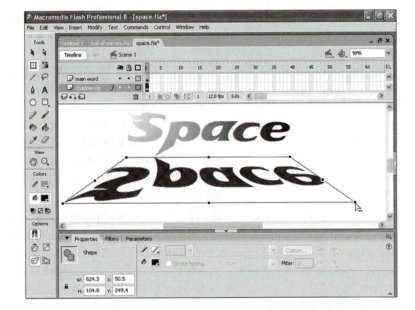

5. Select all the shadow letters and set the color to something a little lighter than the primary letters. With all the shadow selected choose Modify, Convert to Symbol (F8) and select Movie Clip.

6. If you have Flash Professional 8 select the shadow clip and use the Filters panel to apply a Blur effect. In any case you can use the Properties panel to change the alpha to something like 75%.

7. Now change the fill color on the letters. Double-click to enter the primary letters' group. Open the Color Mixer panel and, for the fill color, select the default white-to-black radial gradient (or create your own gradient). Select the Paint Bucket tool and make sure the Lock Fill is not selected. Click in the top left corner of the leftmost letter. Then, turn on Lock Fill and click once in each of the other letters. Finally, use the Gradient Transform tool to control the position and fall off of the gradient. It should spread across all the letters.

8. Now, to push this over the edge, we can animate. First do a Shape Tween with the main letters. Go back up to the main timeline and select the main letters. Choose Edit, Cut (Ctrl+X) and then select Modify, Timeline, Insert Layer (or just click the little "Insert Layer" button at the base of the timeline). Make sure the new layer is active, and select Edit, Paste in Place (or Ctlr+Shift+V). Select the letters again and choose Modify, Break Apart. Finally, go to frame 20 and insert a keyframe. Use the Gradient Transform to move the highlight of the gradient to the right most letter. Select the keyframe in frame 1 and use the Properties panel to set a Shape tween.

9. The shadow is a little bit easier. Click on the cell in the shadow's layer under frame 20 and insert a keyframe. Use the Free Transform tool and skew the bottom of the shadow to the left. You might need to nudge it a bit so it looks lined up with the main letters. Finally, return to the keyframe in frame 1 of the shadow's layer and use the Properties panel to set Motion tween. Don't worry too much about how the shadow looks during the tween—it's really only necessary that it looks good in the last frame.

By the way, in the section on Masking later this hour you'll see an alternative to converting text to shapes when you only need to modify the fill. You can have any color or gradient that gets revealed by a block of text—that is, the text is the mask.

Using Filters for Special Effects

In the preceding task you used the Blur filter to soften the shadow, but notice you didn't use the Drop Shadow filter. In fact, you can't distort the shadow when using that filter. So before you jump into the following examples using Filters, remember that sometimes you just have to draw or animate by hand what you want to show. Filters are like decorations on a cake—the filling has to taste good too.

You've already seen Filters pop up in other parts of this book, and they'll appear again. Here I've just included two general effects that can be enhanced by filters: depth and motion.

Showing Depth with Shadows

You don't need a degree in optical physics to know some basics about shadows. Figure 13.4 shows two simple principles: the closer an object is to a light source the bigger the shadow; and, the farther away from where the shadow gets cast the bigger and blurrier that shadow becomes. For example, in the preceding task the wider you made the shadow the closer the light source seemed to be. Using these two simple relationships in your animations will both add depth and communicate a sense of scale to the user—subconsciously.

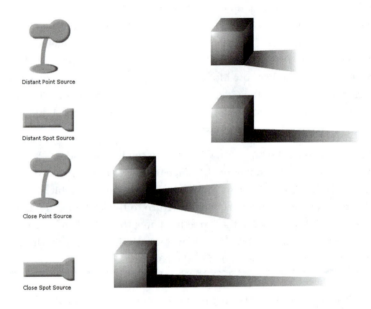

FIGURE 13.4
Understanding how light is cast will help you simulate depth.

Distant Point Source

Distant Spot Source

Close Point Source

Close Spot Source

Adding a subtle shadow can go a long way to add depth to your animations. Here's a great task that proves that.

▼ **Try It Yourself**

Add a Shadow to Show Depth and Distance

1. In a new file draw a circle near the top of the stage, select it, and convert it to a Movie Clip (F8).

2. Click frame 10 and insert a keyframe and another in frame 20. Now that frame 1 and 20 are the same, go to frame 10 and hold shift while you drag the instance of the circle down almost to the bottom of the stage.

▼

3. Select the keyframes in frame 1 and 10 (click one, hold shift, then click the other) and from the Properties panel select Motion tween. Test the movie to see the basic bouncing ball. (In Hour 22 you'll add advanced animation techniques to make this animation more realistic, but we're just looking at the shadow effect for now.)

4. Select the circle instance and copy it (you'll use it for the shadow in the next step.) Name the sole layer Circle then lock the layer and then insert a new layer for the shadow. Name that layer Shadow. You can click and drag to move the stacking order of the layers so that the Circle layer is above the Shadow layer where we're about to animate the shadow.

5. In the Shadow layer select Edit, Paste in Place (Ctrl+Shift+V) and the circle instance you just copied will appear. Move the red current frame marker to frame 10. The shadow must move to the "floor" and that must be below the circle when it hits the bottom. Hold shift and drag the circle down so it's just below the circle. Move the red current frame marker back to frame 1 to edit the way the shadow will appear at the start.

6. Back in frame 1, select the shadow and use the Free Transform tool to squash it and widen it just a tad. Use the Properties panel to set the color style to Tint, 100%, and pick the black swatch. If you have Flash Professional 8, keep the shadow selected and use the Filters panel to set a Blur. Set both the X and Y direction to 50.

7. Click the cell in frame 10 of the Shadow layer and insert a keyframe (F6). Before modifying the shadow, also insert a keyframe in frame 20. This way the first and last keyframes will match. Move the frame 10 and select the shadow. Use the Filters panel to set the Blur X and Y to a value near 40. You can use the Free Transform tool to make the shadow a little smaller.

8. Click the keyframes in frames 1 and 10 and set Motion tween. Test the movie. It's okay, but I think the shadow should be both tinted black *and* have an alpha effect. To add both, select the shadow in frame 1 and use the Properties panel to change the Color Style to Advanced. Click the Settings button that appears and change the alpha percentage from 100 down to, say 30 (or whatever looks good). Change the alpha the same for the instance in frame 30. You're welcome to change the alpha similarly for the instance in frame 10, but I'll bet it will look best with its alpha set higher.

Adding a Motion Blur

The Blur filter is great for making an out-of-focus version of an instance, but it's not so great for showing motion with direction. While you can set the X and Y Blur factors independently, the blur appears on both sides (left and right or top and bottom) in equal amounts. To show that something is both moving fast and going in a particular direction, the blur should only appear on one side—the trailing side—like a comet.

You already know that animation is a series of still images, so any motion blur you add is added to a single frame at a time. Naturally, you can tween filters so Flash does the interpolation between keyframes. The point is that any blur you add is added to a single frame at a time. (And, I should add, is used in addition to keyframes where the object appears in different locations.)

There are three general ways to add a trailing blur:

▶ Have two objects: one with the Blur filter and another on top with no blur. The blurred object can even be a different shape. Figure 13.5 shows an example.

▶ Simply use the Drop Shadow filter. Simply set the shadow color to match the object and set the direction to the position from which the object is supposed to be leaving (that is, behind the object). Figure 13.6 shows an example.

▶ Draw lines or some other custom graphic. You can make the lines long to make the object look like it's moving faster, or short to make it slower. Figure 13.7 shows an example.

FIGURE 13.5
The Blur is applied to the object underneath while the object on top is left unchanged.

plain object

blur filter
on another instance

You'll have to wait until Hour 22, "Advanced Animation Techniques," for a task that steps you through using one of these motion blur techniques (namely, the Drop Shadow). In addition, Hour 22 teaches you other ways to imply motion as well as add depth. There are so many subtle touches you can do to communicate an idea.

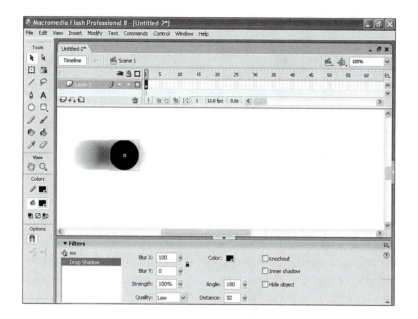

FIGURE 13.6
A Drop Shadow
filter in the
same color as
the object is a
very effective
way to show a
motion trail.

FIGURE 13.7
You might think
a few simple
lines won't
work, but simply
watch an old
cartoon frame-
by-frame and
you'll see it real-
ly does.

Masking Effects

As you should remember from Hour 11, the shapes you draw into a layer with its Layer Properties set to Mask will show through to the objects in any layer or layers directly underneath with their Layer Properties set to Masked. That is, the mask layer defines what is visible in the masked layers. One of the tasks in Hour 11 was the spotlight effect where the spotlight (the mask) moved to reveal a bright version of a skyline. To add realism you added a third layer—not masked or a mask itself, just a normal layer—containing a dim version of the skyline so that the user would see a darkened version of the skyline where the spotlight was not revealing the bright sky-line. I'm bringing this up because masking often requires you carefully plan out your layers. And, often, the important layers are the ones that aren't part of the mask! In any event, it can be tricky to work things out in your head—but I think you have to.

One of the apparant limits of masking is the fact masks are a all-or-none effect. That is, the mask is either on or off. What if you wanted the mask to have a gradient? It's actually very simple: add another (non-mask) layer on top containing a gradient. If the mask moves (as in the case of the spotlight) just move that gradient at the same rate. The next task does nearly the same thing, but this time the mask will look like a magnifier (to reveal a larger version of some text in a lower—non-masked—layer). To add realism you'll make the magnifier have a reflection like a regular lens would. That reflection will simply follow the same path as the actual mask. Check it out.

▼   **Try It Yourself**

Create a Magnifier Effect with Masking

1. In a new file draw a circle. Convert the circle to a Movie Clip named Circle. Name the sole layer Circle.

2. Insert a new layer (Insert, Timeline, Layer) and name this layer Big Text. Select the Text tool, set the font about as tall as your circle was drawn, and set the text type to Static. Click on stage and type one long word. Use the Selection tool to move the text so the circle covers the first letter in your word; then convert the block of text into a Movie Clip named MyText. Drag the Big Text layer so it's underneath the Circle layer. Set the Circle layer to Mask.

3. Because we want the mask to reveal a large version of the text, we need a small version of the text underneath everything else. Insert a new layer and name this layer Small Text. Drag that layer so it's below the other two layers. If the Small Text layer is set to masked then use Modify, Timeline, Layer Properties to set it back to Normal. (You can also click and drag the layer down to the left.) Unlock all the layers and copy an instance of the MyText symbol. Turn all the layers invisible except for the Small Text layer. Choose Edit, Paste in Place (or Ctrl+Shift+V). Select the Free Transform tool, hold shift, and resize MyText instance (in the Small Text layer) so it's about 80% of the original size.

4. Make all the layers visible and lock all the layers in order to see the masking effect as shown in Figure 13.8. The first issue is that while the large text is revealed by the mask, you can see through to the small text underneath. You only want to see through where the mask isn't. It's actually really simple to fix: the text needs an opaque background. So, open the Library and access the master version of MyText. Select the Rectangle tool, choose white for your fill color (or whatever you plan for the background color) and "no stroke." Then draw a rectangle at least as big as the block of text. Select the drawn rectangle and choose Modify, Send to Back. Go back to your main timeline and the masking effect should look good.

▼

FIGURE 13.8
You'll need the three layers oriented as shown.

5. At this point we can tween the Circle. For each layer click the cell in frame 30 and insert a frame (F5). For the Circle layer add a keyframe at frame 15 and another at frame 30. Go back to frame 15 and move the circle so that it covers (or when masking, reveals) the right most letter in your MyText instance. Set the tweening for frames 1 and 15 in the Circle layer to Motion Tween. Test the movie. The mask works fine but there's really no way to "see" the edge of the mask.

6. Go inside the master version of the Circle symbol via the Library. Select the circle and use the Color Mixer to select the default white-to-black radial gradient. With the Circle's fill selected, use the Color Mixer to edit the gradient so the white is 0% alpha (click the little arrow above the white portion and change the alpha value to 0). Test the movie again and you should see no change because the mask is either on or off.

7. Go back to your main timeline and insert another layer. Drag the new layer above all other layers. Click once on the Circle layer's name (to select all the frames), then right click on any frame in the Circle layer and select Copy Frames. Right click into frame 1 of the new (empty) layer and select Paste Frames. The new layer will probably get extended longer than all the others. In that case remove the excess frames by holding Ctrl and dragging the end frame all the way to the left.

8. Test the movie. It's pretty cool. There's one last issue you might adjust and that's if the large version of MyText doesn't seem to line up perfectly. Go to the Big Text layer and add a keyframe in frame 30. Then, in frame 1, set Motion tween. Finally, nudge the MyText instance in frame 1 and 30 (of the Big Text layer) until the magnifier effect looks best.

In the preceding task you started with large text and then scaled it down for the smaller version. It wouldn't have made any difference if you started with the small text and scaled it up because text inside Flash behaves like a vector graphic. If, on the other hand, you want to use a raster graphic in place of the MyText I would definitely recommend leaving the revealed (larger) version at 100% of its normal scale.

Then, for the smaller one, scale it down. A scaled raster graphic never looks great, but enlarging a raster graphic always looks grainy.

Before you move on to explore still another masking effect, try to ponder how the preceding magnifier task is nearly identical to the spotlight task in Hour 11. In both cases you had two layers under the mask: one with the large text (or bright buildings for the spotlight task) and one with small text (or dim buildings) that doesn't get masked at all. In the task above, there was one extra step to make the non-mask version of the Circle follow the same path as the mask version.

Next you'll get to play with a pretty cool masking trick that's actually very effective. It's a way to reveal an image using a hand-drawn effect. Basically, the mask is going to build one frame at a time, but look like someone is changing an image by painting one line at a time. I'm sure you've seen the effect before but there's still plenty of room to make it original looking.

▼ **Try It Yourself**

Create a Hand-drawn Masking Transition

1. In a new file import two photos that are the same size. Place each one at 0x 0y in its own layer. Name the layer on top End and the layer underneath Start. You'll initially see the image in the Start layer and then it will transition to the image in the End layer. Make both layers last 60 frames by clicking in frame 60 of each layer and pressing F5 (to insert a frame).

2. Insert a third layer above the other two layers, name the layer Transition. You'll do the rest of this task in this layer (so you're welcome to lock the other layers). The Transition layer should automatically last 60 frames as the other layers. Use the Brush tool to draw a small blob offstage. Click frame 20 (or whenever you want the transition to begin) and insert a blank keyframe (F6). Make sure the Brush size option is nice and large. Paint one little blob in the top left corner of the stage as Figure 13.9 shows. Now keep the Brush tool in one hand (well, your mouse) and place the other hand on the F6 key. Press F6 (which will duplicate the blob you have in frame 20). Then draw a little more to cover up the photo. You can go pretty fast because you have another 40 frames (or how ever many frames it takes you to cover the photo entirely—add frames in all three layers as needed).

3. When you're done with your frame-by-frame animation that covers the photo simply set the Transition layer to Mask; the End layer to Masked; and make sure the Start layer stays as Normal. Test the movie.

▼

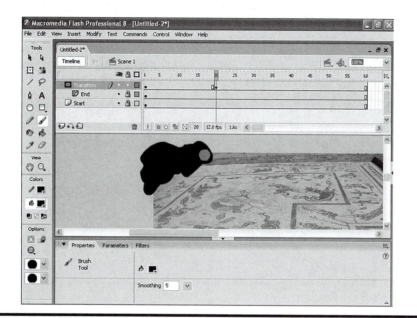

FIGURE 13.9
A blob, drawn freehand, is the start of the mask that will fully engulf the stage size to reveal a second photo (on top of the first).

The hand-painted feeling in the preceding task is not the only way to do a transition. For example, you could do a Shape tween or even just a simple Motion tween where a small circle tweens to be bigger than the entire stage. No doubt you've seen this sort of wipe in old movies. Transitions are easy: have one layer with the starting content below everything else. Then have the masked layer go from having a tiny part revealed through its mask to having it entirely revealed because the mask grows.

In case you think masking can't do much, I've included one more example. When I visualize how the layers work in the next task I think of a stencil. That is, we're going to have a gradient that does a shape tween but only reveal through a mask (the stencil).

Try It Yourself

Use a Mask As a Stencil

Perhaps you'll be more psyched if I called this task "adding an animated glow" because that's what you'll be doing. Here are the steps:

1. In a new file select the text tool, pick a large bold font, set the color to red, and set the text type to Static. Click and type a short headline. Use the Selection tool to select the block of text and convert it into a Movie Clip and name it Headline. Name the sole layer Base. Click frame 60 and insert a frame (F5). (This simply makes the rest of the layers 60 frames long.) Select the instance of Headline and copy (Ctrl+C).

2. Insert a new layer and then select Edit, Paste in Place (Ctrl+Shift+V). Name this layer Stencil and set the layer properties to Mask.

3. Insert a third layer and name this layer Glow. Arrange the layers so that Glow is in the middle (and set to masked) and Headline is at the bottom (and set to Normal) as Figure 13.10 shows. Lock all the layers except for Glow. Also, make the Stencil layer invisible.

FIGURE 13.10
You'll need the layers oriented as shown.

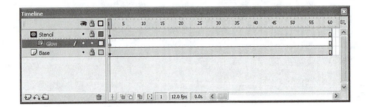

4. In the Glow layer draw a rectangle with no stroke that's slightly bigger than the entire Headline instance. Use the Color Mixer and select a linear gradient for the rectangle's fill. Edit gradient so that it has three steps: 0% alpha yellow on both ends and 100% alpha yellow in the center as shown in Figure 13.11.

FIGURE 13.11
The three-step gradient (clear-yellow-clear) will be used in the masked layer starting as a diagonal band at the top left.

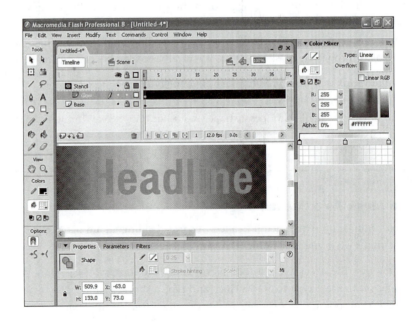

5. Use the Gradient Transform tool to rotate, move, and set the falloff so that the gradient appears as a small diagonal band over the top left of the Headline instance (also shown in Figure 13.11).

6. Select frame 20 of the Glow layer and insert a keyframe (F6). Use the Gradient Transform tool to just move the position of the gradient's center to the right— just to the right of the last letter in your Headline instance.

7. Go back and click frame 1 of the Glow layer and use the Properties panel to set Shape tween. Test the movie.

Looking back I realize many of these special effects involved text. There's no rule written that says you can't apply special effects to other shapes including logos or anything else for that matter.

Summary

Hopefully this was one of the more fun chapters—it certainly was for me. It's nice to combine the little bits of information learned and create something! The good news is there's still more to learn.

In this hour you explored a few special effects as a way to solidify and apply concepts including how shapes work, how to use Flash Professional 8's Filters, and Mask layers. Specifically, you saw how to paint with bitmaps and how to turn text into a shape in order to treat it like any other shape. When you used filters this hour it was only for specific and practical applications.

Gaining a more complete understanding of using Mask layers will ultimately prove to be the most valuable part of this hour. It's not so much the details of how the Mask layers work but rather the way you must wrap your brain around a problem and work out the layer orientation. Even if you end up using Blends instead of masking, the thought process is the same as with masking.

Q&A

Q *You showed a few fancy ways to change the fill and stroke for text once it was a shape, but can't you also effectively "fill" any shape by using the stencil mask technique?*

A Yes. You can have your pattern in the Masked layer and then the text (or any shape you want to reveal) in a Mask layer. In fact, this approach leaves open the possibility to edit the text—which is impossible once you convert text to a shape (by breaking apart twice). The only disadvantage of using masks is that you need to manage multiple layers.

Q *You finally mentioned Blends in the last sentence of the Summary. Shouldn't they be part of a chapter on special effects?*

A For sure, but these were covered in both hours 4 and 5. This chapter focused on effects that you can animate. While you can apply a Blend to any Movie Clip instance, including clips that animate, you can't tween the Blend effect. That is, Flash can't interpolate between two frames with clips that use different Blends. Having said all this, you can definitely use Blends in conjunction with any of the tasks this hour. (Though, do realize they only apply to clip instances—not text or shapes.)

Workshop

The Workshop consists of quiz questions and answers to help you solidify your understanding of the material covered in this hour. You should try to answer the questions before checking the answers.

Quiz

1. What happens when you take a Dynamic Text block containing the word "Flash" and select Modify, Break Apart?

    A. Nothing. You can only break apart Static text.

    B. The characters turn into shapes.

    C. Each character turns into an individual Dynamic Text block.

2. How do you create a 3D special effect in Flash?

    A. You can't. You either need to purchase a plugin or wait until Flash 9.

    B. Use the 3D Filter (only available in Flash Professional 8).

    C. Use any trick you can think of such as adding a shadow that suggests depth.

3. How can you make a gradient mask?

    A. You can't, but you can add an extra layer above the mask with any sort of gradient you want.

    B. You can't, but using the Invert Blend on a symbol containing a gradient is the same thing.

    C. Simply put a gradient inside the mask layer as we did in the task "Create a Magnifier Effect with Masking."

Quiz Answers

1. C. You need to select Modify, Break Apart twice to turn a text block (containing multiple characters) into a shape.

2. C. The point is that you learned 3D using an essentially 2D media, paint, a long time ago. You'll see more traditional approaches to animation in Hour 22.

3. A. Although the mask in the magnifier task did contain a gradient, it acted the same as if it were a solid. The extra layer on top is how we made the gradient portion show up.

Exercise

Try to deconstruct a small portion of any special effect you've seen on the Web—preferably in a Flash website, but that's not necessary. Break it down to small pieces. Think about it in super slow motion if that helps. And start to map out the layers and individual components needed to build it. Try to actually build it if you want, but that's almost the least important part of the exercise. Just don't start building it too early.

PART III

Adding Interactivity and Advanced Animation

HOUR 14

Making Buttons for the User to Click

What You'll Learn in This Hour:

▶ How to create simple buttons

▶ How to create multistate buttons that include a down state and an over state

▶ How to create buttons with advanced features such as animated states and sound effects

▶ How to control what area on a button is clickable

▶ How to create invisible buttons

Now that you've learned how to create basic drawings and simple animations in Flash, we can move on to what's possibly the most compelling attribute of Flash: interactivity. A plain linear animation can be quite powerful on its own. When you add interactivity, though, the users are engaged. They become part of the movie. In this hour, and the next two, you'll learn how to add interactivity to movies.

The most straightforward way to add interactivity is by adding buttons. This way, users can click buttons when they feel like interacting—maybe they want to stop and start an animation at will. Or maybe you would like them to be able to skip ahead past an intro-duction animation.

Flash makes it easy to create very sophisticated buttons using any shape. In addition, it's easy to add visual enhancements, including animation and sound effects. This hour you'll learn how to create the visual elements of buttons. Then, in Hours 15, "Using ActionScript and Behaviors to Create Nonlinear Movies," and 16, "Using ActionScript for Advanced Interactivty," you'll start making the buttons do things.

Button States

Button states are simply the different visual versions of a button as a user interacts. For example, all the dialog boxes that appear in Flash contain an OK button. That button has a **down state**—what it looks like when a user clicks it—that is slightly different (visually) from the normal **up state** for the button. The buttons that you create in Flash can also have a down state. Actually, you can also easily create an **over state**, which is the visual look of the button while the user puts his cursor over it. For example, all the buttons in the Tools panel in Flash have an over state that looks like a raised box. You'll learn to create this kind of effect in this hour.

Making a Button

Any time you create a new symbol, you must specify the behavior as a Movie Clip, Button, or Graphic. So far you've only chosen Graphic or Movie Clip. Creating a button is actually no more difficult than selecting Button as the behavior. The following task looks at creating a button in more detail.

▼ **Try It Yourself**

Make a Super Simple Button

In this task you'll make the simplest button possible:

1. In a new file, draw an oval or a rectangle that will become your button.

2. Use the Selection tool to select the entire shape.

3. Convert the shape to a symbol by selecting Modify, Convert to Symbol (or pressing F8).

4. Name the symbol MyButton, make sure that you select the Button behavior, and then click OK.

5. Test your movie (by using Control, Test Movie or pressing Ctrl+Enter) and notice the way your mouse cursor changes when you place it over the button (as shown in Figure 14.1).

6. Save this file because you'll add to it in the next task.

FIGURE 14.1
Any shape can be used as a button. The user's cursor changes to a hand when it's over the shape.

Enabling Simple Buttons

It's actually possible to preview buttons without testing a movie. To do this, you select Control, Enable Simple Buttons. However, this feature is more trouble than it's worth. You have to turn it off in order to modify your button (if you want to click to select it you don't want it behaving like a button). The best way to "see" the button is to use Test Movie.

Making a button looks easy, doesn't it? Even though you did make a button in the preceding task, it probably falls short of your expectations in two general ways: It doesn't look like a button (with various states) and it doesn't act like a button (causing something to happen when it's clicked). We'll address the issue of making the button *do* something in Hour 15. For now, though, you can complete the following task to make the simple button look better by adding an over state and a down state.

Try It Yourself

Add Multiple States to a Simple Button

In this task you'll refine the simple button you made earlier this hour:

1. In the file that contains the MyButton symbol you created in the previous task, double-click the instance of the button, and you are taken into the master version of the symbol. If you're having trouble clicking the button because you keep getting the hand cursor every time you go over the button, select the Control menu and make sure that the menu item Enable Simple Buttons does not have a check mark next to it.

   Now that you're in the master version of the MyButton symbol, you should notice that this symbol has only four frames—and instead of being numbered, they're named Up, Over, Down, and Hit (see Figure 14.2). They are still four frames—they just all have names. Into each frame, you'll draw how we want the button to appear for various states. The up state already contains how the button looks normally.

The Four States

The up state contains the visual look of the button in its normal state. Over contains the look for when the user hovers his cursor over the button. Down is when the user clicks. Hit is a special state in which you place a visual representation of what portion of the button you intend to be clickable. This is what the user must "hit" in order to see the over and down states.

FIGURE 14.2
Inside the button symbol are four named frames.

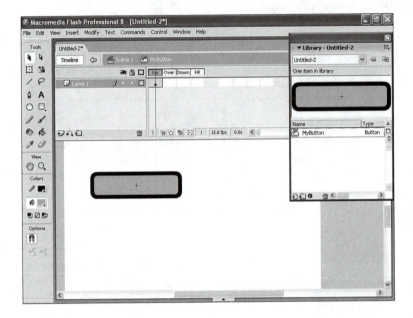

2. In the Over frame, draw how the button will look when the user's cursor hovers over it. To do this, insert a keyframe into the second frame of the button by clicking in the Timeline under Over and pressing F6 or selecting Insert, Timeline, Keyframe. Select the Paint Bucket tool and a color similar to but slightly lighter than the color currently filling the rectangle shape. Fill the shape in the Over frame with the lighter color.

3. Insert a keyframe in the Down frame by clicking in the Timeline under Down and pressing F6 or selecting Insert, Timeline, Keyframe.

4. Select the entire contents of the Down frame and—using the arrow keys on your keyboard—nudge the shape down and to the right three pixels (click three times with the right arrow and three times with the down arrow).

5. You're done editing the master button, so get back into the main scene (either by clicking Scene 1 at the top left of the Timeline or by pressing Ctrl+E) and test the movie by selecting Control, Test Movie.

This task proves you can create a pretty advanced button with very little effort. The various states contain the graphics for how the button will look in different situations: Up is the button's normal state, over is when the user passes the cursor over the button, and down is when the user presses the button. In the preceding task you had the states change just the color and location of the graphic, but you can put anything you want in each state (and you will later this hour).

Defining a Button's Hit State

In the preceding task you saw that there are four states. In addition to up, over, and down, there's one called hit. The hit state is never visibly seen by the user. It defines where the user must position her cursor to show a button's over state or where she must click to see the button's down state. Imagine that you had a doughnut-shaped button. If you didn't set a hit state, the user wouldn't be allowed to click anywhere in the hole (similar to Figure 14.3). However, if you inserted a keyframe and drew a solid circle (no doughnut hole) in the Hit frame, the user could click anywhere within the solid circle. This can also be useful when you want a small button but you don't want to frustrate the user by requiring her to have the precision of a surgeon. I say, "give them a break," and make the hit state big enough to easily click even if that means that it's bigger than the button itself. You can practice this in the following task.

Hit State Is Always Present

The first four frames of a button are used, regardless of whether you place keyframes (or even frames) into all four of them. Compare this to a normal Timeline in which you insert only two frames. By the time the playback head reaches Frame 3 or beyond, you don't see anything on the Stage. However, buttons break this fundamental concept by effectively inserting frames (not keyframes) in all four frames—at least that's a good way to think about it. Therefore, if you draw only into Frame 1, that image will remain as the visual element for all four frames (Up, Over, Down, and Hit).

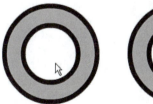

FIGURE 14.3
Changing the shape contents of a button's hit state affects what portion is clickable.

Try It Yourself

Make a Button with an Extra Large Hit State

In this task you'll create a large hit state so the button is easy to click:

1. In a new file, use the Text tool to draw the word *Home*. Because this text will appear inside a button, use the Properties panel to ensure the Selectable option is not selected as shown in Figure 14.4. Because this text is not going to change, also set the Type to Static Text.

FIGURE 14.4
Text appearing in buttons should always be unselectable. For this exercise, you'll also want to use Static text.

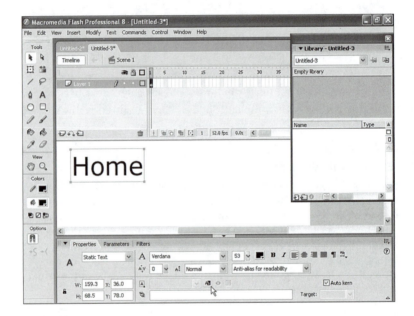

2. Using the Selection tool, select the text block you just created and convert it into a symbol (by pressing F8 or selecting Modify, Convert to Symbol). Name it Home Button, make sure that you select Button behavior, and then click OK.

3. Test the movie (by selecting Control, Test Movie) and notice how the button is sensitive to where you move your cursor. You see the hand cursor only when you're exactly on top of the text. Back in the file, you can fix this by creating a larger hit state for the button.

4. Double-click the button so you can edit the master button. Inside our button, insert a keyframe in the Hit frame by clicking in the Hit frame and pressing F6 or selecting Insert, Timeline, Keyframe. Realize that the Home text in the Hit frame is just a copy of text in the Up frame; inserting a keyframe copies the contents of the other frame.

5. While in the Hit frame, use the Oval tool to draw a filled oval that's slightly larger than the text. When you have your oval, you can delete the text (from only the Hit frame). (After you draw the hit state, you can delete the Home text because the user never actually sees anything that's in the Hit frame.)

6. Test the movie now by selecting Control, Test Movie or pressing Ctrl+Enter, and you see that the button gives the user a break because it's much easier to click.

For the button in the preceding task, you used a hit state to create a larger area for the user to click. Often you can forgo creating a hit state, and the button's solid areas will define the clickable (or "hot") area. Just remember that without a hit state, the closest keyframe to the left of the Hit frame will define what's hot—that is, the graphics in the down state.

Minimizing a Button's Impact on File Size

Regardless of how fast everyone's Internet connections are getting, there's no excuse for a file that's bigger than it has to be. And just because you're creating buttons this hour doesn't mean that you can ignore file size considerations. For example, in the previous task, I instructed you to insert three keyframes and use the Paint Bucket to color the shape in each differently. I didn't want to diverge from the main task, but hopefully you were thinking, "Hey, if all we're doing is changing the color or location, we should be using symbols instead of a new shape in each keyframe."

Using Symbols Inside Buttons

Although most people understand why symbols are useful and important, many don't use symbols as much as possible. For example, if a multistate button has three nearly identical keyframes, the contents of each keyframe are duplicated. This isn't a problem if you use instances of a symbol on each frame. People often mistakenly think that because a button is a symbol, editing its contents will take full advantage of symbols. You need to consider using symbols while you're inside symbols. Anytime you copy and paste (which happens when you insert a keyframe), you should consider using symbols, even if you happen to be editing a symbol's contents.

Did you Know?

In the following task you can try creating a multistate button again—this time using the symbols in each state instead of new shapes.

▼

Try It Yourself

Remake a Multistate Button by Using Symbols in Each State

Start this task from scratch, by following these steps:

1. In a new file, draw a rectangle with no stroke. This will become your button.

2. Use the Selection tool to select the entire rectangle you just drew. Convert the oval into a symbol by selecting Modify, Convert to Symbol or pressing F8. Name it MyButton, make sure that the behavior is Button, and then click OK.

3. Next, you need to edit the master version of the button you just created. Double-click the instance of the button and you are taken inside the master version. Inside the master button, you should see the shape you drew. Notice that it's not a symbol—it's a shape or Drawing Object. After all, you just told Flash to convert the shape into a symbol, so inside the symbol you have a shape. This will be an issue if you start adding keyframes inside the button.

4. To be totally efficient, convert the rectangle shape itself to a symbol before you add any more keyframes. Select the entire shape, select Modify, Convert to Symbol, name the symbol Rectangle, be sure to select the Movie Clip behavior (it will be Button by default because that's the last symbol type you made—this exercise won't work if you put a button inside a button), and then click OK. If you have Flash Professional 8 select the rectangle clip you just created and use the Filters panel to apply a Bevel filter.

5. Now that the first keyframe contains an instance of the Rectangle movie clip, insert a keyframe in the Over frame. For Flash Professional 8 users add a Glow Filter (in addition to the Bevel already on the instance). If you only have Flash Basic 8, simply Tint the Rectangle instance by selecting the Rectangle and from the Properties panel choosing Tint in the Color Styles drop-down list.

6. Insert a keyframe in the Down frame. Flash copies the contents of the previous frame. Next you can modify the Bevel that's already been applied (each new keyframe just copies the instance from the previous frame). Change the value for Angle from 45 to 225. If you have Flash Basic 8 simply nudge the tinted instance of Rectangle in the Over frame down and to the right.

7. Go back to the main scene and test your movie. It should look like Figure 14.5, and the file size should remain small because you did it all with just one shape.

▼

FIGURE 14.5
A visual change occurs in the three states of the button.

Hopefully, you're beginning to get excited about the power you have to create buttons. Even the quick-and-dirty buttons you're making in this hour's tasks are looking pretty good. Add the Filters in Flash 8 Professional and you've really got some major power.

We're *still* going to wait until next hour to make the buttons do anything when they're pressed. In the meantime, you'll see that there's lots more you can do with buttons.

Advanced Buttons

If you think the buttons you've been making are exciting, just wait. You're about to make some very sophisticated buttons, and you'll have a chance to apply both your new knowledge of basic buttons and a little of what you've learned about animation from previous hours.

Animated Buttons

Creating an animated button in Flash is easier than you might imagine. Do you want a button that is animating at all times? or one that just animates when the cursor passes over? How about both? You can do anything you want; as you'll see in the next task, you just put an animated movie clip in the appropriate states of the button. That's it.

Try It Yourself

Create an Animated Button

In this task you'll create a button that animates when the user rolls over it:

1. In a new file, use the Text tool to type the word Home on the Stage (make it fairly large). Select the text with the Selection tool, convert it to a symbol (by selecting Modify, Convert to Symbol), name it Plain Text, be certain to select the Movie Clip behavior (chances are good it's still defaulting to Button from an earlier task), and then click OK. You will use this symbol extensively.

2. The text onscreen is an instance of the Plain Text symbol, and now you can create a Movie Clip symbol that animates the Plain Text symbol on the Stage. With the Plain Text symbol selected, select Modify, Convert to Symbol, name the symbol Animating Text, select the Movie Clip behavior, and then click OK.

3. Now you can edit the Animating Text symbol. Access the contents of this symbol by double-clicking. Make sure you're in the Animating Text symbol before you do anything else (look at the edit bar to make sure).

4. Inside the master Animating Text symbol, insert a keyframe at Frame 30 and one at Frame 15. (Create Frame 30 before you change the instance at Frame 15—so it ends in the same location as where it starts.) Scale the Plain Text symbol instance in Frame 15 so that it's noticeably larger. Go back and set tweening in Frame 1 and Frame 15 to Motion (by right-clicking each keyframe, individually, and selecting Create Motion Tween). Scrub the Timeline to get a feel for the animation.

5. Go back to the main scene (by clicking Scene 1 at the top left of the Timeline or pressing Ctrl+E). Delete everything on the Stage (by selecting Edit, Select All, and then selecting Edit, Clear—or better yet, by pressing Ctrl+A and then pressing Delete). You're not deleting any symbols; they're both safe in the Library. Open the Library by selecting Window, Library or pressing Ctrl+L. Drag an instance of the Plain Text symbol onto the Stage.

6. Now you're ready to create your button. Once again, with the Plain Text symbol selected, convert it to a symbol (by selecting Modify, Convert to Symbol), name it Animating Button, select the Button behavior, and then click OK. By converting the existing Plain Text symbol into the Animating Button symbol, you're using an instance of a symbol to create the button.

7. Now you can edit your button and make it animate. Double-click the Animating Button symbol instance on the Stage; you're taken inside the button—which you can confirm already has an instance of the Plain Text symbol in Frame 1.

8. Next, you will place an instance of the Animating Text movie clip in the button's over state (Frame 2). You could drag it from the Library and align it to the Plain Text instance in the up state. However, you're going to do it another way that won't require any manual alignment. Insert a keyframe into the over state (by pressing F6). This copies everything from the Up frame (an instance of the Plain Text symbol).

9. In the Over frame of the button, access the Properties panel and select the Plain Text instance on the Stage). Click the Swap button in the Properties panel, and the Swap Symbol dialog box appears (see Figure 14.6).

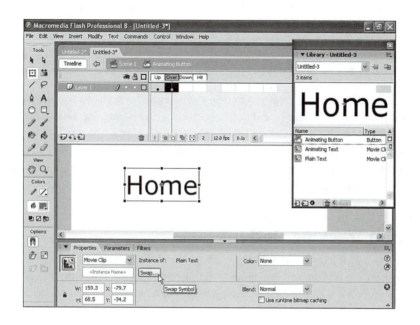

FIGURE 14.6
You can swap
the symbol to
which an
instance is
linked without
changing any
other properties
(such as posi-
tion) of the
instance.

10. The Swap Symbol dialog box shows all the symbols in your Library and a dot
next to the one the current instance is linked to (see Figure 14.7). Click
Animating Text and then click OK. You've now swapped the instance (previously Plain Text). You should see that the name of the current symbol listed in
the Properties panel (next to Instance of:) has changed.

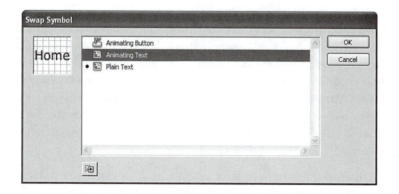

FIGURE 14.7
In the Swap
Symbol dialog
box you can
select a differ-
ent symbol.

11. The button is lacking a nice large hit state. It has a hit state, but it's kind of a
moving target and difficult to access. In the master version of the button's Hit
frame, insert a keyframe and draw an oval that is at least as big as the word

Home. After you draw the oval, delete the instance of Animating Text that was automatically placed in the Hit frame when you inserted the keyframe; it's not necessary. (Note that you could have used Onion Skin tools to align the oval to the text in the previous frame.)

In the preceding task you created a button that uses a movie clip in its over state. However, instead of creating from the "top down" (that is, making the button and then putting a movie clip in the button), you did it from the "specific to the general" (or from "inside out"). First you created a symbol with text (Plain Text). Then you animated Plain Text in the movie clip you named Animating Text. Finally, you created the button and used the Plain Text symbol in the Up frame and the Animating Text symbol in the Over frame.

Button Tracking Options

A button's tracking option is a subtle attribute that gives you additional control over exactly how the button acts. In Figure 14.8 notice that in the Properties panel, while any button is selected, there's a choice between Track as Button (the default) and Track as Menu Item.

FIGURE 14.8
The Properties panel lets you specify whether a button will track as a button or as a menu item.

The easiest way to understand tracking is to have more than one button and make sure the buttons have over states that are visually different from their up states. (You could have several instances of the same button.) If you leave them all with the default setting Track as Button, when testing the movie, you can click and hold one of the buttons, and you won't be able to access any other button while you keep the mouse down. Many Flash buttons work this way. For example, if you click a button and keep the mouse pressed while you roll over other buttons, only the one that you clicked initially will be affected. This is the action caused by the default setting Track as Button.

Now, if you set several buttons to Track as Menu Item and test again, you'll see that even if you've started to click one button, if you hold your mouse down and roll over other buttons, they will react (and register if you let go). This is similar to regular menus: When you click and hold and then move up and down, you're able to let go on any item in the menu.

The difference between these options is very subtle, but you should realize that they're available. It comes up if you design several button from which a user is likely to click, hold, and move their mouse to the preferred button before letting go (in which case you should select Track as Menu Item). Usually the default Track as Button is fine.

Sounds in Buttons

The simplest way to associate a sound with a button is to place that sound in a keyframe within the button. For a sound to occur when the user's cursor goes over a button, just put a sound in the over state. Fancier effects can get more complicated. For example, making a sound loop *while* the user's cursor is over the button takes a few more steps. Ultimately, however, to create complicated sounds and effects, you need to learn about ActionScript, covered in Hour 15 and expanded on in Hour 16. For now, we'll cover two basic forms of sounds in buttons: simple sound effects in the over state and looping sounds within a button.

Try It Yourself ▼

Create a Button with a Rollover Sound Effect

In this task you'll make a button that plays a sound when the user rolls over it:

1. In a new file, draw a rectangle shape, convert it into a symbol (by selecting Modify, Convert to Symbol or pressing F8), name it Audio Button, select the Button behavior, and click OK.

2. Double-click the instance so you can edit the master button.

3. Inside the master version of the button, you can concern yourself with the over state (where you'll include a sound). Of course you need a new keyframe in the over state because sounds are only placed in keyframes. However, before you insert a keyframe (which, if inserted now, would copy the shape from the Up frame), you need to convert the shape in the Up frame to a movie clip by selecting it all, selecting Modify, Convert to Symbol, naming it Shape of Button, selecting the Movie Clip behavior, and clicking OK. (Be sure to choose Movie Clip because Button is the default after step 1.)

4. Insert a keyframe in the Over frame. (You can tint Shape of Button or scale it if you want a visual effect when the user rolls over the button.) Then, with the Over frame selected, access the Properties panel. Notice that you don't see any sounds listed in the Sound drop-down list because you haven't imported any (see Hour 11).

▼

5. Either import a short sound from a file or use one included in the keyframing. fla file (downloaded from www.phillipkerman.com/teachyourself/sourcefiles). There are several ways to take an audio file out of one Flash file into another. Keep open the file you're working on for this task then open the keyframing.fla file. Open the Library (by selecting Window, Library or pressing Ctrl+L). Press the New Library Window button (at the top of the Library) then select the other file name (perhaps "Untitled-1" if you haven't saved yet). With both Libraries open drag the Breaker Switch sound item into your file's Library. Now select the Over frame and use the Properties panel to select Breaker Switch (because it's been imported into your file), as shown in Figure 14.9.

FIGURE 14.9
On the over state of the button, you specify a sound to play.

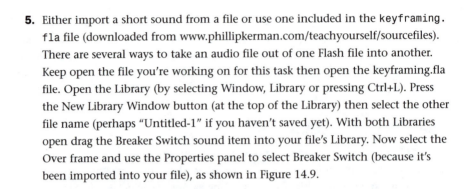
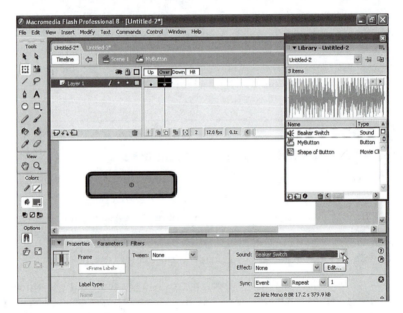

6. Test the movie to see (and hear) if it works.

7. Save this file because you'll use it in the next task.

That task wasn't so bad. Just put a sound in the keyframe of the over state of a button! In the preceding task you used the Breaker Switch sound in particular for two reasons. First, it saved you the hassle of finding a sound. Also, it is a short sound. Had you chosen a longer sound, such as Beam Scan, you might have noticed that there's enough time to roll over the button, roll off, and roll back on quickly, which causes a layering effect on the sound that is not exactly pleasant. You can fix that by changing the Properties panel's Sync setting to Start (as you did in Hour 10, "Including Sound in Animations").

You'll see how a long sound (or worse, one that loops forever) requires such additional consideration in the next task. Generally, I suggest that incidental sound effects—such as rollover sounds—be very short so that they don't become tiresome for users. A gratuitous sound effect that's cute the first time can become really annoying when it repeats.

Try It Yourself ▼

Create a Button with Looping Sound

In this task you'll make a sound loop while the mouse is over a button:

1. Edit the master button you created in the previous task. If you aren't already inside the master button, double-click the instance of the button.

2. Select the keyframe in the over state. Change the Repeat drop-down list to Loop. (See Hour 10 for more information on this.)

3. Test the movie. There are some problems. The sound Breaker Switch doesn't loop well. However, that's the least of the problems—and one that could easily be rectified with an alternative sound. The serious problems that we'll address are (1) the sound will layer on top of itself every time you roll off and then roll back on the button and (2) when the sound starts, it never stops.

4. You might recall from Hour 10 that three other Sync settings exist besides the default Event. In this case, you want the sound in the over state to start playing only if it isn't already playing. In the master Button symbol, set the Sync setting for the sound in the Over frame of the button to Start (that is, while the frame is selected, use the Properties panel to select Start from the Sync drop-down list). Test the movie again, and you see that you fixed the problem of the sound starting again after it has already started.

5. The sound still continues forever once started. The opportune time to stop the sound is when the user rolls off the button—the up state. There happens to be a behavior called Stop All Sounds, but what if you want other sounds to continue playing? You only need the particular sound that's looping to stop. In the up state's keyframe, add the same sound. But this time, select the Stop setting in the Sync drop-down list, to cause only that particular sound to stop. To do this, select the first keyframe (in the up state), and then in the Properties panel, select the same sound you're using in the over state (Breaker Switch) from the drop-down list of sounds available, and set the Sync drop-down list to Stop.

6. Test the movie, and it should work. ▲

Invisible Buttons

Invisible buttons are very useful. They're easy to make, too, as you'll see in the next task. You'll create an invisible button, and Flash will let you (the author) see the invisible button as semi-transparent cyan; the user won't see anything.

It might seem useless to make a button the user can't see, but it's actually quite useful. The only trick is that you'll probably want to place the invisible button on top of something visual. For example, what if you had a map on which you wanted the user to be able to click specific areas (maybe cities) and learn more about the one she clicked? All you would need is one big picture of the map and lots of invisible buttons placed in key locations. This would be more practical than cutting the map into little pieces and making buttons out of each piece.

▼ Try It Yourself

Make an Invisible Button

In this task you will create and use an invisible button:

1. Select Insert, New Symbol, name the symbol Invisible, select the Button behavior, and then click OK. This takes you to the master version of the symbol you're creating. Flash expects you to draw something here in the master version of the Invisible button symbol.

2. Leave all the frames of the button blank, but in the Hit frame insert a keyframe. (Because the previous keyframe is blank, this is the same as inserting a blank keyframe.)

3. Draw a circle around the center (the plus) in the Hit frame. (To center it, you can draw a circle and then cut and paste or use the Info panel to set the center to 0,0.) Your button's Timeline should resemble the one in Figure 14.10.

4. Go back to your main scene and drag an instance of this Invisible button from the Library to the Stage. Check it out; it's cyan. Test the movie, and you see nothing (except that your cursor changes when it reaches the button's location).

5. In the main scene, draw a large box and then a few circles in different locations on the box (as shown in Figure 14.11). Imagine that this box is a large map and each circle indicates a city. Then drag an invisible button from the Library for each circle you drew. Line up the buttons and scale them appropriately to cover each circle.

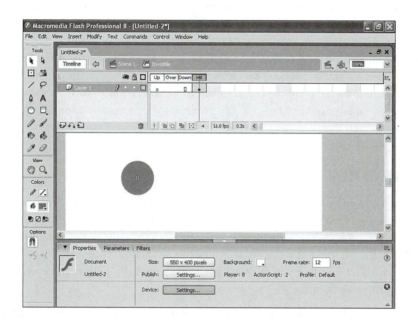

FIGURE 14.10
An invisible button looks like this—nothing in any frame except the Hit frame.

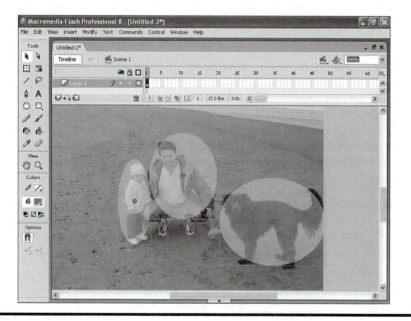

FIGURE 14.11
Invisible buttons can be placed on top of any drawing.

For something you can't even see, invisible buttons are actually quite powerful. It's safe to say I've never done a project without them. Their main advantage is they keep the visual elements separate from the button's functionality. You can place invisible buttons on top of anything to effectively create a button the user can see and click. In Hour 23, "Working on Large Projects and in Team Environments," you'll learn how such code–data separation can make you more efficient. For now, just realize that invisible buttons (or any buttons, for that matter) don't do anything until you attach behaviors or ActionScript to them.

Summary

Now you should understand how to create buttons from any shape in Flash. In this hour you also learned how to make a button change visually when the user's cursor rolls over or clicks it. You learned how to control exactly what part of the button is clickable (the hit state) as well as how to make an animated button. Not only did you learn visual stuff, but you learned how to put sounds in buttons and even how to make invisible buttons.

You should be able to apply many of your animation skills to make compelling buttons. However, you've only learned the first half—how to make the buttons *look* cool. In the next hour you'll embark on making the buttons function—making them do things by attaching behaviors.

Q&A

Q *I accidentally dragged a movie clip to the Stage and used the Properties panel to change it to Button behavior. Now my movie clip doesn't play, and it kind of works like a button. (There's an over state, and a hand cursor appears when the user moves his mouse over the button.) What's up with that?*

A Remember that the fact that the master version of a symbol is a movie clip (or any other symbol behavior) doesn't prevent you from changing the behavior of individual instances on the Stage. If you change an instance that has the Movie Clip behavior to Button behavior, the first frame of the movie clip acts as the up state, the second frame is the over state, the third is the down state, and the fourth is the hit state. You won't see the labels in the master version of a symbol unless the default property of that symbol was Button in the first place (or if you change the properties of the master symbol by way of the Library's Options menu). (There's more information about this in Hour 4, "Using the Library for Productivity.")

Q *My buttons aren't working when I click Play. Why?*

A If you haven't learned it already, forget about using Play to really see what the user will see. Use Control, Test Movie. Alternatively, you can turn on Enable Simple Buttons in the Control menu; however, this is a pain because you must turn that option off before you can click to edit a button instance. (With the option on, the button will act like a button, not like an instance on which you can click.) Finally, the feature refers to "simple" buttons, meaning that more complex ones won't work. So you should just use Test Movie.

Q *I noticed in my Components panel there are already a few buttons available, why are we bothering making them from scratch?*

A Those components are very useful and, in fact, you'll learn how to use them in Hour 17, "Using Components." They're very consistent but can tend to look almost too commonplace. You can customize them, but that almost always takes more work than just making a custom button. Both types of buttons (components and the homemade type you made this hour) have value.

Q *I swear I followed the directions, but some of these exercises are just not working. What's a likely cause?*

A The biggest oversight I've seen is accidentally putting buttons inside buttons—which won't work. When you're trying to be efficient by using symbols inside the different states of a button, make sure you're selecting the Movie Clip behavior.

Q *The invisible button isn't quite "invisible" because the user's cursor changes. What can I do if I want to really hide a button?*

A There's a property that, provided you write a script, will turn off the hand cursor for a button. You'll learn more about ActionScript in the next hour, but for now let me show you how to turn off the hand cursor for a single button:

1. Give the button instance an instance name via the Properties panel. Say, "myButton."

2. Put this script in the first keyframe where the button appears:
   ```
   myButton.useHandCursor=false;
   ```

   To turn off the cursor on all buttons put this script in the first keyframe of your movie:
   ```
   Button.prototype.useHandCursor=false;
   ```

Workshop

The Workshop consists of quiz questions and answers to help you solidify your understanding of the material covered in this hour. You should try to answer the questions before checking the answers.

Quiz

1. How many frames can appear to animate when you roll over a button?

    A. It depends on how many keyframes are in the button.

    B. No more than four frames.

    C. As many as you want because you use a movie clip.

2. Can I have a different sound in two different instances of one button?

    A. No.

    B. Yes.

    C. It depends on whether the sound loops—for looping sound, yes; for nonlooping sound, no.

3. What happens if a button has no graphics in any state except the hit state?

    A. It won't work.

    B. You'll have an invisible button.

    C. Flash will crash.

Quiz Answers

1. C. Although in the master button itself you only have the space of one frame for each state, in each frame you can place a multiframe movie clip (of any length) and, like all movie clips, it will play on its own.

2. A. If you put a sound in the master version of a button, that sound will be heard in each instance of the original button. However, if all the visual contents of buttons are instances of other symbols, you can have two master buttons without affecting file size negatively. That way, you can have a different sound in each master button. (Of course, two different sounds will add to file size.)

3. B. That's how you make invisible buttons.

HOUR 15

Using ActionScript and Behaviors to Create Nonlinear Movies

What You'll Learn in This Hour:

▶ How to put scripts in keyframes and on objects such as buttons

▶ How to edit ActionScript to make it do exactly what you want

▶ How to apply behaviors and modify them to suit your needs

Flash's programming language is called **ActionScript**. Like any programming language, ActionScript lets you write instructions that your movie will follow. Without ActionScript, your movie will play the same way every time. If you want the user to be able to stop and start the movie, for example, you need ActionScript. In addition, Flash includes **behaviors** which are snippets of ActionScript that you can add without needing to know all the details behind the code. It turns out that, even with behaviors, you can do much more if you invest just a little bit of time learning ActionScript. Last hour you learned how to create buttons. This hour you'll learn how to attach ActionScript to those buttons so that something happens when the user clicks a button.

The topic of scripting is very deep. We won't cover it all this hour. Rather, we'll cover the basic concept as well as look at typical applications for scripting. This way, you'll build a good foundation on which to grow at your own pace.

Using ActionScript

Scripting is nothing more than writing instructions. Each instruction tells Flash to do something very specific. For example, "play," "stop," or "set that movie clip's alpha to 50%." By keeping each piece of ActionScript very specific, you can easily piece together more advanced instructions. But at the core, each "sentence" (or line of code) is a single instruction.

All your ActionScript is typed into the Actions panel. Open the Actions panel and follow along as we explore. Select Window, Development Panels, Actions (or press F9). Take a quick look at Figure 15.1, and then we'll cover a few more details before you do a few exercises.

FIGURE 15.1
The Actions panel has several components.

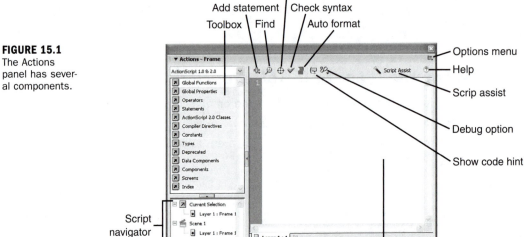

The Actions panel has the following features:

▶ **Toolbox**—The Toolbox list provides access to all installed actions. It is organized like folders.

▶ **Script Category**—simply narrows the actions listed in the toolbox to ActionScript 1.0 & 2.0 or one of the two FlashLite versions (for delivering Flash to various mobile devices such as cell phones). Leave this on the default ActionScript 1.0 & 2.0.

▶ **Script pane**—In the Script pane, your actions will appear in order of execution.

▶ **Navigator pane**—In the script navigation pane, you can see all the scripts in your movie.

▶ **Current Script tab**—The Current Script tab indicates which script is currently being edited. Figure 15.1 indicates that the script is for Layer 1. Compare this to how the Properties panel shows you the currently selected instance.

▶ **Pin Script**—The Pin Scrip button adds a tab for a particular script so that you don't have to first select the object or layer into which you want to add a script. Normally, the Actions panel acts like other panels—always reflecting the settings for the currently selected item (in this case, the script for the selected keyframe or object, such as a button).

▶ **Script Assist**—When the Script Assist button is pressed you no longer type free-style into the script pane, but rather you make selections from options that will appear above the script pane (for example, as Figure 15.7 shows). This is the return of "Normal Mode" last seen in Flash MX (version 6). Script Assist ensures your scripts are free of syntax errors.

▶ **Options menu**—The options menu (as on any panel) contains additional settings. Preferences such as script font typeface are available.

▶ **Help button**—The Help button (also known as the Reference button) provides online help with any selected piece of ActionScript.

▶ **Options toolbar**—The Options toolbar includes the following buttons:

> ▶ **Add Statement**—This button, which I call the "plus button" throughout the rest of this book, pops up a menu that provides the same script elements found in the Toolbox. The menu also shows the key combination for each script that has one (see the later tip).
>
> ▶ **Find**—This button let you search scripts (and optionally replace parts) as you would in a word processing program.
>
> ▶ **Insert Target** Path—This button helps you address specific objects, such as particular clips. You'll learn that scripts can apply to individual clips (say you want to play or stop just one clip—you have to target that particular clip). This button helps you specify a target clip.
>
> ▶ **Check Syntax**—This button checks that your ActionScript has no syntax errors and displays details (in the Output panel) if not. (This won't guarantee that the movie will behave as you had in mind—only that you have no show-stopping errors.)
>
> ▶ **Auto Format**—This button cleans up your code by adding indentation where appropriate. This makes it much easier to read.

▶ **Show Code Hint**—This button re-triggers the code-completion helper that appears as a ToolTip to help you complete ActionScript (when Flash knows what you're about to type).

▶ **Debug Options**—This button lets you add and remove **breakpoints** where you purposefully make Flash pause on a specified line of code so that you can investigate how it's playing (or, most likely, not playing the way you expected). You can also add and remove breakpoints by clicking in the gutter to the left of any line of code. You'll see a red dot appear to the left of the line of code.

Keyboard Shortcuts for Actions

In the Actions panel under the Add Statement (+) button, you'll find key combinations such as Esc+go. This means the action can be inserted by simply pressing the following keys in sequence (not at the same time): Esc, go. If you find yourself inserting the same action repeatedly, you might use this method instead because it's quicker than typing the code manually.

Syntax is unique to each programming language. Every piece of ActionScript has a very specific syntax that must be followed. As an analogy, consider how every email address has to have the form name@domain.com or it won't work. Flash has no mercy for invalid syntax—you'll see errors appear in the Output panel until you resolve the errors. Even after you perfect the script, the movie may not play exactly as you had in mind but syntax errors are show-stoppers because you must correct them. Luckily, there are plenty of ways to ensure that your scripts have perfect syntax.

You can easily add an action from the Toolbox by double-clicking or dragging it to the right side of the Actions panel (the Script pane). You can build a complex set of instructions, one line at a time. A **statement** is a code sentence that uses only words from the ActionScript language.

Again, **actions** are instructions. Flash will follow each line of code in sequence. Some actions are complete pieces of instruction, with no additional modifications on your part. For example, you can add a stop action, and when Flash encounters it, the playback head will stop advancing. However, many actions require that you provide additional details (called *parameters*). For example, an action such as gotoAndPlay requires that you provide the additional detail about what frame number or frame label you want to go to.

Specifying Actions by Using Parameters

Now you can try out actions and parameters. You'll see that some actions are quite simple. In the following task is a quick exercise that uses actions and parameters. After you complete it, we'll step back to analyze what you did in the task.

Try It Yourself ▼

Make an Action That Loops Part of Your Movie

In this task you'll make the last few frames of an animation loop. Here are the steps:

1. In a new file, use the Text tool to create a text block containing the word *Welcome*. Make sure the text type is Static. Select the block and convert it to a symbol. Make it a movie clip and name it Welcome Text.

2. Position the movie clip instance in the center of the screen, and insert one keyframe at Frame 20 and another at Frame 30.

3. Move the current-frame marker to Frame 1 and move Welcome Text all the way off the Stage to the left. Set motion tweening for both Frame 1 and Frame 20. In Frame 20, use the Properties panel to make the tween rotate one time clockwise (CW) on its way from Frame 20 to Frame 30. See Hour 8, "Using Motion Tweens to Animate," for a review of this. Test the movie. Notice that the whole movie loops over and over. Instead of leaving the animation as is, you're going to make the rotation part (from Frame 20 to Frame 30) loop forever.

4. You can add actions to any keyframe, but instead of mixing scripts with your animation, you can just make a whole new layer exclusively for actions. Name the single layer you currently have `Animation` and then choose Insert, Layer and name the new layer `Actions`. Make sure the current layer is Actions (you'll see a pencil in the layer). Select Frame 30 in your Actions layer, insert a keyframe (by pressing F6), and then access the Actions panel (by pressing F9). Make sure Frame 30 remains selected when you edit the Actions panel by noting that the tab reads "Actions:30" and has the keyframe icon (as shown in Figure 15.2). This confirms the script you're about to write will execute when the playback head reaches Frame 30.

▼

FIGURE 15.2
The Actions panel is opened right after Frame 30 is selected so that you can set an action to execute when the playback head reaches that frame.

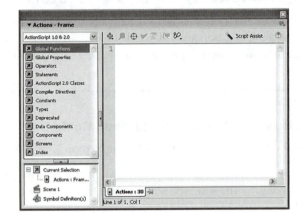

5. To insert a `gotoAndPlay` action, select Global Functions, Timeline Control and then double-click `gotoAndPlay`. You should see a `gotoAndPlay` action added to your script in the Script pane on the right (see Figure 15.3). Because this action requires parameters, a code hint will appear to help guide you. If it goes away, just click inside the parentheses following `gotoAndPlay` and press the Show Code Hint button.

FIGURE 15.3
Right after you insert gotoAndPlay, the Actions panel is populated as shown here.

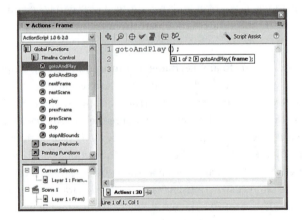

6. You always type any required parameters inside the parenthesis. In this case, type **20** because that's the frame number to which you want to go and play. Therefore, the finished action in the script area should read `gotoAndPlay(20);` (as shown in Figure 15.4).

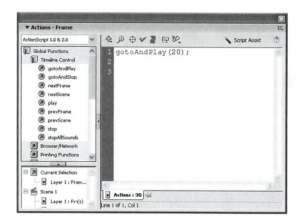

FIGURE 15.4
This is how the complete code looks. Every time the playback head reaches Frame 30, it goes back to Frame 20 and plays.

7. Test the movie (don't just play in the authoring environment). It plays once, and then every time it gets to Frame 30, it goes back to Frame 20 and plays again.

As easy as the preceding task was, there is one thing in particular that could make it better. Consider the amount of work involved if you changed the location of the keyframes. For example, what if the second keyframe (Frame 20) had to move to Frame 25? Of course, the initial tween would take longer to play, and the rotation would be quicker, but the loop would also stop working properly. To fix it, you would need to remember to edit the action in Frame 30 so that it read `gotoAndPlay(25);`. You would have to repeat this fix every time you changed the location of the keyframe where the rotation starts.

Naturally, there's a better way. Instead of making the destination of `gotoAndPlay` an explicit frame number, you can change the parameters to make the destination a named frame label, which will be the same for the frame, no matter where it is located in the Timeline. You'll use frame labels in the next task.

Try It Yourself

Use a Frame Label as the Destination of a `gotoAndPlay` action

In this task you'll improve the `gotoAndPlay` action by supplying a frame label instead of a frame number. Here are the steps:

1. In the file created in the preceding task, click Frame 20 of the Animation layer. In the Properties panel you should see a place where you can type a frame label. Label this frame Loop Start (see Figure 15.5).

FIGURE 15.5
If you label
Frame 20 (via
the Properties
panel), the des-
tination of the
gotoAndPlay
action can
change from an
explicit number
(20) to a label
name (Loop
Start).

2. Click Frame 30 in the Actions layer and open the Actions panel.

3. You're going to modify the gotoAndPlay line in the Actions panel. Change 20
   to "Loop Start" (with the quotation marks). The final script should read
   gotoAndPlay("Loop Start");, as shown in Figure 15.6.

FIGURE 15.6
This new ver-
sion of the
gotoAndPlay
action is better
than the original
because the
destination is a
frame label.

4. Test the movie; it doesn't look any different from the old version to the user. Now go back to the Timeline and click Frame 20, and then click and drag it so Loop Start is now Frame 10.

5. Test the movie again. The animation now loops back to Frame 10, where you moved the Loop Start keyframe. The power of using a label as the destination of the `gotoAndPlay` action is that it means you can go back and move the location of the Loop Start keyframe to any frame you want, and it still works! (Save this file for the next task.)

Using Script Assist

If Script Assist truly helps novices write scripts then I suppose I shouldn't have to explain anything here. Interestingly, when Macromedia removed "Normal Mode" (the old name for Script Assist) in the previous version of Flash, an uproar came from many people who were far from novices—so, in fact, Script Assist is a perfectly legitimate tool. In my opinion, however, you shouldn't use it exclusively. That is, a great way to work is to toggle Script Assist on and off as needed. For example, if you're not sure how to write a particular script, turn it on in order to help create the script and then turn it off.

Here's a quick explanation of how to use Script Assist and then a short task that gives you a better flavor for how it works. When you press the Script Assist button you're taken into a mode where you no long make edits by simply typing into the script area—you can't. Once you add scripts (by using the toolbox or plus button) you make changes by editing the options revealed in the section above the script area. That area is only revealed when you're in Script Assist mode (as Figure 15.7 shows).

The area above the script only displays options available for the currently selected line of code. That is, while your entire script area could have many lines, only one is selected at a time and that's the one you can edit by changing the options. Additionally, those options vary depending on the script you're editing. The advantage is that these options can guide you through modifying your scripts and will always enforce perfect syntax. In some ways it's restrictive because you may feel like typing into the script area, but you can't—you do everything in the options area. Even changing the sequence in which the actions appear (that is, the line order) requires that you select the line then press the "move up" or "move down" arrows. In many ways, Script Assist mode is actually similar to the free-style mode (that is, when the Script Assist button is not pressed in). In both modes you create instructions by adding statements in the toolbox or via the plus button. It's just making edits to the scripts you've added is more structured in Script Assist mode.

FIGURE 15.7
Script Assist mode reveals an options area above your script where you can make changes to the selected line of code from the available options.

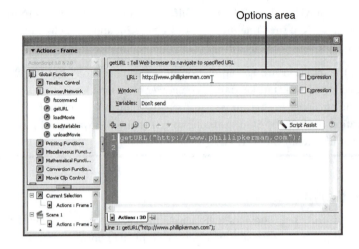

Options area

By the Way

Switching Into Script Assist Mode

While I encourage you to toggle between Script Assist and (what I'm calling) free-style mode, you can only enter Script Assist mode when all your syntax is correct. That is, if when not in Script Assist mode you add or edit a script and leave it with a syntax error, you won't be able to enter Script Assist mode. You'll see a warning dialog and a detailed explanation in your Output panel. If you're planning on making lots of changes and you're not sure about the syntax, then only make one change at a time and switch back to Script Assist (or press the Check Syntax button) to confirm you didn't make any errors. Alternatively, I suppose you could try to spend your entire time in Script Assist mode though I think that will prove restrictive.

The way Script Assist ensures perfect syntax is only half of the benefit. The other way (and in my opinion the more valuable way) Script Assist helps you is by guiding you filling in the scripts. The code hints that appear (when not in Script Assist mode) are similar but quickly disappear and certainly don't enforce the correct syntax. Open up the file you created during the previous task, "Use a Frame Label as the Destination of a gotoAndPlay action," so you can take a quick tour of what I'm talking about.

Open the Actions panel and select the keyframe in frame 30 in the layer you named Actions. Switch into Script Assist mode by pressing the Script Assist button. You can see the options area appears above the script area as shown in Figure 15.8.

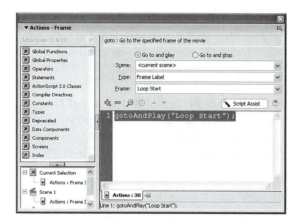

FIGURE 15.8
You can make changes to an existing script using Script Assist.

Keep an eye on the actual script (in the script area below) as you explore to the options area. Go ahead and change the option between Go to and stop and Go to and play and watch the script below update. Now, here's a really useful feature: click the down arrow on the right side of the Frame combo box and you'll see a list of all the frame labels in your movie (though, for now, you'll only see "Loop Start" as that's the only one we added. If you had more labels, they'd all be listed here and there would be no way you'll make a typo if you select the label from this menu.

In many ways, I think it's hard to try to learn by only using Script Assist mode. However, I will bring your attention to it again later this Hour when you learn about putting actions directly onto buttons (in the section Button Actions).

Frame Actions

In the previous task you saw how placing one action in a keyframe and changing its parameters makes the playback head jump to a different frame. Step back a second and consider what else you've learned. Actions are instructions that you want Flash to follow. Actions do things. You can modify actions by changing their parameters. This is all good information; however, if actions are instructions, exactly when does Flash *follow* those instructions?

The answer depends on where you put the actions. You can put actions both in keyframes and on any object type, such as button instances, movie clip instances, and components (covered in Hour 17, "Using Components"). In the preceding task you placed an action in a keyframe. In that case, the action was executed (that is, the instruction was followed) when the playback head reached that frame. If you put an action in Frame 10, it would not be followed until the playback head reached Frame 10.

With an action in a keyframe, the user doesn't do anything but wait for the playback head to reach the appropriate frame to see the action happen. Although this isn't exactly interactivity, it's quite powerful. For example, often it's useful to place a `stop()` action in the first frame so that your movie initially appears paused and won't play until a `play()` action is encountered (perhaps after the user clicks a button). Another example might be when you want to stop in the middle of an animation. All you need is a keyframe and a stop action. There are many more examples of keyframe actions, which are good for when you want something to happen at a certain moment in the animation—not just when a user clicks.

Notice that in the previous task you simply used frame actions. The actions were executed when the playback head reached that frame. This is just one of the three places you can put actions; you're about to see the other two—button actions and movie clip actions.

Code "on" Buttons

I'm about to introduce putting code on objects (starting with buttons) but keep in mind there are two parts: the concept of associating code with buttons and the exact implementation (that is how you physically select the button and then type into the Actions panel). It's actually possible to do the implementation differently... namely, type the code into a keyframe, but refer to a button. I'll show both ways, but regardless of how you do it the concept of associating code with a button is the same.

Button Actions

Putting an action in a keyframe causes the action to execute when that frame is reached. However, putting an action on an instance of a button makes the action execute when the user clicks the button. The decision of whether to put an action in a keyframe or a button is simple. If you want an action to occur when a particular frame is reached, put it in a keyframe. If you want an action to occur when the user acts (for example, when he clicks a button), put the action on an instance of the button.

Keyframe actions are pretty straightforward: You just assign them to keyframes. Button actions, however, require that you specify to which *mouse event* you want the action to respond. Do you want the action to respond when the user presses the button or when the user releases the button? Maybe you want the action to execute when the user rolls over the button. This level of detail gives you the power to make an action perform exactly as you want.

Mouse events are specific situations that refer to exactly how the user is to interact with a button. For example, one mouse event is `press` and another is `release`. When you specify to which mouse event you want an action to respond, you are specifying exactly when the action is to execute. Only in actions attached to objects do you need this extra level of specificity because actions in keyframes simply execute when the keyframe is reached. All mouse events include the word on followed by the actual event name in parentheses (for example, `on(press)`).

The best way to see how mouse events work is to try it out. In the following task you'll add to the preceding task buttons that let the user stop and continue the animation while it plays.

Try It Yourself ▼

Add Buttons to an Animation to Stop and Continue Playback

In this task you'll add buttons that let the user stop and continue the animation from the preceding task while it plays. Here are the steps:

1. Either use the file created in the previous tasks or make a new file with a motion tween over several frames (make sure you can see something moving while the animation plays).

2. Insert a new layer for the buttons. You don't want to place buttons in the layer that has the animation; that would affect the tween. Name the new layer Buttons.

3. Into the new Buttons layer, draw a rectangle that will become a button. Select it, and then convert it to a symbol (by pressing F8). Name it MyButton and make sure the behavior is set to Button.

4. You're going to need two buttons, so either copy and paste the instance that is already on the Stage or drag another instance of the MyButton symbol from the Library onto the Stage in the Buttons layer. Apply a Tint color style to each instance—one red (for Stop) and one green (for Play). As you recall, you do so by selecting the button instance on the Stage and using the Properties panel to select Tint from the Color drop-down list and then selecting a color and percentage.

5. Give each button a memorable instance name (say "green" and "red"). Use the Properties panel to set the instance names. This step is only necessary for the upcoming note "Keeping All Code in One Place."

6. Now you need to attach an action to each button individually. Select the red button and access the Actions panel. The tab should read "red" and have an ▼

icon of a button. This way you know you're editing the script for that button instance. For this button, make sure the Script Assist is turned off. Click the plus button and select Global Functions, Timeline Control, stop.

7. Unlike a keyframe action, which can appear as a single line of code, a button action requires at least two extra lines of code: one before and one after the main script so that the script is wrapped inside an event. Think of the main script (in this case, `stop()`) as the meat of a sandwich, but it's not complete without pieces of bread above and below the code. Any code attached to a button has to be surrounded by an `on` event. Therefore, place your cursor in front of the `s` in `stop` and then type the following:

```
on(press){
```

Then press Enter.

8. Click after the last line of code (that is, after `stop()`), press Enter, and type this:

```
}
```

The resulting script looks like this:

```
on(press){
 stop();
}
```

Notice that you should indent the second line for clarity. This is a very good habit to adopt. You can always clean up your code by pressing the Auto Format button in the Actions panel.

9. The preceding steps are painful because they step through every last detail. For the green button let me show you a neat trick that Script Assist supports. Select the green button and open the Actions panel. Confirm that the green button appears in the current script tab at the bottom of the Actions panel. Turn on Script Assist (by clicking the Script Assist button). This time you'll insert a play but because you're in Script Assist mode it will automatically add the mouse event. Click the plus button and select Global Functions, Timeline Control, play.

10. Notice the play() action is added—no surprise there. However you should also see the necessary `on(release){` code added above (and `}` below). Click the first line and you can modify exactly which event will trigger the stop (for

example, you can change it to on(press)). The nice part about Script Assist is that you see all the available mouse events.

11. Test the movie, and you'll find that when you press the buttons, the movie will play and stop.

What Do You Want to Do, and When Do You Want to Do It?

Did you Know?

Before you write a script you need an idea. But then, converting the idea into ActionScript can be challenging. I use the following question when helping students write a script: What do you want to do, and when do you want to do it? That is, the "what" could be "stop the movie" and the "when" might be "when the user presses the button." The "what" is always your raw script (such as stop() or play()) and the "when" is tied to where you put the script (for example, on a button if you want it to happen when the user presses or in a keyframe if you want it to happen when the playhead reaches that frame).

Keeping All Code in One Place

By the Way

In many ways, putting code right on buttons (as you did in the preceding task) makes perfect sense. You find the instructions for the actions when you select the buttons, and that gives you a bit of context. However, it can also mean you're running around selecting different instances to reveal their scripts—sort of like the card game Concentration. I have mixed feelings about whether this is the best way to learn. In any event, it's not the ultimate way to program.

Just so you can see what I'd call a better solution, I'm going to show you an alternative to the preceding task. All you do is make sure you give your buttons instance names (as you did in the preceding task: green and red) and type the following code into the first keyframe of the movie (with Script Assist turned off):

```
red.onPress=function(){
 stop();
}
green.onPress=function(){
 play();
}
```

Translated, this says that the instance named red shall execute the code stop() when the onPress event occurs. You always leave the word function as is. Notice that onPress in this syntax is equivalent to on(press) when placed right on the button. I'm sure you can guess that the last three lines make the green button trigger the script play() when it gets pressed.

From this point forward, if I say "put an action on a button," I mean you can either use on(press) right on the button or .onPress, as shown above.

Movie Clip Actions

This hour you've seen how to place actions in keyframes and on button instances. Most of the actions you'll encounter are likely to fall into one of those two cases. However, there's a third place where you can attach actions: in instances of movie clips. It's a little confusing because, unlike with buttons, you can also put actions on keyframes inside a master movie clip in the Library. However, the rule that you can only put actions in keyframes, button instances, and movie clip instances remains— so if you put any actions *inside* a movie clip, you have to put them in one of those three places (keyframes, nested buttons, or nested clips) inside the clip. We've already discussed putting actions on buttons and in keyframes—and those techniques will work inside master movie clips. But now you're going to see how actions can also be placed on instances of movie clips.

Actions on movie clips are powerful. It would get complicated to fully explore this feature now, but you can do a task that gives you a taste.

▼ **Try It Yourself**

Place Actions on a Movie Clip Instance

This task shows you how to attach actions right onto clip instances. Here are the steps:

1. Create a movie clip that contains several frames and some kind of animation inside the clip (so you can see whether it's playing). That is, add frames inside of a symbol.

2. Place this movie clip on the Stage and test the movie (to verify that it's animating). Your main Timeline should have only one frame.

3. Back in Flash, select the instance of the movie clip on the Stage and open the Actions panel. (Confirm that you've got the movie clip selected by looking at the current script tab.) Do the next few steps with Script Assist turned off.

4. In the Toolbox insert onClipEvent, which is listed under Global Functions, Movie Clip Control. The code and code hint will appear as shown in Figure 15.9.

5. Like buttons requiring that you use on events, clips require that you use onClipEvent events. Select (from the code completion popup, it's still visible) or type load. This event will trigger when the clip first loads.

▼

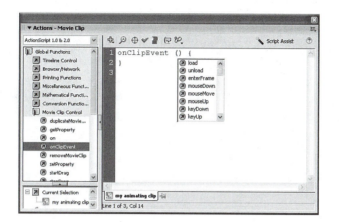

FIGURE 15.9
The skeleton for
onClipEvent is
similar to that
of an on event.

6. Between the two curly braces insert a `stop` action. The resulting code so far should look like this:

```
onClipEvent(load){
  stop();
}
```

Feel free to type it by hand, but be sure to type it *exactly*.

7. You will add two more actions that respond to the `mouseDown` and `mouseUp` events. For this example, when the user clicks `mouseDown`, the movie clip should start to play. When the user stops clicking (that is, when `mouseUp` occurs), the movie clip should stop. With Script Assist turned off, you need to add this below the closing curly brace. That is, the separate events must appear as independent sandwiches (well, starting and ending curly braces). Just so you can experience Script Assist, turn it back on now. Click the last line in your script (the closing curly brace) and add another `onClipEvent` (under Global Functions, Movie Clip Control) and it will appear after the code you already have. This time you can select the event `MouseDown` from the options area as shown in Figure 15.10.

8. In order to make the Movie Clip stop when the user presses their mouse, add a `play()` action (from Global Functions, Timeline Control). The `play()` needs to appear between the two curly braces for your `MouseDown` event. While in Script Assist mode, actions always get added after the selected line, so you want to select the line with `MouseDown` (line 4). If the `play()` happens to get added to the wrong place, you can select that line and use the up or down arrow buttons to move it to the correct place. You can also drag actions from the toolbox.

FIGURE 15.10
By selecting the
onMouseDown
event, the script
that follows will
only trigger
when the user
clicks.

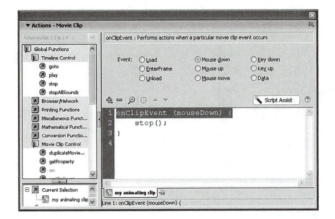

9. Finally, in order to experience yet another feature of Script Assist mode, try to
   add a stop() action below all the code you have in place—that is, below the
   last closing curly brace. What happens is the stop() that you add automatically gets surrounded with the required onClipEvent elements. Go ahead and
   make it so the stop() action triggers when the user does a MouseUp (by clicking the onClipEvent line and selecting the Mouse Up option). The complete
   script should look like this:

```
onClipEvent(load){
  stop();
}
onClipEvent(mouseDown){
  play();
}
onClipEvent(mouseUp){
  stop();
}
```

10. Test the movie. It's actually pretty sophisticated, despite the simplicity of the
    script. Go back and reread the script (in the Script area of the Actions panel)
    attached to the movie clip instance.

There are a few important things to note about the preceding task. First, you could
have just typed the entire script without ever visiting Script Assist mode—I just
wanted you to experience the way the options area displays the available settings
and how scripts attached to clips (or buttons) always must appear within either an
on() event (for buttons) or onClipEvent() event (for clips). Also notice how the
movie clip events mouseDown and mouseUp respond to any mouse click—not just to
clicks on the movie clip itself. If you want something that responds to clicks right

on a graphic, use regular buttons (which support the on(press) and on(release) events).

Also notice the actions you attach to a movie clip instance apply only to that instance. It might be more explicit if you precede `stop()` and `play()` in all cases in the preceding task with `this.`, as in `this.stop()` and `this.play()`. This makes more sense when you think about it because it means just that one movie clip will stop or play. You can prove this to yourself several ways. Drag another instance of your movie clip from the Library (and don't attach any actions to this instance). When you test the movie, the `stop` and `play` actions apply to (that is, "target") only the clip with the actions attached.

Finally, this example shows that you can write code to respond to various events (in this case, `load`, `mouseDown`, and `mouseUp`). For each one, you have the two pieces of bread plus the meat in the middle. What I haven't mentioned yet is that you can stack the sandwich with many layers of meat. That is, for one event, you can trigger several lines of code. For example, when the `mouseDown` event occurs, you could have a sound start playing in addition to the `play()` action triggering. As long as you put your code between the two curly braces, one event can trigger as many lines of code as you want. (This is also true with buttons and on events.)

The basic things to remember are that just as with buttons, actions on movie clip instances are wrapped inside events. Buttons respond to the on event, whereas movie clips respond to the `onClipEvent`. Finally, actions attached to movie clip instances affect only the particular instances to which they're attached.

Using Behaviors

You've got enough of the basics of scripting down to move on to behaviors. I realize that behaviors are intended to make programming easier for novices, but in my opinion, you'll get a lot more out of them if you understand what they're doing. Behaviors simply insert several lines of ActionScript in one swoop. For scripts that require you to specify parameters, the behavior will prompt you for data. Another interesting feature of behaviors is that even after you've inserted a complete script, you can come back and make edits to it without touching the code. That is, you can use the Behaviors panel as your interface to edit the underlying code.

All this can make a programmer very nervous because she can feel out of control. In any event, I do believe it's important to see what's happening. For that reason, during the following discussion and tasks, be sure to keep open your Actions panel and watch the changes that occur in the Actions panel when you make changes to the Behaviors panel. Let's first take a tour of the Behaviors panel. Open the Behaviors panel (by pressing Shift+F3 or selecting Window, Development Panels, Behaviors) and take a look at Figure 15.11.

FIGURE 15.11
The Behaviors panel has several components.

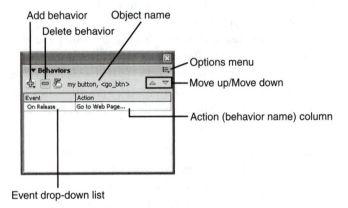

The Behaviors panel has the following features:

▶ **Add Behavior**—You always select a behavior to add by clicking the Add Behavior (plus) button. This reveals a hierarchical menu of all installed behaviors.

▶ **Delete Behavior**—The Delete Behavior button lets you remove a behavior. Alternatively, you can just select and delete any row containing a behavior that you want to remove.

▶ **Move Up and Move Down**—These buttons let you reorder multiple rows of behaviors (you can add more than one).

▶ **Event**—The Event drop-down list lets you specify a trigger for any added behavior. Remember that when attaching actions to objects, you have to specify events such as press or release.

▶ **Action column**—The Action column simply presents the name of any added behavior. In addition, you can double-click any row in this column to repopulate a behavior after it's added.

The whole idea of the Behaviors panel is that it will insert the ActionScript code for you. Most behaviors prompt you for additional details so that parameters can be set. Also, if you need to re-edit a behavior, you can do it through this panel. Actually, you can tweak any behavior by editing the resulting code by using the Actions panel. If you edit the code through the Actions panel, however, you not only potentially break it, but the Behaviors panel can't access code after you've changed it.

(Please don't let this prevent you from trying to learn from mistakes here—it's not like you'll cause some sort of meltdown.)

Using the getURL Action

Whereas the gotoAndPlay action jumps the playback head to another frame, getURL jumps the user to another web page. If you're familiar with how a hyperlink works in HTML, you should know that getURL is the same thing. With gotoAndPlay, you need to specify as a parameter the frame to which you are navigating. With getURL, you need to specify to what URL you want to navigate.

URL stands for *uniform resource locator* and is the address for any web page. If you want to use the getURL action to jump to my home page, for example, you need to know the URL (which is http://www.phillipkerman.com).

The following task teaches you how both getURL and the Behaviors panel work. You'll actually learn more about getURL in Hour 19, "Linking a Movie to the Web." In the following task, you'll quickly use this action to see how easy it really is.

Try It Yourself ▼

Make a Button That Hyperlinks to Another Web Page

You'll build a hyperlink in this task. Here are the steps:

1. In a new file, create a Button symbol called myButton and place an instance on the Stage. Give this instance the name go.

2. With the button instance selected, open both the Actions panel (by pressing F9) and the Behaviors panel (by pressing Shift+F3). Move the Actions panel to the side because you're only going to use it to watch what's happening behind the scenes.

3. Make sure the button is selected by ensuring that you see myButton, <go> in the Behaviors panel (as shown in Figure 15.12).

4. Click the plus button in the Behaviors panel and select Web, Go to Web Page. Into the URL field that appears in the dialog box, type **http://www. phillipkerman.com**. (Leave the Open In option set to the default, _self.)

5. Test the movie. Or, better yet, select File, Publish Preview, Default or press F12—so you can watch this in a browser. Just click the button in the Flash movie and, if you're connected to the Internet, you'll hyperlink to my home page.

▼

FIGURE 15.12
When you select
the button, you
see its symbol
and instance
name in the
Behaviors
panel.

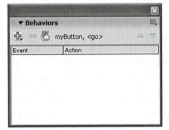

You can see that the ActionScript produced by the preceding task is the same as if you had created it using the steps in one of the earlier tasks. That is, you can also select getURL in the Actions panel toolbox under Global Functions, Browser/Network. The getURL action is nearly the same as gotoAndPlay(), except that the parameter needs to be an URL. If you want to change the event that triggers this behavior, click On Release in the Behaviors panel, and you can select from the other events available to buttons, as Figure 15.13 shows.

FIGURE 15.13
The Behaviors
panel lets you
change the
event trigger
without affecting
the underlying
code.

You can also change the destination URL by double-clicking in the Action column in the Behaviors panel. That will redisplay the dialog box that appeared in the first place. You can actually do all these modifications (change the event, change the URL, and even delete the whole behavior) through the Actions panel. You get the same results either way.

You can expand the set of behaviors installed on your machine. Actually, it's not terribly difficult to make your own. A behavior is really just a template of code. It gets a bit more involved when you define the dialog boxes that pop up, but it's all fairly straightforward. My point here is that you might not like the set of behaviors that ships with Flash at this point, but you'll surely see more over time.

Behaviors are simply a tool that guides you through ActionScript. But they can become more trouble than they're worth, especially when you know exactly what you want to do. Sort of like cookie cutters, they're great for holidays, but sometimes you just have to use your fingers and shape the cookie yourself. However, there are some really great benefits to behaviors, too, as discussed in the following sections.

Addressing Movie Clips

The navigation actions you saw in the preceding section are good for jumping around within a Timeline or throughout the Web. However, you know that movie clips have their own Timeline. What happens when you want to jump around within a movie clip? If you put an action inside the movie clip or if you attach an action to the clip, it's pretty straightforward. If you have a `stop` action on a button inside the movie clip, for example, it will cause the movie clip to stop (provided that it has multiple frames). So scripting is easy when you put an action in the master clip or on a clip instance.

Your job gets a little more complicated when you want to send an action to another clip remotely. For example, say you have a movie clip and a button on the Stage (the button is not inside the movie clip). If you put a `stop` action on the button, it will cause only the main Timeline to stop; the movie clip won't stop. To direct an action to a clip, you first address, or "target," that particular instance of the movie clip (remember, you could have several instances on the Stage at once). You can do this in Flash in several ways.

Consider that you have to do two things: address the clip and tell it what to do. Remember from Hour 12, "Animating Using Movie Clip and Graphic Symbols," that instances of movie clips can be named (via the Properties panel). You can only address named clip instances. So addressing a clip is simply stating its name. That is, you don't say `stop()` but you say `clip.stop()` (where `clip` is the instance name of the clip you want to stop). If the clip is nested inside another clip, you must address its entire path (or full address). You place the action immediately following the clip's address.

It might be easiest to understand this by using pseudo-code. You can use the programmer's trick of writing scripts in your own words—being as clear as possible—just to get things sorted out. Then you translate to real code. For example, if you wanted a clip instance named ball to stop playing, you might say (in pseudo-code): "ball, you stop." In English, you might say "stop ball," but remember that you have to address the object first and then tell it what code to execute.

The syntax to address an object uses what's called *dot syntax*. For example, this code would actually make a clip instance named ball stop playing:

```
ball.stop();
```

If that sounds simple, then you've got about one-third of ActionScript under your belt. In the following task, you can practice addressing.

▼ **Try It Yourself**

Target Nested Instances

In this task you'll address and stop instances of wheels that are inside a clip of a car:

1. You'll need a car with rotating wheels, like the one you made in Hour 12, in the task titled "Use a Movie Clip to Make a Rotating Wheel." Remember that you achieved this by working from the inside out. First, you made a clip of a wheel called Plain Wheel (a circle with lines that would be noticeable when it rotated). Then you used an instance of Plain Wheel to create another clip called Rotating Wheel. Rotating Wheel contained an instance of Plain Wheel in Frame 1 and one in Frame 20. You set a motion tween to rotate the wheel in the first keyframe of Rotating Wheel. Finally, you used two instances of Rotating Wheel in the creation of the car. At this point, either revisit that task in Hour 12 or create the Rotating Wheel clip.

2. Drag one instance of Rotating Wheel to the Stage. Test the movie to confirm that the wheel is rotating and take note of the direction in which it's rotating.

3. Drag another instance of Rotating Wheel and place it to the left of the other instance. With the Properties panel, name one of the instances front_wheel and the other back_wheel, as shown in Figure 15.14.

4. Draw a car body (nothing fancy) around the two wheels. Select everything and choose Insert, Convert to Symbol (or press F8). Name this new movie clip Car.

5. On the Stage you have an instance of Car, but it has no instance name yet. Use the Properties panel to name this instance the_car. (Note that a clip instance name should have no spaces and should not begin with a number.)

6. Insert a keyframe at Frame 40 and move the_car to another place on the Stage. In the first keyframe, set motion tweening.

▼

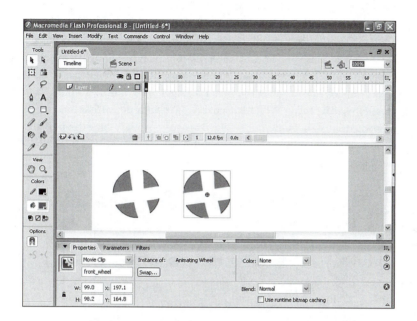

FIGURE 15.14
Using the Properties panel, name each instance of Rotating Wheel so that each can be addressed individually.

7. In a new layer, draw a rectangle to be used as a button. Select it and covert it to a symbol called myButton, making sure to set its behavior to Button. Copy and paste this button so that you have two instances. Set the Properties panel's Color drop-down list to Tint and pick a green color for one instance and a red color for the other. Then name the button instances green and red.

8. Select just the red instance of myButton. Open the Actions panel (confirm that the tab name matches the instance name). Type the following code (either by hand or by dragging pieces from the toolbox):

```
on(press){
 stop();
}
```

9. Test the movie, and you'll see that the stop button stops the car from moving across the screen, but it doesn't stop the wheels from spinning. You need to add additional actions to stop the wheels.

10. Back in Flash, access the actions for the red button and add two additional lines of code. Make sure you're not in Script Assist mode and change the code so that it reads as follows:

```
on(press){
 stop();
 the_car.front_wheel.stop();
}
```

Because you want the `front_wheel` instance to stop, and that instance is inside the instance `the_car`, you need to include that entire path when you address `front_wheel`. You'll need a third line of code to stop the `back_wheel` instance, too, but you can insert it a different way. Click right after the semicolon that ends either `stop` action and press Enter. In order to address the `back_wheel` instance, click the Insert a Target Path button (it looks like a crosshairs). The Insert Target Path dialog box pops up, with a hierarchy of the named clip instances in your movie. Next to `the_car`, click the plus sign to see the named clip instances inside it. Click `back_wheel` and then click OK (see Figure 15.15). Notice that the address `this.the_car.back_wheel` appears.

FIGURE 15.15
Using the Insert Target Path dialog box, you can target an individual instance.

11. Now you have to say what you want to do with the `back_wheel` instance. The easiest way is to just type `.stop();` so that it matches the code that stops the front wheel. The only tricky part is that you must remember to follow `stop` with parentheses. The finished code appears in Figure 15.16.

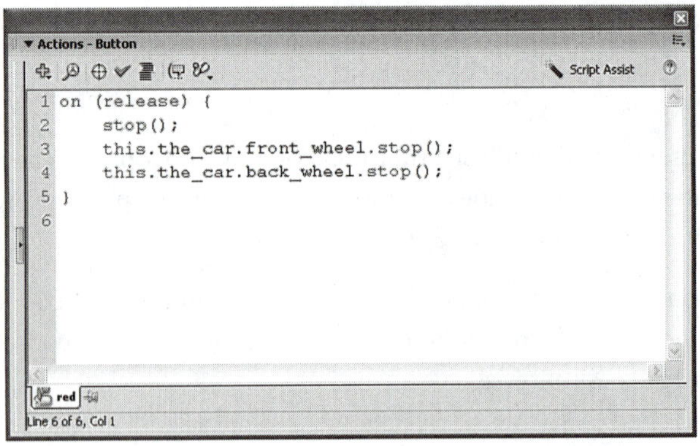

FIGURE 15.16
The code for the stop button includes these three lines of code.

```
1 on (release) {
2     stop();
3     this.the_car.front_wheel.stop();
4     this.the_car.back_wheel.stop();
5 }
6
```

12. Test the movie. When you click the red button, the car and both wheels stop. You could repeat this process with the play action (that is, play()) on the green button to allow a user to make the car move again.

Addressing clips is simple, as long as you remember to name your instances. (Just make sure each instance name is just one word and does not begin with a number.) Using the Insert Target Path dialog box is a nice way to learn the syntax for addressing. When you choose the clip from the hierarchy, Flash automatically puts it in the correct syntax. Addressing clips goes from the general to the specific, as in this.the_car.back_wheel, but until you know these conventions, it's probably safest to use the Insert Target Path dialog box.

Action Efficiency Tricks

When you have an idea how to insert actions, you can work on fine-tuning the technique. Besides the general suggestion to be deliberate and include no more actions than necessary, there are a few more specific ways to be efficient.

The first technique is to use a separate layer for all frame actions, as you did in the first task in this hour. You can put an action in any keyframe, but sometimes you want an action to execute when the playback head reaches the middle of a tween. Instead of inserting a keyframe (and effectively messing up the tween), you can use a separate layer to insert all new keyframes. Not only will this prevent tweens from breaking, but you'll have only one layer in which to manage your frame actions. Otherwise, you might be hunting through all your layers looking for actions.

Another similar technique is to use a separate layer for all frame labels. In the second task in this hour, you saw the beauty of using labels as destination points for the goto actions. Just as you don't want to restrict the design of your tweens to accommodate frame actions, it's nice to keep all your labels in a layer of their own. There's no reason to be stingy with layers—insert them as needed. Layers don't affect file size, and they can help organize your movie.

There are many more efficiency tricks, but these are just a few that apply to actions. You'll learn more throughout the rest of the book.

Summary

This hour touched on the fundamental things you can do with actions. You have learned how an action can be placed in a keyframe to execute when that frame is reached and on instances of buttons to execute when the user clicks. You have learned that the exact mouse event to which you want to respond needs to be specified. You have also learned how actions can be placed inside movie clip events attached to instances of movie clips.

Not only have you learned where actions go, but you have learned that many actions require further specification in the form of parameters. If you understand this simple concept, you'll be able to apply that knowledge to almost any action you encounter because most actions require parameters. This hour just scratches the surface of how to use actions, but hopefully the concepts covered make sense to you because the same structure and terms apply to all kinds of scripting in Flash.

Q&A

Q *I put an action* (`gotoAndPlay(5)`) *in the last frame of my movie, and I swear the movie is never reaching the last frame, because I have some text that is supposed to appear briefly on the Stage—on just that last frame. It works only if I put the graphics one frame before the* `gotoAndPlay` *action. Why?*

A This is a critical concept: Frame actions are executed *before* the on-the-Stage graphics of that frame are displayed. If your action says to go to another frame, it goes to the other frame before it draws graphics on the Stage.

Q *Why does my movie loop (effectively doing a* `gotoAndPlay(1)` *on the last frame), even though I haven't put any actions in it?*

A The option to automatically loop is set by default when you test a movie (and when you publish a movie). While testing, you can uncheck the option to loop from the Control menu of the Flash Player (not the Control menu of the Flash authoring program). If you turn this off, you most certainly won't see the movie loop unless you include an action to make it loop. By the way, normally you don't need a `stop` action at the end of your Timeline; if you simply uncheck the Loop option (when you publish), the movie will automatically stop on the last frame.

Q *Which action do I use to create a commercial video game?*

A I hope it's obvious that we are taking baby steps first. It's amazing the kind of powerful things you've done this hour. It's going to take a lot more work before you're cranking out video games; although you can create amazing games by using Flash, it takes a lot of work. For now, we're just laying the foundation.

Workshop

The Workshop consists of quiz questions and answers to help you solidify your understanding of the material covered in this hour. You should try to answer the questions before checking the answers.

Quiz

1. Where can actions be inserted in Flash?

  A. Inside Button symbols, on keyframes, and inside Movie Clip symbols.

  B. In any keyframe except Frame 1 (plus buttons and movie clips).

  C. On keyframes, on button instances, and on movie clip instances.

2. What is an action, anyway?

  A. Anything that moves on the Stage

  B. An instruction snippet that tells Flash what to do

  C. What programmers call a *function*

3. How many actions can you place in one button?

  A. One for each mouse event

  B. No more than two

  C. As many as you want

Quiz Answers

1. C. Remember you don't put actions inside master button symbols! Of course, within master movie clips you can have actions in keyframes and buttons, but Answer C covers those places.

2. B. *Action* is a pretty generic term, so Answer B is the best of these definitions. (In fact it's so general that I cringe every time I say *action*—but it sure is easier than defining dozens of other terms.)

3. C. There's really no limit to how many actions you can place in one button, although there are some restrictions against illogical sequences (for example, you can't have two `gotoAndPlay` actions in a row). One event could result in many actions being executed, and you can have several events within one button.

HOUR 16

Using ActionScript for Advanced Interactivity

What You'll Learn in This Hour:

- ▶ How to create draggable objects
- ▶ How to create variables to track user data
- ▶ How to change visual properties of clip instances
- ▶ How to change onscreen text dynamically

You saw last hour how a few strategically placed actions can control how a movie plays. An action on a button instance gives the user the power to make that action execute when he or she clicks the button. Also, you can place actions in a keyframe to make the movie jump back to another frame—effectively looping. Last hour was fun, but it was just the tip of the iceberg!

This hour continues on the subject of adding interactivity via ActionScript. You won't spend time learning exactly how to place actions (that was covered last hour); instead, you'll forge ahead into applying scripts for more complex tasks.

You have a huge task in front of you! Even if you don't see yourself as a programmer, this hour should give you a sense of Flash's potential. If you're already into programming, this hour may not challenge you, but it will give you the fundamental tools with which you can grow on your own.

Making Drag-and-Drop Interactions

One of the most effective ways to give your users the power to interact is by letting them drag items around the Stage. This is essential for the creation of most games, and it's also a particularly effective teaching method because some people are "tactile" learners (whereas others might be visual or aural learners). For whatever reason, you might want to let your users move items around the Stage. This is simple to do in Flash.

There's a slight dilemma, however. In Flash, the simplest way to determine when a user clicks a specific area involves the use of buttons. However, movie clip instances give you a few additional capabilities. The good news is that you can make movie clips respond to events originally designed for buttons (such as press and release). The bottom line is that buttons and movie clips can behave like each other; ultimately however, movie clips can do more than buttons. The time to use a button is primarily when you want different effects for the up, over, and down states. In any event, in this hour you'll use movie clips whenever you can—including for the draggable object task that follows.

Try It Yourself

Make a Simple Draggable Object

In this task you'll create a simple draggable object. Here are the steps to follow:

1. In a new file, draw a rectangle, select it, and convert it to a symbol. Call the symbol MyClip and make sure its behavior is set to Movie Clip. Also, use the center registration option, as shown in Figure 16.1.

FIGURE 16.1
When creating the draggable clip, select the center registration option.

2. Select the clip instance and use the Properties panel to give it the instance name box. Next you'll attach an action to it that effectively says "drag me." Select the box instance and open the Actions panel. Make sure Script Assist is not active and type the following code:

```
on(press){
 startDrag(this);
}
```

This basically says, "When the user clicks this clip, start dragging this object."

3. Test the movie. It should be apparent what else you have to do. As it is now, the clip starts dragging, but you can never let go.

4. To fix the problem, go back to the box instance and add the following code (below the code you already have):

```
on(release){
  stopDrag();
}
```

If you use Test Movie now, you'll see that it works fine.

Interestingly, in the preceding task, you don't need to specify any parameters with stopDrag (the way you do with startDrag)—Flash just stops dragging anything.

Controlling Drag and Drop

The preceding task was fairly simple. There are two refinements that can make it much more interesting. Specifically, you can first constrain the area in which the user is allowed to drag. For example, you should prevent the user from dragging the object offscreen. Second, it would be nice if you could check whether the user dropped the object onto another object. Maybe you want to ask the users to put several objects in order, as Figure 16.2 shows. To do this, at the moment the user lets go, check whether she has dropped the object on the target. In the next task you'll constrain where the object is dragged, and then later you'll calculate where the user drops the object.

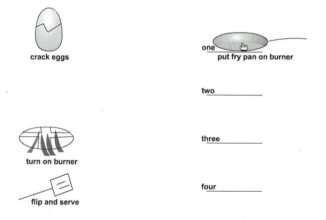

crack eggs

put fry pan on burner

one

two

turn on burner

three

flip and serve

four

FIGURE 16.2
Asking the user to place these objects in the correct order is a perfect case for a drag-and-drop interaction.

Try It Yourself

Constrain the Draggable Area

In this task you'll constrain the draggable object to a specific rectangle shape. Here are the steps:

1. The `startDrag()` action accepts five additional parameters. In addition to the parameter you included that specifies which object to drag, you can also opt for the "lock to center" feature, as well as specify four values for maximum and minimum x and y values inside which the user will be able to drag. Go back to the code on the box instance from the preceding task and edit it so that it reads as follows:

```
on(press){
  startDrag(this, true, 0, 0, 550, 400);
}
on(release){
  stopDrag();
}
```

Notice that only the `startDrag()` action is edited. The second parameter (`true`) says *do* lock to center, meaning the object's center point will appear where the mouse moves. This option may pose a problem if your object isn't using the center registration, as specified in step 1 in the preceding task. If your object didn't use the center registration when you created it, change the code `true` to read `false`. `0, 0, 550, 400` specifies left, top, right, and bottom, respectively. Because the default Stage size is 550×400, this will keep the object on the Stage. If you don't remember which parameter is for which value, press the Show Code Hint button, as shown in Figure 16.3.

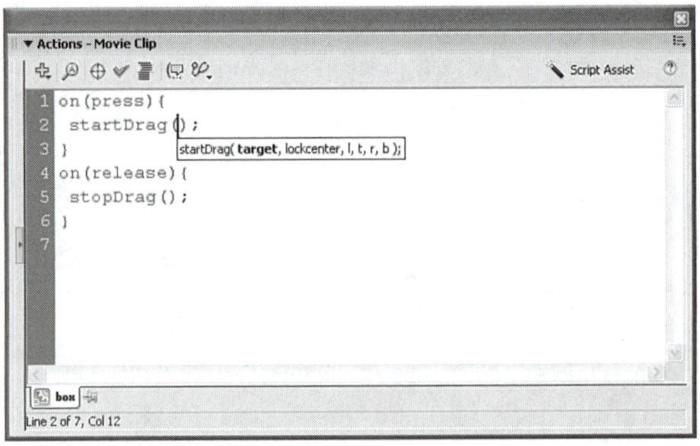

FIGURE 16.3
Pressing the Code Hint button will make re-editing the `startDrag()` code easier because it reveals the syntax.

2. Press F12 to see a publish preview. I suggest doing this rather than using Test Movie only because the edges of the Stage will be more apparent. You might notice that although you can't drag the box completely off the Stage, you can drag it so it's hanging halfway off. That's because the coordinate parameters limit the center of the clip's location. Instead of 0 for the left, you should have said "zero plus half the width of this box." You can use ActionScript for this (that is, `0+this._width/2`). Alternatively, you can first gather the locations by hand and enter them manually.

3. To manually gather locations, first position the box in each of the four locations (one at a time) by using the Align panel. That is, select the box, make sure To Stage is selected in the Align panel, and then click the top-left button (Align Left Edge), as shown in Figure 16.4.

Align left edge

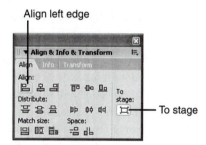

To stage

FIGURE 16.4
The Align panel can position an object to align perfectly with any edge of the Stage.

4. From the Info panel determine the locations of the box for each of the four locations (left, top, right, bottom). Write down these locations. Be sure to have the center registration option selected in the Info panel so that it reflects the clip's center location (see Figure 16.5).

Display top-left coordinates

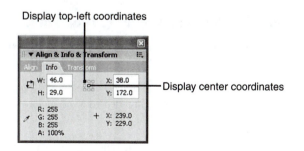

Display center coordinates

FIGURE 16.5
The Info panel can reflect the top left or center of any object. In this task, use the center option.

5. Use the numbers you came up with in step 4 to replace just the start drag line of code. Here are the numbers I came up with by using the Align and Info panels:

```
startDrag(this, true, 50, 25, 500, 375);
```

My box was 100_50, which accounts for the 50 added to 0 (and subtracted from 550), as well as 25 (added and subtracted appropriately).

6. Because, this hour is about scripting, you can use the following alternative to bypass the manual steps you followed in steps 4–5:

```
startDrag(this, true, 0+this._width/2, 0+this._height/2,
          550-this._width/2, 400-this._height/2);
```

Feel free to experiment using other values besides those shown in the preceding task in the startDrag action's parameters.

Now that the user can't drag the box off the Stage, you can add a feature that will check whether the user dropped it on top of the correct target. For example, say you put text inside the clip that said "Oregon" and then you had a map with the outlines of the United States state borders. Depending on whether the user dropped the label on the correct state, you could give him appropriate feedback. The trick is that you need to think about both *how* to check whether it's right and *when* to check it. In addition, you have to decide how to respond to the user dropping the box correctly or not. After you got this working for Oregon, you could make 49 more boxes if you wanted! The following task walks you through the steps of doing one of these.

Try It Yourself

Ascertain Where an Object Is Dropped

For this task, you can add to the same file used in the preceding task. Follow these steps:

1. Make a clip to serve as a target. Draw any shape, but make sure it's noticeably bigger than your box. Convert it to a movie clip and then give it the instance name correctSpot.

2. Next, you need to determine when to check where the user dropped the box, whether the user dropped it in the right spot, and how to respond in either case. The time to check is right after the user lets go of the object—that is, inside the on(release) curly braces. You can add an if statement after stopDrag. To start, edit the code so that it reads as follows:

```
1 on(release){
2    stopDrag();
3    if(correct){
4        trace("correct");
5    }else{
6        trace("wrong");
7    }
8 }
```

Lines 3–7 were added. This is the skeleton for an if-else statement. The idea is that normally, every line of code executes (when the release event occurs). You use the if statement and if-else statement when you want to skip certain lines of code. In this case, only line 4 or line 6 will actually execute—never both. When you simply want Flash to either execute or not execute some code, you use a plain if statement, which looks like this:

```
if(condition){
 trace("will do this when condition is true");
}
```

In this example, however, you want Flash to always execute one thing or the other (so you use if-else).

3. Line 3 (if(correct){) won't work as is. This is sort of like pseudo-code because it makes sense when you read it. However, Flash doesn't know what correct means. You need to replace just that word with an expression that results in true or false. The hitTest action will turn into true or false if one clip's center is hitting any portion of another clip. Here's what you type in place of correct in line 3:

```
this.hitTest(_parent.correctSpot)
```

This is just an expression that's either true (if this clip's center is within the area of the correctSpot clip) or false (when this clip's center is not on the correctSpot clip). Unfortunately, you can't just use correctSpot because this code is on the clip. That is, there is no correctSpot clip inside the box. Rather, you use parent because it's up one level. Here's the complete code:

```
on(release){
   stopDrag();
   if(this.hitTest(_parent.correctSpot)){
      trace("correct");
   }else{
      trace("wrong");
   }
}
```

By the Way

> ### Expressions in ActionScript
>
> An **expression** is like a phrase or partial sentence in English. Expressions can always be evaluated, but they're never complete thoughts or statements. For example, 2+2 is an expression. When evaluated, it turns to 4. In the case of an if statement, you need to write an expression that results in true or false. In English you might say, "age is greater than 21." That's just an expression because it has a value (true or false), but by itself it's not a complete statement. if statements often use logical operators (such as > and <) in their expressions.

4. At this point you can test the movie, and Flash will accurately report correct or wrong, depending on where you drop the box. However, the trace actions will only work while you're testing. You can just snap the box to the center of the correctSpot clip (when it's right) or back to its original location (if it's wrong). First, use the Info panel to determine the box clip's initial x, y location. Edit the on(release) code one last time so that it reads as follows:

```
on(release){
    stopDrag();
    if(this.hitTest(_parent.correctSpot)){
        this._x=_parent.correctSpot._x;
        this._y=_parent.correctSpot._y;
    }else{
        this._x=10;
        this._y=20;
    }
}
```

You'll want to replace the 10 and 20 in lines 7 and 8 with the x and y values you found for the box clip's initial location. Lines 7 and 8 simply say, "set this clip's x to 10" and "set this clip's y to 20." Lines 4 and 5 say the same thing, but instead of using hard numbers (such as 10 and 20), they say "set this clip's x to the correctSpot clip's x."

▲

The last step in the preceding task required that you use a technique that's covered in the next section of this hour—how to set properties (such as x and y location) of clips. Actually, after you learn some more techniques, you can come back and decide to give the user different or additional feedback for dropping the box in the right place or the wrong place.

Programming in Flash

It seems like there's a lot to draggable objects. This hour has included a lot of detail so far because using draggable objects is one of the most advanced features that doesn't require a lot of programming. The term *programming* gets tossed around a lot, but my definition of programming is using the ActionScript language to make a Flash movie play back differently based on user input, user interaction, timing issues, or data found outside Flash. If you want your movie to play back the same way each time (like a narrative or a cartoon, for example), you don't need to do any programming. Even if you want relatively sophisticated interactivity (buttons, draggable objects, and so on), you can achieve it with basic actions or behaviors. However, for a much more dynamic (changing) movie, you need to do some programming. Fortunately, ActionScript is fairly easy to use. Behaviors insulate you from the actual code. Also, the Actions panel includes helpers such as code hints, code completion, and Script Assist. When you approach the process of programming in small steps, you will probably find it easier than you would imagine after looking at the cryptic code some programmers create. It doesn't have to be difficult.

The rest of this hour introduces you to most of the programming capabilities of Flash. An entire book could be devoted to this topic (actually, I've written several), so naturally, it can't be fully covered in just this hour. I'm just going to point the way. If you have little interest in programming, it's safe to skip the rest of this hour. You can always come back later if needed. There's plenty more information in later hours, so only jump ahead to Hour 17, "Using Components." (Don't skip the rest of the book!)

Variables

Variables are a safe (yet temporary) place to store information. Imagine each variable as an individual whiteboard. You can write whatever you want on the whiteboard, erase it, and then write something else in its place. Variables are similar. Variables are useful because you can use them to save data while a movie plays.

A key concept with variables is that each one has both a name and a value. With a whiteboard, whatever is written on the whiteboard is the current value. If you have several whiteboards—maybe one has a phone number, another has an address, and so on—you would want to name (or label) the whiteboards so you know which one is which. If you name one phone_number and the other address, you could simply find out the value of phone_number. It would be less complicated than trying to remember which whiteboard is which. Transferring this analogy to real variables, imagine that you have a variable named phone_number whose value is whatever number you put into it.

You can do two things with variables:

▶ Set or change their values

▶ Ascertain or check their values

Notice that I didn't mention that you can create variables. You don't need to take a formal step to create them; they simply exist as soon as you set the value for one. However, the way you create a variable is to start with the keyword var followed by the variable name as in:

```
var myVariableName;
```

In practical terms, common tasks that you'll need variables for might include the following:

▶ Asking the user for his or her name (so you can use it later)

▶ Counting how many times the user has been to part of your movie (so you can change the course after he or she has seen something several times)

▶ Quizzing the user and tracking his or her score

▶ Displaying text that changes frequently, such as a prompt. You can use the Dynamic Text option to reflect the current value of a variable that you keep changing.

In the following task, you'll learn how to use a variable to get a user's name.

▼   **Try It Yourself**

Use a Variable to Get the User's Name

This task involves letting the user input data (his or her name), and it also shows how you can monitor the user's input. Here are the steps:

1. In a new file, select the Text tool and then open the Properties panel. Set the Text Type drop-down list to Input Text (the default is Static Text). Also, select the Show Border Around Text button (as in Figure 16.6). Click once to create a block of text. The little square at the bottom right of the text can be used to change the margins of the text box. One thing that's interesting about the Input Text and Dynamic Text settings is that with them, you can create text blocks with nothing in them.

2. With the text block selected (using either your I-beam cursor in the field or the Selection tool), select the entire block. Then use the Properties panel to set the instance name to username_txt (see Figure 16.6).

▼   **3.** Put a stop action in Frame 1.

Instance name

Show border around text button

FIGURE 16.6
The user will
type his or her
name into this
input text block.

4. Create a button and put an instance of it next to the text block you created in step 1. You're basically going to let the user advance to the next frame when he presses this button. However, it will be especially nice to let the user advance by simply pressing Enter on the keyboard. Open the Actions panel and select your button instance. Type this code in it:

```
on (press) {
 username = username_txt.text;
 nextFrame();
}
```

5. Before you go on to the next frame, you need to make sure Flash stops on the first frame. Also, we'll formally declare a homemade variable called username. Click once on Frame 1 in the Timeline (make sure the Actions panel tab says Layer 1:1) and type this code:

```
var username;
stop();
```

6. Click once on Frame 2 and insert a blank keyframe (by pressing F7). In Frame 2 create another text field. This one should be set to Dynamic Text (so the user can't edit it).Give this field the instance name message_txt.

7. Now you're going to put a couple actions in the keyframe on Frame 2. The first thing you do is populate the text field—or, more specifically, change the text property of the instance named message_txt. (You saw earlier this hour how you can change the _x or _y of a clip; text instances happen to have a property called text.) Select the keyframe and then open the Actions panel. Type the following code in it:

```
message_txt.text="Welcome " + username;
```

Translated, this means "set the text property of the message_txt instance to the string "Welcome " followed by the value of the variable called username."

If you put a word such as `Welcome` in quotes (as a string), it's taken literally. When you refer to a variable name (such as `username`), the value is used. The plus sign actually performs a concatenation when used with strings. (**Concatenate** means to connect.)

By the Way

> **Populating Fields**
>
> **Populate** is a popular term for the process of filling in data. It can be a manual process that you follow while editing, or it can be done at runtime with scripting.

8. Using Test Movie, see how your movie works.

The preceding task lets you experiment with two basic features: controlling variables (by setting values) and controlling the text the user sees in a field. You let the user directly affect `text` property of the field (by typing right into the input text).

The next task shows you how to increment a variable. It's very simple: A variable named `count` will increase every time the user clicks a button. Then, just to prove it's working, you'll have another button that reveals the current value of `count`. This task might seem simplistic, but it's very useful. What's more, incrementing variables is so common that you need to know how to do it.

Try It Yourself

Increment a Variable

This task demonstrates how to increment a variable and then reveal it to the user. Here are the steps:

1. In a new file, create a button and a dynamic text block. Give the text field an instance name `counter_txt`.

2. Create a button and give it an instance name `counter_btn`.

3. This time we'll put all the code in a single keyframe, so select the keyframe (not the individual button or text field instance) and type this code:

```
var count = 0;
counter_txt.text = count;


counter_btn.onPress = function(){
 count++;
 counter_txt.text = count;
}
```

Translated, this code says we'll be using a variable called `count` with an initial value of `0`. The second line pre-populates the `counter_txt` instance. Then, every time the user clicks the `counter_btn` instance you increment the `count` variable and update the `counter_txt` instance's `text` property.

4. Test the movie, and you should see the `count` variable increment. There's nothing wrong with this code, but I want to emphasize you don't need to continually display the value of variables for the user's benefit. For example, if you're tracking user's scores there's no requirement that you show them their running score. Let's keep track of the user's clicks but only reveal that value when they click another button.

5. Create another button and give it an instance name `reveal_btn`.

6. Completely change the code (in the keyframe) to read as follows:

```
var count = 0;
counter_txt.text = "";

counter_btn.onPress = function(){
  count++;
}

reveal_btn.onPress = function(){
  counter_txt.text = "You clicked " + count + " times";
}
```

7. You can test the movie again. This time, the user doesn't see anything until they press the `reveal_btn` instance.

Increment Shortcut

To increment the value of the variable `count` in the preceding task, you simply used the script `count++`. You can also decrease the variable's value by using the script `count--` (that is, use your variable's name followed by two minus signs). Finally, if you want to increment by a larger number than one, you use `count+=5`, which increases the variable `count`'s value by five. To decrease in larger numbers, use `count-=5`, replacing 5 with whatever number you want the increments to decrease by. Just realize that `++` and `--` work only when the value of `count` is indeed a number (not a string).

You might notice that when the Properties panel is set to either Dynamic Text or Input Text, there are a bunch of extra options. Of particular interest is the Embed button (shown in Figure 16.7). When you click this button, you can opt to embed character outlines for any particular glyph (or letter) in your typeface. These options only apply to dynamic text and input text because the actual words and letters that appear may change. Flash needs to know whether you expect the user to have the font installed already. If you use a fancy font that your users don't have (and you leave these buttons deselected), another font will be used as a substitute. The overall look and the spacing may change drastically if you do this. (Of course, it won't be an issue on your machine when you test because you have the font installed.)

If you're not sure your users have the selected font (the safest bet is that they don't), you can opt to embed the entire font outline (well, uppercase, lowercase, numerals, and punctuation) so it will appear properly, no matter what the contents of the text block may become. This, naturally, adds to the file size significantly. As an alternative, you can even specify just the characters you type into the field under Include These Characters. Including the minimum necessary will help maintain a small file size.

FIGURE 16.7
Clicking the Embed button reveals the Character Options dialog box.

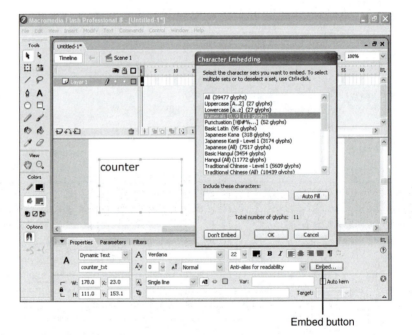

Embed button

Properties

Every object changed during authortime. You can think of **properties** as visual attributes (although some properties are not visible). For example, every object has two position properties (one for x and one for y). Common built-in properties include _x (x position), _y (y position), _alpha (current alpha setting), and _rotation (current rotation of a clip). All the built-in properties are listed in the Properties category of the toolbox list in the Actions panel. Clip instances, button instances, and dynamic or input text objects work differently from other objects in Flash. Not only can you set these objects' properties during authortime in Flash, but through ActionScript you can change them dynamically during runtime, too. For instance, you can effectively move a movie clip instance by changing its _x and _y properties.

Setting Properties

Although instances of Graphic symbols can have color styles and other properties changed during authortime, only instances of the three object types (button instance, clip instance, and dynamic or input text) can change during runtime. To change a property of an object with ActionScript, you simply address the object (that is, target it), specify the property, and set it to a new value. The following task shows you just how easy this can be.

Try It Yourself ▼

Change the Alpha Property of a Movie Clip Instance

In this task you'll change the alpha of a movie clip when the user clicks a button. Here are the steps to follow:

1. In a new file, place a button and a movie clip on the Stage. Select the movie clip on the Stage and use the Properties panel to name the instance of the clip theClip.

2. On the button instance, use the Actions panel to add this code:

```
on(press){
 theClip._alpha = 50;
}
```

3. Test the movie, and you should see the instance theClip change to 50% alpha when you click the button. ▲

Rotating or Changing Alpha on Dynamic Text

If you want to do the preceding task with a text object (that is, change the _alpha or _rotation property of a text object), you need to embed characters for the font used (as discussed earlier). This isn't necessary with static text, but then again, you can't give static text an instance name.

By the Way

The seemingly cryptic line of code you put into the button in the preceding task (theClip._alpha = 50) is actually pretty simple. It uses "dot syntax." This syntax is a little funky at first, but after you get it, there's no stopping you. It always follows the form `object.property`. In this case, you want to change the alpha of an instance called `theClip`. The object is the clip instance, and the property you're changing is `_alpha`. (Notice that many—but not all—built-in properties are preceded by an underscore.) Translated, `theClip._alpha = 50` means, "`theClip`'s alpha is assigned the value 50."

The fact that you're referring to the clip from outside (that is, from the button, which is not inside the movie clip) means you had to address the clip. To be more technical, I should have said the form is `path to object.object.property`. Say you want to target a clip that itself was inside another clip; you can address the clip in the form `theClip.clipInAClip._alpha=50`, where `clipInAClip` is the instance name of the clip inside the movie clip. Notice that addresses and properties are all separated by periods (when speaking, you say "dot," which is why it's called "dot syntax"). Remember from Hour 15, "Using ActionScript and Behaviors to Create Nonlinear Movies," you addressed a clip within a clip to make it stop the same way you're now addressing clips to change their properties.

It's not always so tricky. You could change the code to read `_alpha=50`. Unless the code begins with `_root`, you can assume that the keyword `this` is implied in front of any address. That is, `_alpha=50` is the same as `this._alpha = 50` (which means "this Timeline, you set your alpha to 50"). Go ahead and try it. First, draw a circle or something on the Stage (so you'll see more than just the button and movie clip). Then change the script inside the button to `_alpha = 50`, test the movie, and notice that everything on the Stage changes! Now go back and cut the button from the main scene and paste it inside the master movie clip. Now when the button is clicked, everything inside the clip instance (including the button) changes to alpha 50. Copy and paste the clip so you have multiple instances of the clip (now with the button inside each one). You'll see that the button only changes the alpha of the instance in which you clicked. This is kind of cool, considering you don't even have to name any instances or specify the clip you're targeting. In conclusion, you can target specific clip instances by name, or (if you omit the target) Flash will consider that an implied `this` precedes your object. By the way, starting any address with `_root` (as in `_root.clip._alpha = 50`) targets the main Timeline, from which you can address any object. This is called an **absolute address** (as opposed to all the relative addresses we've used so far).

Getting Properties

Besides setting properties (like how you set the alpha of the clip), you can also ascertain—that is, *get*—the current value of any property. In fact, you can get the value of any property but set the property of only some (albeit most) properties. For example, you can't set a clip's `_totalframes` property at runtime. To access a property, you use the same form as in the preceding example (you'll just check it, not change it). For example, say you have a dynamic text block with the instance name `message_txt` and an action that reads

```
message_txt.text = "The current alpha is " + theClip._alpha + "%"
```

Because `theClip._alpha` is not within quotation marks, Flash will get the current alpha value of the clip and stick it between the two parts of a string. Then the whole (combined) string is placed in the `text` property of the `message_txt` dynamic instance. Access to properties follows the same form whether you're setting the property or getting the property. It's always `object.property`.

Getting a property can be combined with setting a property. In the following task, you'll use two buttons that change the alpha of a clip. One button reduces the alpha, and the other increases it. Obviously, this will require more than just setting the alpha. You can't just set the alpha to "10 less." You have to know "10 less than what." Therefore, you'll first get the current alpha and set the alpha to 10 less than that. (This is easier to understand when you try it.)

Try It Yourself ▼

Make Buttons That Increase and Decrease the Alpha Setting of a Clip

This task involves both setting and getting properties of a clip. Here are the steps:

1. Place two buttons and one clip on the Stage. Name the clip instance (as before, not the name in the Library) `theClip`.

2. Use the Actions panel to put the following code on one button:

```
on(press){
 theClip._alpha = theClip._alpha - 10;
}
```

This means `theClip`'s alpha should be assigned the value of "`theClip`'s alpha minus 10."

3. The other button will have nearly the same code, except it will add 10:

```
on(press){
 theClip._alpha = theClip._alpha + 10;
}
```

4. Test the movie!

▲

Summary

When you understand it, programming in Flash is pretty easy. The hard part is organizing the job at hand—that is, deciding what you have to do and when you have to do it. When you know what you need to do, it's almost routine to execute it. When you have a good handle on targeting, variables, and properties, you'll be unstoppable.

As a warm-up in this hour, we explored draggable clips extensively. You actually made the start of a pretty sophisticated interaction.

This hour also covered two significant programming concepts: variables and properties. Variables store data while a movie plays. You can change variables, watch them change (in dynamic text blocks), let the user change them (via input text blocks), and ascertain their values any time by simply referring to them in a script. You have learned how to set and get properties of clip instances. Setting built-in properties such as _x, _y, and _alpha will have immediate and visual effects on clip instances. You have learned the object property syntax for referring to or changing properties of specific clips.

Q&A

Q *I'm having trouble figuring out why I keep getting the following error: "Statement must appear within on/onClipEvent handler". What does that mean, and how do I avoid it?*

A That's one of the most common errors. Basically, it's saying that the code you've directly attached to a button or Movie Clip instance must appear within an event sandwich. That is, for buttons between on(someEvent){ and } or, for Movie Clip instances between onClipEvent(someEvent){ and }. Note that this doesn't apply to code placed in keyframes—only when you select the button or clip and type into the Actions panel.

Q *I'm not clear which method is better: putting code right on buttons or putting everything in a keyframe. Is one better, and, can I mix and match?*

A Whichever one you're more comfortable with is better for you. Personally, I put all my code in a keyframe (or in external .as files which is another topic altogether). I like having everything in one place. The only hassle is that you have to name all the button instances (in order to refer to them and assign the onPress behavior from inside a keyframe). You can mix and match. You can even have both at once, code in a keyframe and on buttons—they'll both execute.

Workshop

The Workshop consists of quiz questions and answers to help you solidify your understanding of the material covered in this hour. You should try to answer the questions before checking the answers.

Quiz

1. When does the `startDrag()` action execute?

    A. When the user first clicks (and holds onto) the object.

    B. When the movie starts.

    C. It depends where you put the action.

2. How do you create a new variable?

    A. Wait until the playback head has at least reached Frame 2.

    B. Just start using them as you need them, any time you want.

    C. Insert the action `newVariable`.

3. Do you have to use ActionScript to change the alpha of a clip instance?

    A. Yes. You do it via the `_alpha` property.

    B. No. You can use the `_visible` property.

    C. No. You can do it by hand via the Color Styles drop-down list in the Properties panel.

Quiz Answers

1. C. You could make the `startDrag()` action execute at any time you want. It's up to you where you put the code (in a keyframe or a button, for example).

2. B. Although it's possible to initialize a variable other ways, it's not necessary. You can just start using variables as you need them.

3. C. This is, of course, a trick question. There is a `__visible` property, but you haven't learned about it yet. When `_visible` is set to `false`, the clip disappears. When `_visible` is set to `true`, the clip is fully visible. I just wanted to point out that you can change properties by hand during authortime (by using the Properties panel, for example), although this doesn't enable you to see properties change at runtime.

HOUR 17

Using Components

What You'll Learn in This Hour:

▶ How to use the user interface components that ship with Flash

▶ How to populate components with customized data

▶ How to make components trigger your own ActionScript

Last hour you studied programming. For some, it was probably more technical than you'd prefer; for others, it wasn't technical enough. This split is natural. Some people like to express their creativity by solving puzzles, whereas others like more artistic endeavors. One of the great things about Flash is that it can appeal to both types of people—and components are a great example of this fact.

A **component** is a version of a movie clip that has programming code encapsulated in it so that a nontechnical person can use it without having to know how it works. Anyone can use a component. Depending on the features built in to the component, it can do some pretty fancy stuff.

This hour you'll mainly learn how to use components. First, though, it's important to get one concept straight: You use components while authoring Flash, but someone had to create them. It's not as simple to say *the developer* and *the user* anymore because there's another developer who created the component to begin with. I often refer to the *using developer*, meaning the person who's using the component while authoring her Flash file (not to be confused with the developer who created the component).

What Is a Component?

I just described components as movie clips with code in them. However, a movie clip with actions inside (maybe on a button or in a keyframe) doesn't automatically become a component. A Movie Clip symbol becomes a component when the component developer identifies parameters that can set differently for each instance. It's similar to how you can scale or tint any movie clip. In the case of components, you can set other properties in addition to the scale and tint. For example, you can set the label on each instance of a Button component (to change the word that appears on the button). The most common components are used for user interface (UI) elements such as buttons and menus. However, a **component** is just a clip with code and the ability to set initial values differently for each instance.

You'll usually follow this order to use a component:

1. Place it on the Stage.

2. Populate it with data (for the Button component, you might change its label).

3. Define the ActionScript that gets triggered when the component's event fires (say, how you want to handle the `click` event for the Button component).

4. Place additional components that may work together (say, the RadioButton component, of which you'll always want two or more).

We'll spread out all these steps into separate tasks in this hour, but this helps to know where you're headed. The first series of tasks this hour uses the ComboBox component. This is basically a drop-down menu from which the user can select any option, as shown in Figure 17.1. As with any component, you can define exactly how the ComboBox component is populated (that is, what's listed in the drop-down list) as well as how it will behave (that is, what it will do when the user makes a selection). You'll do just that in the next task.

FIGURE 17.1
You can use the ComboBox component to let your users make selections.

▼　　**Try It Yourself**

Manually Populate the ComboBox Component

Later this hour you'll build on this task, but at this stage you'll just populate the component. Here are the steps:

1. In a new file, open the Components panel by selecting Window, Components. It's possible to install sets of components, so make sure that the User Interface components section is fully expanded, as shown in Figure 17.2.

▼

Expand/Collapse option

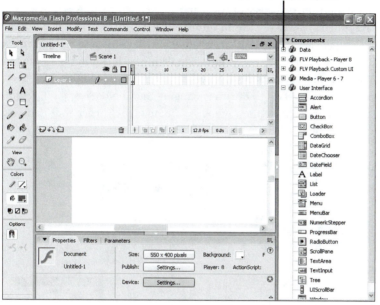

FIGURE 17.2
Make sure the
User Interface
components are
fully expanded,
as shown here.

2. Drag the ComboBox component onto the Stage as if you were dragging an instance from the Library. You can use the Free Transform tool to change its width, and you won't cause it to distort (but don't rotate or skew it). With the instance on the Stage still selected, open the Parameters panel. (If the Parameters panel is not in its default location adjacent to your Properties panel, select Window, Properties, Parameters.)

3. Before you populate the parameters, give this instance a unique name so that later you can access it by using ActionScript. Name the instance myComboBox. Then click the Parameters tab so that you can populate this component uniquely.

4. In the Parameters panel, select the line Labels. Click the magnifier button at the right of this line (see Figure 17.3).

5. In the Values dialog box that appears, click the plus button and then replace the text defaultValue with Macromedia. This will be the first item to appear in the ComboBox component. Repeat the process of clicking the plus button to create two more items—one for Microsoft and another for Sams. You can click any value you have created and move it up or down in the list by pressing the arrow buttons. Click OK when you're finished.

6. Test the movie, and you'll see the ComboBox component function. This is a pretty sophisticated piece of code, and all you had to do was provide unique data. You can likely use this in future projects. The only problem is that nothing happens when the user selects an item. That's because you've only set values for the "labels." In addition to populating each slot in the ComboBox with labels you must also supply a "data" for each slot. In addition, you need to write code that reacts to the user changing the ComboBox. You'll resolve all this in the task "Make the ComboBox Component Trigger Your ActionScript," later this hour.

FIGURE 17.3
Each named property (in the left column of the Parameters panel) can > be populated with unique values (in the right column). In the case of labels for a ComboBox component, you will enter several values.

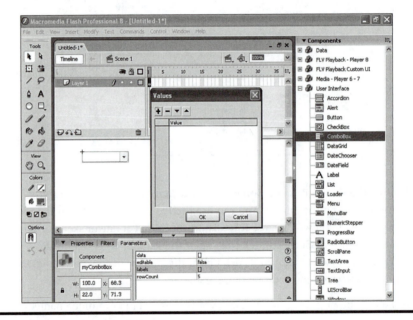

A common attribute of many components is the way they can contain both labels and data. The user sees the labels, but only your ActionScript can see the data. The data give you a convenient place to store additional details that the user doesn't need to see. In the case of the ComboBox component from the preceding task, the labels are what the user sees onscreen, and the data will be the actual web addresses to which we'll jump. In the end, you simply need to populate the data parameter with a list of three URLs that match the three companies listed in the `labels` parameter (which you just populated). You can do this manually in almost the same way you did in the preceding task, except that you enter values into the `data` parameter instead of the `labels` parameter. In order to demonstrate a different way that populates *both* data and labels, you'll do it by using ActionScript in the next task.

Try It Yourself ▼

Populate the ComboBox Component by Using ActionScript

As the next step toward letting the user navigate using the ComboBox component, you'll populate both the data and labels by using ActionScript. Follow these steps:

1. The following code will replace any labels you entered by hand via the Parameters tab of the Properties panel. It uses the addItem action, which accepts two parameters: the label and the data. Because your ComboBox component has the instance name myComboBox, you can put the following code into Frame 1. That is, select Frame 1, open the Actions panel, and then type this code:

```
var myComboBox:mx.controls.ComboBox;
myComboBox.removeAll();
myComboBox.addItem("Macromedia", "http://www.macromedia.com/");
myComboBox.addItem("Microsoft", "http://www.microsoft.com/");
myComboBox.addItem("Sams", "http://www.samspublishing.com/");
```

   The first line tells Flash that myComboBox is an instance of the ComboBox component. Actually, it helps you more than it helps Flash because anywhere you type myComboBox., the period will trigger a code hint for all the actions related to ComboBox components. The second line (removeAll()) will remove what you typed by hand. The last three lines each set a label and a corresponding value for data.

2. Test the movie at this point, but it will appear no different than it did at the end of the preceding task. In the next task you will include the ActionScript to actually jump to those URLs. As you probably can imagine, this involves the getURL action. However, the next task will show you exactly when to trigger that script as well as how to determine the parameter (so you go to the right website). ▲

Although populating a component manually or by using ActionScript is important so that the user sees your content, you'll almost always need to tie the component to your movie by letting it trigger scripts. In the case of the ComboBox component, when the user makes a selection, you want to trigger the getURL action. Just as a button can respond to a variety of different events (such as press and release), each component has one or more events to which a script can respond.

There are two basic ways to assign a script to a component's events: by using the Behaviors panel or the ActionScript panel to attach code directly to the component or by using the addEventListener() action. Personally, I recommend using addEventListener(), despite the fact that it's slightly more complex. If you use this method, when you have several components (say, a row of radio buttons), you won't have to physically add code to each one. Because both approaches are fairly easy, we'll look at both in the following task.

▼   **Try It Yourself**

Make the ComboBox Component Trigger Your ActionScript

In this task you'll add ActionScript that the ComboBox component triggers each time the user makes a change. Here are the steps:

1. With the file from the preceding task, select the instance of your ComboBox component and open the Actions panel. Begin by typing on(. You should immediately see a code completion hint that lists all the various events available for this component, as Figure 17.4 shows.

FIGURE 17.4
Typing on(triggers a code completion hint, which lists all available events for the selected component.

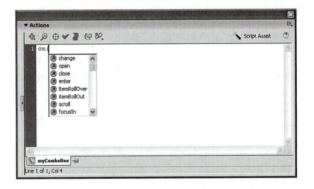

2. Select the event change, which triggers every time the user changes the ComboBox component. Notice that there are many other events that you can trap. Make sure the skeleton for the on(click) event looks like this:

```
on(change){
}
```

By the Way

> **Trapping Events**
> **Trap** means that you can prepare a script that triggers when a particular event (that you want to trap) occurs.

3. You need to add a getURL action after line 1 and before line 2. Click after line 1 and press Enter. Then, from the plus button, select Global Functions,

▼

Browser/Network, getURL. The code hint should appear to help you fill it in, but for now just use Macromedia's address. The code should look like this:

```
on(change){
 getURL("http://www.macromedia.com/");
}
```

If you select Control Test Movie now, it will work only insofar as you'll hyper-link to Macromedia, no matter which selection you make.

4. Open the Actions panel and make some edits to the script the behavior produced. Replace the entire parameter in the getURL action (quotation marks and all) with code that says "the data for the item that's currently selected in this ComboBox component." Naturally, that's pseudo-code. In the Actions panel, change the code to read as follows:

```
on (change) {
 getURL(this.selectedItem.data);
}
```

Although that code might look a bit complex, it uses dot syntax, as discussed last hour. In English you might go from specific to general, like "the data of the selected item in this component." But in script it goes from general to specific: this.selectedItem.data.

5. When you test the movie now, it should work great. Whenever the user changes the ComboBox component selection, the currently selected item's data value (set way back in each addItem() action) will be used as the getURL action's first parameter.

Code hints helped you in the preceding task because they displayed the available events for the ComboBox component. Naturally, you'll also find complete details in the Help panel. Another way to trigger code hints is by declaring the instance name of your component, like this:

```
var myComboBox:mx.controls.ComboBox;
```

In effect, this tells Flash that the name myComboBox is going to be a ComboBox component, so you want all code hints that come with it. To see how you can do the whole preceding task by using ActionScript (that is, not putting any code "on" the ComboBox itself), check out the following code. All you need is to have a ComboBox instance named myComboBox and the following code:

```
var myComboBox:mx.controls.ComboBox;
myComboBox.removeAll();
```

```
myComboBox.addItem("Macromedia", "http://www.macromedia.com/");
myComboBox.addItem("Microsoft", "http://www.microsoft.com/");
myComboBox.addItem("Sams", "http://www.samspublishing.com/");
myComboBox.addEventListener("change",doChange);
function doChange(evt){
 getURL(evt.target.selectedItem.data);
}
```

The last four lines replace what you did in the preceding task, but they use script (that is, you don't want any code ComboBox component instance itself). You don't have to use this all-script approach. It's just that, as you'll see with the RadioButton component in particular, it's easier to add an event listener to several buttons than to put code on each one. Plus, a custom function such as doChange() can also serve as the clearinghouse for several different buttons. Notice the code uses the selectedItem of evt.target (not this or myComboBox)—that is, the particular component instance that changed. You'll see this in a minute, but I wanted to show you that there's always an all-script alternative to putting code right on components.

Using the RadioButton Component

With radio buttons (like the old mechanical buttons on car radios), you can select only one button at a time. Selecting which radio station to play requires that you pick just one. If you change your mind, that's fine, but you can't play two stations at once. It's important to use radio buttons only for this kind of situation—for instance, when the user selects from mutually exclusive choices, such as male and female. On the other hand, check box buttons (for which there's another User Interface component) allow for multiple selections.

You always use RadioButton components in groups; for example, two buttons (male and female) in a gender group and three buttons (novice, intermediate, expert) in a skill level group. Like other components, each RadioButton component has a label and a value. Depending on the interaction you're building, you might want to trigger code immediately when the user makes a selection or wait until the user is satisfied with his selection and clicks Continue. The one thing I'd suggest you avoid is proceeding to a new screen immediately after a user clicks. That's because the user might have made a mistake, or might want to change her mind. You'll explore all these details in the following task.

Try It Yourself ▼

Use the RadioButton Components

In this task, you'll use a radio button to ask the user to specify his skill level (novice, intermediate, or expert). Follow these steps:

1. In a new file, open the Components panel and, one by one, drag three instance of the RadioButton component onto the Stage.

2. Arrange the three RadioButton component instances vertically. You can use the Align panel (by pressing Ctrl+K) to space out or line up the buttons. Select the top instance and access the Parameters tab in the Properties panel, as shown in Figure 17.5.

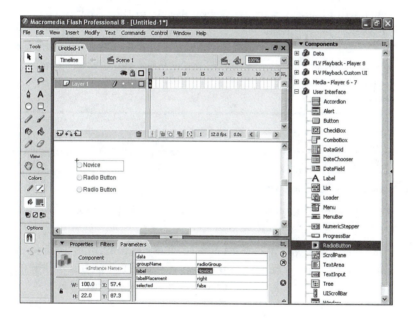

FIGURE 17.5
You populate the three RadioButton component instances one at a time by using the Parameters panel.

3. Change the value for the label to Novice. Also set the value for the data to novice. Finally, notice the group name radioGroup. Just leave this alone because the other buttons have the same name—so only one option in the group can be selected at a time. If you add another group later (say, with Male and Female buttons), you'd want all buttons in the other group to share a different group name (say, genderGroup). Give the first RadioButton component the instance name novice_option. (This is only because later you'll learn how to re-create this whole task entirely in ActionScript.)

4. Change the label, data, and instance name of the second button to
Intermediate, intermediate, and intermediate_option, respectively. Set
the label, data, and name for the last button to Expert, expert, and
expert_option, respectively.

> **Numbers for Data**
>
> You might prefer using some code system for the different levels (such as 1 for
> novice, 2 for intermediate, and 3 for expert). In this case, you'd want to set the
> data values accordingly. Don't do that for this example, but note that using num-
> bers for data is less touchy than using string values.

5. Notice that unlike with the ComboBox component, each of your RadioButton
component instances changes to reflect its current label. That is, you can see
the labels Novice, Intermediate, and Expert without even testing the movie.
This feature is called Live Preview. You can turn it on and off from the Control
menu. Go ahead and test the movie. You'll notice, now, that only one
RadioButton component can be set at a time (that is, when you select one, the
others deselect).

Try It Yourself

Apply the Radio Buttons

Although your radio buttons are nice, they don't really *do* anything. Follow these
steps to give the buttons some practical use:

1. Using the movie from the preceding task, drag a Button component onto the
Stage. Use the Parameters tab in the Properties panel to set this button's
label to Continue. Give the Button component the instance name
continue_button.

2. Make sure the button is on the Stage in Frame 1 (with the three instances of
radio buttons). Go to Frame 2 and insert a blank keyframe (by pressing F7). On
the screen, create a dynamic text block and give it the instance name message.
Go back to Frame 1, and you'll make it so that when the user clicks Proceed,
the user's skill level is determined and then the second frame displays an
appropriate message.

3. Click Frame 1 and open the Actions panel. Type this code in it:

```
stop();
continue_button.addEventListener("click",doClick);
function doClick(evt){
```

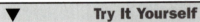

```
theMessage="Welcome " + radioGroup.selectedData;
nextFrame();
}
```

Notice that `stop()` will just prevent the movie from advancing to Frame 2. The second line says that for the `continue_btn`'s `press` event, you want to execute two lines of code. The first line sets a variable called `theMessage`. It combines the string `"Welcome"` with `selectedData` from `radioGroup`. The `selectedData` is the data of the currently selected radio button in that group. Finally, `nextFrame()` just advances to Frame 2 (where you'll put some more code).

4. Finally, with your variable `theMessage` assigned with a value, you can go to Frame 2 and populate the text field. Select Frame 2 and type this code into the Actions panel:

```
message.text=theMessage;
```

This just says, "set the text property of the message field to equal the value of the variable `theMessage`."

5. Test your movie!

In many ways I wish that components required even less scripting than they do. Even this simple example took a bit of work. And, in fact, there's a few loose ends. For example, test what happens when you press the button before selecting a radio button. One way to address that is to disable the continue button until after the user has made a selection. An easier way is to set a default for the user. That is, use the Parameters panel to set the "selected" parameter for one of the radio buttons to true (say, the novice button). Despite the fact that complex applications take more work, components can save a ton of time. Also, many of the scripting conventions for the various types of components are consistent, so it's not like you have to learn new conventions for each one.

Changing Component Styles

Components include code and graphics. However, you can change the styles that components use, such as the typeface or font weight. In addition, you can change the colors used in components. You can also create your own custom themes by editing every last graphic used in the components. The following sections show a little bit of code to apply text and color styles to all components used in your movie.

You can try any of these with the tasks from this hour. Or you can just drag a few components on the Stage and see the results. However, I suggest that you experiment by testing one example at a time so that you can see the impact of each script. You can type all these examples into the actions for Frame 1.

Styles Only Work at Runtime

Note that you won't see any style changes until you test the movie.

Setting the Style of a Single Component Instance

You can affect a single instance by using this form:

```
myInstance.setStyle("theStyle", value);
```

You have to replace *myInstance* with the instance name of your component, replace "*theStyle*" with the supported style (found in the Help files), and replace *value* with an actual value. For example, if you had a RadioButton component instance named rb, you could use the following code to change the text color (style name "color") to red:

```
rb.setStyle("color", 0xFF0000);
```

Hex Values

Notice that Flash uses the prefix 0x to signify that what follows is a hexadecimal (also called hex) value for color. You'll see the hex values for colors when you use any of Flash's color selection tools. However, those tools use # as the prefix for hex.

Setting the Style of One Component Type

You can affect all instances of a particular component by using this complex code:

```
var myStyle = new mx.styles.CSSStyleDeclaration();
myStyle.color = 0x0000FF;
_global.styles.CheckBox=myStyle;
```

It's really only the second line where you can customize things. If you want to also affect another style, just insert a line like this:

```
myStyle.fontFamily="Times New Roman";
```

To find what styles are supported, just search the Help file for "supported styles."

Setting the Style of All Components

The way you set a style for all instances of all components is shown here:

```
_global.style.setStyle("theStyle", value);
```

You can only change "theStyle" and value (to the style and value for the style you want to set). For example, the following code sets the color of all components' text to red:

```
_global.style.setStyle("color", 0xFF0000);
```

Using Themes

The topic of themes can become rather involved, but I want you to quickly notice that one style type is called themeColor. You can use any one of the following lines of code to change the overall theme color of your components:

```
_global.style.setStyle("themeColor", "haloGreen");
_global.style.setStyle("themeColor", "haloOrange");
_global.style.setStyle("themeColor", "haloBlue");
_global.style.setStyle("themeColor", 0x00FF00);
```

Naturally, you can apply the theme color to any single component type or instance by using the same basic syntax shown earlier this hour. Notice that the last line above uses a hex value, whereas the other three use one of the new preset halo colors.

Summary

Components have really grown up since their ancestors first appeared in Flash 5 as Smart Clips. Components should bridge the separation between programmer and nonprogrammer. A real programmer can create a sophisticated component that can enable the nonprogrammer to use sophisticated features in her projects without learning all the ActionScript necessary. Realize that the components that ship with Flash are just a taste of what's possible. You can find many more at the Flash Exchange site (www.macromedia.com/exchange/flash) as well as at other sites listed in Appendix B, "Resources."

This hour you have learned how to populate components manually (by using the Parameters tab in the Properties panel) as well as populate components by using ActionScript. In addition, you have learned how to use on() events or addEventListener to make components trigger your own custom code.

This hour you have seen details of the ComboBox, Button, and RadioButton components. There are many more components, but these are a good start. This hour you have also learned the basic scripts for changing the styles of components.

Q&A

Q *I decided to add a Button to the task "Make the ComboBox Component Trigger Your ActionScript." (Mainly because it only triggered when the user changed the option; I figured the user might want to click a button to go to the current selection.) In any event, here's the code that I put right on the Button instance:*

```
on (click) {
  getURL(this.selectedItem.data);
}
```

A That's pretty close. But instead of accessing the data for the selectedItem of "this" (the button, which has no selectedItem) you want to refer to the instance myComboBox. Change the code on the Button instance to read as follows:

```
on (click) {
  getURL(this._parent.myComboBox.selectedItem.data);
}
```

This says to grab the data for the selectedItem in the myComboBox but that instance is up one level from inside the Button—hence the code `this._parent`.

Q *Do components have to be complicated?*

A Of course not. The examples in this hour are relatively basic—they could be much more sophisticated. When you get the hang of using components, you will start seeing lots of consistencies between the various components.

Q *Are components just for user interface elements?*

A No. There happen to be some pretty fancy media components for playing back video and audio. These include all the user interface controls needed. It's just that the User Interface components are the most versatile because you snap them together for your own needs.

Workshop

The Workshop consists of quiz questions and answers to help you solidify your understanding of the material covered in this hour. You should try to answer the questions before checking the answers.

Quiz

1. Components are simply movie clips that have properties the author can edit via the Parameters panel.

    A. True.

    B. False. You edit the properties via the Components panel.

    C. False. Components require that you code in C++ or Pascal.

2. Flash ships with only a few components, so after you exhaust their possibilities, you'll have to wait for the next version of Flash for any new ones.

    A. True. Unless an interim release comes out, such as Flash 8.1.

    B. False. Components can be used to create more components (called *component mutation*).

    C. False. You or any other talented programmer can create components from scratch, so it's likely that you'll find a variety of components on the Internet.

3. You should use radio buttons only when providing the user with a selection of audio tracks.

    A. True. Why do you think they're called *radio buttons*?

    B. False. Radio buttons can be used for any purpose you want.

    C. False. Radio buttons should be used only for mutually exclusive choices.

Quiz Answers

1. A. That's a perfect definition.

2. C. Anyone can make a component. I'm sure that you'll be able to find many of them online for free.

3. C. Radio buttons should be used only for mutually exclusive choices (such as male and female). Check box–type buttons are for situations in which multiple selections are possible (such as pepperoni, olives, and sausage).

HOUR 18

Using Video

What You'll Learn in This Hour:

▶ How to import and use video in movies

▶ How to build scripted controls to play videos

▶ How to optimize for high quality and low file size

▶ How to use cue points to synchronize a video to the graphics in your Flash movie

In the not-too-distant past, it was impossible to display video inside of Flash without something short of a miracle. The video support in Flash 8 has really come of age. You can import video, trim it, and compress it, using the state-of-the-art VP6 codec from On2 that keeps files small and quality high. Even though most of the technical details are handled automatically, you're given enough control to vary the results greatly. If you want the best quality and most features, you need to use Flash Professional 8. There are a few workarounds that you can take if you only have Flash Basic 8 but, in short, Flash Basic 8 falls flat if you want to do video.

Codec is short for *compressor/decompressor*. Basically, videos need to be compressed so they download quickly. The same video needs to be decompressed for the user to view it. Many different technologies are available to compress and decompress. The codec that Flash Basic uses is called Spark (from Sorenson) while Flash Professional 8 also includes VP6 (from On2).

Flash Basic 8 Versus Flash Professional 8

You're about to learn nearly every option available for preparing and displaying videos inside Flash. Because the differences between Flash Basic 8 and Flash Professional 8 are most striking when considering video, I've produced the following table as an overview.

Don't worry if you don't understand every technical term—you will by the end of this hour. You can use the following table as a reference as you go through the rest of this hour.

Technique	Flash Basic 8	Flash Professional 8
Embedding a video into your .swf file	Supported.	Supported.
Encoding a video as an .flv file for external playback	Workaround: embed it first, then export. Note, these .flvs are CBR, not VBR.	Supported Also included is a standalone application for batch .flv creation.
Playing an external .flv (including those produced in outside applications)	Only with the "no-frills" video object.	Can use video object, Media Components, and the new FLVPLayback component with skin chooser.
Customized encoding settings (instead of presets)	Unavailable.	Supported.

Embedding Video Versus Playing External Video

There are two general ways to play video inside Flash: either embed where you import, compress, and then place the video inside your main file or, compress the video into an .flv file and play it externally. The video file has to download in either case, but by keeping it external you can control when it downloads. Perhaps you can give the user a choice of three different videos and only download the one they select. Embedding the video not only makes your main file bigger, but the quality isn't as good as playing an external .flv. Generally, the best route is to create an .flv to play externally. However there are two cases where embedding the video is a better option. One is when the video is very short (say, less than 30 seconds) and you don't want to bother with maintaining several files (the .swf and the .flv). I say short because a long embedded video with sound will begin to drift out of synchronization. The second reason to embed video is when you need frame-by-frame control. An external .flv can only pause on keyframes (which get added automatically, but may only appear a few times per second—much less frequently than every frame of video). If you want to let the user step frame-by-frame through a video clip of your golf swing, embedded video is a better choice.

Regardless of whether you plan to embed the final video or play an external `.flv`, you need to compress the video. That is, your source can be one of many video formats (such as MPEG or QuickTime) but it must be compressed using one of the Flash Player's two supported codecs. Namely, the older Sorenson Spark (which works in Flash Player 7 and Flash Player 6) or the newer, and much better quality, On2 VP6 codec (which requires users have Flash Player 8 or later).

Compressing a video (for embedding or to make an `.flv`) is only slightly more involved than importing other media types, such as sound or graphics. It really is as easy as selecting File, Import and then selecting a video. But as with sound and graphic files, there are different types of video files—each with its own attributes. In addition, the tasks of making a video look good, play well, and download quickly can all require some work. The first step—always—is concentrating on your source video.

Making Video Look Good

We'll look at the supported video types and how to get them into Flash in a minute, but it's worth noting that the entire creation process for video involves many specialties. Even if you don't employ a Hollywood crew, you will always have the responsibilities of sound engineer, camera operator, casting agent, writer, and so on. Also, technical issues such as background noise, camera shake, and lighting all affect the final outcome. There's not enough room in this book to teach you everything about video making. Just consider learning about traditional movie making.

When you're selecting or creating videos, there are a few considerations specific to video on the computer. The entire viewing experience is much different on a computer than in your living room. The following tips come down to the fact that video on the computer has restrictions:

▶ Only use video when appropriate. Three particular cases stand out: celebrity endorsement (that is, when the face is recognizable or important to add credibility to your message); call to action (when the video or sound can actually motivate someone to physically get up and go do what you're pushing); expert demonstrations (for example, a cook showing you how to fold eggs is something you could never really describe with pictures or words, you really need a video).

▶ As far as video content is concerned, you should refrain from using many fine details, such as small text; it can become illegible in a small video window.

▶ Changing viewpoints and camera angles (such as going from close up to far away) is always good. Just be aware of details that may be difficult to see on a small screen.

▶ Be conservative with special effects; everything has a "price"—be it lower per-formance, large files that download slowly, or gratuitous effects that become tiresome. Although the limits of computer videos may appear restrictive, they are really just challenges to overcome. In some ways, the restrictions of regular TV are removed. For example, you can use nearly any aspect ratio (that is, the shape—wide or narrow). You can even mask the video to make any shape you want, as Figure 18.1 shows.

In addition to these tips, you need to consider other optimization issues, as discussed later this hour.

FIGURE 18.1
Despite digital video's restrictions, you can do cool stuff such as change the viewing window's shape.

Supported Formats

Flash can compress video in various file formats. These are all digital files saved on your computer. For example, if all you have is a videotape, you'll need to digitize it first. This involves video capture hardware, which basically records the analog video into the computer's hard disk. However, if your source video is already in a digital format (such as a mini DV video camera), making a digital copy on the computer takes little more than a cord to connect the camera to the computer (naturally, this is also a piece of hardware). Finally, although your favorite movie on DVD is in fact already saved as a digital file, you'll find it next to impossible to convert this to a digital file that Flash will import (besides the fact that you may break copyright laws to import it).

There's much more to say about the way you create high-quality digital video files on the computer. However you do it, you must create one of the following digital file formats:

▶ QuickTime (.mov)

▶ Digital video (.dv)

▶ MPEG (.mpg or .mpeg)

▶ Windows Media (.asf or .wmv)

▶ Video for Windows (.avi)

Installing Video Support

By the Way

It's possible that your system configuration won't list this many digital video formats. To increase the types of video your computer will support, install QuickTime (from www.quicktime.com). In addition, if you're using Windows, be sure to install DirectX 9 or later (www.microsoft.com/directx/). You can see which version, if any, you already have by selecting Start, Run, and then typing dxdiag and click OK.

Although the list of video formats is relatively long, you'll probably use only one of the first three. Although each format has its unique purpose, when it comes to importing video into Flash, you always want to start with the highest-quality source. That's because Flash always compresses the video (a little or a lot—but always some). Video is like images in that quality degrades when you compress a file that's already compressed. Unfortunately, true uncompressed video files are huge. For example, the source videos I used in a recent project were about 200MB to 300MB per minute. Starting with such high quality really made a difference, even though the compressed version was less than 1MB per minute. In practice, a video that's only slightly compressed will still be high in quality but not nearly as big. Keep in mind, however, that the compression stage can be *very* time consuming. The On2 VP6 codec is particularly asymmetric meaning it takes longer to compress than decompress. That's usually the case with any codec, but here you could be tying up your machine for hours if not days!

Professionals creating source digital video files should have no trouble creating a QuickTime video with little or no compression (for example, the codec called "Animation"). Also, if you're copying video directly from a digital video camera, you can use one of the digital video formats (.dv). Also, many cameras will let you save a QuickTime video. Although MPEG can be high quality, there are actually several versions of it, so you'll have to test your entire process to make sure that it imports into

Flash correctly. I suspect that many MPEGs you'll find have already been compressed, so you really should find a higher-quality original. The same can be said for Windows Media. I think you'll be hard-pressed to find noncompressed high-quality .asf or .wmv files. Finally, Video for Windows (.avi) files are simply not as good as QuickTime files. They're old technology. This isn't to say that you can't make a decent .avi, but just that you'll do better with QuickTime.

Don't think this section is a rule book for how you should progress. The only universal rule is that you always want to start with the highest-quality original.

Now that you have your computer set up with video support, you'll see how to import video into a Flash movie in the following task.

Try It Yourself

Embed a Video

In this task, you will embed a QuickTime video into your Flash movie. Here are the steps to follow:

1. To make this go quickly, I'm going to use the sample movie that came with the free version of QuickTime (which you can find at www.quicktime.com), but you can use any footage you can find. Start a new Flash movie and select File, Import, Import Video. Click the Browse button and select the file sample.mov, which is located in the QuickTime folder (that is, Program Files/QuickTime). Then click Next.

2. The Deployment step of the video import sequence will appear as shown in Figure 18.2. Select the Embed option so that the compressed video will get saved inside the .fla and then click Next. (In fact, Flash Basic only has two options, but I'll cover all 5 options available to Flash Professional 8 after this task.)

3. The next step, Embedding, lets you select various details about how the video will appear in your file. Most of these settings are purely for convenience. For example, I recommend simply leaving the default symbol type "Embedded video" because it's simple to make the other types (Movie Clip or Graphic) by hand. For this exercise, leave the Symbol type and Audio track options as is and uncheck the two checkboxes. The only setting here that has any lasting impact is when you want to chop up your video. We'll take a quick side trip to see the video split feature so click "Edit the video first" and press Next.

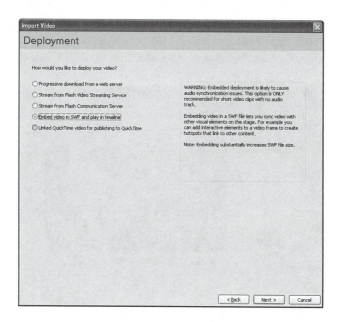

FIGURE 18.2
The Deployment dialog is where you decide whether to embed or create an external .flv.

4. The Split video dialog appears as shown in Figure 18.3. This is perhaps the simplest video editor of all time. Set the in and out points (by clicking the right facing and left facing arrow buttons) and then click the plus button to add the clip. You can reorder the clips as well. I just wanted you to see this dialog but for this exercise click the Back button so that we don't trim the video. (If you happen to have only a very long video go ahead and make a short clip so the encoding process won't take all day.) Back at the Embedding dialog (first seen in step 3) change the radio button at the bottom to "Embed the entire video." Then click Next.

5. The final screen, Encoding, lets you select the quality and corresponding bandwidth requirements from a variety of preset profiles. Only Flash Professional 8 lets you access the Advanced Settings for the On2 VP6 codec. There you can fine tune the compression settings. Select one of the Flash 7 profiles from the drop down menu and notice the details that appear underneath the menu list Sorenson Spark for the codec. This is the only codec that will work when you publish to Flash player 7. Select "Flash 8 - Low Quality (150kbps)" and you'll be taking advantage of the new On2 VP6 codec—though this also means only users with the Flash Player 8 will be able to view it. The 150kpbs data rate means that the file will use 150 kilo*bits* (not kilobytes) for every second. That is, a 10 second video will be 1500 kilobits. The idea is that if your internet connection can maintain at least 150kbps (for example, most DSL connections are approximately 256kbps) then the video can play without interruption. When you're finally ready to encode click the Next button. You'll see one more dialog reviewing what you're about to and then click Finish.

FIGURE 18.3
You can make rough edits to your video during the import process.

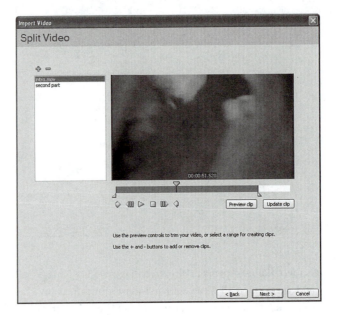

6. You'll have to sit through the encoding process (which is, luckily, way longer than the decoding stage at the time the user watches your video). When it's done, the video you just embedded will appear in your Library. Drag the video on to your main Stage. You'll see a dialog box (see Figure 18.4) that asks if you want to extend the Timeline to accommodate the video's total number of frames (in this case, 60). Click Yes.

FIGURE 18.4
When you place a video on the Stage, Flash asks whether you want to extend the Timeline to accommodate the video's length.

7. Test the movie so you can hear the audio play. (Note that the sample I used had white on the first frame, so you won't see anything if you're on Frame 1 unless your Stage is a different color.)

If all you wanted was a video inside Flash, you could stop after the preceding task. However, like I mentioned earlier, embedding the video inside your movie the way you did in step 2 above is not always the best choice—creating an external .flv is usually better. In addition to the benefits already mentioned, .flvs can also be posted on a streaming server (namely, Flash Media Server). This way, users will have hyper access to any point in the video. That is, embedding the video or playing .flvs without any special server does what is called progressive download which means users can watch the beginning of a video while the remainder downloads. The premise is that by the time the user needs to view the later portions, those frames will have finally downloaded. In the case of a true streaming server, you can jump to any point in the video and the server sends just those bits. This means users can jump ahead which is not the case in traditional progressive downloading.

I threw in this discussion of the two ways to play .flvs (progressive or streaming) because back in step 2 of the preceding task, I promised to explain the other deployment options shown in Figure 18.2. In addition to the Embedded option that you selected in the preceding task, Flash Professional 8 has two "Stream" options plus an option "Progressive download from a web server." (Plus an option for creating QuickTime which is no longer supported in Flash Player 8 so I'm not going to cover it.) Interestingly, the first three options all create the same .flv. That is, instead of embedding the video, they output a separate .flv file that loads into your movie at runtime. The only difference between these three options is how they pre-populate the parameters for the FLVPlayback component. Basically, to produce an .flv the process is nearly identical to the task above—you're just outputting an .flv instead of a new item in your library. In addition, you get to select which FLVPlayback skin to use as shown in Figure 18.5. If you have Flash Professional 8 you can do exactly this in the task later this hour "Create an .flv and Use the FLVController Component."

FIGURE 18.5
When using
Flash
Professional 8
to produce an
`.flv` you can
select from a
variety of skins
for the
FLVPlayback
component.

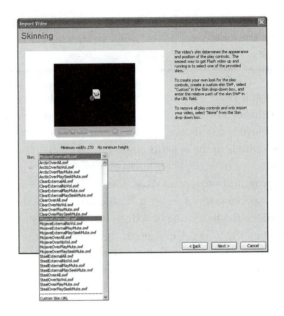

Using Video

Next you'll learn some of the ways to display videos—both embedded into your
`.swf` and created as an `.flv` that resides outside of your file. In this section you'll
see how to control the playback of your videos (like giving the user a stop and play
button) as well as using special effects such as masking. The creative side of displaying a video is much more interesting than the technical details. But, because the
technical details vary between embedded and external video I've separated the two.

Playing an Embedded Video

As a review, a sound in a keyframe that is set to Event begins to play when that
frame is reached, and it continues to play until it's finished—even if the Timeline
slows down to display all the frames. Stream sounds are locked to the Timeline. This
means that you need to make sure that the sound has enough space in the Timeline
to finish. The reason to review Stream sounds at this point is that an embedded
video placed in a keyframe needs enough space in the Timeline to finish playing the
audio portion. For example, if the video is 10 seconds long and the frame rate is 12
fps, you need 120 frames in the Timeline. Flash will tell you exactly how many
frames are needed if you drag an embedded video into a timeline that's too short.
Another reason to remember Stream sounds is that by default all the audio in an
embedded video is affected by the global publish setting for stream audio (which

you set by selecting File, Publish Settings to open the Publish Settings dialog box and then selecting the Flash tab).

The visuals in your video behave like Graphic symbols. In fact, embedded videos are not really the same as graphics, buttons, or movie clips because you can't tween videos or tint them through the color effects, as you can other symbols. However, of the symbol types, videos are most like Graphics in several respects. You can scrub to see a preview of videos. Also, you must extend the Timeline far enough for all the video frames to play (as you did in step 4 of the preceding task).

These concepts are just discussed here to help you understand a few of the technical details that follow. You're about to see how easy it is to build controls for an embedded video.

Try It Yourself ▼

Make a Playback Controller for an Embedded Video

In this task, you'll add some standard video buttons that give the user a way to control the video. Follow these steps:

1. Create a new movie and import a video as you did in the task "Import a Video" earlier this Hour. That is, make sure you select embed on the deployment dialog that appears when you import and compress the video. Then drag it onto your main timeline and let Flash add frames needed.

2. You're about to create buttons (Stop, Pause, and Play). Put those buttons in their own layer on the main timeline. Lock the layer the video is in and then make a new layer for the buttons.

3. Instead of drawing your own buttons select Window, Common Libraries, Buttons. Inside this Library is a folder called rounded. Drag each of the following buttons from that folder to the Stage: Rounded Green Pause, Rounded Green Play, and Rounded Green Stop. You can align these buttons underneath the video any way you want (consider using the Align panel).

4. Open the Actions panel and select the rounded green pause instance. Then type the following code:

```
on(release){
  stop();
}
```

For a review of ActionScript, revisit Hours 15 an 16.

▼

5. Keep the Actions panel open but select the rounded green play button instance and type this code:

```
on(release){
 play();
}
```

6. Finally, for the rounded green stop button, type this code:

```
on(release){
 gotoAndStop(1);
}
```

7. Select the keyframe, and type this code into the Actions panel:

```
stop();
```

8. Test the movie, and you'll be able to control the embedded video.

By the way, it's very easy to add step forward and step backward buttons. Just use this code for your step forward button:

```
on(press){
    nextFrame();
}
```

And this for your step back button:

```
on(press){
    prevFrame();
}
```

One fair criticism of the previous task is that it sure did dirty up the main timeline. That is, the timeline has as many frames as the video does. Normally I'd suggest putting the video inside a Movie Clip; let that clip grow as long as it needs to be; then place the Movie Clip instance in the main timeline where it will only use 1 frame. The problem with that approach is that when Flash reaches the frame containing the Movie Clip it must download all the frames contained in that clip before displaying anything. If the clip has a big video this could mean a long delay. So, doing it the way you did in the task is appropriate for embedded videos. By the way, you can save the preceding task as built and then, in Hour 20, use the MovieClipLoader to load the movie at runtime.

Before we move on to playing external .flv videos, I should mention that all the cool stuff—such as masking the video into an odd shape—works with embedded videos. This is covered later this hour in the Special Effects section.

Playing an External `.flv` Videos

Earlier this Hour you heard that Flash can play external `.flv` files. Naturally, you need to first create the `.flv`. There are four general ways to produce an `.flv`:

▶ Import a video into Flash Professional 8 and select one of the first three deployment options listed (that is, not the option to embed the video). The advantage of doing it this way is that it also configures a component for you.

▶ Use an outside application to produce the `.flv`. Either the Flash 8 Video Encoder (that ships with Flash Professional 8) or the third-party products On2's Flix or Sorenson Media's Squeeze 4.2 for Flash.

▶ Export directly from a supported video editor on a machine with the Flash Video Encoder (which ships with Flash Professional 8) installed. (More about this option and which applications are supported are in the section, "Using Outside Video Editors.")

▶ Use any version of Flash 8 (including Basic) to first embed the video and then export an `.flv` via the video item in the library. By far, this renders the lowest quality but it works if you don't have Flash Professional 8 and want to follow some of the tasks that would otherwise require the Pro version.

The tasks that follow concentrate on how to play an external `.flv` once it's produced. In the next task, "Create an `.flv` and Use the FLVController Component," you'll use Flash Professional 8 to generate the `.flv` and use it immediately. In "Create and Play an `.flv` the No-Frills Way," you'll use any version of Flash to export an `.flv` and then play it externally without any components. Realize you can use any `.flv` (even if it's not the best quality possible) and then replace it later with a better one.

What's Wrong With Videos Produced in Flash Basic 8?

By the Way

When embedding video inside Flash Basic 8 the minor disadvantage is that you must select a compression profile from a variety of presets—Flash Professional 8 has the advanced settings where you can fine tune things. In every other way, embedded videos are the same for either product. However, embedded videos (even if you export it as an `.flv` from the Library) always use CBR (Constant Bit Rate). A video using VBR (Variable Bit Rate) is always better quality than an identically sized CBR video. That's because every frame in a CBR is the same size. A VBR will use more bandwidth of the frames that need it (say, ones with detail) and make up for the increased size by sacrificing frames that don't need the bandwidth (perhaps blurry or frames with lots of motion). Producing `.flv`s using the first three options above (that is, not embedding and exporting) use VBR.

However you produce the `.flv`, playing an external `.flv` will definitely give you the best results—most notably the audio and picture remain synchronized. Playing external `.flv`s is a bit more involved, however. For one thing, you have to remember to upload both the `.swf` and the `.flv` file (plus an additional `.swf` if you use one of the FLVPlayback component's skins). Plus, you only get a preview of the video frames when the video is embedded. If you want to draw animations on top of live action video, you'll need to work with embedded video (at least at the stage where you're producing the animated overlay—you can delete the embedded video once you get the animation done). All I'm saying is that there are additional restrictions when playing `.flv` files.

The following task will probably seem suspiciously simple after the preceding explanation. You'll need Flash Professional 8 for this task, but in it you'll experience the easiest, fastest, and most advanced way to play `.flv`s.

▼ **Try It Yourself**

Create an `.flv` and Use the FLVPlayback Component

In this task, you'll create an `.flv` and advanced controller with no programming. Here are the steps:

1. Make a new folder in a known location so that all the files you'll need to track are easy to find.

2. Create a new file and save it in the above folder as "my_movie_player.fla." Select File, Import, Import to Stage. Point to a source video file such as a QuickTime.

3. On the Select Video dialog, click Next; on the Deployment dialog, select "Progressive download from a web server" and click Next; on the Encoding dialog, select "Flash 8 - High Quality (700kbps)" (and, if the video is really long, trim the length by dragging the end point triangle next to the preview to the left), then click Next.

4. You should see the Skinning dialog as in Figure 18.5. Select the skin "ArcticExternalPlaySeekMute.swf" (or, any one that strikes your fancy with a name ending "...ExternalPlaySeekMute.swf"). Click Next. Finally, feel free to read the Finish Video Import dialog and then click Finish.

5. Sit back and wait for the compression to complete. (It can take a long time as the VP6 codec is very asymmetric meaning it takes a long time to compress and much less time to decompress.) When it's done compressing open the folder where you saved your movie and notice a new `.flv` file.

▼

6. Back inside your Flash movie you should notice the FLVPlayback component sitting onstage. Select that Component instance and open the Parameters panel. There are lots of parameters you can feel free to modify—including the skin (in case you want to use a different skin than the one selected in step 4). The main parameter, which has already been set for you, is the contentPath (which, you can also change if you change the .flv's file name).

7. Now for the fun part. Test the movie. Pretty sweet how that component works. When you're done watching your video there's one last step that's super important to understand.

8. Go back to your file folder and notice that in addition to the .flv and the my_movie_player.swf based on your .fla, there's another .swf (ArcticExternalPlaySeekMute.swf) for the component. You need to upload all three (plus an .html file when you publish) when you deploy this to the Web. (More about publishing in Hours 19 and 24, but don't forget that piece for the component—plus the .flv file.)

As great as the FLVPLayback component is, you still might want to make your own controls. The FLVPlayback component can be set to no-skin and you can use ActionScript to make your own buttons control the video. While it's actually a very powerful component (even without the skin) you still need Flash Professional 8 to use it. If you only have Flash Basic 8 you can still play external .flvs produced elsewhere—just not using the FLVPlayback component.

I should note, too, that the FLVPlayback component requires your users have the Flash 8 Player. This is also a requirement any time you select the On2 VP6 codec. If you want to deliver to the Flash 7 Player not only do you have to select a different codec (Sorenson Spark) but you have to either use one of the Media Components (also only available in Flash Professional) or use no component.

The following task shows how to play an external .flv without using components.

Try It Yourself

Create and Play an External .flv the No-Frills Way

If you already have an .flv produced with Flash Professional 8 or one of the third party tools, you can skip to step 3.

1. Embed a video as you did in the task "Embed a Video." That is, select File, Import and from the second import dialog (the one for Deployment) select Embed Video. If you want this task to work in Flash Player 7, be sure to select

a supported profile from the Encoding dialog (everything else you do here won't require Flash Player 8).

2. Once the video is embedded, find the video object in the Library. Double-click on it to access its properties. Click the Export button and save a `.flv` named `my_file.flv`. You can close this Flash file now because you were just using it temporarily.

3. Start by making sure your `.flv` is named `my_file.flv`. Create a new movie and save it in the same folder as the `.flv`.

4. Create a video object on the stage. Open the Library window and, from the library's options menu, select New Video. Drag the video object onto the stage and name the instance `my_video`. You can resize the instance to match your actual `.flv`'s dimensions.

5. Create two button instances and name them `stop_btn` and `play_btn`, respectively.

6. Open the Actions panel and click the first keyframe in the timeline, then type this code:

```
my_nc = new NetConnection();
my_nc.connect(null);
my_ns = new NetStream(my_nc);
my_video.attachVideo(my_ns);
play_btn.onPress = function(){
    my_ns.play("my_file.flv");
}
stop_btn.onPress = function(){
    my_ns.play(false);
}
```

There's a ton more you can do with the NetStream object, such as monitor how fast a video is downloading. The only catch is that, unlike using the FLVPlayback component (which also has much more to it), you'll have to do most of the coding by hand. You're welcome to read all about in a Flash Video paper I wrote at www.phillipkerman.com/wholestory.

Special Effects

Now for the fun part. Once you've embedded a video or set up a component of video object to display an external `.flv`, you can perform countless special effects that can dramatically change the way a user experiences your video. We'll look at just a few.

Rotoscope (Draw Frames of a Video)

In this task you'll combine frame-by-frame animation with live action video. Here are the steps

1. Embed a video like you did in the task "Embed a Video" earlier this hour. At the end, I'll show you how to convert this task to work with an external .flv, but you have to start by embedding the video. If you are planning on playing an external .flv select Modify, Document and set the framerate to match the framerate at which you're going to render the video.

2. If you're planning on leaving this as an embedded video, place the video object in the main timeline. If you're planning on the converting this to an .flv then first make a new Movie Clip and put the video object inside the clip. In either case, make sure you say "OK" to the dialog asking to add more frames to accommodate the video's duration (as earlier in Figure 18.3).

3. In the timeline where the video appears, insert a new layer (which should appear above the video's layer). Ensure the new layer is both above the video and extends the entire length of the video. (If not, just move the layer and click a cell above the last frame in the video and press F5.)

4. Click the layer name of the empty layer to select the entire span of frames and press F6. You'll now have an empty keyframe above each frame of the video where you can draw.

5. Select the Brush tool and pick a bright color. Hold the mouse in one hand and put the other hand on the > button. Draw right into the empty keyframe of frame one (perhaps draw an outline around an object in your video such as a person's face). After you draw press > and draw another frame. Even if you have hundreds of frames to draw you can do it quickly. It's definitely possible to insert pauses (by removing the keyframes) or even do tweens that match the video, but it might be just as fast to simply draw every frame. For this exercise feel free to stop after 10–20 frames and come back after you've had some practice to finish them all.

6. If you're going to leave the video embedded, you're done. Go ahead and test the movie. If you want this animation to work with an external .flv you've

▼

got two steps left. First, remove the video from the timeline and create an .flv named my_file.flv (as you did in "Create an .flv and Use the FLVController Component" if you have Flash Professional 8 or as you did in "Create and Play an External .flv the No-Frills Way" if you only have Flash Basic). And second, write the code so that the animation syncs up with the external .flv.

7. Instead of actually deleting the video, simply access its layer properties and set it to Guide so that you'll always have the video for reference. If the video object isn't being used anywhere then it won't add to the file size. Drag on to the stage an instance of the Movie clip containing your animation. Name this instance my_animation.

8. From the options menu in the Library select New Video. Drag an instance onstage and name the instance my_video. Select the first keyframe in the movie, open the Actions panel and type this code:

```
my_nc = new NetConnection();
my_nc.connect(null);
my_ns = new NetStream(my_nc);
my_video.attachVideo(my_ns);

my_animation.stop();
my_ns.play("my_file.flv");

var framerate=12;
onEnterFrame=function(){
   my_animation.gotoAndStop(Math.floor(my_ns.time*framerate));
}
```

Note that you'll need to set the framerate variable to match your movie's actual framerate (shown here as 12). The code that runs every enter frame ensures the my_animation clip remains in sync with the time of the NetStream (that is, the external video).

There's a lot more you can do with synchronizing animation with a video. In the task above, every frame of the animation was synchronized with a frame in the video. Often, you only need to update an overlaying graphic once in a while. For example, you could display a caption containing the speaker's name or bullet points that match what the speaker is discussing. In such situations you don't need *every* frame synchronized. Such cases are more appropriate for cue points. In Flash Professional 8 you can actually inject cue points into an .flv at the time you encode it (Figure 18.6) or use the Media Components to set cue points (shown when you do the next task in Figure 18.7).

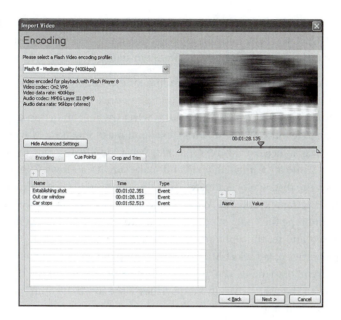

FIGURE 18.6
You can inject cue points right into the .flv when you encode using Flash Professional 8.

Inserting cue points is fairly intuitive. In fact, there's a third-party tool called Captionate (www.captionate.com) which I'd highly recommend for injecting .flvs with cue points and complete captioning data. In all cases, the code to actually make something happen when the cue points are triggered is slightly more involved. One exception is cue points for which you set the type column to Navigation. When you use the FLVPlayback component users can jump to those cue points using the next and back buttons. In the following task you'll set up a Movie Clip to display bullet points in synch with a video. After you have it set up, you can take one of three approaches: synch to cue points injected into the .flv, manually input cue points into the MediaPlayback component, or do everything manually (the old-school way).

Try It Yourself ▼

Use Cue Points

You can download an .flv for this exercise from www.phillipkerman.com/teachyourself/samplefiles/.

1. Create a new Flash file and save it adjacent to the colors.flv you downloaded.

2. Select Insert, New Symbol and name it Bullets and pick Movie Clip then press OK.

▼

3. You should be inside the Bullets Movie Clip. Create some static text that reads "Blue." Click the keyframe and use the Properties panel to type blue into the frame label field. Insert a blank keyframe in frame 2.

4. In frame 2 we'll do something a bit more fancy. Namely, we'll place a symbol which itself contains an animation that plays once and stops. Start by creating some static text that reads "Pink Stuff." Select the text and choose Modify, Convert to Symbol. Name it "Pink Text" and make sure it's a Movie Clip. Now, with that instance of Pink Text selected, select Modify, Convert to Symbol (again). Name it "Animated Text" and make sure it's a Movie Clip. Now, double-click the instance of Animated Text. Inside this clip click on frame 10 and insert a keyframe (press F6). While frame 10 is selected, open the Actions panel and type the code: stop(); Go back to frame 1 and move the instance to the left and set the alpha to 10%. Click the keyframe in frame 1 and from the Properties panel select Motion. Go back up one level (so you're inside the Bullets symbol). Finally, give frame 2 (of the Bullets symbol) the label pink. Now when the user arrives in frame 2 they'll see the "Pink Stuff" text animate into place and stop.

5. Inside the Bullets symbol, go to frame 3 and insert a blank keyframe (press F6). Type some static text that says "Green Leaves". You're welcome to make this animate too—just make sure you nest any animation. When you're done be sure to give the third frame (here inside the Bullets symbol) the label green.

6. Place an instance of the Bullets symbol on stage and give it an instance name bullets.

7. Here's the cool part. You can take any one of the following three steps: You can follow step 8 that uses the new FLVPlayback to sync the bullets to the cue points that I already embedded into the .flv. Alternatively, go straight to step 9 to use the older Media Components to input the sync points manually (which will work with any .flv). Finally, if you don't have Flash Professional 8, you can jump to step 10 where you can use a video object and use an array—definitely the most home rolled approach (but it works with Flash Basic 8).

8. Approach 1: Drag an FLVPLayback component on to the stage and place it next to the bullets instance. Give the FLVPlayback an instance name playback. Select the first keyframe and type this code into the Actions panel:

```
playback.contentPath = "colors.flv";
bullets.stop();
myListener = new Object();
myListener.cuePoint = function(evt) {
  bullets.gotoAndStop(evt.info.name);
};
playback.addEventListener("cuePoint",myListener);
```

9. Approach 2: Drag a MediaPlayback component onto the stage and place it next to the `bullets` instance. (Remove the old playback instance if you performed step 8.) Give the MediaPlayback an instance name `playback`. Select Window, Components Inspector and select the MediaPlayback instance. Click the plus button three times to add three sync points. Name the three sync points blue, pink, and green respectively. Set the times to `0:0:0:0`, `0:0:4:4`, `0:0:7:2` respectively. The populated component inspector should look like Figure 18.7. Finally, select a keyframe in your movie and type this code into the Actions panel:

```
playback.contentPath = "colors.flv";
bullets.stop();
myListener = new Object();
myListener.cuePoint = function(evt) {
  bullets.gotoAndStop(evt.cuePointName);
};
playback.addEventListener("cuePoint",myListener);
```

FIGURE 18.7
The MediaPlayback lets you set cue points from inside Flash.

10. Approach 3: From the Library's options menu, select New Video. Drag an instance of the video object on to the stage. Give it an instance name `my_video`. Open the Actions panel, select a keyframe and type this code:

```
bullets.stop();
my_nc = new NetConnection();
my_nc.connect(null);
my_ns = new NetStream(my_nc);
my_video.attachVideo(my_ns);
```

```
myPoints=[0, 4.4, 7.2];
myLabels=["blue", "pink", "green"];
onEnterFrame=function(){
  if ( my_ns.time > myPoints[myCounter] ){
    bullets.gotoAndStop(myLabels[myCounter]);
    myCounter++;
  }
}
//every time you want to restart the video, do these three lines:
myCounter=0;
bullets.gotoAndStop(1);
my_ns.play("colors.flv");
```

If you don't mind requiring Flash Player 8, the first approach (step 8) is best. If you have Flash Professional and don't use the On2 codec you can deliver to Flash Player 7 using the second approach (step 9). Finally, with Flash Basic 8 you're limited to the last approach (step 10). In that case, you can decide whether the On2 codec warrants requiring Flash Player 8.

Optimizing Quality and File Size

With all this talk of encoding options and coding tricks it might be easy to lose sight of the core goal: namely, to produce the best looking video that downloads fast. It may seem quaint to study traditional techniques (developed decades ago) but that's exactly what you should do if you want good looking video. For example, use a tripod and shade the camera lens to reduce flare which can desaturate the colors. Consider a few strategic cuts instead of special effects that can make transitions long and arduous. The point is there's a wealth of experience photographers and film makers can share that all translate to digital video.

I also have a few technical tricks that can reduce the file size without having a huge impact on quality. The two biggest factors that have an immediate impact on file size are the video's framerate and its pixel dimensions. For example, a 12 fps video will be nearly exactly half the size as a 24 fps video. A lower framerate will not only be smaller, but it won't look quite as good—especially if there's a lot of motion. The best thing to do is to take a small representative sample and test different framerates. Keep going lower and lower until the quality is unacceptable then back off.

Just like any raster graphic, you can also render videos at different dimensions. Similar to how low framerates make for a smaller video, smaller dimensions make the file smaller too. But here's a great tip that can have a surprising effect. Often, you can render a video at half its final size and then stretch it during playback. For example, you want a video to display at 240×320. You can render it at 120×160 but just stretch the video holder (video object or component) to 240×320. Test it out! Make a video at 240×320 at a particular bandwidth and make another at the same bandwidth but only 120×160. Naturally, the smaller one will be sharper until you stretch it. But the paradox is that often the stretched one looks way better than the same file sized unstretched one.

Lastly, as a bit of a repeat from Hour 10, "Including Sound in Animations," stereo sound is twice as big as mono. Just be sure you really need stereo before you include it in your video. By the way, when you embed video inside your Flash movie, you set the compression level via the Publish Settings for Stream sound.

Using Outside Video Editors

Flash Professional 8 comes with both the Flash 8 Video Encoder and a plugin to let other video editors create .flvs directly. These get installed automatically when you install Flash (or you can run the installer later) and it works in conjunction with various popular video editors. The idea is that video professionals can best make final edits and other sweetening in their favorite video editor and then export directly to the Flash video format (.flv). In addition, you can use the stand-alone version of the Flash 8 Video Encoder to compress raw videos into .flvs in batches.

To use the plugin you just need to launch one of the supported video editors on the same machine where you have Flash Professional 8 installed. The supported software includes Adobe After Effects, Apple FinalCut Pro, Avid Xpress DV, and Discreet Cleaner among others. Once you're finished editing the video, simply select something like File, Export, Flash Video (though the exact menus differ for each product). You'll see a dialog identical to the Encoding dialog you saw when you used Flash to do the compression.

The stand alone version should be installed in a folder adjacent to where Flash 8 Professional is installed (C:\Program Files\Macromedia\ for example). Again, the available options are identical to those found when using Flash to perform the compression. However the stand alone version adds a batch feature that will, at your convenience, compress a long list of videos you've added to the queue. This means you can take several videos, add them to the queue—even add the same one but select different compression settings for comparison—and then let them compress overnight. Video compressors are always slow and the On2 VP6 codec is extra slow when compressing.

Summary

Some messages are simply best suited for video. In my mind, only video reveals the personality of a subject. Also, when a demonstration is needed, there's just nothing like a video. The majority of this hour dealt with the technical limits of video. Don't let that stop you. The price (extra work on your part and extra download time for the user) can definitely be worth it when necessary.

In this Hour you learned how to embed a video right into your file as well as how to create a Flash video file (.flv) and play it externally. Embedding a video may be easier and does provide the ability to step through each frame but when the video is longer, the added file size (to your main movie) isn't worth the cost of embedding it. Keeping an external .flv not only provides the best synchronization and video quality but the user only downloads the video's they request. There really are many more topics worth studying in Flash Video but this chapter touched on the primary points.

Q&A

Q *I realize that you recommend against using* .avi *files, but that's all I have. Should I first convert an* .avi *file to a QuickTime file by using a tool such as the QuickTime player?*

A First, if the only source file is an .avi file, you might as well use that. If it's good quality, great. If it's not, oh well. But converting it to a QuickTime file can't make it better.

Q *I've embedded a video with a great music track. Why does the audio sound so terrible?*

A You need to set how the audio is to export via the Stream compression in the Flash tab of the Publish Settings dialog box. See Chapter 10 for more about sound compression. The key here is that the Stream setting is what affects the audio in an embedded video.

Q *I know that the compression stage can take a long time, but even after I've compressed the embedded video, my Flash movie takes forever to export. Why is that?*

A Audio takes a long time to compress, and it's likely that Flash is compressing the audio at the time you publish. You can temporarily change the Audio Stream setting (in Flash's Publish Settings dialog box on the Flash tab) to Raw so that every time you do a test movie, it goes quicker. Just remember to set it back to a reasonable compression level before you export the final time.

Q *Every time I attempt to compress a particular video (regardless of whether I select to make an external* `.flv` *or embed the video), Flash reports that the audio can't be imported. What's the problem?*

A Depending on the type of audio track in your video, Flash may simply not support it. You'll need to get an new source file.

Workshop

The Workshop consists of quiz questions and answers to help you solidify your understanding of the material covered in this hour. You should try to answer the questions before checking the answers.

Quiz

1. If On2's VP6 coded yields better results than the Sorenson's Spark codec (which it does), why would you ever select Spark?

    A. You don't want to pay the additional license charges which accompany the VP6 codec.

    B. You are planning on delivering to Flash Player 7 and the VP6 codec only works on Flash Player 8 or later.

    C. You don't like the fact the VP6 encoded videos are at least twice the size of Spark encoded videos.

2. How do you change the compression on a video that you've already embedded?

    A. You can't. Instead, you could re-embed and recompress at that time.

    B. You simply access the video item (in the Library), select its Properties option, and then click Recompress.

    C. You simply need to modify the Video tab of the Publish Settings dialog box.

3. On2's VP6 is which of the following?

    A. An old technique where rock bands would begin to play "on two" instead of "on four" as in "one, two, three, four"

    B. The compression technology included with Flash 8 and the decompression technology used in the Flash player

    C. An option (that costs extra) to compress your videos with "supercompression"

Quiz Answers

1. B. Requiring users to upgrade to the latest player is definitely an issue, especially when it's so new. In addition, the VP6 codec requires more resources from your users' computers.

2. A. Answer B makes sense, in fact most imported media lets you reimport via the Update button on the item's Properties dialog box—but that is not supported for video and simply displays a warning.

3. B. A codec has both compression and decompression components. There is a version called Spark Pro (that costs extra), but realize that users with the Flash player will still be able to view Flash videos that use this version.

PART IV

Putting It All Together for the Web

HOUR 19

Linking a Movie to the Web

What You'll Learn in This Hour:

- ▶ How to publish a Flash movie with the required HTML document
- ▶ How to incorporate hyperlinks inside a movie to enable the user to jump to other pages or send an email message
- ▶ How Flash and HTML can be combined
- ▶ How to upload files to a web server

Now that you've explored all the basics of creating images, animations, buttons, and inter-activity, you can move on to putting it all together for the Web. In the first hour of this part of the book, you'll learn about getting Flash movies into web pages and linking them to other pages. The knowledge you've acquired up to this point will make the task at hand easy. It helps, however, if you've seen a few Flash websites so that you have an idea where you're headed.

A Flash movie can simply be played on your computer (as is the case every time you use Test Movie). The fun part comes when you upload a Flash movie to a web server so any-one who has a browser and the free Flash player can see it. Not only can your movie be seen by anyone in the world, but you can include links that give the user a way to jump to other sites. You'll do all that this hour!

A **hyperlink** is often just a word or static picture in a web page that you can click to navi-gate to another web page. In Flash you can put hyperlinks on buttons or even in keyframes. This way, the viewer will have a chance to jump to other parts of the Web.

Basic Publishing

Flash's Publish feature makes the process of preparing a movie for the Web a snap. I know I've said that a lot of tasks you perform in Flash are simple, but publishing in Flash really is both simple and quick. Basically, you just select File, Publish. Publish will not only export a .swf, but it will also create the HTML file that's necessary.

HTML stands for Hypertext Markup Language. An HTML file is a text file that uses special code to describe how a web page is to be displayed. A user's browser program will first download the HTML, and the code included in it describes how the web page should display. The reason HTML is important is that every web page that you visit is really an HTML file that describes what is to be included in the page layout. Therefore, to upload a web page, you don't just upload a Flash .swf. You upload an HTML file (with an embedded .swf), and that is what the user visits.

It's interesting to know that when you type in a web address (www. phillipkerman.com, for example), your browser looks for a file named index.html (it also looks for other similarly named files if it can't find index.html). The index.html file is read in by the browser, which makes sense of its contents. Besides containing the actual text that appears onscreen, the index.html file contains the details about which size and style text to use (such as italic or bold). Because the HTML file doesn't actually have images in it, if the web page includes photographs, the HTML must specify the name and location of the image file (such as trees.jpg). The browser accumulates all the information specified in the HTML file and shows it to the user as an integrated layout of images and text.

In the case of a page that includes a Flash movie, it works almost the same way. The HTML file specifies where the Flash movie (that is, the .swf file) is located and how to display it onscreen. This is almost the same as how it specifies a static image, such as a .gif or a .jpg. In the case of the .jpg or .gif image, additional information can be included—parameters such as the height and width of the image. Similarly, the HTML referring to a .swf can include parameters such as width, height, but also details such as whether the movie loops, whether it should be paused at the start, and more. This HTML basically says to put an image here, a Flash movie there, and so on. The actual code is relatively easy to learn, but it's not exactly intuitive. Besides, it's unforgiving if you make mistakes.

Fortunately, Flash's Publish feature will create the HTML file for you, so you don't really have to learn HTML. However, it is a good idea for you to learn some HTML, and one of the best ways to learn is to take a peek at the HTML Flash creates. Regardless, Publish is a neat feature—you just select the Publish command, and Flash does all the work.

Publishing in Flash has three aspects. For now, we'll concentrate on Publish and Publish Preview, with which HTML and .swf files are exported; the only difference between the two is that with Preview, you see the results right away in your browser. An important component of publishing involves how you can modify every detail via the Publish Settings command (under the File menu). As you'll see in Hour 24, "Publishing a Creation," the Publish Settings command lets you specify details as well as decide what media types to export (because Flash can export more than just Flash and HTML files). The third aspect of publishing involves using, modifying, or creating templates and profiles, which give you extensive control over the HTML created when publishing. (Templates and profiles are also covered in Hour 24.)

In the following task you'll try out the File menu commands Publish and Publish Preview.

Try It Yourself ▼

Publish a Movie

In this task you'll quickly (and easily) publish a movie for viewing in a browser. Here are the steps to follow:

1. In a new file, create a simple animation. Save the file to a new or empty folder (maybe a folder called Test on your desktop). Call the file testmovie.fla.

2. Select File, Publish Settings to open the Publish Settings dialog box, select the Formats tab, and ensure that Flash and HTML are the only options selected (this is the default). Click OK (see Figure 19.1).

3. Select File, Publish. What happens? Nothing much seems to appear, but if you look inside your Test folder, you should find (in addition to your source .fla) two files—one .swf and one .html. Both have the same base name as your original .fla file. If you double-click the HTML file, you launch your default browser and see your movie play. (Seeing a movie in a browser is exciting to many people.)

4. If you simply upload the .html and .swf files to a web server, anyone can see your movie, provided that he or she is given the address and has the Flash player.

▼

FIGURE 19.1
The Publish
Settings dialog
box lets you
specify what
kind of files will
be created
every time you
publish. The
default simply
exports a Flash
.swf and the
HTML that
holds it.

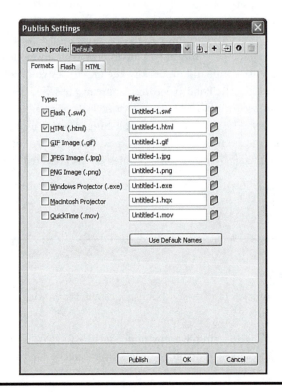

When you used Publish Settings in the preceding task, you made sure that both an HTML and Flash (.swf) file would be exported upon publishing. Not only does the Formats tab allow you to specify more file types to export, but for each format you select, you're given another tab. For example, because you have HTML and Flash selected, you see a tab for each. If you look in those tabs, you see several parameters you can modify. We'll spend more time on this in Hour 24, but for now you can go ahead and check out these tabs if you like; most of the settings are pretty self-explanatory.

A few final notes on publishing: First of all, after you selected Publish in the previous task, you found the files Flash exported. Instead, you could have—in one fell swoop—exported the file and launched it in your browser automatically. To export the appropriate files and view them in a browser in one step, you select File, Publish Preview, Default (or press F12). You'll likely use this method in more ways than this, so it's good to understand exactly what's happening.

Second, you'll notice that the name of both the `.html` and `.swf` files match your source `.fla` file's name. If later you want to change the `.html` file's name to, say, `index.html`, you'll have no problem doing so. However, if you want to change the `.swf` file's name, you'll have to be careful. The HTML file points to the `.swf` file. If you open the HTML file in a text editor (such as Notepad), you'll find two references to the `.swf` file's name. (To open the file in Notepad, either drag the file onto the Notepad icon or open Notepad and select File, Open, making sure you change Files of Type to All Files, as shown in Figure 19.2, and point to the `.html` file.)

FIGURE 19.2
If you want to view `.html` files through Notepad (to see what Flash created), you just need to specify All Files in the dialog box after you select File, Open.

The two references to the `.swf` file's name correspond to the HTML code created for Netscape Navigator and Internet Explorer. Although the following code is just part of the HTML file created, you'll find the two parts in it:

```
src="testmovie.swf"
PARAM NAME=movie VALUE="testmovie.swf"
```

I won't explain the HTML entirely, but both lines of code need to point to the correct file. If your Flash file's name is indeed `testmovie.swf`, this code works. If you change your file's name, you must change these lines in your HTML code to match the new name.

Another thing to keep in mind: You don't have to export both the `.html` and the `.swf` file every time. You can select File, Export Movie to just create a new `.swf` based on the latest edits in your source `.fla`. Maybe you've already created the HTML, or maybe you've made some edits to it that you don't want overwritten by publishing again. All you need to do is select File, Export, Export Movie and then select Flash Movie from the Save As Type drop-down list in the Export Movie dialog box. When you export this way, you see one more dialog box, which lets you specify details of the Flash movie. This dialog box is identical to the Flash tab in Publish Settings dialog box (for now, just accept the defaults). Probably the easiest way is simply use Test Movie, which immediately exports only the .swf part of your Publish settings. Test Movie uses the most recent .swf options under Publish Settings.

This might sound like a lot of options, but the main decision is whether you want to export just the .swf (as in Export Movie) or both the .swf and the .html (when you use Publish).

Simple Hyperlinks

This hour you've seen how to publish your movies to a browser. But what good is a Flash movie in a browser if it doesn't do "web stuff"? There's nothing wrong with making a Flash movie that simply entertains. But if your users are already on the Web, you might as well give them a way to hyperlink to other web pages.

There's only one script you really have to learn to create a hyperlink: getURL (also called Go to web Page found under the web category when you press the plus button in the Behaviors panel). (If you already know how to create a hyperlink in HTML, you can think of this action as the same as a href.) Specifically, when Flash encounters the getURL action, it takes the user to a new web page, either within your site or to another website altogether. That's the simple explanation. Naturally, there are more details. You'll use this action to see how it works in the following task.

▼ **Try It Yourself**

Use getURL to Create a Hyperlink

In this task you'll create a button that, when clicked, takes the user to another website. Here are the steps to follow:

1. Create a new file and save it in an empty folder. (This step isn't absolutely necessary, but it is useful when you're creating complex websites because all the files and folders can get out of hand; therefore, I like to start with a nice clean folder.)

2. Drag a Button component onto the Stage and use the Properties panel to change its Label parameter to Go.

▼

3. Attach a behavior to the button by selecting the instance of the button on the Stage, opening the Behaviors panel, and finding Go to web Page. Just press the plus button and find it under web.

4. When the dialog box appears, you need to indicate the web address to which you want the user to navigate. In the URL field, type `http://www.samspublishing.com`, as shown in Figure 19.3. You'll learn about the other parameters later, so leave them alone for now.

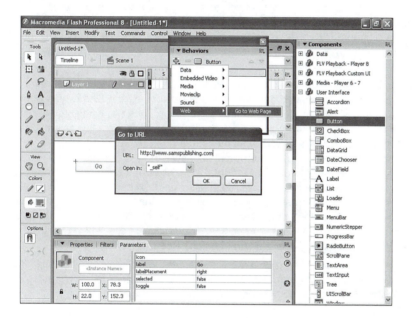

FIGURE 19.3
The Go to Web Page behavior requires that you specify the address to which you want the user to navigate.

5. Select File, Test Movie. When you click, you are taken to the Sams Publishing website.

6. Next try File, Publish Preview, Default (or press F12). This time the Flash movie plays in a browser, and when you click the button you'll probably see the new extra-secure warning dialog added in Flash Player 8. The issue is that a file on your hard drive (after all you haven't uploaded this movie yet) can be either local files or files on the internet, but not both. You can click the Settings button and then explicitly authorize this file. Click the Edit Locations drop-down and select Add Location then click Browse for folder and select the folder you created in step 1. Next time you select Publish Preview it should work.

Flash 8 Security

The new security change that can make the tasks in this hour difficult to test have to do with the new rule that a `.swf` running on your desktop (that is, not on a web server) may only access other files on your desktop (but not the Internet). You can change the Local playback security setting (in the Flash tab of the Publish Settings) to "Access network only" and the `.swf` will only be able to access the Web. The first point to understand is your `.swf` (running locally) can access the Web or local file—but not both. I'm not going to suggest changing the local-only default because while that will let you test the Go to web page behavior (`getURL()`) locally it will disable other features such as loading locally stored images runtime (as you'll do next hour). Remember that once you upload your `.swf` (even with the local-only setting) it will be able to load external images *and* jump to other web pages.

You may think that because you only plan on delivering files to the Web all this is unimportant. However, in order to test without uploading the files (which would be a big pain, say, every time you did a test movie) you need to configure your computer for testing. It's pretty easy. First, realize none of this applies when you do a test movie because Flash's security measures don't apply (although you may see an informational message in the output window—though everything still works). For testing locally in the browser (and for the rest of this chapter) you should set up a `.cfg` file that defines a folder on your computer where the Flash Player knows the content is trusted by you (thereby disabling the security restrictions for just that folder). (In fact, that dialog you saw in the previous task only appeared because of a file called FlashAuthor.cfg that effectively says "show warnings because I'm authoring"—end users shouldn't see that dialog.)

Anyway, you can specify individual .swfs or an entire folder where it's okay for files to access both the internet and local files. So, pick a folder for projects in this book: for example, I'll use `C:\Documents and Settings\Phillip\My Documents\STY Book\`

Next, you need to find the Flash Security folder. On Windows it will be in:

`c:\Documents and Settings\<user name>\Application Data\Macromedia\Flash Player\#Security`

Mac:

`/Users/<username>/Library/Preferences/Macromedia/Flash Player/#Security`

Create a folder inside the #Security folder named FlashPlayerTrust. Finally, make a text file and name it with the .cfg extension. For example: `book.cfg`. Inside this text file type the path to the folder you're okaying. For example:

`C:\Documents and Settings\Phillip\My Documents\STY Book\`

You can add as many locations as you want (and, in fact, add as many files as you want to that FlashPlayerTrust folder).

That's it. Now you can simply save all your projects while testing in that folder and they'll behave as the will when posted on a real web server.

Now that we have the security issue out of the way, let's look at two other ways (in addition to using getURL) you can create hyperlinks inside Flash, and they both involve using text. Any static text can have a URL associated with it automatically. You'll learn about this method in the following task.

Try It Yourself ▼

Create a Text Hyperlink

In this task you'll use an automatic feature to associate a hyperlink with a block of text. Here are the steps:

1. Create a block of text using any font you like—just make it big enough to read.

2. With the text block selected, access the Properties panel. First make sure the text type is Static (not Dynamic or Input), and then type a legitimate URL into the URL Link field (next to the chain-link icon). In Figure 19.4, http://www.phillipkerman.com is used. The text becomes hyperlinked text, also called hypertext.

FIGURE 19.4
You can make a selected block of text a hyperlink by specifying a URL link in the Properties panel.

3. Select Publish Preview. I like this method because it doesn't involve any behaviors; it's just a built-in text property. Notice that the new page replaces the browser window. As you'll see in the "Targeting Windows" section later this hour, it's possible to change the target window to blank to see the linked page appear in a new window instead. ▲

Now you'll learn the third way you can create hyperlinks: using dynamic text. This method, like the previous one, applies only to text. Dynamic text also has an option for HTML that allows you to populate a text block (through setting the associated variable) with actual HTML code. You'll see how this is done in the following task.

▼ Try It Yourself

Use Dynamic Text to Create a Hyperlink

In this task you'll create HTML within a Flash text block. Follow these steps:

1. Use the Text tool to create a long block of text. It doesn't matter what you type because the text will be replaced.

2. With the text block selected, use the Properties panel to set the text type as Dynamic and give this instance the name `my_txt`. Also, make sure you have Render as HTML selected and Selectable unselected (see Figure 19.5). (You can effectively click the Render as HTML option using the script: `my_text.html=true`)

FIGURE 19.5
Selecting dynamic text and the HTML option for the text block allows you to create HTML in Flash.

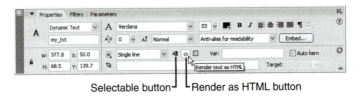

Selectable button⌐   ⌐Render as HTML button

3. In the first keyframe, populate the `my_txt` instance by selecting the first frame and accessing the Actions panel. Then type the following code:

```
my_txt.htmlText="This is <A HREF='http://www.yahoo.com'>Hot</A>."
```

4. (Note that you set the `htmlText` property, not the text property as you do when populating with plain text.) If you understand the HTML, great. Otherwise, just accept it for now. It will make sense later. Select Publish Preview.

▲

By the
Way

Quotes Within Quotes

Notice the single quote marks for the nested string around the web address. If you need to include regular quote marks within a string (which always begins and ends with quote marks), you have to "escape" the nested quote. In other words, `my_txt.text="I said "No""` won't work because Flash will think the quotation mark right before No is the ending quotation mark for the string started before I. To make it work, precede the literal quote mark with a backslash character (\), like this: `my_txt.text="I said \"No\""`. Using single quotes when possible is much easier.

Using Style Sheets

Although you can't display every type of HTML inside Flash (only the most basic tags are supported), Flash supports a limited version of Cascading Style Sheets (CSS). (You can view the whole list by searching for "Supported CSS properties" in Flash's Help panel.) You can use CSS to define text styles like a word processor. When you change the CSS definition, the text that uses the styles automatically updates.

You can store CSS definitions within Flash or in external .css files. To get you started, the following task exploits the main features of CSS.

Try It Yourself ▼

Display Text by Using CSS

In this task you'll control text display by using CSS code:

1. For this task, we'll store the CSS declaration in a .css text file. Use Notepad or a simple text editor to create a file with the following contents:

```
bodyText {
  font-family: Verdana;
  color:#000000;
  font-size: 10px;
}
headline {
  font-family: Verdana;
  color:#006600;
  font-size: 24px;
}
a:hover{
  color:#FF0000;
  font-size: 10px;
  text-decoration:underline;
}
```

2. I'll give you a quick translation, even though this is standard CSS. We've defined two styles "bodyText" and "headline". In addition the a:hover defines how the text with hyperlinks shall appear when the cursor hovers over the link. Save the text file in a new folder and name it styles.css.

3. Create a new Flash file and save it in the same folder as the CSS. You can name it usesCSS.fla.

4. Place onstage a dynamic text field and make the margins as wide as the stage. Give this text an instance name myCssText_txt.

▼

5. Select the first keyframe and open the Actions panel (or press F9). Type the following code into the Actions panel:

```
//set some properties and clear the field
myCssText_txt.selectable=false;
myCssText_txt.html=true;
myCssText_txt.text="";

//define a new style sheet and attach it to the text field
myStyles= new TextField.StyleSheet();
myCssText_txt.styleSheet = myStyles;

//define what happens when it loads
myStyles.onLoad=function(){
    //populate the text field using our new styles
    myCssText_txt.htmlText = "<headline>this is a headline</headline>";
    myCssText_txt.htmlText += "<bodyText>this is the body </bodyText";
    myCssText_txt.htmlText += "<bodyText>this is a ";
    myCssText_txt.htmlText += "<a href='#'>link</a></bodyText>";
}
//commence loading
myStyles.load("styles.css");
```

The comments (text appearing after //) should help explain what's going on. First, I set the `selectable` and `html` properties and clear the text field. Next I define a style sheet and apply it to the text field. The last line begins loading the .css file. But, not until it's fully loaded (inside the onLoad method), do we populate the text field.

Incidentally, to let the user navigate to a new web page, you can replace the # with an URL of your choice.

6. Test the movie.

I know you typed a lot of code in the preceding task, but it's just so cool, I really wanted to include this feature. Remember that when you publish to the Web, you'll need to include the .swf and the .html (as usual) but also the styles.css file. It gets loaded every time the user visits the site. What that means is you can change the styles (by editing that .css file) users will see the changes the next time they visit. You never have to touch the source .fla file and republish. In some ways, this task is a good introduction to next hour where you learn about modularizing your Flash site. Here, you're keeping the layout style separate from the actual content which is a great way to make updates easy.

What Other Web Tasks Can Flash Do?

For the rest of this hour, you'll learn some useful and powerful ways to combine Flash with standard HTML. If you already know HTML, you should be able to take this information and run with it. If you're not familiar with HTML, the rest of this hour should still be useful because you'll see some examples of what's possible. In addition, you'll see some code snippets that you can probably use in the future. If you want to learn more about the concepts discussed this hour, you can look to any good HTML resource.

Targeting Windows

You probably noticed that when you clicked the button you created in the second task this hour, "Use getURL to Create a Hyperlink," not only were you hyperlinked to another page, but the page you were viewing (the one with your Flash movie) was actually replaced with the new page. This is the default behavior for any hyperlink (as is the case with the HTML equivalent, A HREF). Alternatively, you can specify the window parameter to change the behavior from "replace this page with another" to "jump to a new web page and put it in new window."

In HTML, **window** refers to the rectangular frame into which the user views a web page. Some pages just have one big window whereas others are made up of an arrangement of several windows. Windows can be given names so that you can specify into which window particular content should go. There are also some generic window names. Compare this to how you can refer to houses in your neighborhood specifically by using addresses or you can use generic terms such as "next door" and "across the street."

The Go to web Page behavior's Open In setting (which is getURL's second parameter) lets you specify a target window into which the specified URL will load. If you set this parameter to "_self", the hyperlink loads the new web page directly inside the same browser window. If you edit the getURL script, you can specify a window name (which generally applies only when you've previously named windows, as in HTML frames), into which to load the new web page. For example, suppose your Flash movie has several buttons, each one causing a different window to change its contents. As you click the buttons, the Flash movie stays in its own window, and other windows pop open as necessary.

One way to arrange several windows in HTML is by using framesets. One frameset can have as many **frames** as you want. Each frame can be designed to have specific dimensions and features such as a menu bar or title bar.

In addition to author-named windows, there are four reserved "generic" target window names. If you click the Open In drop-down list, as shown in Figure 19.6, you'll see _self, _blank, _parent, and _top. Most of these names apply to frames (which you can learn about in an HTML reference), and one name comes in handy when frames aren't being used. The name _blank causes the selected URL to load into a new browser window, and it leaves the current window open. To see this in action, select the button created in this hour's second task, open the Behaviors panel, and double-click the row you added (it should read Go to Web Page...). Then change the parameter to _blank. When you publish, you should notice that when the button is clicked, a whole new browser window is created.

FIGURE 19.6
The Go to Web Page behavior provides the generic target window options in a drop-down list.

Sending Email: The `mailto:` Command

Although you have to use more advanced techniques to actually send email from a web page, here's a quick-and-dirty way to do something close. The HTML command mailto: can be used in conjunction with getURL to automatically open a user's email program with a preaddressed email message. The user just needs to type a message and then send the email message.

It's really simple. You can just make another button (perhaps with the label Email Me) and then use the Go to Web Page behavior again. But this time, be sure to select _self and put the following text in the URL field:

```
mailto:flash8@phillipkerman.com
```

Here, flash8@phillipkerman.com is the email address. If you select the Publish Preview command, when the action is encountered, you should see that a new email message that's already addressed is created. The user only needs to type the message and click Send. The only catch is that the user must have a default email program identified on his or her computer (most people do).

If you want the email message to pop up with the subject and body content already created, you can change the simple mailto string (for the URL field) to something like this:

```
mailto:flash8@phillipkerman.com?subject=Subject goes here&body=Body goes here
```

Simply replace flash8@phillipkerman.com with the address you want the message sent to, replace Subject goes here with whatever subject line you want, and replace Body goes here with whatever message you want in the body of the email message.

Using Flash Inside a Larger Website

Although you can create a website entirely in Flash, sometimes it's not necessary or even desirable. Often you'll just want to use Flash to supplement a more conventional website. In the following sections, you'll learn several ways to use Flash within a larger website. This should help spark some ideas that you can use in your own site.

Pop-up Windows

You can supplement a plain HTML website by simply including a link to a Flash web page. Imagine a web page that has text, images, and a simple hyperlink (in HTML, A HREF) that points to a page you created with Flash's Publish command. This is the basic hyperlink you've seen a million times on the Web. Somewhere in your HTML file you include this:

```
<A HREF="published.html">Click for Flash sample</A>
```

This creates a line of hypertext on your website that, when clicked, opens up the HTML file that contains your published Flash movie. You can even make this link cause the Flash site (in this case, published.html) open up in a new (blank) window:

```
<A HREF="published.html" target="_blank">Click for Flash sample</A>
```

If you're creating your web page by using Macromedia Dreamweaver, you simply use the Properties panel to specify the link and target settings, as shown in Figure 19.7. The Link and Target fields are equivalent to the URL and Window fields, respectively, in the getURL parameters of Flash.

Okay, so that's easy enough. You can add some sophistication to this link from a regular site. The preceding methods simply cause the browser to hyperlink to another page (perhaps in a new, blank window). However, one technique that might be appropriate is to pop up a new browser window that has specific features. For example, the pop-up window can be sized to your specifications instead of being the same size as the current browser window. You can specify other features to remove or disable certain browser attributes (such as resizing, viewing the buttons, and so on). This involves a little JavaScript (which I won't explain in detail but will provide here) attached to a line of hypertext. Here's an example:

```
<A HREF="#"
script language="JavaScript"
onMouseDown="window.open('animation.html', 'thename', 'width=300,height=335');">
click here!</A>
```

FIGURE 19.7
Using
Dreamweaver,
you can turn
text into hyper-
text via the
Properties
panel.

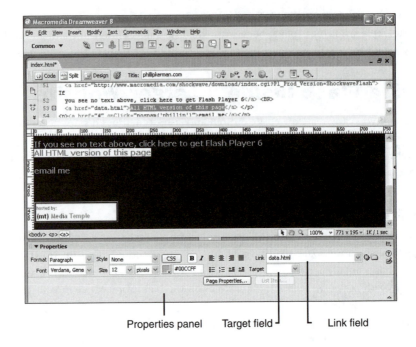

Properties panel   Target field   Link field

The key portion of this script is `window.open()`. The first parameter is the filename you want to open (in this case, `animation.html`). The second parameter is the arbitrary name you're giving this window, and the third parameter is a string full of the features you're including. In this case, only the width and height are specified (in pixels). (You can find more features that can be included here in a good JavaScript reference.)

If you want to let the user close the window that has popped up in another way besides using the browser's close button, you can provide some simple JavaScript to perform the task. For example, you can make a Flash animation file called `animation.fla`, with the movie size set to 300_300, and then publish it to `.swf` and `.html` files. Then you can open the HTML file you created (`animation.html`) by using a text editor (such as Notepad). At the very end of the file are these lines:

```
</OBJECT>
</BODY>
</HTML>
```

You're simply inserting some JavaScript (to close the window) between `</OBJECT>` and `</BODY>`. Here's the result:

```
</OBJECT>
<A HREF="#"
script language="JavaScript"
```

```
onMouseDown="window.close();">Close</a>
</BODY>
</HTML>
```

Note that although the movie is 300×300, the `window.open` code creates a window that's 300×335 to make room for the hypertext (`Close`).

This shows how a little JavaScript in an HTML file can close a window, but what does it have to do with Flash? Not much, except that it's an effect you may want to try. However, let's now look at a technique that lets you execute JavaScript from inside Flash. For example, what if you want a button created in Flash that executes the `window.close()` code? There are two basic ways: the "javascript:" method which works when you publish to Flash Player 6 or 7, and the new ExternalInterface object. You can simply use the Go to Web Page behavior and, in the field for the URL parameter, type `javascript:window.close()` (see Figure 19.8). All you do is start with `javascript:` and follow with the actual JavaScript code! This technique works pretty well on all the modern browsers.

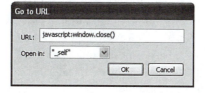

FIGURE 19.8
You can send code through the Go to Web Page behavior. Just precede the actual code with `javascript:`.

The new ExternalInterface object approach is much more elegant, but does require a bit of code. The advantages, however, include the fact it's much easier to pass parameters. For example spawning a new window via `window.open` is very tricky using the `javascript:` method. To trigger JavaScript directly from inside a Flash 8 `.swf` you use the `call()` method— but you need to first import the ExternalInterface class. Here's code you can put right on the button—instead of the Behavior:

```
on(press){
  import flash.external.ExternalInterface;
  ExternalInterface.call("window.close");
}
```

The `window.close()` JavaScript is pretty simple—it doesn't require any parameters. Where the ExternalInterface becomes easier is when you do need to pass parameters. For example the following code will let the button spawn a new window (like the code I showed earlier, but this code goes inside your Flash movie):

```
on(press){
  import flash.external.ExternalInterface;
  ExternalInterface.call("window.open", "animation.html", "thename",
"width=300,height=335");
}
```

One last detail related to pop-up windows: The HTML that the Publish feature creates is solid and works great. However, it's not necessarily what you'll want to use in every case. You'll learn in Hour 24 how to change the exact behavior of Publish. However, there's one tiny adjustment I make almost every time—and it's especially applicable to the `animation.html` file used in the example. I would change the top part of the HTML file (`<BODY bgcolor="#FFFFFF">`) to this:

```
<BODY bgcolor="#FFFFFF"
leftmargin="0" topmargin="0" marginwidth="0" marginheight="0">
```

This edit simply positions the Flash movie with no margins. Without this adjustment, the 300_300 Flash movie would get cut off in a 300_300 window. (In Hour 24 you'll learn how this edit can be incorporated as the default so you don't have to make the edit by hand every time.)

Including Flash Within HTML

This hour you first learned how to publish a Flash movie (which created the `.html` and `.swf` files). Then you learned how to make links that let the user jump out of Flash. Finally, you learned how to make links from a plain HTML page to a Flash page (including popping up a sized window). So far, it might appear that the conventional HTML pages have been kept separate from the Flash pages. Actually, the "all-Flash" page you published was really an HTML page with nothing but Flash on it (no text or images). It's easy, and more practical, to have your HTML host more than just a sole Flash movie. You can have the Flash parts living along with the text and images of your regular HTML page.

Here are the three basic approaches:

▶ Let the Publish feature create an HTML file and then add to that file in a text editor.

▶ Copy a portion of the published HTML file and paste it inside an HTML file created elsewhere.

▶ Insert a Flash file into a web page by using a web layout tool that supports Flash such as Dreamweaver.

To add regular HTML to the file that Flash's Publish feature created, first open the `.html` file with a text editor such as Notepad or Simple Text. Then you need to decide whether you want the content you're adding to go above or below the Flash animation. If you want to put content above the Flash file, simply add it after the `<BODY bgcolor="#FFFFFF">` tag and before the `<OBJECT classid=...>` tag. To add content under the Flash file, insert your content after the `</OBJECT>` tag but before the </BODY> tag. What you must remember is that everything between the <OBJECT> and </OBJECT> tags specifies details about the Flash file, and you should not edit this. Later, when you learn to extract a portion of this file, you'll be taking everything between `<OBJECT...` and </OBJECT>, inclusively. Figure 19.9 shown an example of an `.html` file opened in Notepad.

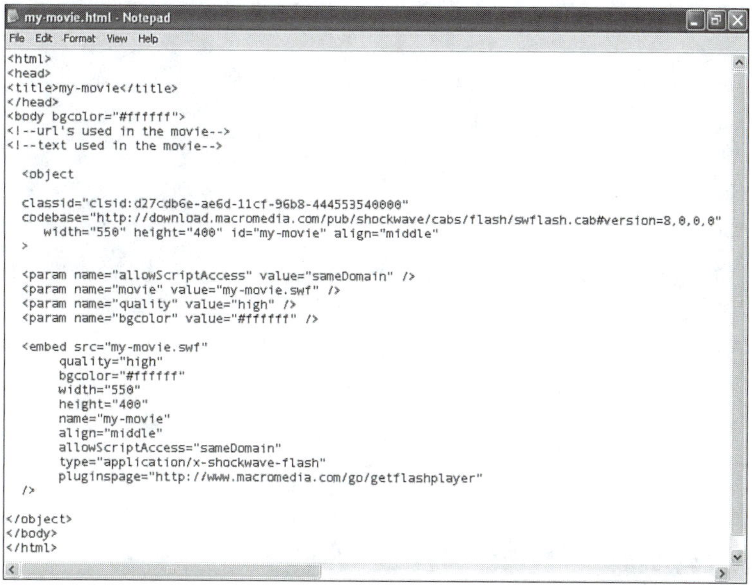


```
<html>
<head>
<title>my-movie</title>
</head>
<body bgcolor="#ffffff">
<!--url's used in the movie-->
<!--text used in the movie-->

  <object

  classid="clsid:d27cdb6e-ae6d-11cf-96b8-444553540000"
  codebase="http://download.macromedia.com/pub/shockwave/cabs/flash/swflash.cab#version=8,0,0,0"
     width="550" height="400" id="my-movie" align="middle"
  >

  <param name="allowScriptAccess" value="sameDomain" />
  <param name="movie" value="my-movie.swf" />
  <param name="quality" value="high" />
  <param name="bgcolor" value="#ffffff" />

  <embed src="my-movie.swf"
       quality="high"
       bgcolor="#ffffff"
       width="550"
       height="400"
       name="my-movie"
       align="middle"
       allowScriptAccess="sameDomain"
       type="application/x-shockwave-flash"
       pluginspage="http://www.macromedia.com/go/getflashplayer"
  />

</object>
</body>
</html>
```

FIGURE 19.9 You can extract the portion of HTML between `<OBJECT...` and </OBJECT> to use it elsewhere.

If you're using Dreamweaver, this entire process is extremely simple. All you do is decide where you want to insert the Flash movie and select Insert, Media, Flash (or press the Insert Flash button). The Properties panel lets you specify parameters (almost identical to those in the Flash tab in the Publish Settings dialog box). If you use this method, you don't need to publish the HTML code from inside Flash because this creates the same HTML code that Publish would have otherwise created (but it does so inside the file currently open in Dreamweaver). See Figure 19.10 for an example.

Therefore, just as you can insert images in HTML, you can also insert Flash movies. What's more, the HTML that Publish creates has room for you to make edits and add HTML content (such as text and images). Consider that you can embed Flash `.swfs` anywhere you can embed images. For example, inside tables or html frames. All in all, you can combine HTML and Flash quite seamlessly.

Insert Flash media button

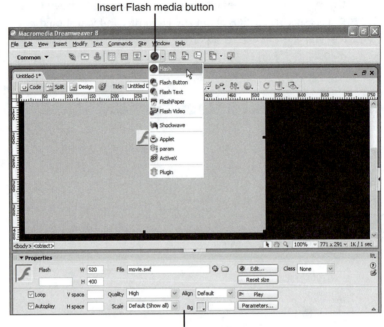

Flash movie properties

Uploading Files to a Web Server

Probably the most critical step in this entire hour involves actually uploading all the
necessary files to a web server. Although you can test your files on your computer,
other people won't be able to see your creation unless you put it on a web server.

A **web server** is a computer that is connected to the Internet and is configured to let
others view files through common Internet means (such as a browser). Your computer is likely connected to the Internet, but unless you're running server software (and
have the right kind of connection), other people won't be able to browse the web
pages on your hard drive. Many service providers, however, provide space on their
web servers for subscribers to upload files.

The process of uploading may be simple if you are running a web server on your
computer. Maybe you work at a company where the process is as simple as copying
files to another computer's hard drive. In the simplest of cases, you just copy the
.swf and .html files to the hard drive, making sure you put them both in the same
location.

If you have an Internet service provider (ISP) that gives you a certain amount of disk space on its web server, you can simply copy the files to the appropriate location. Your ISP should be able to give you more information, but the most common way of uploading files involves using a File Transfer Protocol (FTP) program. There are several popular (and free) FTP programs that let you specify an FTP address, a login name, and a password to gain access to a server, where you can copy and move files. Also, Dreamweaver has a built-in feature to upload files. A simple (although not ideal) way to upload files is to use Internet Explorer and type into the address box `ftp://login:password@ftp.server.com/`, where `login` is your login name, *password* is your password, and *ftp.server.com* is your ISP's server name. Check with your ISP, but this method should allow you to copy files from your hard drive to the ISP's server— all you do is drag files into the Internet Explorer window, as shown in Figure 19.11.

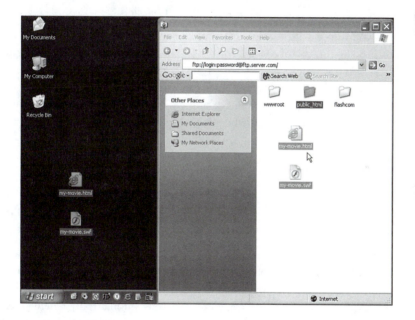

FIGURE 19.11
Although this isn't the best method, you can use Internet Explorer to upload files to a server.

Many Web Servers Are Case-Sensitive

Because many web servers use Unix file-naming conventions and Unix is case sensitive, your best bet is to keep all your filenames lowercase from the start. For example, if your `.fla` is called `myMovie.fla` and you publish it, Flash will create files named `myMovie.html` and `myMovie.swf`. This is asking for trouble because if you change the `.swf` to `mymovie.swf`, the HTML file may not find it. The general rule is simple: Keep all filenames entirely lowercase.

Watch Out!

Summary

You've learned a lot this hour—and not everything you learned involved Flash! That's okay because the emphasis of this hour was on what to do with your Flash movies when you're ready to distribute them to the world. Although you can certainly create amazing Flash movies that never go on the Web, it doesn't take much effort to get them onto the Web when you're ready.

Although some of Publish's details won't be discussed until Hour 24, you did see how it exports the necessary .swf and .html files through Publish and Publish Preview. Displaying your Flash content on a web page can be as simple as clicking a button. However, you also learned how to use the Go to web Page behavior (which uses getURL) to include hyperlinks to other web pages. You can also use the same technique to send JavaScript commands straight from Flash.

Besides JavaScript, you also explored several aspects of HTML, including the A HREF tag (which is the equivalent of Flash's getURL action), tables, and frames. Hopefully, this overview has inspired you to learn a little more about HTML and try using it with your Flash projects. In any case, the tricky part isn't figuring out how to get something done—it's figuring out and deciding what you want to attempt. As with many things in life, after it's clear where you're headed with a web page, it's usually easy to get your task done.

Q&A

Q *When I use Publish Preview, everything looks great, but when I put the files on my web server, they don't work. Why?*

A Well, the reason could be due to one of a million things. Here's a rundown of a few of the common problems. Did you use any uppercase characters in any of the filenames? If so, you should try using all lowercase because your server might be case-sensitive, and some FTP programs automatically rename files to all lowercase. Did you copy all the correct files to the server? Did you put all the files in the right locations (such as the .swf file in the same folder as the .html file)? Is your server properly configured for Flash's MIME setting? (If you want to learn more about this setting, check out Macromedia's TechNote 4151—just type 4151 into the search field at www.macromedia.com.)

Q *Can I have more than one Flash movie on a web page?*

A Of course. You can have as many as you can track. For example, it might make sense in a table to have a Flash movie in two different cells. You could also design a frameset where one Flash movie is contained in a frame that never reloads (and contains background music) and a bunch of other Flash movies load into frames that change. Whatever you want, it can probably be done.

Workshop

The Workshop consists of quiz questions and answers to help you solidify your understanding of the material covered in this hour. You should try to answer the questions before checking the answers.

Quiz

1. If you select the Publish command and nothing seems to happen, is there something wrong?

    A. Yes. Publish has a bug and doesn't actually work.

    B. Possibly. You need to be connected to the Internet for this command to work.

    C. No. Publish simply exports the files selected in the Publish Settings dialog box. If you want to see the results, try using Publish Preview (or find the exported files).

2. Is it necessary to use the Go to web Page behavior (or `getURL` action) only on buttons?

    A. Yes. Otherwise, you wouldn't know exactly when the user wanted to navigate to a new web page.

    B. No. You could also put the behavior on a keyframe so it goes to another page as soon as the frame is reached.

    C. No. You can use Go to web Page on keyframes but not on button components.

3. True or false: If you read all the material in this hour, you should have a good grounding in HTML.

   A. True. It was concise yet comprehensive.

   B. False. If you didn't know HTML before this hour, you probably still don't—but at least you know some of the potential.

   C. False. Only when you finish this book will you become an HTML pro.

4. Is using the Go to web Page behavior (or `getURL` action) the only way to create a hyperlink?

   A. Yes. Except if you do it in HTML.

   B. No. There are at least 20 other behaviors that ship with Flash under the web category.

   C. No. There are also some ways to create hyperlinks with text.

Quiz Answers

1. C. Publish creates files, but you won't see anything unless you first find the files created. Publish Preview creates files and immediately previews them in your browser.

2. B. The Go to web Page behavior can be attached to buttons, and keyframes as well as clip instances. It makes sense that you might want to automatically load a new page, say, after an animation finishes.

3. B. The idea of this hour wasn't to teach HTML but rather to point those with some HTML experience in the right direction and give others an idea of what's possible.

4. C. When the Properties panel is set to Static Text, you can specify a URL to jump to. Also, the Dynamic and Input styles can have HTML style, effectively letting you write HTML in Flash.

Designing a Website to Be Modular

What You'll Learn in This Hour:

▶ How to use the `MovieClipLoader` to play one movie inside another or display an external image (`.jpg`, `.gif`, or `.png`)

▶ How the `loadSound` action lets you play external MP3 sounds

▶ The benefits of and how to use shared libraries

It's possible to create a huge website entirely with one giant Flash file. However, separating the site into modular segments has distinct advantages. Just to name a few, you can have portions of the site load as needed (instead of making every visitor download everything), several team members can work on the same site simultaneously, you can update portions of the site as they change instead of having to reedit one master file, and you can create different versions of the site for different languages by just swapping out portions with language-specific content. There are other reasons modularity is good, but it comes down to efficiency, your productivity, and the user experience.

This hour covers several ways a Flash site can be modularized as well as some of the issues you'll need to consider in deciding when and where tomodularize.

Although the technical concepts covered this hour are not particularly difficult, the Flash features discussed are strict and unforgiving. As long as you use the correct syntax, you'll be fine. Ultimately, the difficulty comes in deciding the appropriate use of such features. That is, it's easy to learn *how* these features work, but it's more difficult to decide *when* to use them and *where* to use them. For each feature, you'll first learn how it works and then look at practical uses.

Loading Movies or Images

The `MovieClipLoader` lets one Flash movie play another. Effectively, the second movie plays on top of the first. It's easiest to understand, though, if you think of one movie as the *host* and the other movie (the one that's loaded on top of the host) as the *submovie*. Think of a big entertainment system—a wall of stereo and TV equipment. The movie you put into your VCR can play on only the TV screen. Think of the TV as the host Flash movie, and the video you put into your VCR is loaded on top of it.

One reason to do this is because you might have several submovies that only play one at a time. You might want to give the user the choice as to which submovie to play. All you need to do is trigger the `MovieClipLoader` when the user clicks a button. It's sort of like a jukebox, where each record or CD is a separate submovie. The reason the `MovieClipLoader` is beneficial is that only the submovies the user requests have to download.

Let's look at some of the technical issues with the `MovieClipLoader`; then you can try it. First, only `.swf` files can execute the `MovieClipLoader`'s `loadClip` action. Therefore, not only will you have to use Test Movie to see the results, but if you plan to load movies they need to first be exported as `.swf` files (in the case of loading image files, you simply need to have those JPGs, GIFs, or PNGs available). Second, when you use the `MovieClipLoader`, you must specify into what target to load the movie. Movies are loaded into one of two basic targets: a clip instance or a level number. If you load a movie into a clip, the clip is replaced with the movie that's loaded. If you load a movie into a level, anything that happens to be in that level currently is replaced by the movie.

By the
Way

> ### Levels: The Hidden Layer
>
> **Levels** are the numbering system Flash uses to describe the stacking order of loaded movies. The host movie is always in Level 0 (referred to as `_level0`). If you load one movie into `_level1` and another into `_level2`, the `_level2` movie will appear on top of everything else.

Finally, remember when I said that when you load a movie, it gets loaded "on top"? That's not entirely true. When you load a movie into a clip, the loaded movie actually replaces the clip, so the loaded movie resides in the same level where the clip was. That is, if the clip was in front of something or behind something, the loaded movie will be, too. In the case of loading a movie into a level, the loaded movie will be in front of everything else that happens to be assigned lower-level numbers and behind items assigned higher-level numbers. The `_root` Stage is always `_level0`. Therefore, if you load a movie into `_level1`, it will be on top. However, if you load another movie into `_level2`, it will be on top of everything else—the first loaded movie (`_level1`) will be sandwiched between the Stage and the new l loaded movie. In the next task you'll see that there's actually a way to avoid levels and load movies into actual clips.

Try It Yourself

Load a Movie

In this task you'll use the `MovieClipLoader` to selectively let the user download just the segments he or she is interested in. Here are the steps to follow:

1. The name of the game for this task is organization. Remember, haste makes waste. Create a new empty folder into which you'll save and export all your movies. You'll be making three colored tweens plus the main hosting file.

2. Create a new file and set both the movie's width and height to 300. Use Modify, Document (or Ctrl+J) to do this. Make sure that Ruler Units is set to Pixels.

3. Create a simple tween of your choice, and make the tweening object entirely red. Save the movie as `red.fla` in the folder you created in step 1. Use Test Movie, which exports a movie called `red.swf` to the same folder as your `red.fla` file.

4. Use Save As to name the file `green.fla`, and change the color of the tweening object to green. (You might need to change the color in each keyframe.) Remember to save and then use Test Movie to create the `.swf`.

5. Repeat step 4 but create a file with everything blue.

6. You should have three `.fla` files and three `.swf` files (red, green, and blue for each) as shown in Figure 20.1. Close all the Flash files. Then create a new Flash file and save it as `main.fla` in the same folder. Set this document's size to 500×500. This "main" file will load movies into a clip.

red.fla   green.fla   blue.fla

red.swf   green.swf   blue.swf

FIGURE 20.1
From each of your three `.fla` files you'll need to create a corresponding `.swf`. ▼

7. Draw a l square exactly 300×300 by drawing any rectangle and then using the Info panel to change its dimensions to 300×300. Make sure there's a line around the box and then delete the fill. Select the entire outline and convert to it a symbol (make it a movie clip, name it box, and select the top-left Registration option). Name the instance on the Stage theClip_mc in the Properties panel while the box is selected.

8. Drag a Button component onto the Stage and open the Actions panel with the button selected (by pressing F9). Type the following code:

```
on(click){
  _root.theLoader_mcl.loadClip("red.swf","theClip_mc");
}
```

This tells the MovieClipLoader instance (named theLoader_mcl) to begin loading the red.swf file into the theClip_mc instance in the _root Timeline. We'll make the theLoader_mcl in the next step. (You can change _root to this._parent if you prefer.)

9. Select the first keyframe in the movie and open the Actions panel. Type the following line of code:

```
theLoader_mcl = new MovieClipLoader();
```

10. Test the movie. Notice that the loaded movie is registered perfectly. That's because the loaded movie loads with its upper-left corner aligned with the clip's registration point (in this case, it's the upper-left as specified when you created the clip in step 7).

11. Make two more buttons and use the same basic script as before, except change the string for one to "green.swf" and to "blue.swf" for the other.

You can tweak l the task you just completed to display images. In addition to loading .swf files, Flash Player 8 can load images in the following formats: .jpg (both regular and progressive encoded JPGs), .gif, and .png. Flash 7 supports only .jpg and .swf. The .gif format has been used very widely, and .png is great because it supports alpha channels—meaning portions of the loaded image overlay (and see through to) objects underneath. Anyway, to load images just change the first parameter in the loadClip() method. For example, in step 8, change "red.swf" to read "someimage.png". You'll need an image (named "someimage.png") in the same folder, of course.

Before we look at more advanced variations, I want to point out that you can use the MovieClipLoader to load into levels instead of clip instances. Change the second parameter in the loadClip() method (step 7 previously) to read: "_level1" (or "_level2", "_level3", and so on). One advantage of loading into levels instead of clip instances is that you don't need to first create a clip, place it onstage, and give it an instance name. Personally, I still prefer to load into clip instances. I just think it's more intuitive because you can visually position the instance on stage or set any other property (such as rotation or alpha). Levels require that you keep track of which level is being used for which loaded image. That is, at any one time you can load only one object (image or .swf) into a single level, or clip instance, for that matter). Also, you should be aware that loading into _level0 replaces your whole movie. Normally, you'll want to load into level 1 or higher (or, better yet, into clip instances you've placed onstage).

Determining When a Movie Is Fully Loaded and How to Unload It

Now that you know how to load an image or .swf, it's a good idea to learn how to unload it. But first, you should learn how to determine whether a movie that's loading has completed loading! This will be important if the movie that's loading is large. It's nice to let the user see that a movie is indeed downloading. You might actually want to *make* the user wait for it to fully load. All these things require you to determine whether a loading movie has downloaded.

The best way to determine whether a movie has loaded is to set up a so-called listener that waits for the onLoadComplete event. But that doesn't happen until the .swf or image is fully loaded. You can use the onLoadProgress event to get up-to-the-minute information about how the downloading is progressing. This way, you can display information to the user (such as a progress bar). That's just what we'll do in the next task.

Try It Yourself ▼

Use the MovieClipLoader Object to Display Progress

In this task you'll use the built-in features of the MovieClipLoader object in order to display the download progress in a standard horizontal graphic:

1. First, create the submovie that will be loaded. Set the document properties (by pressing Ctrl+J) to 300×300. Then create a linear animation that starts in Frame 2. That is, click Frame 2, select Insert, Timeline, Keyframe (or press F6), and then build the animation that plays through many more frames (maybe out to Frame 60). Using an imported video clip would be ideal because you want something that takes a little while to download. To that end, consider importing a sound and making it start on Frame 2 (again, to make the file big).

▼

2. Select the first frame of this submovie and open the Actions panel. Type using stop(); so that this movie stops on Frame 1 while the rest of the movie downloads.

3. Make a new layer and in the last frame of that layer (Frame 60) click and then insert a keyframe (by pressing F6). With the last frame selected, open the Actions panel and type gotoAndPlay(2); so that the movie will loop but not all the way back to the start (where there's a stop action).

4. In a new folder, save this movie as submovie.fla and then use Test Movie (by pressing Ctrl+Enter) to create a .swf named submovie.swf. When you use Test Movie, the movie just sits on Frame 1; you'll control this issue from the movie into which it loads.

5. Now in a new movie, draw a box that's exactly 300×300, remove the fill, select Modify, Convert to Symbol (or press F8), name the box Holder, and make sure it's behavior is set to Movie Clip and the top-left registration option is selected. Next, in the Properties panel, name the instance now on the Stage my_mc.

6. Next, you'll draw a rectangle (for the progress bar). Select the Rectangle tool, turn off Object Drawing, and then draw a rectangle. Select only the fill, and then select Modify, Convert to Symbol (or press F8). Select the upper-left registration point so that when the rectangle scales, it scales from the left. You can call the symbol Progress and then name the instance progress_mc.

7. Finally, select the first keyframe in the main movie and type the following code (which I'll explain next) :

```
1 theLoader_mcl = new MovieClipLoader();
2 myListener = new Object();
3 myListener.onLoadStart = function(mc) {
4     progress_mc._visible = true;
5 };
6 myListener.onLoadProgress = function(mc, bytesLoaded, bytesTotal) {
7     progress_mc._xscale= bytesLoaded / bytesTotal*100;
8 };
9 myListener.onLoadComplete = function(mc) {
10    progress_mc._visible=false;
11 };
12 theLoader_mcl.addListener(myListener);
13 theLoader_mcl.loadClip("submovie.swf", "my_mc");
```

The first line creates a new MovieClipLoader instance (theLoader_mcl), and the last line initiates the loading—you really only need those two lines. But the object myListener has three events that it's going to listen for: onLoadStart, onLoadProgress, and onLoadComplete (all built-in features of the MovieClipLoader). The key is line 12, where we associate that listener instance (myListener) with the MovieClipLoader instance (theLoader_mcl). Notice that line 4 does the work of setting progress_mc's scale to a percentage based on how much has loaded divided by how much will load. (In the workshop section of this hour, I've included some code for making a custom animation instead of simply stretching a bar.)

8. Test the movie. The movie should work great. If you *really* want to test it, put it on a web server and try running it from a slow connection. While testing, you can select View, Simulate Download, but that feature doesn't work reliably when using the MovieClipLoader. Note that if you do upload the files, it might appear to download instantly the second time. That's because the loaded movie has already downloaded to your browser's cache. Basically, you either have to clear the cache or delete the .swf files from the folder that contains downloaded files. For example, with Internet Explorer, select Tools, Internet Options to open the Options dialog box, and then click Delete Files on the General tab. Alternatively, you can trick the browser into not using the cache by changing line 13 to read:

```
theLoader_mcl.loadClip("submovie.swf" + "?ran=" + Math.random(), "my_mc");
```

Unfortunately, you can only use this code in a file posted on a web server. That is, it won't work when you do a Test Movie.

It turns out that you can pull off a similar effect with less code by using components, as the following task demonstrates.

Try It Yourself

Use Components to Load a Movie

In this task you'll use the Loader and ProgressBar components to reduce code:

1. Start a new file and save it adjacent to the submovie.swf file from the previous task.

2. Drag a Loader component and a ProgressBar component onto the Stage. Give them instance names myLoader and myProgress, respectively.

3. Select the myLoader instance. On the Parameters tab in the Properties panel, set contentPath to submovie.swf and scaleContent to false.

4. Select the myProgress instance. Change its parameter for source to read myLoader.

5. Select the first keyframe, open the Actions panel, and type this code:

```
myLoader.addEventListener("complete", removeBar);
 function removeBar(){
 myProgress._visible=false;
 myLoader.contentHolder.play();
 }
```

When the "complete" event triggers, the homemade function removeBar() will hide the progress bar and tell the contentHolder instance to play. Notice that submovie.swf will load into contentHolder, which is inside myLoader.

Shared Library Items

The whole idea of storing items in your Library is that they're only stored once, regardless of how many times they're used in a movie. However, an item in one movie's Library isn't automatically recycled if you copy it into another movie. Flash has two (confusingly similar) features to let you share Library items among your movies. There are two ways to do it: runtime sharing and authortime sharing. **Runtime sharing** involves storing Library items in a single source movie (that gets exported as a .swf). Then, one or more user movies can access the source .swf's items. This way, if the source .swf ever gets updated, the changes will be reflected in all user files. This is just like making an edit to a master symbol, except in this case, multiple movies will reflect the change instead of just multiple instances within one movie.

Authortime sharing is slightly less complex than runtime sharing. You still have one source movie containing Library items. But with authortime sharing, the shared items get recopied into each user file every time you use Test Movie. That is, the user files copy the shared Library item at the time of export. So if a change occurs in the source item, all user files have to be reopened and exported to reflect the change. Plus, each copy of the source adds to the file size of the user files. It's true that authortime sharing is not as modular as runtime sharing, but it's appropriate for larger common elements that you want copied into each user file. One limit of runtime sharing is that the entire shared Library has to fully download before a user file can begin playing. In this way, runtime sharing isn't good for many or large items.

You're about to learn the steps to create and use shared items in the runtime mode. In Hour 23, "Working on Large Projects and in Team Environments," you'll walk through a task involving authortime sharing.

How to Share Library Items at Runtime

Sharing items at runtime involves two basic steps. First, you need to create the Library containing items to be shared. Then, in each file that will use the shared items, you need to establish a link to the source.

Try It Yourself ▼

Prepare Items to Share at Runtime

In this task you'll create a Library containing items that can be shared. Follow these steps:

1. Create a new file and immediately save it as shared.fla in a folder called RuntimeSharing. Import one bitmapped image (.jpg, .bmp, or .pct, for example). Delete the bitmap on the Stage (don't worry—it's still safe in the Library). Also, import one sound file. Finally, create a rectangle and convert it to a symbol (by pressing F8). Then make it a movie clip, name it clip and click OK.

2. You should now have a Library with three items. Rename the items image, sound, and clip. Generally, the next step is to simply export a .swf containing these three Library items. However, normally when you export a .swf, all unused Library items are excluded so that they don't contribute to the file size. Normally, this is a good thing. The problem is that in this case, you want all the items in the Library to export with the file. Sure, this will add to file size, but you want these assets to be available to many user files. To ensure that each item is included in the .swf export process, you define the linkage properties for each item.

3. To define the linkage for the sound you imported, find it in the Library, select it, and then select Linkage from the options menu (or right-click). Select the Export for Runtime Sharing check box. This exposes three other required fields: Identifier, AS2.0 Class, and URL. You can accept the default name for Identifier (you should always use something easy to remember). Into the URL field type shared.swf because that's the name for this movie after it is exported. Leave the AS2.0 Class field blank. Figure 20.2 shows the linkage settings you should use.

4. Define the linkage for the bitmap and the box movie clip the same way: Click Export for runtime sharing and type shared.swf into the URL field.

5. Save (by pressing Ctrl+S) and then export this file. ▼

FIGURE 20.2
You set a
Library item's
linkage to
Export for run-
time sharing.
This way, the
item will defi-
nitely export,
even if it's not
being used in
this file.

6. Use Test Movie (by pressing Ctrl+Enter) because the movie is already saved in
   the right folder. Your source items are now ready to be shared. You can think
   of this as your shared Library.

Now you can use the shared items in any other movie. Inside the other movies, the
items simply need to have the Import for Runtime Sharing check box selected. In
the following task, you'll start *using* the items from the shared Library, and then it
should start to make sense.

Try It Yourself

Start Using a Shared Item

In this task you'll create a user file that can access the contents of the shared Library
you created in the previous task. Here are the steps:

1. Create a new file (by pressing Ctrl+N) and select File, Save As. Name the file
   user1.fla and save it in the RuntimeSharing folder (from the previous task).
   Now you have to get those shared items into the new movie. You *could* copy
   instances from the shared.fla file, but that would involve first creating
   instances (by dragging from the Library) and then pasting into user.fla.
   That's not really sharing—that's copying. Instead, you want to open

shared.fla as a Library. To do that, make sure you're editing user1.fla and that you've closed shared.fla then select File, Import, Open External Library and then select shared.fla. You should see the Library from shared.fla, but notice that it's darkened a bit to represent that it's from another file. You can now use instances from this movie without adding to the file size of the user1.fla file.

2. Drag items from shared.fla's Library to the Stage of user1.fla. Drag the bitmap onto the Stage. Then open the Library for user1.fla (by pressing Ctrl+L) and notice that the bitmap looks like it was copied into the Library. Try dragging the sound from the shared.fla file's Library to user1.fla's Library. Finally, drag the clip onto the Stage. The file user1.fla now seems to have three items added to its Library (see Figure 20.3). However, these are really just instances pointing to the master version in the file shared.fla.

3. Double-click the clip named clip in your user1.fla movie. You should see a dialog box like the one shown in Figure 20.4. Click No. The point is that you can only make edits to the master when you open shared.fla. By the way, you can drag instances from user1.fla's Library onto the Stage, and you're still using instances of the masters saved in shared.fla.

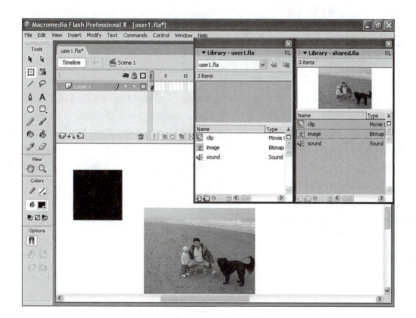

FIGURE 20.3
After you bring assets from a shared Library into a user file, they appear to be included in the user file's Library.

▼

FIGURE 20.4
Trying to edit a clip set up for runtime sharing causes this dialog box to appear. It basically says that if you want to edit the clip here, it won't be linked anymore. Editing the original is done through the source movie.

4. Use Test Movie and then look at the file sizes. The shared.swf file should be rather large (it has a bitmap, a sound, and a movie clip). The user1.swf file should be tiny because it only points to the shared.swf file. By the way, it also assumes that shared.swf is adjacent to user1.swf. If you move shared.swf or change its name, user1.swf won't know where to find it.

5. While you're inside user1.fla, take a look at the linkage settings under each item's linkage properties. You should see Import for Runtime Sharing selected, and you should see the Identifier and URL fields filled in. These settings mean that, when exported, this movie will look in the file shared.swf for items with the identifier listed.

▲

What's the big deal? In the preceding task, you have two files, and one's bigger than the other. So what? First of all, you can repeat the preceding task, but this time you can name the file user2.fla. You can use instances of the same symbols (maybe in different ways), and user2.swf will be tiny, too! Visitors to your site will download shared.swf only once, regardless of whether they view user1.swf or user2.swf or both. In addition, you can change the contents of shared.fla—maybe change the bitmap or the clip symbol. Making a change and exporting shared.swf again will enable all your user files (user1.swf, for example) to reflect the change. This is just like how you can change a master symbol, and every instance reflects that change. In the next task, you'll give it a try. (If you want to first repeat the preceding task but name your file user2.fla, you may.)

▼   **Try It Yourself**

Update Shared Items in a Library

In this task, you'll learn how to update the contents of a shared Library. Follow these steps:

1. Make sure you've closed all open files and even the Library for shared.fla by selecting File, Close All. Open the source of your shared Library (shared.fla). Take note of what the identifier is for the bitmap by selecting it and selecting

▼

Linkage from the Library's Options menu. Delete this bitmap from the Library and import another bitmap that will serve as a replacement.

2. Access the newly imported bitmap's Symbol Linkage Properties by selecting Linkage in the options menu, select Export for Runtime Sharing, and specify the same identifier as for the old bitmap (probably image).

3. Save the movie and export a .swf (by pressing Ctrl+Enter).

4. Double-click any user files you've made (user1.swf, for example). They should now reflect the change.

The preceding task was almost too easy. You simply created a new Library item in the master shared Library file (shared.fla), made sure it would export, and gave it an identifier name that matched the old one. Then, as soon as you exported the .swf, it worked. Basically, each user file doesn't care what's inside the master shared Library; it simply looks for items that match identifier names. For example, if you have a movie clip that contains English language text and swap it with one that contains Spanish, as long as the identifier is the same, it will work fine (it will just appear in a different language).

Although you are probably starting to see how shared Library items can enhance productivity, remember that their other benefit is file size savings. The shared.swf file downloads only once. This might make you want to include larger items (such as sounds and raster graphics). But you should know that when sharing items, the source (shared Library) must download entirely before the user files begin to play. For this reason, you really should use loadMovie or the MovieClipLoader object for larger elements so that you can control and monitor their downloading (as you did in an earlier task this hour). The most appropriate time to use runtime sharing is when you have lots of small items that you expect might need to change periodically—for example, a seasonal icon used on several different pages of your website. The icon (set to Export for Runtime Sharing) could change from themes for Halloween to Thanksgiving to New Year's.

Basically, all the upfront work in runtime sharing can be very useful, provided that you use the same styles and assets throughout many files. Runtime sharing also means that all the team members could be given copies of the latest version of shared.swf to use on their computers. In the end, when everything is published, the latest version of shared.swf will be used by everyone. All it takes is a little planning.

Playing External Sounds

You can play MP3 sounds that reside outside a movie. This means your movie can stay nice and small and load sounds only as the user requests them. It also means you can swap out and replace the original MP3 files without needing to reimport them into Flash. There are a few subtleties on how it works, but the script is easy enough to learn. The next task shows you how to make a jukebox application.

▼ **Try It Yourself**

Play an External MP3

In this task you'll build a mini jukebox from which users can select songs to play. Follow these steps:

1. Find a few MP3 files and place them in a new folder. Name the files song1.mp3, song2.mp3, and song3.mp3.

2. Drag a List component onto the Stage and give it an instance name songs_lb. Use the Free Transform tool to make the list nice and wide.

3. Put this script in the first keyframe of the movie:

```
1 songs_lb.addItem("Title of song one", "song1.mp3");
2 songs_lb.addItem("Title of song two", "song2.mp3");
3 songs_lb.addItem("Title of song three", "song3.mp3");
4
5 songs_lb.addEventListener("change",playSong);
6 function playSong() {
7     filename=songs_lb.selectedItem.data;
8     my_sound=new Sound();
9     my_sound.loadSound(filename,true);
10 }
```

4. Naturally, you can replace the titles for the songs in Lines 1–3. Notice that the second parameter in each of Lines 1–3 is the actual filename. These filenames will be hidden in the List item's data properties. Every time the user selects a song, the homemade playSong() function triggers. Line 7 sets a homemade variable filename to the data in the currently selected item. Finally, Lines 8 and 9 are really all you need for an external sound. The first one makes a Sound object instance (stored in the homemade my_sound variable). Then, Line 9 loads the sound. The second parameter (true for streaming) makes the sound begin playing as soon as enough has downloaded (instead of waiting for it to entirely download).

▲

Similarly to how Flash only loads images in the .jpg file format, the loadSound action only plays files in the .mp3 format.

Media Components in Flash Professional 8

Just as the Loader and ProgressBar components made loading external .swf files a snap, Flash Pro comes with three special media components. They include everything you need to easily load, play, and even let the user pause or resume external sounds and videos. Of course you can do all this by hand, but these components make it very easy.

By the Way

Summary

This hour you saw several ways to cut up movies into little pieces. Such modularization can have performance advantages as well as productivity value. The perceived download time is reduced if users only need to download segments as needed. The productivity of you and your team is increased when you break a site into smaller files. Not only can several people work simultaneously, but you can impose consistent styles by using shared Library items. This hour you also learned the steps necessary to modularize. However, the challenging and creative part comes as you decide when and where to modularize.

The specific features you learned this hour started with the MovieClipLoader that lets you (at runtime) play another .swf by loading it into a level number or into a clip instance. You also learned about sharing Library items at runtime, with a .swf acting as a Library shared between several files or among several team members. Finally, you got the basics of how to load an external sound. All these techniques can turn your investment of upfront work into productivity down the line.

Q&A

Q *I've created the submovies that I intend to load into my main movie via* loadMovie. *I've saved them all in the correct folder, but when I test the main movie, I get the error* Error opening URL "c:\windows_desktop\ somefolder\submovie.swf *in the output window, and my movies don't load. What's going on?*

A Most likely, when you made your various submovies, you saved them correctly, but you needed to take the extra step of exporting them as .swf files (simply by using Test Movie). Only .swf files and .jpg files can be loaded using loadMovie.

Q *My website is getting pretty messy with all the little submovies and* .jpg *files in the main folder. Is there a way I can keep the movies that load in a separate folder to keep everything straight?*

A Yes. When you specify the movie you want to load, if you simply type **mymovie.swf**, Flash will look for mymovie.swf in the same folder. If you want to store mymovie.swf in a subfolder called movies, you can change the URL field to read movies/mymovie.swf. (By the way, you can use all the standard HTML relative references as well, such as ../ to indicate "up one folder.")

Q *My loaded movies appear down and to the right of the clip into which they load. Is the only way to resolve this to move my clip up and to the left to compensate?*

A No. What's happening is that the loaded movie is orienting its top-left corner in the registration point of the movie into which it's loading. It sounds like the clip into which the movies are loading used center registration (making the loaded clips look like they appear down and to the right because their top left is in the center). You can remake the clip and select the top-left registration point this time. Or you can edit the contents of the holder clip: Select everything and move it down to the right. Back on the Stage, you can move the clip up to the left.

Q *If I know I'm going to use a shared Library item in a project, but I don't actually have the master media elements (such as the bitmaps I want to share), is there any way I can start now?*

A Sure. Bitmap items' Properties dialog boxes have two buttons—Update and Import—which let you reimport (and replace) a previously imported bitmap. The particular scenario of wanting to work without the final artwork is explored in a task coming up in Hour 23, involving authortime sharing (compared to this hour's runtime sharing examples). You might want to explore that task because it should help you fully understand the difference between authortime sharing and runtime sharing.

Workshop

The Workshop consists of quiz questions and answers to help you solidify your understanding of the material covered in this hour. You should try to answer the questions before checking the answers.

Quiz

1. How many movies can you load into a single clip instance?

  A. None. You need to use two clips.

  B. As many as you want.

  C. One at a time

2. If you're having trouble playing an external `.wav` sound file at runtime, what's the likely cause?

  A. Your speakers are not cranked.

  B. You can only play `.mp3` files.

  C. You have to use Publish Preview in the browser in order for sounds to play.

3. How many people can simultaneously edit the master version of a shared item?

  A. One

  B. As many people as you want

  C. A number equal to how many user files you have

Quiz Answers

1. C. You can have only one loaded movie per clip (or level, for that matter).

2. B. Flash only supports the runtime import of sounds in `.mp3` format and images in `.jpg` format.

3. A. Only one person can actually edit the master version of shared items. After the master version is turned into a `.swf`, you can share it throughout a network—or just redistribute copies to everyone involved.

Exercise

Back in the task "Use the MovieClipLoader Object to Display Progress," you displayed a progress bar by scaling from 0% to 100%. Instead, for this exercise, consider making a movie clip containing an animation. For example, you could do a shape tween or frame-by-frame animation of a glass filling up or a sand-timer emptying. The code really isn't too difficult. Instead of taking the percentage downloaded and setting the _xscale, you just do a gotoAndStop(). Imagine if the movie clip you create has 100 frames; you could simply jump to the frame that matches the percentage. In fact, you can jump only to whole number frames when using gotoAndStop(). The following code takes care of that. What's cool about this code is that your movie clip need not be exactly 100 frames.

So, make a movie clip with the multiple frame animation you want and put an instance on stage with the instance name progress_mc. Then, replace line 7 of step 7 of the task "Use the MovieClipLoader Object to Display Progress" with the following code:

```
progress_mc.gotoAndStop( Math.floor((bytesLoaded/bytesTotal) *
progress_mc._totalframes ));
```

HOUR 21

Optimizing a Flash Site

What You'll Learn in This Hour:

▶ How to reduce the file size of a movie without affecting quality

▶ How to remove unnecessary special effects to improve performance

By now, you can draw, animate, and design a site that's both interesting to look at and easy to use. Of course, you can always run either Test Movie or Publish Preview to get an accurate idea of how a movie will play. However, there can still be a marked difference between how a movie plays on your computer and how it plays when viewed by a web audience. Not only do connection speeds vary, but each user's computer may perform differently. The result might be that although a movie instantly plays smoothly on your computer, it takes a long time to download and then stutters as it plays on someone else's computer.

Optimization involves two unrelated issues: reducing a movie's file size to speed download times and improving playback to ensure that the movie plays equally well on different computers, regardless of processor speed. This hour investigates both issues in an attempt to ensure that your movie downloads quickly and plays well on all your users' machines.

File Size Considerations

The fastest way to lose your audience members is to make them wait a long time for a movie to download. In a minute, you'll see how to calculate how long a movie takes to download. An even simpler formula, however, is this: The faster the movie downloads, the better. Even as Internet connections are speeding up (with technologies such as DSL and cable modems, for example), the reality is that the majority of your potential audience members are still connected via dial-up connections (56kbps modems or slower). Even if you decide to target only those people with fast connections, there's no reason to create movies that are larger than absolutely necessary. The natural tendency is to push the technology to the limit and then push it a little further. If you fill a storage closet to capacity and then you are given a larger closet, most likely you will just fill the new closet and think you need even more room—this is natural. Just because you *can* make large Flash files doesn't mean you *should*.

Calculating Download Times

It doesn't take any fancy math to estimate how long a file takes to download. You just need to know how big the file is and the rate at which it downloads. This is similar to estimating how long it takes to travel in a car; you just need to know the total distance and the speed of the car. For example, if the total distance is 30 miles and your rate of speed is 60 miles per hour, your trip should take one-half hour. Total distance in miles divided by miles per hour equals time in hours:

distance / rate = time

Applying this formula to download times is similar:

file size / rate = time

A file size that's 10 units big downloading at 5 units per second will download in 2 seconds. That was easy! We didn't even have to talk about bits, bytes, and kilobytes. All these terms refer to different units—like inches and feet or dollars and pennies. The formula works the same as long as the units for file size and rate are the same. A car traveling 100 kilometers per hour will travel 50 kilometers in one-half hour. We'll eventually discuss bits and bytes, but for now, just keep the size / rate = time formula in mind.

In reality, you can only estimate (not calculate) how long it takes to travel somewhere by car because speed varies slightly, depending on factors such as traffic and weather conditions. The same is true with Flash movies because download speeds vary. Just because you have a 28.8 modem (which, in theory, downloads 28 kilobits per second) doesn't mean an image that is 100KB (that is 800 kilobits because 1 kilobyte is 8 kilobits) downloads in 28 seconds (that is 800 Kbps/28Kbps = 28 seconds). Depending on several factors, including Internet congestion and the performance of the web server, the file might take longer to download. If the actual rate of download is only 23Kbps, for example, that 100KB file will download in 34 seconds. When it comes to calculating download times, realize it's always just an estimate.

What's Big? What's Small?

The formula to estimate download speed can be summed up as this: the bigger the file, the longer the download time. Therefore, a goal to reduce download time is really a goal to reduce file size. In the following sections, you'll learn which Flash features tend to create larger files—and, more importantly, you'll learn alternative techniques to achieve the same effect with less impact on file size. Although a few Flash features should certainly be avoided at all costs (such as the Modify, Shape, Soften Fill Edges feature), you don't need to avoid features that increase file size— you just need to use them only when they're needed.

Lines Take Up Less File Space Than Fills

When you draw either a fill or a line, Flash stores the math required to display your drawing. In the case of fills (drawn with the Brush tool, for example), information is stored for all sides of the shape. You can change just one side of a fill, as shown in Figure 21.1. A line, however, doesn't really have sides—it has two end points, but no thickness. Suppose you draw a green line and give it a stroke of 10. Flash stores just the line, the stroke, and the color. Flash doesn't really store the thickness—only that the line needs a stroke applied to it. The same shape drawn with a brush would require Flash to store information about all sides of the shape. In this case, think of a simple line as a four-sided shape. Check out Figure 21.2, where I drew two lines, turned one into a fill (by selecting Modify, Shape, Convert Lines to Fills), and then selected everything with the Subselect tool. You'll see that there are many more anchor points in the fill, meaning it will result in a larger file.

Breaking Apart Text Can Increase File Size

When you select a block of text and choose Modify, Break Apart (actually, choosing Break Apart *twice* when you have more than one character), the text turns into a shape. Besides the fact that you won't be able to edit the text after it's broken apart, the file size usually increases because Flash stores all the curves in every character of the text. Actually, leaving the text alone also requires that the font outlines be stored as well—but that's handled by the font itself, which tends to be very efficient. For example, the letter *i* might appear twice in the text *Phillip*, but it's only stored once in the font. If this word were broken apart, Flash would store the letter *i* each time. Broken-apart text will almost always add more file space than regular static text.

FIGURE 21.1
Fills take up more file space than lines because Flash must store information about all sides of the shape (whereas lines have no thickness).

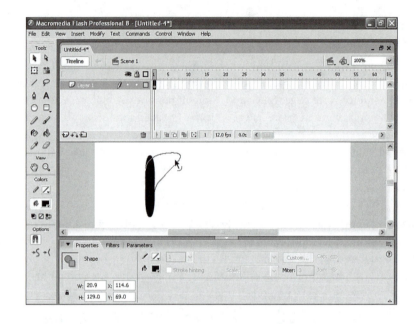

FIGURE 21.2
The line on the right was converted to a fill. The Subselect tool can be used to see the additional complexity of the fill.

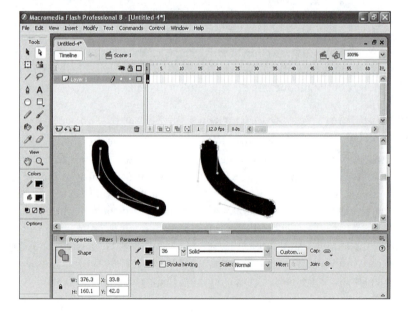

Suppose you have a paragraph of text. Likely, breaking it apart will make your file bigger because Flash must save the shape information for all the characters. However, suppose you have one special font you use for a single character. If you break apart just that letter, you might find that your file is actually smaller! That's because when you use just one character (in static text), the necessary information Flash stores for that font might be more than the shape information had the character been broken apart. The upshot is that if you are using the same font in several places in a movie or if you have a lot of text (in the same font), you shouldn't break it apart. However, if it's used for just one character, you'll probably want to break it apart. (Later this hour, you'll learn ways to measure the difference so that you can just compare the effect of one method over the other.) Of course, the decision between broken-apart text and regular static text needs to include other considerations (such as whether you're absolutely sure you'll never need to edit the text again or you definitely need a shape in order to do a shape tween).

Dynamic and Input Text with Embedded Fonts Can Be Large

There are times when you don't have a choice between using broken-apart text and using static text. If you're using dynamic or input text, there isn't an option to break it apart (otherwise, the text wouldn't be changeable anymore). As you first learned in Hour 5 "Applied Layout Techniques" (and then again in Hour 16), when you use dynamic or input text, you have options as to which font outlines to include (if any). Figure 21.3 shows where you can choose to include font outlines. It's worth mentioning again that you shouldn't embed more font outlines than absolutely necessary because that adds significantly to the file size.

The three situations that justify embedding fonts are

- ▶ You're using a font users might not have installed. Say, you're using a very uncommon or even custom font.

- ▶ The text is being rotated.

- ▶ The text needs to be revealed through a mask or one of the new Blends.

Finally, remember that when you do need to embed a font, embed as few glyphs as possible. For example, embed just the numerals 0–9 and a colon (:) if you're displaying the time.

FIGURE 21.3
Including font
outlines is nec-
essary when
you want a
dynamic field to
display custom
fonts—but it
adds significant-
ly to the file
size.

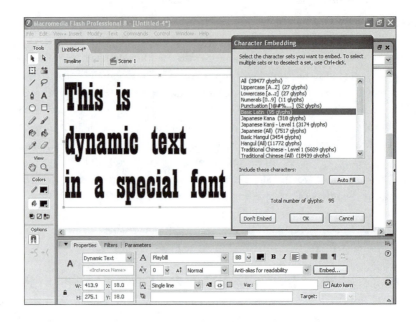

Shape Tweens, Motion Tweens, and Keyframes All Affect File Size

Ignore, for a moment, the visual and functional differences between using the different types of tweens and using keyframes for animation. Generally, shape tweens add
to file size most significantly. The difference between using motion tweens and multiple keyframes is not so cut-and-dried. Basically, you want the fewest keyframes possible. A motion tween, however, requires Flash to effectively create in-between
keyframes (even though you won't see them). In reality, if you use a motion tween
to move a circle across the screen with a keyframe on Frame 1 and another on Frame
10, the effect would be the same as using 10 individual keyframes. (Of course, in
either case, you would be using an instance of the Circle symbol, so there wouldn't
be multiple copies of the shape.) Basically, using frame-by-frame animation conservatively and using motion tweens are about the same. However, when using frame-
by-frame animation, you might find that you can pull off the same effect with fewer
frames. Not only can this make the movement look more believable, but when fewer
frames are used, you get a smaller file size. And just so I don't have to return to this
point later this hour (when we look at performance optimization), frame-by-frame
animations tend to perform better than tweens. To sum this up, avoid shape tweens
and (in all cases) look for ways to use fewer frames.

Take Optimization with a Grain of Salt

Although the preceding tips (and those that follow in this hour) might seem like rules to live by, it's worth remembering that the file size–creating features of Flash do have useful purposes. For example, there's nothing like a shape tween to get a morph effect. Just because shape tweens tend to add to file size doesn't mean you can never use them. Look for alternatives where appropriate, but feel free to use shape tweens when you have to. When you know which features tend to affect file size, you can make more educated decisions. These tips provide a good starting point. Later this hour you'll see how you can calculate the file size impact of each feature.

Sounds and Bitmaps

So far in this hour there has been no mention of sounds and raster graphics (such as .jpg and .bmp files). They have such a huge impact on file size that the following sections are devoted to studying them. The file size savings you gain from other tips (such as using lines instead of fills and Movie Clip instead of Graphic symbols) pale in comparison to the significance of managing sounds and bitmaps. That's not to say that text and vector graphics don't matter, but sounds and bitmaps are more significant. Anything you can do to reduce their size will result in a major savings in the file size of a movie.

Sounds

Flash provides several ways to compress audio and bitmaps. You saw that these compression settings are specified individually via the Library item properties for each imported bitmap or sound in Hour 3, "Importing Graphics into Flash," and Hour 10, "Including Sound in Animations." You'll also see in Hour 24, "Publishing a Creation," how you can set compression settings for all imported bitmaps and sounds at once via the Publish Settings dialog box. Although you know where to set the compression settings, you might not fully understand how this affects your movies.

Different types of compression exist. For audio, you should always use MP3 or Voice. Although Flash supports ADPCM, you should only use this if you are publishing your movie as Flash 3 or lower. (That is, you want the audio in your movie to work for people who have only the Flash 3 player.) If you happen to be delivering your movie to run only on your hard drive (maybe you're creating an enhanced slide presentation that you're not distributing via the Web), you can specify no compression (that is, use Raw). Barring those two situations, MP3 is the best choice.

A simple relationship exists between quality and file size. You learned how to set the compression settings individually for just one sound in Hour 10. Basically, you try one setting and listen to how it sounds. As you try greater and greater levels of compression, you'll both hear the difference and see the file size change. It's just a matter of balancing these two priorities—good quality and small file size.

There are a couple additional ways to optimize sounds. The easiest one to remember is that stereo sounds are twice as big as mono sounds. Therefore, you should let Flash always convert stereo to mono, unless you truly *need* stereo. Keep in mind that you can still use stereo panning effects on sounds that are mono. When a frame with sound is selected, you can use the Effect feature, you can use preset effects (such as Fade Right to Left), or you can make your own effects to give a mono sound stereo-like effects (see Figure 21.4).

FIGURE 21.4
The Edit Envelope dialog box (accessed from the Properties panel) lets you create panning effects using mono sounds.

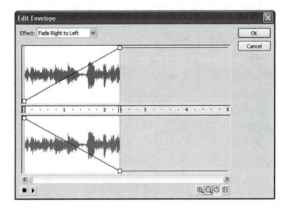

Another great way to reduce the impact of sounds on file size is to trim excessive silence from the beginning and end of every sound. It's customary for audio engineers to pad every sound file with a little silence. However, sounds take up the same file space for every second they're played, regardless of whether they're audible (although compression tends to counteract this). Ideally, sounds should be trimmed before they are imported, but you can trim them inside Flash through the Edit Envelope dialog box. You can review this technique in Hour 10, but for now remember that it means smaller file sizes. For example, by trimming excessive silence in a particular sound, in a recent project I cut the sound by 10 percent. That may not seem like a lot, but because sounds can be very large, 10 percent of a large file can be significant. What's more, because I just trimmed out the silence, I didn't lose anything. Consider, too, that a long fading-out sound could be trimmed and you might not notice the difference because the volume is so low there.

Bitmaps

You can reduce the file size impact of bitmaps in several ways. First of all, consider not using bitmaps at all. Although this might seem like a flippant tip, it's worth thinking about. Of course, you should avoid any unnecessary raster graphics (.jpg, .gif, .bmp, and so on) because each pixel's color is saved in the file, unlike with vector graphics, which store only the math necessary to redraw the shapes. However, certain types of images (such as photographs) only work as bitmaps. Therefore, it's not always a matter of choice. In addition, if you want a bitmap with transparency (also called an *alpha channel*) .png is the only alternative.

One big warning: Using Modify, Bitmap, Trace Bitmap, as explored in Hour 3, does convert a bitmap into all-vector shapes. However, you should use this feature only when the bitmap contains clear and bold sections. If you find it necessary to set the Trace Bitmap dialog box to draw lots of tiny vector shapes instead of large, bold areas, as shown in Figure 21.5, you'll probably end up creating a vector version that's larger than the original bitmap. People tend to think that vector graphics are small and bitmaps are large, but taken to an extreme, vectors can be quite large, too. Therefore, use Trace Bitmap only when the content of your image file is better served as a vector—that is, it contains bold geometric shapes. (Of course if you're trying to achieve a particular special effect, Trace Bitmap can be used—just realize the potential file size impact.)

FIGURE 21.5
Using Trace Bitmap on a photograph would require such small values for Threshold and Minimum Area that the image would increase in size.

Importing High-Quality Media and Then Compressing Them

As a bit of a review, I think it's worth mentioning the difference between the bitmap export options. Although it might seem counterintuitive, it's best to start by importing the highest-quality sound, video, and bitmapped graphics possible. This will certainly add to the file size of your source `.fla`. However, you can let Flash do the compression before publishing your movie. Either through the properties for individual sound and bitmap items in the Library or through the Publish Settings dialog box, you can control how much Flash compresses your media. For example, instead of converting an image into a compressed `.jpg` before importing it into Flash, try to start with the best-quality uncompressed `.bmp` or `.png` file. After it's imported, you can specify how Flash is to compress it upon export. This way, you can always decide how much to compress it. If you start with something that's already compressed (and therefore lower quality), you can't make it any better inside Flash. High-quality sounds should start as `.wav` or `.aif` format (MP3s are already compressed). Raster graphics should be `.bmp`, `.png`, or `.pct` format. (Note that `.jpg` files are always compressed at least a little bit and `.gif` files always have 256 or fewer colors.)

However, if you have a sound or an image that's already compressed (such as an `.mp3` or `.jpg` file) and either you don't have access to a better-quality original or you're confident that the current compression is ideal, there's no need to first covert it to another format. For example, you might have used the Selective JPEG Quality feature in Fireworks to make a great-looking and small JPG. In these cases, just import the image as is, but make sure that Flash doesn't recompress it. For imported compressed images, you see the option Use Imported JPEG Data in the Library item's properties. Using this option prevents Flash from recompressing the file. The only time to recompress an image that's already compressed is when you have no access to the original. Compressing a compressed image will indeed bring the file size down, but the quality will be lower than if you had simply compressed it to the same level once by starting with a high-quality original.

Using the Bandwidth Profiler

Now that you understand how to manage file size by compressing audio and bitmaps and using certain drawing techniques, you need to measure the impact of each. Even if you know audio adds to file size, you still might want to use it. Your decision, however, needs to be based on how much file size the audio adds. If it means the user will simply wait a couple extra seconds, adding audio may be worth it. However, if adding a piece of music means the user waits 10 minutes, you probably shouldn't use the music. In order to decide whether a particular media element is worthwhile, you need to know how much it affects file size. The Bandwidth

Profiler helps you assess exactly how much each media element adds to a file's size. Basically, you try out a file size–reduction technique (such as compression) and then use the Bandwidth Profiler to judge how much the change helped. If you make another change, you use the Bandwidth Profiler again to measure the improvement. The previous sections taught you how to identify ways file sizes grow; this section will teach you how to measure the impact.

Turning on the Bandwidth Profiler is easy, but deciphering the data it provides is a bit tricky. The following task introduces you to the basic features of the Bandwidth Profiler.

Try It Yourself ▼

Use the Bandwidth Profiler to Judge Download Times

In this task you'll learn how the Bandwidth Profiler can help you assess how a movie might play over the Internet. Here are the steps to follow:

1. Download the file `keyframing.fla` from my website, www.phillipkerman. com/teachyourself/sourcefiles/. Use Test Movie (by pressing Ctrl+Enter).

2. As the exported `.swf` plays, select View, Bandwidth Profiler (or press Ctrl+B). Notice that this is an option in the Test Movie Flash Player, not the authoring tool. Therefore, you'll only see it while you're testing.

3. The Bandwidth Profiler provides information in the top section while the movie plays below, as shown in Figure 21.6. You see data on the left and a graph on the right.

4. Look at the first section of data, called *Movie*. Most of this information is simply a recap of the settings you can change in your source movie (such as dimensions and frame rate). In addition, you'll see two values whose numbers will vary: Size (or file size) and Preload. When I tested the movie `keyframing.fla`, I got a file size of 9KB (or exactly 9,292 bytes). Later, when you attempt to optimize this file, you'll see whether the size is reduced. Preload displays how many frames must preload (and how long that takes) before the movie will start playing. Of course, this depends on your user's Internet connection. The Bandwidth Profiler can make estimates based on different connection speeds such as the preload time based for a modem settings (found under the menu View, Download Settings).

▼

FIGURE 21.6
Vital statistics for an exported .swf are shown in the upper-left area of the Bandwidth Profiler.

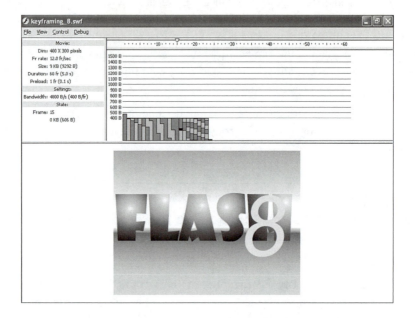

5. Select View, Download Settings. Notice that one of the modem types has a check mark (56K, by default). Change this to 14.4 (for 14.4Kbps modems), and you'll see the Preload setting change from less than 1 second to about 4 seconds!

6. Select View, Download Settings, Customize, which opens the Custom Modem Settings dialog box, as shown in Figure 21.7. Here, you can modify the presets or create your own. Add an option for the common cable modem bit rate of 1.5Mbps. In the sixth field, change User Setting 6 to read 1.5Mbps (Cable) and the number in the bit rate column to 187000. Click OK.

7. Select your new setting from the menu View, Download Settings. You should see the preload time reduce to nearly nothing.

8. The Bandwidth Profiler lets you simulate how long a movie takes to download at the selected bit rate. Select View, Simulate Download. The movie starts over, and you see a green progress bar move across the top of the graph. Change the bit rate to 14.4 (from the menu View, Download Settings) and try Show Streaming again. Even with this relatively basic movie, the current-frame marker in the graph (an arrow) catches up to the green progress bar and must occasionally wait for the content to download. This isn't desirable, but it's an accurate representation of how this movie will look on a slow connection.

(You'll learn ways to address this in the next task, "I̶m̶p̶r̶o̶v̶e a File's Size with
the̶ ... ning how to identi-
fy

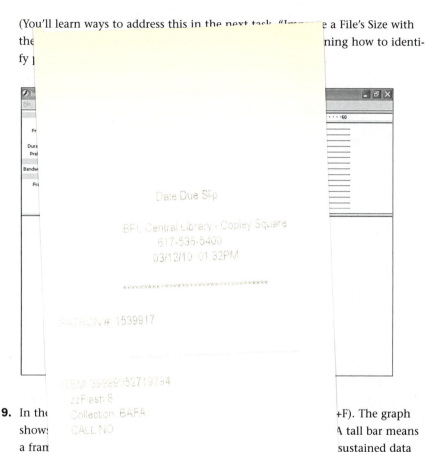

FIGURE 21.7
The Custom
Download
Settings dialog
box lets you
simulate any
Internet connec-
tion speed.

9. In the ... +F). The graph
   shows ... A tall bar means
   a fram ... sustained data
   transf ... if a frame's bar
   is high ... frame while it
   downl ... otice relatively
   high b ... sense. Close the
   test m ... ttle new
   conter ... oad (see
   Figure

FIGURE 21.8
After Frame 16, little new appears onscreen (until Frame 26). This means most data is downloaded by then (as you'll see in the Bandwidth Profiler).

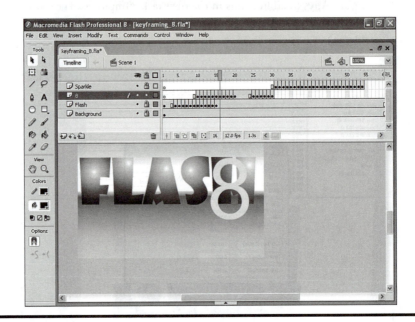

By the Way

Deciphering Bits, Bytes, and Kilos

In the preceding task, you specified 187,000 bytes per second for a 1.5Mbps cable modem. This was calculated based on modem speeds listed as "kilobits per second" (or, in the case of 1.5Mb cable connection, that's 1,500,000 bits per second). Computer file sizes are often displayed in kilobytes or megabytes (not bits). Because 1 bit is one-eighth the size of a byte, you can convert bits to bytes by dividing by 8. Therefore, 1,500,000 bits per second is the same as 167,000 bytes per second. A 320KB image will download in 2 seconds on a 1.5Mbps connection (1500Kbps / 8 = 167KBps; therefore, a 320KB file will download in about 2 seconds at that rate).

Another issue, however, is the fact that an Internet connection might not download at a consistent rate. Note that the presets in the View, Download Settings menu for 28.8Kbps modem and 56Kbps modem are lower than what you would expect (2,400 and 4,700 instead of 3,600 and 7,000). That's because the Flash presets are padded to more accurately represent an actual modem download speed. Generally, you don't have to do a lot of math. In this case, however, doing the math might be interesting.

Use the Bandwidth Profiler's Simulate Download option to watch how the movie will play. Analyze the movie frame-by-frame by scrubbing to view which frames are exceeding the red streaming limit. By the way, just because a vertical line is above the red line doesn't necessarily mean playback will pause at that frame. When possible, Flash starts to download frames before they are encountered. For example, several frames might not involve any onscreen changes, but Flash is still downloading. While displaying these frames, Flash can start to download frames from later in the movie. Frames that have no visual changes don't take long to download; therefore, Flash can concentrate on downloading future frames. This behavior is called *advance streaming* (though, I'd prefer to call it *buffering*).

The Bandwidth Profiler has an option to show such streaming behavior in a graph that is similar to the Frame by Frame Graph view. When you select View, Streaming Graph, you'll still see each frame's vertical box. Basically, each frame is shown as alternating light and dark gray boxes. The red horizontal line represents the maximum data that can be transmitted in the time one frame takes to play (that is, 1/12 second if you have a frame rate of 12 fps). If the first frame (dark gray) can download in less than 1/12 second, you'll see Frame 2's bar in dark gray stacked on top of Frame 1's light gray bar. For example, open the keyframing.fla file again and use Test Movie, select View, Streaming Graph, and select View, Download Settings, 56K. As you click on any of the first several gray or black rectangles, each of the first 13 frames takes 1/12 second or longer to download. But then in the time it takes to play Frame 28 or 29, Flash can download more than two frames (see Figure 21.9). As a result, the entire 60-frame movie is completely downloaded in the time it takes 25 frames to display. (Select View, Show Streaming for a view of this effect in real time.)

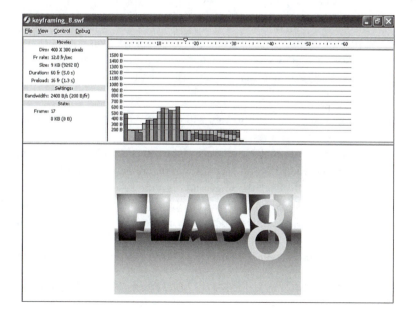

FIGURE 21.9
The Streaming Graph view (not Frame by Frame Graph view) displays how quickly Flash will preload upcoming frames.

The Bandwidth Profiler is very useful. However, it doesn't fix problems; it only helps you discover problem areas. Ideally, you should simply avoid making your file too large in the first place. The Bandwidth Profiler is still worth learning to use, but just remember that it's only for identifying problems that could be avoided. The following task steps you through a scenario of using the Bandwidth Profiler to help identify a problem and solve it.

▼ **Try It Yourself**

Reduce a File's Size with the Bandwidth Profiler's Help

In this task you'll use the Bandwidth Profiler to help improve a file's size. Follow these steps:

1. Open the same movie, `keyframing.fla`, that you downloaded for the last task (available at www.phillipkerman.com/teachyourself/sourcefiles/). Immediately determine the total size of the exported movie. All you need to do is run Test Movie and look at the data at the top-left area of the Bandwidth Profiler (press Ctrl+B if it's not visible). For example, I get 10,746 bytes for the total size. Write down the number you get as a reference for later.

2. Close just the movie you're previewing. Select File, Publish Settings and then select the Flash tab. Notice the JPEG Quality slider. Move that all the way to the left (the lowest quality) and click OK.

3. Test the movie again to see the change in file size that results from using compression. You shouldn't see any change because JPEG compression is applied only to raster graphics, and this file has none. (If this file had raster graphics, you would likely see that this change made the file smaller but lowered its quality.)

4. The change you'll make in this step will cause a difference—you're going to optimize the curves in every drawn shape. Unlock all the layers. Click the Edit Multiple Frames Onion Skin option (so that you can select multiple frames). Now select the Modify Onion Markers menu and pick Onion All, as shown in Figure 21.10. Finally, click the stage and then use Select All (by pressing Ctrl+A). Now choose Modify, Shape, Optimize, slide the Smoothing scale all the way to the right, and select both option check boxes, as shown in Figure 21.11. Click OK, and you should eventually see a message concerning how much optimizing took place. When I tried this, I saw that there was a 39% reduction in the number of curves.

▼

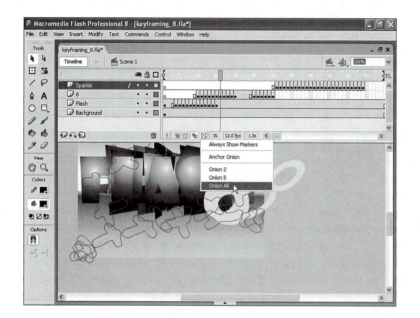

FIGURE 21.10
To select every frame, choose Onion All after the Edit Multiple Frame option is set.

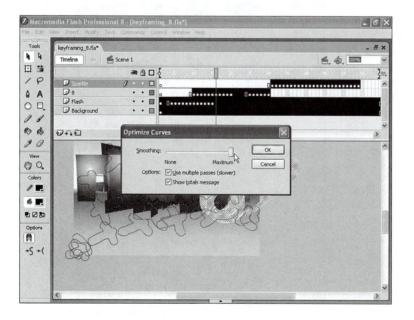

FIGURE 21.11
Using Optimize reduces the file size by simplifying the shapes.

5. Use Test Movie and notice the improvement in the file size. I get 6,730 bytes, which means the file is about 2,500 bytes smaller. It's not really a whole lot, but it's something. What's more, the image looks no worse. (You should notice that the *s* in Flash and the sparkles have changed.)

Although the big lesson from this task might be that using Modify, Optimize can often reduce the file size (simplifying shapes), you're still just in the stage of finding problems. For now, just realize that the Bandwidth Profiler helps find the problems, not necessarily fix them.

You can find a related feature worth knowing about by selecting File, Publish Settings to open the Publish Settings dialog box, selecting the Flash tab, and clicking the option Generate Size Report, as shown in Figure 21.12. The next time you export the movie (by using Test Movie), you'll see an all-text version of the data from the Bandwidth Profiler appear in the output window. In addition, you'll find a text file (named similarly to your movie's name and in the same folder) with the same contents. This provides a permanent record of the data you find in the Bandwidth Profiler.

FIGURE 21.12
The Publish Settings dialog box option Generate Size Report will export a text version of data gathered from the Bandwidth Profiler.

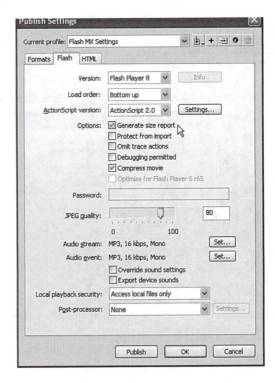

Finally, the keyframing.fla example still pauses periodically during the first 20 frames when you simulate a 14.4Kbps modem. If your target user would have that type of speed, and you can't find any other way to reduce the file size, you'll have to resort to using a preloader, which will load all or part of the movie to your user's hard drive before playing it. The following task shows a quick way to do that.

Try It Yourself ▼

Use a Preloader in the Bandwidth Profiler

To get a sense of how the Bandwidth Profiler works, in this task you'll create a basic preloader to pause playback on the first frame of a movie until most of the movie is downloaded. Here are the steps:

1. Open the keyframing.fla file that you downloaded earlier (from www.phillipkerman.com/teachyourself/sourcefiles).

2. Select Insert, Scene. Open the Scene panel and rename the new scene Preloader. To rename it, just double-click the current name (Scene 2) and then drag the scene order so that Preloader is on top.

3. Click the first frame of the Preloader scene's Timeline and insert two additional keyframes by pressing F6 twice.

4. Select the second keyframe, open the Actions panel, and type the following code:

```
if(getBytesLoaded()<getBytesTotal()){
 gotoAndPlay(1);
}
```

Translated, this means that if the size of the bytes loaded is less than the size of the bytes total, then it'll go back to Frame 1 and loop (where it will continue to reenter Frame 2 with this script).

5. So that the user can see it progress as she's stuck in this screen, go to Frame 1 and place some text onscreen. With the text selected, use the Properties panel to set the text block to Dynamic Text and give it the instance name progress_txt. Now you just have to put a message in that field.

6. Go back to the script you just wrote in Frame 2 (refer to step 4) and add the following three lines anywhere after the open curly brace ({) and before the closing brace (}):

```
percent=_root.getBytesLoaded()/_root.getBytesTotal()*100;
percent=Math.floor(percent);
progress_txt.text=percent+"%";
```

▼

In fact, these three lines could be consolidated to one, but it's easier to read this code as three lines here. First, you calculate the exact percentage downloaded and store it in a homemade variable called `percent`. Then you set `percent` to the "floor" of `percent`, meaning the nondecimal portion. Finally, the last line populates the text field with the value of `percent` plus the % symbol.

7. Run Test Movie, and with the Bandwidth Profiler, select View, Simulate Download. You'll see the percentage display increase until, at 100%, the rest of the movie plays, as Figure 21.13 shows.

FIGURE 21.13
While the content downloads, the movie is stuck in the first two frames of the first scene (where the user can see the percentage downloaded).

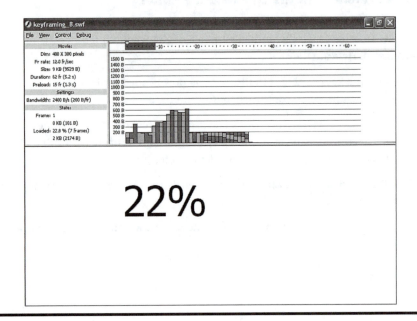

The preloader you built in Hour 20, "Designing a Website to Be Modular," was more sophisticated than the preloader you created in the preceding task. However, this was a good opportunity to use the Bandwidth Profiler.

Improving the Download Experience

I've never heard someone say they enjoy waiting for Flash movies to download, so anything you can do to improve the experience is worth considering. For example, in the previous example a user might find something else to do while the movie preloads. In that case, he could actually miss the entire animation if he didn't get back right in time. Perhaps a better design would be to insert a third frame in the Preloader scene (where the user won't reach until it's fully loaded) and a `stop()`

script plus a button labeled Begin. When the user clicks it, only then would he proceed to the main animation. Another idea is to modularize your movie by using LoadMovie and LoadSound (introduced in Hour 20). Sometimes it's fine to keep everything in your main movie and have the user wait for it all (like in the previous task). The advantage here is that after it's all downloaded, there are no more delays. However, when you have a ton of media, it makes more sense to spread out the delay so that every time the user requests an image or sound, only then does he have to wait for it to download. Besides spreading out the delays, some users might not want to see every bit of content, so there's no reason to force them to sit through a download.

Both these tips are very general, but you can even steal ideas from real life. Think about those coloring placemats restaurants often give kids. Some Flash sites create a simple puzzle to placate users during the initial download. The point is that, if you make these considerations at the start of your project, you can usually hide or minimize the negative side of slow downloads.

Performance Hits

So far, this hour has covered optimization as it applies to making files smaller (so they download quickly). The other side of optimization involves making a movie play quickly—in other words, ensuring that its performance is consistent and smooth on all users' computers. If you set your frame rate to, say, 12 fps, it will never exceed that number. However, on some computers, it might slow to a lower rate. Unfortunately, there isn't a "Performance Profiler" (similar to the Bandwidth Profiler) where you can simulate performance on other machines. There are far too many variables that can affect playback speed. For the rest of this hour, we'll look at ways to avoid common performance hits to ensure the best possible performance on every user's machine.

Avoiding Gratuitous Special Effects

In previous hours you learned how unnecessary special effects can distract users from your core message. However, there's another reason to avoid gratuitous special effects: Having too many effects can cause a movie to play slowly. For example, it might not be necessary to rotate and motion tween each piece of text that appears onscreen. Maybe this is interesting for the first block of text, but it can get tiring to wait for each to do its animation. Plus, if a user's computer slows down for each tween, the effect is even more disruptive.

Although a motion tween involving a change in the Alpha effect may be necessary to communicate a particular message, this kind of tween should be used with caution. Not only does the computer need to display the object that's moving, but it also needs to display a semitransparent version of the object, which means it must display the graphics underneath the object. Simply put, this means slower machines might not be able to keep up with the desired frame rate. Often, an Alpha effect isn't even needed. For example, if your background is white, a simple Brightness effect will look the same and perform slightly better than an Alpha effect.

Another significant performance hit that can often be avoided involves tweens that scale, move, or change the Alpha setting of a bitmap. Generally, Flash does not excel in the display of bitmaps. Changing the size of a bitmap makes the computer do a lot of work. Even if you have a fast machine, you can see this behavior by first setting the frame rate to a high value (such as 60 fps) and then performing a simple motion tween on a bitmap. Select Control, Play (not Test Movie) to watch your movie play inside Flash. Then change the scale of the bitmap on either the keyframe or the tween and play it again. You should see the actual frame rate drop during the tween that involves scale.

Other special effects such as Filters can slow down performance, too. One way to preview such performance hits is by temporarily setting the frame rate very high (say, 60 fps) and then testing before and after you try different approaches to see how they cause the movie to slow or play in a jerky manner. Keep in mind the suggestion earlier in this section and simply avoid *unnecessary* special effects. If you really need to use an effect, go ahead. Just be careful with those that really cause the movie to slow down because they might cause your users' computers to slow down even further.

Avoiding Streaming Sounds

When you place sounds in keyframes, you have a choice between the Sync settings Event and Stream. You should generally use Event or one of the other event-like choices, Start or Stop. These will have the least impact on performance. Stream is useful when you need synchronization to be maintained. When you use Stream sounds, you can hear the sounds play as you scrub the Timeline. Stream sounds are comparable to Graphic symbols, whose animation you can also preview when you scrub. The disadvantage to Stream sounds, however, is that the visual parts of the movie will be sacrificed when a computer can't keep up. That is, Stream sounds are always synchronized, and if the computer can't display the graphics in time, Flash will drop visual frames to keep up with the sound. Therefore, Stream sounds can make the graphics appear to skip and jump. This is simply due to the fact that Flash will never cause the sound to play slowly because it would sound funny if it did.

Event sounds will play as soon as they can. If the computer can keep up, these sounds will play as expected (that is, when the appropriate keyframes are reached). Also, graphics will display as soon as they can. However, on slow machines, the graphics may take longer to display, so the sound may not stay in perfect synchronization. That's not to say you can't achieve a decent result with Event sounds. Consider cutting the sound files into shorter bits before importing them. You can place sounds in the Timeline so that they line up closely with graphics. It still won't be perfect, but at least no frames will be dropped. If you don't need critical synchronization, use Event sounds because both the graphics and the sounds will play smoothly—they just might not be perfectly synchronized.

Graphic Issues

Here are a few tips to assure the best performance possible.

Using Optimize Curves

Earlier in this hour you saw how you can optimize any drawn shape by selecting Modify, Shape, Optimize. Using the Optimize Curves feature will remove curves from a shape, making it look more streamlined. Sometimes the visual impact is subtle but the file size reduction is significant. Other times, the visual change is too great to be acceptable, as is the case in Figure 21.14. Consider optimizing any time the visual change is acceptable. In addition to making the file smaller, it often speeds playback performance (yet another reason to use it).

FIGURE 21.14
Two shapes are shown before and after Optimize Curves is applied. Sometimes the results may be unacceptable.

Never Using Modify, Shape, Soften Fill Edges

Never is a strong word, but it applies in this case. It doesn't take more than a few minutes to calculate both the file size difference and the performance difference for a shape drawn and then softened. Try a test where you create a simple shape tween. Test the movie and note the file size in the Bandwidth Profiler. Play the movie inside Flash and note the actual frame rate. Then, individually select the shape at each end of the tween and use Modify, Shape, Soften Fill Edges. You'll see the file size jump and the performance drop. I suppose the one situation when you might consider using this feature is when you're only exporting a static image (that is, if you're using Flash as a drawing tool). You're much better off using Flash 8 Professional's Blur filter—both for file size savings and performance.

Avoiding Line Styles

You saw in Hour 2, "Drawing and Painting Original Art in Flash," that when you draw a line, the Properties panel drop-down list for stroke style gives you lots of patterns (see Figure 21.15). Try to use only the Solid and Hairline styles. The others tend to make movies much larger. I can't say that with them you'll always see the performance drop, but you'll certainly see your file size increase.

FIGURE 21.15
You should try to use only the Hairline and Solid stroke styles.

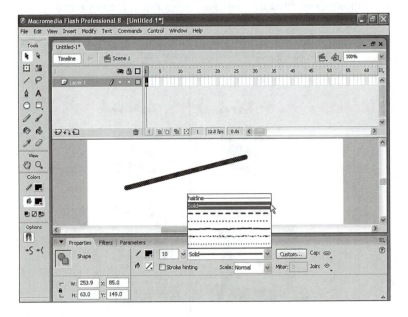

Summary

This hour, you studied two ways to optimize Flash movies. You should optimize file size to make your movies download faster, and you should optimize performance so that they play more consistently. The Bandwidth Profiler and the Generate Size Report option allow you to analyze your movies in several ways. You can use them to simulate download speeds and identify areas in your movies that need extra attention.

In this hour the optimization process was also applied to performance. Even though your movies might consistently play at high frame rates, such as 30 fps, on your machine, they might slow down on your users' machines. Although there's no sure way to see how your movies will look (except to actually try them on other machines), the basic approach to performance optimization is to simply know what types of effects and techniques tend to slow down computers and try to avoid them.

Q&A

Q *I've followed all the performance optimization tips and still find that my animation appears jumpy. What's wrong?*

A It's possible that you're simply trying to move a graphic across a large distance in very few frames. Try extending the total number of frames being used. You can compensate by increasing the frame rate. Provided that the computer can keep up with this increased frame rate, you'll see the same motion but in more (smaller, incremented) steps.

Q *What's the ideal file size for a movie?*

A This is a common question but one that's impossible to answer. I think the best answer is "no bigger than it has to be." Consider, too, that you can cover up a long download time in very creative ways. Of course, you could use a percentage display, as you did in one of this hour's tasks. Better than that, you can occupy your users with some small, interactive (or very small file size) content. Make them watch something interesting (but small) while they wait for the bulk of the movie to download. There are many ways to do this successfully. Finally, consider using the modular technique of the `MovieClipLoader` object (discussed in Hour 20). That way, users have to wait to download only the portions of your site they request.

Q *I used Modify, Shape, Optimize, and it sure cut down the file size, but my image doesn't look very good. What should I do?*

A If the result of using Modify, Shape, Optimize is unsatisfactory, don't use it. Basically, you should just try this option and weigh the file size savings against the sacrifice in the image's quality. Often, an undesirable result isn't as bad as it appears. Consider that in the final movie, the graphic you're judging may only be onscreen for a fraction of a second. The bad quality might not matter in that case.

Q *In the Flash tab of the Publish Settings dialog box I found the option Compress Movie. What's this for?*

A This is really a no-brainer. Basically, it's a way Flash compresses your actions. You'll learn more about it in Hour 24.

Q *My source* `.fla` *file is huge! Even after I deleted unused Library items, the file is much bigger than it should be. Why?*

A When you import media into a Flash movie, the file size grows. But when you delete the media, the file doesn't go back down in size. However, you can simply use Save and Compact to effectively clean up the file. It's almost like defragmenting a hard disk. Incidentally, a big `.fla` is not necessarily a problem for the user—it's the `.swf` that counts.

Workshop

The Workshop consists of quiz questions and answers to help you solidify your understanding of the material covered in this hour. You should try to answer the questions before checking the answers.

Quiz

1. If you reduce a file to half its file size, how fast will it download?

    A. This is impossible to calculate because everyone's connection speed varies.

    B. Twice as fast as it would otherwise.

    C. This is impossible to calculate because you need to know the movie's dimensions (height and width).

2. Why should you avoid using gratuitous special effects?

   A. They can distract the user from your core message.

   B. They can slow down performance and increase download times.

   C. Both A and B are correct.

3. True or false: The Bandwidth Profiler can simulate how a movie will play on a slow computer.

   A. True. Just set your computer's processor speed in the View menu.

   B. False. The Bandwidth Profiler only helps you judge a movie's size and how fast it will download.

   C. True. However, you have to select View, Simulate Computer.

Quiz Answers

1. B. Answer C is just plain false because the download speed of Flash movies doesn't have anything to do with their dimensions (vectors scale). (However, scale can affect playback performance.) Answer A is not entirely false because you really can't say how long a file will take to download. However, if you cut the file size in half, you can certainly say that the download will go twice as fast. Consider if you ordered a half-sandwich—it would take you half as long to finish it as it would take you to eat a whole one.

2. C. Although special effects are fine when necessary, they can be distracting, increase file size, and slow down performance. These are all good reasons to avoid using them.

3. B. The Bandwidth Profiler simply judges file size and download performance. If the question referred to a *slow connection* rather than a *slow computer*, Answer A would be correct.

HOUR 22

Advanced Animation Techniques

What You'll Learn in This Hour:

▶ How to create animations without tweening
▶ How to apply traditional animation techniques like anticipation and overkill
▶ How to simulate depth and perspective

We've explored all the built-in animation tools in Flash. Keyframes, motion and shape tweens, onion skinning, masking, and guides—these should all be pretty familiar. What else is there to learn? How to make really effective animations! This hour we'll study some advanced animation techniques that will make your animations more effective, appear more believable, and maybe even take less work to create (although that's not the highest priority). A lot of the material this hour is just an application of traditional animation techniques developed over the years by conventional animators. Although the concepts you'll learn are not completely new to the world of animation, the techniques you'll be applying to Flash might be new to you.

The two different paths Flash authors tend to follow are application programming and animation. Some people describe the programmers as "technical" and the animators as "artistic." This is a mistake because programming can be very creative, and visual communication can be very technical. The tendency to specialize isn't necessarily because of a natural aversion to one direction or an inclination in another.

It may seem that in this hour we're taking a break from technical issues because in recent hours we've been studying issues such as file size and scripting, but this hour will be just as technical—just applied to making animations.

It's the Result, Not the Technology

When you see a magician saw his assistant in half, no one actually gets hurt. The magician creates an illusion, and you can almost believe the result. Similarly, in animation nothing actually moves. Watching a series of still images can make you believe you're watching something move. In addition to the persistence of vision effect described in Hour 6, "Understanding Animation," animators can use tricks (not unlike magicians) to fool the user into believing he sees something that never happened.

To make someone believe a ball is moving across the screen, for example, really moving it across the screen may not be necessary. That is, a motion tween might display the ball each step along the way—and if the user could slow down the movie, he would see it actually move. However, if the user *thinks* the ball moved across the screen, it doesn't matter whether it really did. Even if you're trying to communicate a principle of physics, being completely accurate in your display is not necessary. It's okay to lie. There's little value in being perfectly accurate if the result doesn't look like you intended.

You're about to look at a few tricks that you can use to enhance your animations. Remember, though, that the techniques are not as important as the results.

Simple Techniques to Use Sparingly

A trick often used in television commercials (especially those played late at night) is to make the screen blink. Sometimes several flashes of white light cause viewers to look at the TV—even if they were not paying attention. This technique is arguably appropriate for TV because people don't tend to give it their full attention.

In the case of a website, you can rely on the fact that the user is more involved than a TV viewer. She is sitting up, maybe even leaning toward the screen—a totally different profile. If you flash the screen, you should do so only sparingly, if at all.

If you want to grab the user's attention, you can use a modified version of flashing the screen—just make a small button or area of the screen blink. For example, if something's about to move, make it blink first. This will draw the user's attention to the blinking object, and then she'll likely be watching when it moves. Technically, this is simply a matter of alternating between filled and blank keyframes.

There are other simple (and potentially annoying) techniques to consider. In the first frame of a movie, instead of starting with the entire interface, animate each element into its final location. If you have an interface with six buttons, you can have each appear, one by one, and move into position. This way, you can control the order in which the user "reads" the interface. Be aware, however, that building in such a way can become tedious and bothersome if it's slow or if the user must sit through the same sequence many times. If the home screen builds again every time the user returns to it, that's probably too much.

Consider also that techniques such as blinking and building are ways to resolve challenges in communication. Sometimes these are good solutions, but the best way would be to simply avoid the problem in the first place. For example, when you find people aren't watching the right part of the screen, don't jump to the blinking solution. Try to first identify whether the problem can be resolved; maybe the rest of the screen is too crowded and that's distracting the users. Cleaning up the interface might resolve the issue. Try to fix the root cause of a problem instead of addressing a single symptom.

You'll probably discover other tricks to solve problems, but use them sparingly. We'll talk about some more dependable techniques later this hour, but always ask yourself if the problem you're trying to resolve can be avoided in the first place. That is, treat the cause rather than the symptom.

Ways to Fool the User

Unlike magic, where the key to success is often found in the art of distraction, animation doesn't need to overcome any physical limits. The challenges in animation include how to show or imply motion where there isn't any, make things look natural, and exploit the user's expectations (either to help you show something that's not there or to create surprises). Pulling a rabbit out of a hat is easy in Flash, but making the rabbit look like it's alive is a real challenge. Let's look at a few ways to address the three goals implying motion, appearing natural, and exploiting expectations. Later this hour you'll apply what you learn.

There are several ways to imply motion. Although it's rare that something moves so fast your eyes see only a blurred image, it's quite common in photographs. People believe a blur is an indicating of motion. Making something appear to streak across the screen can be as simple as drawing lines in the opposite direction of the motion (kind of like exhaust from an airplane). Naturally, Flash 8 Professional's Blur filter implies motion when you apply the blur to just one axis (say, the x axis when the object is moving from left to right). However, the visual impact is often so blurry that the Blur filter can make the object look out of focus . In the upcoming task "Add a Motion Blur" you'll see how the Drop Shadow filter can more effectively communicate motion because the out-of-focus and blurred portion is just the shadow. It's as though you're adding a tail to a comet—sometimes you still want to see the comet.

Making things look natural is possibly the biggest challenge in animation. To animate someone walking is not easy. That's because viewers know how that's supposed to look, and if it doesn't look right, they know. There's no button in Flash that will create natural motion. However, you can learn to animate in a way that looks natural. When you are going to animate something from the real world, study the object you're animating. Carefully watch people walking and ask yourself how you know they're walking. Don't watch just the legs and feet, but look at the arms, hands, and head. Try to identify peculiar and subtle movements. Sometimes overemphasizing unique identifiers, such as the way your hands move while walking, can make an animation more believable.

Here's a good trick to make animations look natural: Insert elements that would be considered mistakes in traditional media. For example, people sometimes simulate dust and scratches to make an animation look like a conventional film. To make something flicker like an old-fashioned movie, just make a two-frame movie clip with a rectangle shape the size of the stage (and the same color as the stage) in Frame 1 and a blank keyframe in Frame 2. Put this two-frame clip in a layer above everything else in the main timeline and apply an Alpha effect of, say, 10%. It will loop continuously to create a flicker effect. People see flickering and they think "old movie." Just study what is peculiar in real life and bring attention to these details—this will make your animation more believable.

Finally, you can exploit the users' expectations in two ways. You can take advantage of their expectations—that is, let them think they saw something because they expected to see it, not necessarily because they did see it. For example, if they see a bowling ball move toward some pins and then they hear the sound of a crash, even if the pins are simply removed from the Stage, they'll imagine the pins fell over. You don't have to animate each pin meticulously. Just remove them. The sound and the expectation are enough to make it believable.

You can also use users' expectations to add more impact by showing the opposite of what they expect. In the case of the bowling ball, imagine a long and drawn-out tween of the ball moving toward the pins. Then, at the last minute, an elf character appears and stops the ball with a screeching sound. Certainly not what the user expects, and that's what gives it impact.

These techniques require some imagination on your part. You'll practice them in the next section. Just don't be afraid to "lie" to the user. They'll thank you later if it means you can make something more believable.

Applying Conventional Techniques

The information in this section isn't unique to Flash. It's years of traditional, conventional animator's techniques that we will apply to Flash. For each technique, we'll do a task.

Adding a Motion Blur

This technique uses Flash Professional 8's Blur filter, but not on the object that's being animated. Instead, it's used on a duplicate instance containing a similar shape. Even if you don't have Flash Professional, you can apply the concept to your own animations. It just won't be as efficient as what I show here.

Try It Yourself   ▼

Add a Motion Blur

In this task you'll use the Drop Shadow filter to add a blurred trail to a simple object. Follow these steps :

1. In a new file, draw a circle, select it, and convert it to a symbol. Name the symbol **Circle** and select the Movie Clip behavior.

2. Move your instance of the Circle to the left side of the stage. In Frame 25, insert a keyframe (F6). In Frame 30, insert a frame (F5).

3. In Frame 10, insert a keyframe (F6), hold Shift, and drag the instance all the way to the right side of the stage. Now, go to Frame 15 and insert another keyframe.

4. Select the keyframe in Frame 1 and set Motion Tween; do the same for Frame 15. The circle is on the left at Frame 1, tweens to the right in Frame 10—where it will wait until Frame 15, where it tweens back to the left (and waits another 5 frames before repeating).

5. Test the movie to see what it looks like with no blur. When you're done, lock the layer and insert a new layer.

6. We're going to start with a Blur filter. Because I only want it blurred while it's moving we can insert new keyframes in the interpolated frames. Namely, click the cell in frame 5 and insert a keyframe (F6) and then again in frame 20. Even if you knew from the start you were putting keyframes there, the order we did it is best because the Circle is in the correct—interpolated—position.

7. Select the instance in frame 5 and use the Filters panel to add a Blur filter. Click the padlock to unlock the Blur X and Blur Y and set Blur X to 20 and Blur Y to 5. Select the instance in frame 20 and add a Blur filter with the same settings. Interestingly, if you select the instances in any of the other frames they now have a Blur filter applied—but with 0 values for the blur. This simply makes them tween from 0 up to whatever you set in frames 5 and 20.   ▼

8. Test the movie and it just looks like the circle is out of focus. That's okay, but to enhance it you can add a Drop Shadow. Select the instance in frame 5 and add a Drop Shadow. Set Blur X to 70 and Blur Y to 10. Now, set the color to the same color as your Circle (or possibly a shade lighter). Finally, set the angle to 180 (that'll put the shadow to the left of "behind" the circle); and set the distance to 30. (You can see the effect in Figure 22.1.) Select the instance in frame 20 and apply the same Drop Shadow settings except set the angle to 0 this time.

9. If you test the movie it probably looks worse. That's because while the frames where you applied the Drop Shadow (5 and 20) should look pretty good, the Drop Shadow that was automatically added to the Circle in frames 1, 10, 15, and 25 don't have the angle (they're all defaulted to 45 degrees). So, click frame 1, click the circle, access the Drop Shadow and set the angle to 180—do the same for frame 10. Finally, click frame 15, click the circle, access the Drop Shadow and set the angle to 0 and repeat for frame 25.

10. Now you can test the movie and it should look pretty good. Feel free to crank up the frame rate. Also, you might consider setting the ease to Ease Out on frames 5 and 20.

FIGURE 22.1
The Drop Shadow filter serves as a suitable motion blur when you set the color to match the object and the angle to appear to trail the object's motion.

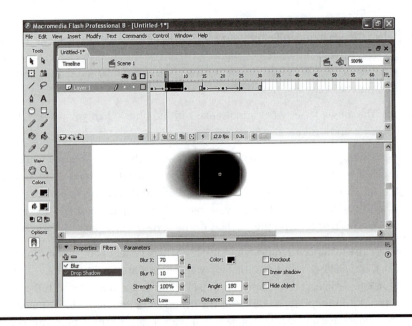

A good deal of this exercise was just tinkering with the Filters panel. It should be easier when it's your idea you're trying to implement. The key points are that filters automatically interpolate and a Drop Shadow (set to the right color and angle) serves as a pretty good motion blur.

Using Anticipation

The blinking technique mentioned earlier this hour is a form of anticipation, drawing the user's attention to something that's about to happen. You can use other forms of anticipation as well. For example, a car with a manual transmission that is stopped facing up a hill drifts back a little bit when it begins to move forward. You can accentuate that effect in your animations to make them more effective. Not only will the users look at the object that's preparing to move (by moving in the opposite direction), but they'll anticipate that something's about to happen. Try it out in the following task.

Try It Yourself ▼

Use Anticipation to Improve an Animation

In this task you'll add a subtle touch of anticipation for a more effective result. Follow these steps:

1. In a new file, draw a circle at the bottom of the Stage and convert it to a symbol (by pressing F8). Name it **Circle** and ensure that its behavior is set to Movie Clip.

2. Insert a keyframe at Frame 10 (you want the circle to sit still for the first 10 frames). Insert another keyframe in Frame 15 and one at Frame 25. You're going to squash the circle between Frames 10 and 15 and then move it up as it goes to Frame 25.

3. Select Frame 25, hold down the Shift key, and then move the instance of Circle close to the top of the Stage.

4. In Frame 15, use the Free Transform tool to compress the circle by scaling it vertically. Also make the circle a little wider because when you squash something in real life, it gets wider, too (see Figure 22.2). Remember, too, that if you hold down Alt while you drag the top-middle resizing handle, the bottom of the circle won't move.

▼

FIGURE 22.2
When you squash the circle, change both the vertical and horizontal scales. (Onion Skin is turned on here for easy comparison to the original shape.)

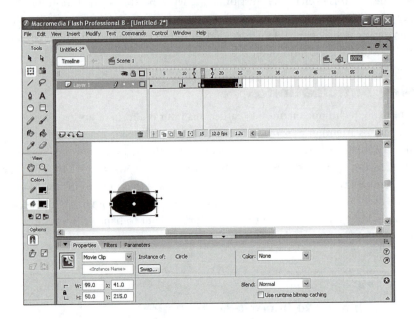

5. You want the bottom of the circle to remain stationary (only the top squashes down). When you select the Transform tool and then the Scale option, you scale the circle around its center by default. You can override this if you hold down Alt while resizing. Therefore, if the bottom moved up, you should now move the circle down. Turn on Onion Skin, and position the bottom of the circle to coincide with the bottom of the circle in Frame 10.

6. Set a motion tween for the keyframe in Frame 10 (so it tweens down to its squashed shape) and in Frame 15 (so it tweens on its way up to the top).

7. Test the movie. It looks all right, but while Circle tweens to the top position, it also restores its shape—but it takes 10 frames to do it.

8. To make the movie more believable, make Circle snap into its normal shape as soon as it starts to move. To do this, go to Frame 16 and insert a keyframe (by pressing F6). It's good that you set tweening for Frame 15 already because the keyframe you inserted at Frame 16 placed the circle in the proper interpolated position. Select the circle in Frame 16 and select Modify, Transform, Remove Transform (or press Ctrl+Shift+Z). The circle immediately returns to its unscaled state.

9. Test the movie to see the final result. Save this movie because in a minute you'll address how to make the end point more believable.

You can use the anticipation technique quite extensively, and it usually means you can get away with using fewer frames (and fewer tweens). You make the user anticipate the movement by including movement in the opposite direction. The task you just did involved squishing the circle down because it was about to go up. If you're moving something to the right, adding a slight move to the left can work, too. The anticipation is usually slower than the movement that follows. That is, during the anticipation portion, fewer frames are used or less distance is covered. There are no hard-and-fast rules for this—you must judge how something looks when you test the movie.

Using Overkill

Whereas anticipation happens before the animation plays, overkill applies to the end of an animation or after it plays. If you're in a car that comes to a stop, you feel as though you move backward just for a moment after the car comes to a rest. Of course you're not moving backward, but you expect to keep going forward, and when you don't, you imagine that you're going backward. A user expects to have that feeling, so you can add this effect to your animations, and it will actually make them more believable. You can try it in the following task.

Try It Yourself ▼

Use Overkill to Make an Animation More Effective

In this task, you'll add the subtle effect of overkill to make an animation more believable. Follow these steps:

1. If you saved the last task, start with it. If you didn't save it, make a simple motion tween of a symbol called Circle that moves from the bottom of the screen to the top of the screen, ending in Frame 25.

2. Insert keyframes in Frames 26, 27,and 28 by clicking in Frame 26 and then pressing F6 three times.

3. Edit the extra frames so that one frame has the circle going too far and becoming stretched (26), one frame has the circle reverberate and actually move lower than the end frame (27), and one has the circle end up in its final resting position (27 where it happens to be already, so that frame won't need to be adjusted). To do this, vertically stretch the circle in Frame 26 so it's extra tall and narrow (as in Figure 22.3). You don't need to make sure the bottom or top lines up with circles in adjacent frames; however, turn on Onion Skin so that you can be sure the stretched circle in Frame 26 is positioned a little higher than the one in Frame 25.

▼

▼
FIGURE 22.3
To make the cir-
cle overshoot
its destination,
you can stretch
it to exaggerate
the overkill.

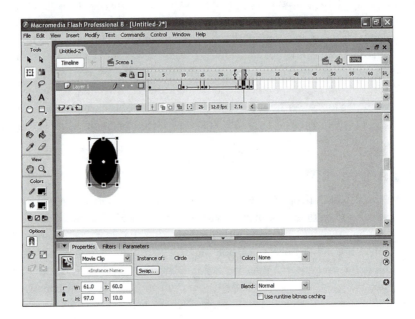

▲

4. In Frame 27, simply move the circle down a few pixels.

5. Test the movie. It's pretty amazing that just a touch of overkill can make this animation so much more believable.

Animation truly is a matter of fooling the user! To prove this, imagine an animation with no tweening but with anticipation and overkill. Say that Frame 1 has a circle at the bottom of the Stage. Frame 10 has a keyframe where the circle is squashed. In Frame 11, a normal circle is moved halfway up the Stage. By Frame 12, it's stretched and past its destination. It's normal (or a little squashed) and a little lower in Frame 13. Finally, at Frame 14, it's in its normal shape in the destination frame—no tweening, and it looks great. Figure 22.4 shows all the frames, with Onion Skin turned on.

Simulating Depth

Despite the fact that Flash is only a two-dimensional program, you can still make the user think your movies have depth. And even though you got to see a few special effects in Hour 13 using shadows there are still more ways to fake depth as you'll see in this section.

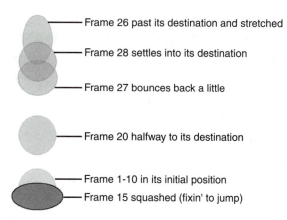

FIGURE 22.4
Just a few keyframes can make an effective animation when you use anticipation and overkill.

Frame 26 past its destination and stretched

Frame 28 settles into its destination

Frame 27 bounces back a little

Frame 20 halfway to its destination

Frame 1-10 in its initial position

Frame 15 squashed (fixin' to jump)

The main way to show depth is with perspective. Simply put, objects appear smaller when they are more distant than they do when they are nearby. When I was a child, I would get scared when I watched an airplane in which my father was traveling take off. As it got smaller and smaller in the sky, I thought my father was disappearing.

We'll look at several subtleties related to perspective, but they're all based on the fact that when you see something get smaller, you think it's moving away. In the following task you'll try to tween an object and change its size. At first it will look plain, but you'll add to it.

Try It Yourself

Add Perspective to a Simple Animation

In this task you'll add just two lines to make the perspective more apparent. Follow these steps:

1. Start by drawing a car and converting it to a Movie Clip symbol. In the keyframe in Frame 1, place the car in the bottom left of the Stage. Add a keyframe in Frame 40, and move the car to the top right of the Stage. Do a simple motion tween between the keyframes.

2. Scale the car larger in Frame 1 and smaller in Frame 40.

3. Test the movie. It probably doesn't look convincing.

4. Insert a layer and draw two converging lines as if they were the shoulders of a road. The animation looks infinitely better (see Figure 22.5).

FIGURE 22.5
The addition of
lines can help
the user see
depth.

5. To add even more evidence that the car is covering great distances, add some
   mountains or bluffs in the road layer. Draw a horizon line toward the top of
   the screen and draw a boxy mountain/bluff on the horizon (see Figure 22.6).

FIGURE 22.6
Adding a hori-
zon line and
mountain (for
scale) makes
the perception
of depth even
greater.

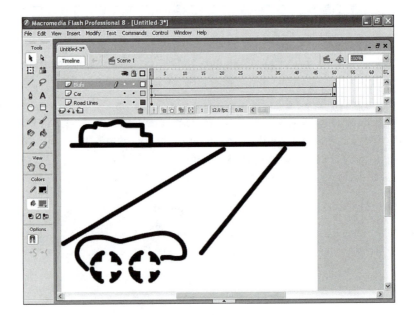

6. Without a reference, the mountain (besides not looking much like a mountain) doesn't have any perspective. Draw another mountain closer (below the horizon) and make it a little bigger. Make an even bigger mountain, partially blocking the road, on the right side. If you fill the closest mountain with white (so it blocks the road and the car), the result is even more believable (see Figure 22.7).

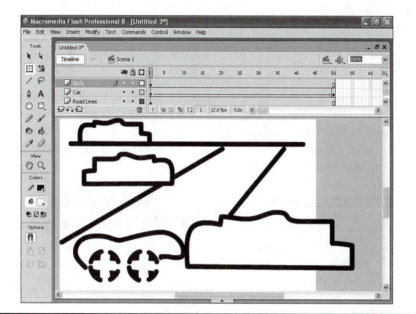

FIGURE 22.7
The repeating shape and changing size of the mountains enhance the perspective effect.

Just imagine how much more believable the previous task would be with realistic-looking graphics. As you've seen, you can use some simple clues to tell the user there is depth. The road shoulders and horizon are there mainly to explain the surface on which the car is traveling. You added mountains that vary in size according to how far away they are supposed to be. The varying-sized mountains actually repeat the converging sense of the lines. Finally, blocking the car with a big mountain leaves little question in the user's brain that the car is going behind the mountain.

You can add even more clues that the car is moving away. Not only do objects get smaller as they move away, but they make smaller and slower movements. If you set Ease to Out, the car would appear to move more slowly the farther away it goes (and that's how a car moving away appears). If you added some bumps in the road (which would have the added benefit of looking more natural), you could make the bumps smaller as the car got farther away. One way to add bumps would be to create a motion guide that gets less jagged toward the end of the car's path. Such tricks just repeat the message that things that are far away are smaller than things that are nearby.

Try another task that simulates depth. This time you'll travel with a car.

▼ **Try It Yourself**

Simulate Depth with Size, Layering, and Relative Speed

In this task you'll travel with a car and create the illusion of depth in several ways. Follow these steps:

1. Draw a rectangle that is taller than it is wide to simulate a log. Convert it into a symbol called One Log, copy it, and paste about 15 copies onto the Stage. Space them evenly so they are twice as wide as the Stage (zoom out and use the Align panel). Select them all and convert them into a movie clip called Logs (see Figure 22.8).

FIGURE 22.8
You'll be moving these logs past the Stage, so the Logs instance needs to be much wider than the Stage.

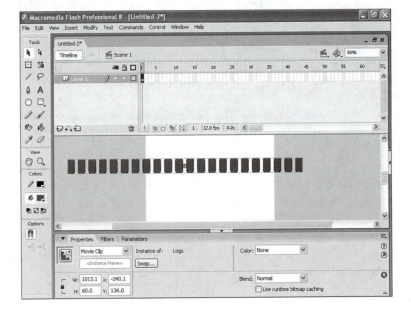

2. Position Logs so that the leftmost log is just touching the left side of the Stage. Scale it slightly larger. Copy this instance and paste it into a new layer. Position the copy similarly on the left side of the Stage, but scale this version smaller than the first and make sure it's positioned higher (as in Figure 22.9). These will be the posts for the guardrails.

▼

3. In a new layer, draw a very wide rectangle (as the guardrail). Convert it to a symbol called Guardrail and copy it into a new layer. Scale the instance in the second layer appropriately to the smaller logs. Position the two instances of Guardrail in a layer between the two layers for logs, so the smaller one is on top of the small logs and the larger is below the large logs (so that the guardrails are on the inside of the road). (Take a peek at Figure 22.9 to see how it should look.)

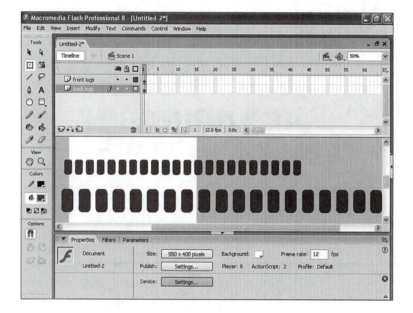

FIGURE 22.9
The two layers for the logs contain the big (close) logs and the smaller (distant) ones.

4. Insert frames for all the layers at Frame 60 (by clicking in Frame 60 and pressing F5). In the two layers with logs, insert a keyframe at Frame 60 (by clicking in Frame 60 and pressing F6). In Frame 60 of the layer with the large logs, hold Shift while you move the logs all the way to the left (so that the right-most log is just touching the right side of the Stage). For the layer with the small logs, hold Shift while you move it to the left—but it won't look like those logs are moving as far (see Figure 22.10).

5. Set motion tweening in Frame 1 of each logs layer. You don't need to tween the guardrail layers because the motion of the logs will imply that the guardrail is moving.

6. Insert another layer for a car. You can draw a car and make it a movie clip. You can even go inside the master version of the car and insert rotating wheel clips. But whatever you do, don't tween the car that's in the main Timeline. It

will remain in the same position, but the logs passing by at varying speeds will make it appear to be moving constantly to the right.

7. Test the movie. The logs that are close to the screen will appear to move faster than the smaller logs because they are closer to the viewer.

FIGURE 22.10
Don't move the smaller logs quite as far as the larger logs.

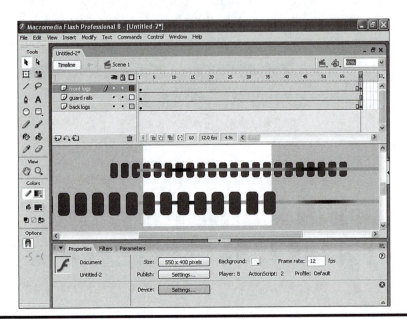

To add to this task, you can draw a mountain or other elements near the horizon. If you add trees in the background, you can have them tween to the left as well—but at a much slower rate. You probably don't need to tween the mountain at all, but if you do, only let it move a tiny bit.

Controlling Point of View

The two tasks you just did with cars involved different points of view (POV). In the first one, the view didn't change; you just saw the car move. In the second task, the view moved with the car, and the foreground and background moved. The first situation was as if a camera were stationary on a tripod as the car moved away. The second case was as if the camera were in a helicopter that was traveling at the same speed as the car. When you watch a movie or an animation, you don't often ask exactly where the camera was positioned—but it's very important.

If the camera is shaking, it gives an entirely different feeling than if it's panning slowly. When you watch a movie, try to note exactly where the director has placed the camera. Of course, in computer animation, you're not limited in physical ways but there's still always a point of view.

Next you'll try a simple task where the point of view affects the user's experience.

Try It Yourself ▼

Control Point of View for Visual Effect

In this task you'll change the point of view during an animation to imply motion. Follow these steps:

1. In a new file, draw the best-looking airplane you can. Convert it to a movie clip so you have one instance of your airplane clip. (If you want to get fancy, you can go inside the clip and add some animated frames—perhaps an animating propeller.)

2. Insert keyframes (by pressing F6) at Frames 50 and 60. In Frame 60, hold Shift while you drag the instance of your airplane to the right until it's off the screen. Set motion tweening in the keyframe at Frame 50.

3. Test the movie, and you can imagine you're filming this from another airplane that is keeping up with your airplane. At Frame 50, your plane stops. It needs something more.

4. Insert a new layer, named Background, and zoom out to 25%. In the new layer, use the Pencil tool to draw a jagged line much wider than the Stage, as in Figure 22.11. Select the line and convert it to a symbol—call it Mountains. In Frame 1 of the Background layer, position Mountains so the left side just touches the left side of the Stage.

5. Insert a keyframe in Frame 50 of Background. Move the instance of Mountains in Frame 50 all the way to the left so its right side just touches the right side of the Stage. In Frame 1 of Background, set motion tweening.

6. Test the movie.   ▼

FIGURE 22.11
Draw a horizon full of mountains, and when they're tweened, they'll make the stationary plane look like it's moving.

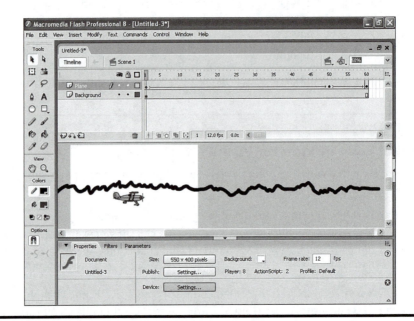

Point of view drives most animation. When you have a clear sense of where the user's point of view is (that is, where the camera is), the potential is great. You can use camera angle and camera shake—all kinds of tricks that actually become visual elements. Most visual elements are concrete and obvious. Point of view may be the most powerful because it's so subtle.

Watch a few movies and pay attention to the location of the camera. It might ruin the illusion you normally get, but it can be educational. For some really great examples of changing point of view, check out the Flash movies at www.bulbo.com.

Beginning with the End in Mind

A common approach animators take is to begin an animation or a tween at the end point. For example, if you're making a title zoom onto the Stage, create the end keyframe first, where the title is scaled and positioned in its end point. Then go back and set up the initial keyframe. It's not so much a technique as an approach.

In this hour's tasks involving anticipation and overkill, you inserted several keyframes (where the circle was not transformed) and then went back to make changes after you had the pristine end keyframes. Know where you're headed, and make plans before you arrive. This may seem vague, but it's so common that it's worth mentioning as an advanced animation technique.

Summary

This hour you saw how just a few touches can make an ordinary animation look rich and believable. Simply giving users a hint that something is about to happen (through anticipation) is enough to make sure they see your animation. Overkill adds a bit of reverberation at the end of an animation to make it more believable. This hour you also learned several ways to create depth and motion.

While some of the examples in this hour might not look advanced, with a bit of work they can become realistic. Of course, an artist can add a few finishing touches to make these exercises look great.

Q&A

Q *I want to create an effect in which the entire Stage effectively zooms really big and then I can transition into another scene. How do I zoom the Stage for the user?*

A Using the Zoom tool to zoom the Stage will only affect your workspace. What you need to do is scale everything on the Stage by using a tween. This can be difficult because you might have several layers. You can solve this a few ways. If you created everything inside one large movie clip, you can just scale an instance of that clip in the main scene. If you've already built everything in the main Timeline, you can effectively take a snapshot of the last frame and then place that inside a clip that gets scaled. To do this, go to the last frame and copy everything on the Stage from all layers at once. Insert a blank keyframe in a new layer and then paste it in place. To make sure the clip you're about to make doesn't include any nested looping movie clips, while everything is still selected, use the Properties panel to set everything to Graphic symbol set to Single Frame, 1. While everything is still selected, convert to symbol (and make this a movie clip). Then it's just a matter of inserting more frames for the tween where you scale this new clip.

Q *Are there any good resources for more animation techniques in Flash?*

A By now, you have most of the technical skills to execute anything in Flash. Studying other Flash books (there are several fine ones) probably won't help you as much as studying traditional animation. With a little refinement, you'll be able to do anything you have clearly defined. If you want some ideas, though, watch animations and movies and study the masters who came long before Flash.

Workshop

The Workshop consists of quiz questions and answers to help you solidify your understanding of the material covered in this hour. You should try to answer the questions before checking the answers.

Quiz

1. When you stretched the circle using the vertical scale, why did you also compress the horizontal scale?

    A. You can't scale a symbol in just one dimension.

    B. It seemed like it would look cool.

    C. In real life, compressing a ball in one dimension will cause it to expand in the other direction—the total volume of the ball never changes.

2. Why did you add extra reverberation to the circle during the overkill task ("Use Overkill to Make an Animation More Effective")?

    A. It seemed like it would look cool.

    B. Real balls always exhibit this behavior.

    C. You wanted the ball to act as the user expects.

3. Is it dishonest to use just a few keyframes instead of a long tween?

    A. Yes. It's not accurately demonstrating the physical movement you're animating and may open you to lawsuits.

    B. Maybe. But if the effect is a believable animation, you've succeeded.

    C. No. In real life, motion involves only two key points: the beginning and the end.

Quiz Answers

1. C. Although it might not be noticeable if you forgo this touch, you might be surprised when you can't figure out why something just doesn't look right. Take a rubber ball and push it on the ground. You'll see it get wider as you reduce its height. By the way, if while using the Transform tool you hold Alt when scaling, you can scale just one side.

2. C. Certainly you shouldn't do something just to make it look cool unless it adds to your message. A real ball might not settle in such a dramatic way, but the user understands the message, and it looks realistic.

3. B. You're not creating animations in order to show physical principles accurately, but to communicate ideas. Remember—it's the result, not how you got to it.

Exercise

Here's a great exercise that I promise will help you become a better animator. Go to the library or video store and rent some classic animated movies to study. If you have a DVD player, you can easily step frame-by-frame through key animated portions. It's really educational.

For something more specific, start with a bouncing ball animation (either a ball bouncing repeatedly or across the screen). Add an ellipse-shaped movie clip to a new layer. Make that shape behave like a shadow—literally shadowing the ball's movement. It should get bigger, darker, and sharper (via a Blur filter) as the ball gets closer, and get smaller, lighter, and blurrier as the ball goes up. Compare the results before and after adding the shadow; the differences should be striking.

Working on Large Projects and in Team Environments

What You'll Learn in This Hour:

▶ How to implement traditional production concepts, such as code–data separation

▶ How to create and use Library items for authortime sharing

▶ How to develop naming conventions and enhance your productivity by using other methods

So far in this book you've been doing all the work yourself—without any help. Although creating an entire Flash site by yourself is possible, a team with a variety of skills can usually do a better job. Instead of trying to do everything yourself, build a team in which each person can specialize. One person could create the audio, another person could design the graphics, and still another could do the programming. The roles can be divided even further. Not only does this mean your end product will be better, but you can also produce more output in a shorter time period because many people are working simultaneously.

The result of a team effort can be great. However, doing a team project well is not easy. There are countless opportunities for extra work and conflicts—technical conflicts that can cause some components of a project to simply not work. This hour, you'll study some general ways to work in a team environment and learn many Flash-specific approaches.

Production Methodologies

Great work has been produced for many years by creative people working in team environments. Although Flash websites have come about only recently, you can learn from more traditional production methodologies. Film production, for example, is not a bad model to follow. Although film is quite a different industry, it has many similarities to Flash. Even more traditional software production can seem quite different from Flash website production; however, you can still learn from the knowledge gathered in that field. This hour you'll look at a few basic concepts and apply them to Flash. These are not original ideas, but how they're applied to Flash is unique.

Defining Roles

It's very important that everyone involved in a project have clearly defined responsibilities. Not only does this prevent two people from doing the same work, but it actually prevents problems. The entire project should be analyzed as a series of tasks. Then the responsibilities should be divided up among the team members. Each team member can take on more than one task, but each task should involve only one team member. You can even change the roles during the project, but just make sure when you do that the new roles are clear to everyone involved.

Sometimes people think that the purpose of role definition is to help identify who is at fault when problems arise. This is a negative way to look at it. In a way, role definition can help identify the person at fault, but mainly it helps to solve the problem. It's too much to expect that problems can be prevented. Therefore, when one arises, having a clear idea who to address allows you to solve the problem without involving (and distracting) other team members.

Testing the System and Doing Full-Path Reviews

After you've defined roles, the next step you should take is to confirm that all aspects of the system are working. It's amazing how many problems this simple step can uncover. For example, if one person is supposed to record some narration and then send it to the animator, an actual test run should be performed. The test would involve the narrator recording some audio. (It can be anything—it will just be a placeholder.) The narrator should make sure it's recorded the same way he will record the real thing. When the animator receives it, he should try to incorporate it. Next, the team can analyze the results. If there's a problem in the process, this is a great time to find a solution. Maybe the audio engineer has emailed the files incorrectly and the animator is having trouble importing them. You'll be glad if you find a problem earlier in the process instead of later. It's almost like a dress rehearsal. Just remember that everyone must act like it's a dress rehearsal—not just a rehearsal—and do everything as they will in the real project.

By the
Way

Using Placeholders While You Work

A **placeholder** is a piece of media that is used in place of the final media. It doesn't have to be pretty or clean, just representative of the final version. For example, if you plan to have a picture of the president in your movie but the election isn't over, you don't need to wait. Just use a picture of your dog—or anything else, as long as it's the same size and placement as the final. When you receive the final picture, you can replace the placeholder.

A similar step you can take early in a project involves a **full-path review**, which is simply a prototype of the entire project, but only a certain portion of it. It's important to flesh out a "full path" (that is, it's important to go all the way down one representative path). As an analogy, imagine that you're testing the process of preparing 20 envelopes. Each one needs to be addressed, sealed, and stamped. A full-path review would involve addressing, sealing, and stamping one envelope. You wouldn't, for example, address each envelope and then try to make a judgment of your process. Instead, you would just use one envelope and take it through the entire process.

If a Flash project has four sections that each have five subpages, for example, as a full-path test you should build one section all the way through, with its five subpages, instead of building one page for each section. Be sure to select the most representative section. If necessary, use two paths. The point is that you want to go deep, not wide.

Using Code–Data Separation

The concept of code–data separation is one of the most valuable in any kind of production environment. The idea is that you try your best to keep the code (the scripting and structure) separate from the data (the unique content). The more you can separate code from data, the more you can make changes to either without affecting the other. Imagine a company whose employees install wood siding on new homes. Naturally, they don't paint the wood until after it's installed. They keep the wood (the *code*, if you will) separate from the colored paint (the data). It makes perfect sense in this case, so certainly there's a way to apply code–data separation to Flash. In fact, you already have on several occasions in this book. In Hour 19, "Linking a Movie to the Web," you used an external CSS file to define the text format. And, in Hour 20, "Designing a Website to Be Modular," you loaded external images and sound files.

Here's a specific case. Suppose you've created a very interesting tween that involves moving text from off the Stage into the middle of the Stage. The code, in this case, could be thought of as the *motion*. The data would be the actual text. In Flash, replacing the data (with no effect on the code) is quite simple. The following task demonstrates one feature that enables this type of separation. After you complete this task, you'll learn some more sophisticated techniques.

▼   **Try It Yourself**

Use the Swap Symbol Technique As Applied to Code–Data Separation

This task uses a built-in feature of Flash to demonstrate how the motion of an animation can be separated from the symbol being animated. Here are the steps to follow:

1. Create a block of text and convert it to a symbol called Holder Text. Create a motion tween. Add some easing and scale it at the first keyframe—anything to make the motion obvious.

2. Test the movie. Now, imagine that the movie is perfect for one section of your site, but you want some other text to follow the same path in another scene. Click the Layer 1 layer, which should select all the frames of this layer. Then select Edit, Timeline, Copy Frames.

3. Create a new scene by selecting Insert, Scene. Click the first frame and then select Edit, Timeline, Paste Frames. You've just copied everything about the first tween into the new scene. However, you want the duplicate frames to animate a different symbol.

4. Create another block of text (it doesn't matter exactly in which frame or layer you create it because you'll trash the instance in a minute). Select the text and convert it to a symbol named Replacement. Now delete the instance of Replacement onscreen. (Don't worry, it's safe in the Library.)

5. Swap out the Holder Text symbol. To do this, in Frame 1, select the instance of Holder Text and, in the Properties panel, click the Swap button (as shown in Figure 23.1). Clicking this button opens the Swap Symbol dialog box, which allows you to exchange the selected instance with a different symbol in your
▼   Library.

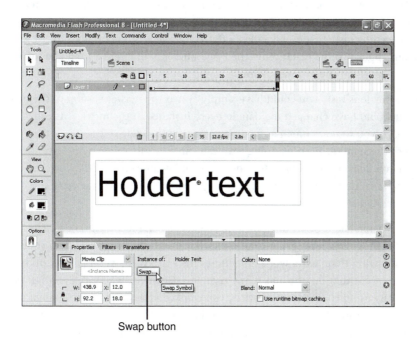

FIGURE 23.1
The Properties panel's Swap button allows you to exchange the selected instance with a different symbol in your Library.

Swap button

6. The Swap Symbol dialog box, shown in Figure 23.2, lists all the symbols in your Library and places a dot by the one currently linked to the instance you have selected. Select the Replacement symbol and then click OK. If there are instances of Holder Text in any other keyframes of your animation, you need to replace each of them the same way.

FIGURE 23.2
The Swap Symbol dialog box provides a list of all the items in the Library and a dot next to the one with which the selected instance is currently linked.

Swap Symbol provides a way to exchange the instance on the Stage with a replacement master symbol without losing any attributes of that instance. For example, in the preceding task, if you had added a tint color effect, scale, or anything, it would remain applied to the instance on the Stage; the only difference would be the master symbol to which the instance points.

In the previous task, you could have simply edited the master version of the text, which would have changed the data in every instance in the movie. Instead, the approach you took, as much as possible, separates the code of the tween from the data of the symbol. With planning, you can carry this to any extreme. Eventually, when you deliver your movie, the code and data will be connected. However, if you plan to separate these items, making changes will be easier because code and data are separated at this point.

Often when a client or art director wants to make a change, it can mean a lot of work for those involved. If you plan for such a situation, you can protect yourself against having to do extra work. Sometimes the extra work won't pay off (in the unlikely event that no one makes any changes). However, when it pays off, it pays off big. By using code–data separation, you can keep the program as modular as possible. Recall from Hour 20 that the MovieClipLoader provides a way to combine and reuse image files among many movies. For instance, your site could use a separate .jpg file containing just a background image. You can include that image (the data) in several movies via the MovieClipLoader (the code). If you need to make a change to the background, you just have one file to edit. A change there will be reflected in each movie that loads the .jpg file. Imagine the amount of work you would have to do if you had to replace the same image in 10 different movies.

Code–data separation is a great concept to keep in mind as you plan a site. Constantly ask yourself, "Can this content easily be separated from the structure?" Keeping code and data completely separated is impossible, but the more you can work in this mode, the better off you will be. Code–data separation is valuable when you're working alone, but the potential productivity is even greater when you're working in a team environment. You can take advantage of Flash's modular features (discussed in Hour 20) to apply code–data separation to team projects.

Applying Productivity Techniques

When you understand some productivity methodologies and their benefits, you need a way to apply this knowledge to Flash. For example, exactly how do you allow separate team members to work on the same project? That's what you'll learn in the remainder of this hour. You'll learn to use built-in Flash features as well as some general techniques that are not specific to Flash but are valuable nevertheless.

Using Shared Library Items

In Hour 20, you saw two ways to share Library items. Basically, one main file's Library items can be shared among many other "user" files. If a change is made to the Library file, that change is seen in all the user files. If runtime sharing is used for the Library items, visitors to your site download those items only once. You can probably imagine how the productivity of shared Library items can help in a team environment.

A common issue in website creation is that an enormous amount of work is needed to create the artwork for a site. While the principal artist comes up with the graphics, the assembly person (animator or programmer) just sits and waits. Then, when the final graphics are complete, the project must come together in an instant. Shared Library items can help by letting the assembly people use a placeholder (or *proxy*) graphic, which allows them to work even while waiting for the graphics from the principal artist. The following task walks you through a scenario so that you can get the idea.

Try It Yourself ▼

Use Shared Library Items to Start Assembling a Movie Without Final Graphics

In this task's scenario, you'll use a shared Library item in order to let the assembly people start working before the artist is finished creating the graphics. This technique is called *authortime sharing* because everything is copied into your movie upon export—before runtime. Imagine that the programmer wants to start working, but the graphic artist hasn't finished creating the graphics for the background. The artist can create placeholder graphics (really, Library symbols) that can be replaced later. Here are the steps to follow:

1. Create a new file and save it as source.fla. Draw a box around the text HOLDER. Select everything and convert it to a symbol. Name the symbol Background and select Movie Clip, but before you click OK, make sure to set the default registration point to the top left, as shown in Figure 23.3. This will make registration easy if the size needs to change (new contents in the clip will only grow—also said to "bleed"—to the right and down).

▼

FIGURE 23.3
When creating a symbol, you can select any of nine points around which the symbol will be registered.

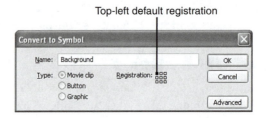

Top-left default registration

2. Select the instance of Background that is on the Stage and copy it. Start a new file (by pressing Ctrl+N) and then use Save As to save the new file with the name user.fla.

3. While in the new user.fla file, paste. Open the Library (by pressing Ctrl+L) and notice that Flash copied the Background symbol into user.fla's Library. (Make sure you're looking at the Library for user.fla; it's possible to have the Library from source.fla open as well.) Select the Background item and from the Library's options menu select Properties. (Alternatively, you can right-click—or use control+click on the Macintosh—to access the item's properties.) If the dialog box is not expanded already, expand it by clicking the Advanced button. The dialog box should look as shown in Figure 23.4.

FIGURE 23.4
A Library item's Symbol Properties dialog box can be expanded to show advanced settings that include author-time sharing options.

4. Notice in the Source section that the original `source.fla` is listed. Flash knows from where you copied this item. Select the option Always Update Before Publishing, which basically means "Recopy the original symbol (in `source.fla`) every time I test or publish this movie."

5. At this point the programmer or animator can use the Background symbol in `user.fla` as needed—as if it were the final version. Scale it, position it in the center of the screen, and then make a tween in a new layer on top of it.

6. Now, let's say you want to see what happens when the graphic artist replaces the original Background in `source.fla`. Simply open `source.fla` and edit the master version of Background. Make a clearly visual change (pretend you're the artist putting finishing touches on the image). Be sure to save `source.fla`.

7. When you return to `user.fla`, you still see the old Background. However, just use Test Movie, and you see that the new version of this symbol is copied into the file. When you're done testing the movie, you should also notice that the change remains.

The cool thing about the scenario you explored in the preceding task is that several files can use the same background. If the graphic ever changes, you just need to re-export all "user" files that use the symbol, and it will be updated automatically. In the case of Swap Symbol, you need to swap every instance used. Authortime sharing is much easier than runtime sharing, so it's more appropriate when you expect graphics will be replaced.

By the way, the *other* shared Library feature (runtime sharing) differs from author-time sharing in that with runtime sharing you would only need to re-export the `shared.fla` file instead of every user file. (Runtime sharing has other advantages and disadvantages, as discussed in Hour 20, but it's worth thinking about how this task would be different using runtime sharing.)

Using Documentation and Naming Conventions

As you build a large, complex project, documentation is important. All media elements should be clearly identified and, if necessary, an accompanying paper document should detail how everything works. Think of documentation as an instruction manual. It can be used by any team member to quickly view an entire project. If documentation is well done, someone outside the project could study it and then begin working on the project.

Not only does a clear paper trail help other team members, but even when you're working solo, documentation can help you sort through your own project if you need to revisit something you built in the past. Documentation doesn't actually need to be on paper, either. You can include notes right inside your Flash movie. For example, because Guide layers don't export with the movie, they're a great place to include notes or maybe just a quick explanation of the more complex features involved in that file. Even the process of creating documentation will help you sort out how a project works.

Specifically, a basic set of documentation includes a text description of every file used in a project. You could have a folder that, by the name you give it, explains what's contained. For example, a folder's name could be sounds. Perhaps it contains .swf files with audio that's loaded into the main movie via the MovieClipLoader. Every file dedicated to a project has a purpose—and if a file doesn't have a purpose, maybe it should be deleted or archived. You just need to explain each file.

Really great project documentation would also include a description of the process. Although something as vague as "create the animation and be very careful to make it look good" may be too general, you don't need to be really specific, either. It's a balance between being clear and being so detailed that you're creating more work for yourself than it's worth. Common sense can help you make this decision. However, realize that if you have to revisit your own work at a later time, you're going to value such documentation.

Documentation should be done during the project—not at the end. The incentive to sit down and document a project that's complete is lost because the project is done. When you reach logical milestones, you should document what you just finished. Think of it as protection. Imagine that you could be audited and you want everything in order, just in case.

One way to document as you go is by using careful, strict naming conventions. Symbol names are important because they enable you to sort Libraries alphabetically. If each team member precedes the name of the symbols he creates with his initials, you can quickly sort items based on author. You could also decide to precede symbol names with the section where a given asset is used. This is the technique that is used in the lesson file found under Window, Common Libraries, Learning Interactions (see Figure 23.5). All the assets for the DragDrop section have names that start with DD_, assets for the HotObject section start with HO_, and so on.
You can use whatever makes sense for your project; it just takes a little bit of organization.

Naming conventions are a set of rules you apply to the names that folders and files are given. You can specify a convention without specifying each filename. For example, your naming convention could specify the following: `SectionNumber_SubSection.swf`. With this convention, for example, for Section 2, Subsection 3 the name would be `2_3.swf`. This convention can accommodate any numbers that arise.

In addition to the names given to symbols in the Library, the instances used on the Stage have names, too. Instance names have little benefit for documentation, but naming conventions can still be critical. If, for example, you have three instances of a symbol named box initially, the instances don't have unique names. If you name them box_1, box_2, and box_3, you could have a script that sets properties for one box at a time. For example, the following code sets a selected box's x position to 10:

```
function move(boxNum){
  _root["box_"+boxNum]._x=10;
}
```

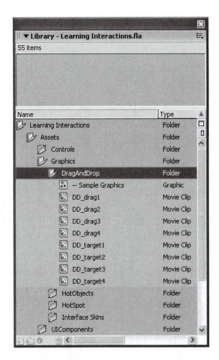

FIGURE 23.5
A Library is organized automatically when you use folders and a consistent naming convention.

Naturally, boxNum needs to be either 1, 2, or 3. "box_" + boxNum dynamically changes to box_1 if boxNum is 1. This idea brings up a lot of scripting issues that are beyond the scope of this hour, or even this book. However, you should be able to see how naming the instances in such a logical manner makes more sense than naming them boxOne, boxTwo, and boxThree because it would be harder to dynamically address any one of the instances.

Documentation and naming conventions are just good housekeeping. Even if they seem like a lot of work during a project, they can actually save a lot of time—not just when there are problems, but also when you want to make structural changes or track progress. Often you can complete a large project with no regard to documentation or naming conventions; you'll just be more be efficient in that case.

Summary

This hour you saw some general approaches to working on large files and in teams. Adapting these general tips to suit your project productivity and efficiency is a topic worth addressing in every project because time is saved; when applied to a large project, this can be even more time saved.

In addition to theories and methodologies, you learned about a few built-in features of Flash that can be applied to productivity. You used some features just as they're designed to be used—such as Swap Symbol. You learned how to tailor other features for special purposes—such as using components for templates. Often, people tend to get rolling on a project and forget the old proverb "Haste makes waste." If you take the extra time to analyze workflow issues, your project will run more smoothly.

Q&A

Q *I have a lot of symbols to swap. Is there an alternative to using the Swap Symbol feature individually on each instance in the Timeline?*

A Well, you can't select several instances and swap them all at once. However, if you are planning to replace an entire tween this way, you can take advantage of an interesting Library feature. Say the instances you want to replace are all based on a symbol called box. To quickly swap them all with another symbol called circle, first either create the circle in a new file or copy it into a new file. In the new file rename the circle symbol (the symbol, not the instance) to box. Now the new file has something called box that actually contains a circle shape. Then copy or drag box from the new file back to your original movie's Library. A Library Conflict dialog box appears, asking you whether to rename the new box or to replace the existing box. Choose to replace, and you see every instance change. Play around with this trick to fully understand it because it will replace every instance used in the entire movie.

Q *Every time I open a* `.fla` *file that my co-worker created, I see a Missing Font Warning dialog box. What does this mean and what should I do?*

A It means your co-worker created a text block (of any type—Static, Dynamic, or Input) that includes a font that you don't have installed on your machine. If you're careful never to touch any of those text blocks and if you send the file back to your co-worker when it's time to publish (or you install the font on your machine), then there's really no problem. However, if you need to edit those text blocks and you're not going to buy the font, this dialog box provides a way for you to specify (in one swoop) which font Flash should substitute for each instance. Just realize that this is an authortime issue and is unrelated to the character options for dynamic and input text.

Workshop

The Workshop consists of quiz questions and answers to help you solidify your understanding of the material covered in this hour. You should try to answer the questions before checking the answers.

Quiz

1. Which of the following is *not* a benefit of code–data separation?

    A. Bugs in the code are eliminated.

    B. Code can be reused in a new project.

    C. Artwork can be replaced without affecting the code.

2. What's a full-path review?

    A. A situation in which everyone involved in the project is present for a review

    B. A situation in which you step through the entire project once (going down each path)

    C. A situation in which one path is completely developed and reviewed

3. What happens if you click a keyframe and select Edit, Copy?

    A. Nothing. You should select Edit, Copy Frames.

    B. The onscreen contents of that layer are copied to the Clipboard.

    C. Flash will quit.

Quiz Answers

1. A. Although good code–data separation practices may tend to make fixing bugs easier, it won't have much impact by itself.

2. C. It probably doesn't hurt to have everyone present, but the idea is to simply go through one completely developed path.

3. B. You might have wanted to use Copy Frames, but simply selecting Copy will copy the selected items on the Stage (and clicking the keyframe selects everything in the layer). To copy the keyframes, select Edit, Timeline, Copy Frames.

Exercise

As a way to solidify your understanding of shared Library items, try to redo the task "Use Shared Library Items to Start Assembling a Movie Without Final Graphics"—but this time use runtime sharing instead. In the end, you'll have the Background symbol with its properties set to Export for Runtime Sharing inside a single `.swf`. Then create as many "user" files as you want; each file should contain the same Background symbol but should be set to Import for Runtime Sharing. You should keep track of file locations and names carefully.

To do this, I followed these steps, in this order:

1. I created the Background symbol in a file named `source.fla`.

2. I set the symbol's properties to Export for Runtime Sharing with the URL field set to `source.swf`.

3. I used Test Movie.

4. Finally, I copied an instance of Background from `source.fla` into as many other files as I wanted. The setting Import for Runtime Sharing was automatically set for every copy.

The cool part is that you'll be able to make changes to the source Background symbol (and re-export `source.swf`), and every user file (the `.swf` files, anyway) will reflect the change without needing to be re-exported. This is different from the task you did earlier in this hour, but doing it will help you understand the differences between runtime sharing and authortime sharing.

HOUR 24

Publishing a Creation

What You'll Learn in This Hour:

► How to use the various publish settings

► How to use templates to publish variations on the default formats

► How metadata can make your projects easier for people to find when searching the Web

► How to publish other media types, such as QuickTime videos

The final step in any Flash production is publishing. In Hour 19, "Linking a Movie to the Web," you learned the minimum steps required for publishing, but that was just in order to quickly get your movies to play in a browser. There's a lot more that the Publish feature can do. In addition to exporting a .swf file and the corresponding HTML file, you can use Publish to export other media types, such as QuickTime, plus traditional formats, such as GIF and JPG. All these formats will be discussed this hour.

How to Publish

Recall from Hour 19 that publishing is as easy as selecting File, Publish. In practice, however, you'll want to first save your files in a known folder and then step through all the publishing settings before finally publishing. The following task steps you through a scenario using Publish.

Try It Yourself

Set Up the Publish Settings and Then Publish a Movie

This task walks you through using the Publish Settings dialog box. Here are the steps to follow:

1. Either open a movie you've created in the past or create a simple animation. Make sure there's some visual change; for example, a movie clip might tween across the screen.

2. Select File, Save As and save this file in a new folder that contains no other files.

3. Select File, Publish Settings. The Publish Settings dialog box appears. Note that any changes you make in the Publish Settings dialog box will only be saved with this file. However, you can save your settings as a profile that becomes available to other files.

4. Select the Formats tab of the Publish Settings dialog box so you can specify which formats will be exported. For every format you select, an additional tab will appear (see Figure 24.1). The options in this dialog box will be covered in depth later this hour. For now, select Flash, and HTML. Notice that each file has the same name as your source file (with a different extension). You can override this setting, but leaving it is probably easiest—you can always rename files on your hard drive before you upload them. (Clicking Use Default Names restores any changes you make to the filenames.)

5. Click the Flash tab and take a quick look at the Version option. Determining which setting to choose for this option is subjective. For this task, suppose you want your movie to work for users who have the Flash Player 6 plug-in or later. Change the Version drop-down list's setting to Flash Player 6. Also, for the sake of demonstration, select Optimize for Flash Player 6 r65. The completed Flash tab is shown in Figure 24.2.

By the Way

Using User Interface Components

If you're using any of the user interface components (also known as V2 components), it's easiest to publish using Flash version 7 or greater. It turns out, you can also make these components work in Flash Player 6, but only revision 65 or later. In any event, you'll also have to select the option ActionScript version 2.0.

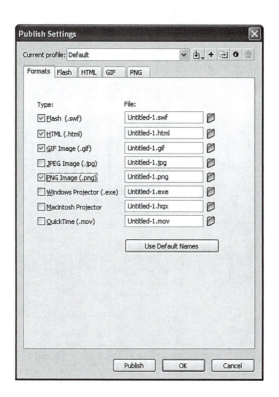

FIGURE 24.1
The Formats tab
of the Publish
Settings dialog
box allows you
to specify which
file formats you
plan to export.

6. Click the HTML tab. Here you can make some adjustments to the HTML that
Flash will create. From the Template drop-down list, select Flash Only. Next,
select the Detect Flash Version check box. The Major version is fixed at 6 (to
match what you set in the Flash tab). However, you can edit the next two
fields to read 0 and 65, respectively. The HTML generated when you publish
will have additional code to ensure visitors have at least the Flash Player
6,0,65. (In the next task, I'll show you how you can control what happens to
those visitors who don't meet this requirement.)

7. Set the Dimensions option to Percent and then type **100** in both the Width
and Height fields so the movie will entirely fill the browser window. You can
come back later and make changes to any of these settings. For now, just make
sure the check boxes Loop and Display Menu are unchecked. (Unchecking
Display Menu prevents users from seeing the extended options when right-
clicking your movie.)

FIGURE 24.2
You can ensure
that your movie
will work with
older versions
of the Flash
Player by chang-
ing the Version
setting in the
Flash tab.

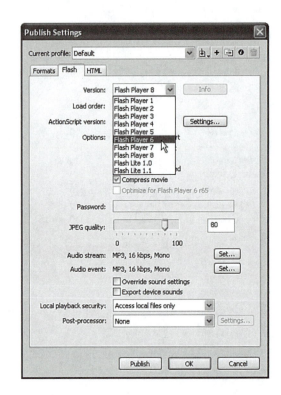

8. When you've gone through both tabs (for the two formats you selected), click OK. The publish settings are saved. Save your Flash file now, too. Select File, Publish. It might not seem like anything happens, but a .swf and the corresponding .html file are exported into the folder where the source file resides. Go into that folder and double-click the HTML file that matches your movie's name.

Using Off-Limits Features

If you are using a Flash Player 8–only feature such as Filters or Blends and you set the Publish settings to target an earlier version of the Player, those features will be turned off and grayed out. So many new features are added with each Flash Player update that sometimes you won't see that you're using an off-limit feature until you publish. For example, Flash Player 1 doesn't even support movie clips. At the time you publish, a warning dialog appears and the Output window contains complete details of the problem. In addition, all the off-limit features of the ActionScript language are highlighted in yellow, as shown in Figure 24.3.

Unsupported actions are highlighted in yellow

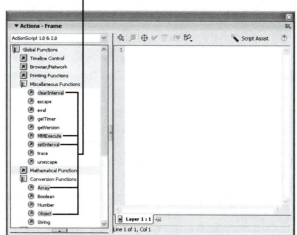

FIGURE 24.3
When you specify an older version of Flash for export, all the unavailable actions for that version are highlighted yellow.

Compared to using Test Movie, the preceding task was a lot of work. Realize, though, that when using the method described in this task, you get to step through each detail and decide how it should be published. By the way, selecting File, Publish Preview (or pressing F12) is the same as using File, Publish, except that immediately following the export process your default browser is launched with the HTML file.

The preceding task walked you through each tab of the Publish Settings dialog box, and you made changes as you went. This is the typical approach. Although you might not choose exactly the same settings in real life as you did in the task, the process is the same. After a few more details about this particular task, you'll take a look at the rest of the options later this hour. The point is that this was just an exercise. The options chosen are not necessarily the ones you'll always want to use.

Testing All Player Versions

In order to see what users with older Flash Player versions will experience, you need to uninstall the Flash Player. Macromedia has a Flash Player Uninstaller (at www.macromedia.com/shockwave/download/alternates/) plus a Tenchnote that links to an archive of the older Flash Player versions that you can install (just type **tn_14266** into the search field at www.macromedia.com).

By the Way

Ensuring Users Have the Flash Player

In the preceding task, you selected Detect Flash Version to require version 6 r65 (6,0,65). What happens to those users who don't have the required Flash Player or have an older Flash Player? Obviously, they won't see your content until they install the latest player, but you can control the exact sequence of events they experience.

Here's a detailed overview of possible scenarios:

▶ **Rely on the browser's auto-install features**—Even if you do not select Detect Flash Version from the Publish Setting's HTML tab, the generated HTML will still indicate the version you selected from the Flash tab. Normally, that's 8,0,0,0 or 7,0,0,0 or 6,0,0,0 but there's also the special case of 6,0,65,0 when you say Optimize for Flash 6 r65. In any event, this version number appears in the HTML and, by itself, means the browser will handle upgrading the user. Depending on the browser, the user will usually see one or a combination of the following: the Flash Player automatically downloads and then is installed after the user approves a security dialog box; a missing plug-in button appears that helps the user select and install the Flash player; or a box the size of your Flash movie appears but not the Flash movie (because the user doesn't have the player). Although this is not the most seamless experience, it works pretty well on most modern browsers.

▶ **Use a script in the HTML to gracefully send users to alternative content**— This relates to selecting the Detect Flash Version option (from the HTML tab in the Publish Settings dialog box). Basically, if the users don't have the correct Flash Player (or if the script can't detect it), the users see different content. By default, the published HTML says something generic like `Alternate Content, please click here to upgrade`. However, in the next task, you'll learn how to replace this with a custom message. Some custom script-sensing approaches go a step further by beginning with an all-script page and then redirecting users to another HTML page—either one with Flash content or one with alternative content (such as an upgrade prompt). Check out Macromedia's Flash Detection Kit at www.macromedia.com/go/fp_detectionkit.

▶ **Use Flash to attempt to detect the Flash version**—This approach requires that the user has some version of Flash. Using ActionScript, there are several ways to see the user's exact Flash version. Unfortunately, it gets complicated when you consider there are different ActionScript approaches for different versions of Flash. Plus, the entire approach depends on users having at least a version of Flash. I recommend using Flash itself to detect which version the user has only as a last resort—and only for checking the revision number, not the major version. For example, if you're using an esoteric feature that's supported only in version 6,0,79 (such as masking device fonts), use a different approach to check that users have Flash to begin with; then use Flash to see whether they lack the exact revision (in which case jump to a frame where you warn the user that certain features are turned off or you recommend they upgrade).

Unfortunately, all these approaches have their limits. Several security settings and user preferences wreck havoc on these technologies. For the definitive word on this subject please download and read the recently updated "Flash Detection Kit" (listed above) which goes into much more detail on all of these approaches. The kit also discusses future technologies that will make the process even easier for versions after Flash 8.

Personally, unless my client wants to use a custom script (such as one in Macromedia's Flash Detection Kit), my preference is to simply rely on the browser's auto-install features. It works for a large majority of users, most people already have Flash, and the new versions get adopted quickly (you can find statistics at www.macromedia.com/software/player_census/flashplayer). My attitude is based on the idea that I don't want to spend 90% of my time attempting to accommodate 1% of the audience. (Granted, I made up those numbers and I often don't have the same stake in a project as my clients do.) Ultimately, you can always place a link underneath the Flash content that says, "If you can't see this, click here to install Flash." That's a surefire approach, albeit a bit clunky.

The next task shows you how to edit the alternative content produced when you selected Detect Flash Version in step 6 in the task "Set Up the Publish Settings and Then Publish a Movie."

Try It Yourself ▼

Address Users Without Flash

In this task, you'll display alternative information (basically a prompt to upgrade) for users who lack the required Flash version. Follow these steps:

1. First, you can simulate what users who lack Flash Player 6,0,65,0 will experience by editing the .html file produced in the previous task. Launch a text editor such as Notepad and then open the .html file. On line 11 you should find the following script:

```
var requiredMajorVersion = 6;
```

Change the 6 to a 9, meaning you'll need Flash Player 9 (which isn't out at the time of this writing).

▼

▼

2. Save the .html file and then double-click it again to launch your browser. You should see a generic message and a link labeled Get Flash. You can edit this message, as I'll show in the next step.

3. Return to the .html file in your text editor. Basically, you'll just find the generic text and modify it. However, it appears twice—once in the string that gets written (lines 143–145) and once in the HTML that appears for those who don't even have JavaScript support (153–154). Notice the `alternateContent` variable is started on line 143 and continues (think appended) on lines 144 and 145. Completely replace lines 143–145 with the following code:

```
var alternateContent = 'We detected you need '
+ ' Macromedia Flash Player.'
+ '<A HREF=http://www.macromedia.com/go/getflash/>Click here to
➥download</A>';
```

If you know HTML, you could get fancier and include a graphic or really anything you want.

4. Completely replace lines 153 and 154 with the following code:

```
We detected you need Macromedia Flash Player.
    <A HREF="http://www.macromedia.com/go/getflash/">Click here to
    download</A>
```

5. Save the .html file and launch it one more time to test it. Finally—and this is important—be sure to go back and reset the `requiredMajorVersion` variable to 6 (like it was before step 1).

▲

Granted, the changes made in this task were pretty minor. But now you know where you can make edits to the published .html file. There's one last point about using this scripted solution: It supercedes the browser's auto-install features. For example, say the user has a browser that can unobtrusively install Flash. If this user has no Flash installed or only Flash Player 5, she'll still see the previously mentioned alternative content. Then, after visiting Macromedia's site to install Flash, she'll have to know enough to return to your site. In many ways, this scripted approach is not ideal because it gives you plenty of opportunity to explain things to the user (in the alternative content) but requires that the user take more steps. I should mention that some other scripted solutions (such as the Flash Detection Kit, mentioned earlier) automatically redirect the user, which makes it hard for her to use her back button to return to an earlier site she visited. I guess the bottom line is that each approach has its own limits.

Using Publish Templates

There are other templates available in the HTML tab. These correspond to files installed in the HTML folder inside the Configuration folder. You can add to these templates by making your own templates. It takes some knowledge of HTML, but instructions are available if you search the help panel for "Customizing HTML Publishing Templates."

You can make minor adjustments to the built-in templates rather easily, as shown in the following task.

Try It Yourself ▼

Customize a Template

In this task you'll improve on one of the built-in templates by removing the natural padding around your Flash movie. Follow these steps:

1. Find the First Run folder adjacent to your installed copy of Flash 8 (in a sub-folder called en, for English). Inside the HTML folder you'll find the templates used by the Publish Settings dialog box. The default location in Windows is C:\Program Files\Macromedia\Flash 8\en\First Run\HTML. (The en is for English; your installation might use a different two-letter language code, such as es for Espanol.)

2. Start by creating a movie that includes an animation of a clip instance of a box moving from the top-left corner of the Stage to the bottom-left corner. Use the Align panel's To Stage option or the Info panel to align the box to the edge of the Stage in both keyframes.

3. Select File, Publish Settings and choose both HTML and Flash. From the HTML tab, select the template Flash Only. (Leave Detect Flash Version unchecked.) Click OK.

4. Press F12 to use Publish Preview. Notice that the square doesn't actually reach the left edge of your browser.

5. Close the browser. Save the movie and then close Flash. Find the file called Default.html inside the HTML configuration folder (identified in step 1) and copy and paste it.

6. Rename the copied file myDefault.html and then open it in a text editor such as Notepad.

▼

▼

7. Change the very first line from this:

   ```
   $TTFlash Only (Default)
   ```

   to this:

   ```
   $TTNo Padding
   ```

   This changes the template name to No Padding. You can name it whatever you want; just be sure to retain the first three characters, $TT, when you do the renaming.

8. Change the part in the 12th line from this:

   ```
   <body bgcolor="$BG">
   ```

   to this:

   ```
   <body bgcolor="$BG" topmargin="0" leftmargin="0"
   marginwidth="0" marginheight="0">
   ```

   This changes all the margins to 0 pixels wide.

9. Save and close this file. Restart Flash and open the movie you created earlier in this task.

10. Select File, Publish Settings. From the Template drop-down list on the HTML tab select the template you just created: No Padding. Click OK.

11. Press F12, and you should see a preview—this time, with no padding around the movie.

▲

You can make more significant changes to the templates than shown in the preceding task. In addition, there are many other places where Flash allows customization to the Actions panel and pre-installed templates through the First Run configuration folder. It's worth snooping through and reading the help files on this topic.

Adding Metadata to Your Flash Creation

There are two primary ways you can expose your Flash creations to search engines: You can add keywords into the .html file's comments or add a title and description to the .swf file. The first (metadata in the HTML) has been around for a while, and every search engine should be reading this data already. That is, while search engines are continually crawling the Web, they pick up words that you place in the .html. You can insert keywords you think apply to your content, and search engines will point to your page. You can increase the likelihood your page will get linked to by studying search engine optimization (SEO) techniques. In addition to stuffing keywords into your .html, Flash 8 does not support embedding metadata in the form of a title and description. Search engines are just beginning to extract these two elements from a .swf. (In fact, users can already search the contents of .swf files by adding the text filetype:swf to the end of their search, but this isn't very useful because it includes everything in the .swf—not just keywords.) You should follow a couple standard guidelines for what to put into the title and description. Specifically, put a clear and concise name into the title and a detailed overview into the description.

Try It Yourself ▼

Add Metadata for Search Engine Optimization

In this task, you'll embed both keywords into the .html and metadata into the .swf itself. Here are the steps:

1. Create a new movie and place the text **click me** onstage. With the text selected, open the Properties panel and make sure the text is set to Static. Also, fill in the URL link field with a URL of your choice, say http://www. phillipkerman.com. Save the .fla in a known location.

2. Select File, Publish and click the Formats tab. Select the check boxes next to Flash and HTML. From the HTML tab, ensure the Detect Flash Version is not selected. (The additional script just makes it harder to edit the .html file—you can still add metadata when detecting the Flash version.)

3. Select Publish and then use a text editor to open the .html file. Notice the following comment, starting on line 9 (comments are separated by <!-- and -->):

```
<!--url's used in the movie-->
<!--text used in the movie-->
```

4. Flash inserts another comment right after this that includes, in HTML format, the click me text and the corresponding link. Provided the search engine looks at comments, it will digest this as if the text and link were regular HTML (not hidden inside the .swf). You're welcome to modify or add to these comments. Just remember that each comment needs to begin with <!-- and end with -->.

5. Because some search engines won't bother reading (and then indexing) your comments, you need to go a step further. Return to your Flash file and select Modify, Document. Fill in the Title field with **Phillip Kerman's Best**

▼

Animation and the Description with **A riveting and entertaining Macromedia Flash animation created by Phillip Kerman, author of Sams Teach Yourself Flash 8 in 24 Hours and other books**. Obviously, you can use any text you want, but the main idea is you want a short title and complete description.

6. Click OK in the Document Properties dialog and select File, Publish again. You won't notice anything new in the .html file, but it effectively has two new lines in the HEAD section. Like I say, it's not really in the .html but rather in the .swf, but if it were in the .html it would look like this:

```
<meta name="title" content="Phillip Kerman's Best...">
<meta name="description" content="A riveting and entertaining...">
```

At this point you can upload your files (as you learned in Hour 19) then sit back and wait for the world to beat a path to your site. I'm half joking because, like I said earlier, there are other general search engine optimizations that you might want to employ. At this point, however, you've done what you can with Flash: injected comments into the .html and metadata into the .swf.

Deciding Which Media Types to Publish

Comparing the different media types available in the Publish Settings dialog box's Formats tab is really a case of comparing apples to oranges. You can export a JPG image or you can export a QuickTime movie. The former is a static image, and the latter is a digital video. This encompasses quite a range of options, making a comparison difficult. The only two media types comparable to GIF are JPG and PNG because they are both static image types. Therefore, instead of comparing the media types, the following sections cover each individually.

Publishing Flash (.swf) Files

.swf is the format you'll likely choose every time. It's the reason you're reading this book—to make scalable vector animations that play well over the Internet. If there's one disadvantage to using this option, it would be the fact that a few potential users don't have the required (but free) Flash Player.

You'll find some interesting options in the Flash tab (see Figure 24.4) of the Publish Settings dialog box:

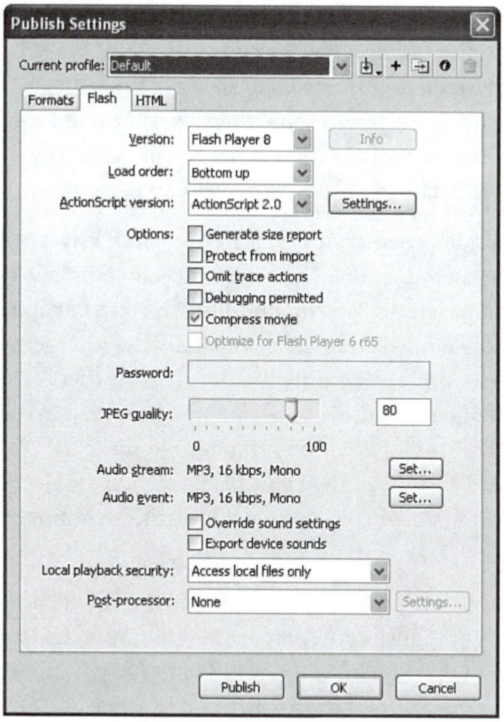

FIGURE 24.4
The Flash tab of the Publish Settings dialog box contains all the export settings for the .swf file you're publishing.

▶ Load Order affects in what order the layers appear as the movie downloads. Bottom Up, for example, causes the lower layers to become visible first. In reality, many users won't notice a difference with different load orders because they affect just the first frame and become apparent only on slow connections.

▶ Generate Size Report exports a text file that contains the same information you learn when using the Bandwidth Profiler, as discussed in Hour 21, "Optimizing a Flash Site." You should recall that when you're testing a movie that includes the Trace action (as you did in Hour 16, "Using ActionScript for Advanced Interactivity"), the output window appears with a message parameter that you provide. Omitting Trace actions won't make any difference if you play the movie in a web browser because Trace has no effect in a browser. The output window will only pop up while you're authoring, so, really, this is more of an authoring preference than a publishing setting.

▶ The Protect from Import option prevents others from importing the .swf file into their own Flash files. Keep in mind that the .swf file you post on your website does download to every user's machine (in a folder such as Temporary

Internet Files in the Windows folder, for example). In my opinion, the Protect from Import option has limited value. First, when someone imports a .swf file, each frame is imported as a separate keyframe. No ActionScript is retained. Second, just because some users import your file doesn't mean they're allowed to use it. Realize, too, that your .swf is by no means hack-proof. Sensitive data such as passwords should never reside in a movie.

▶ The Local playback security option is new to Flash Player 8. It applies only to .swf files that users download and run on their desktops—that is, not .swf files posted on a website. When publishing to Flash 8, you have to choose between making a movie that can access only the Internet or only local files (not both). Note this applies only to .swf files the user runs in the Flash Player 8. Also, if you want to make an application that accesses both the Internet and the user's hard drive, you need to make a Projector (which is an .exe), as described later in this hour in the section "Projectors." (You'll find more information about configuring your work environment to deal with this issue in the Flash 8 Security section of Hour 19.)

▶ The Compress Movie option is a no-brainer: You should always leave it checked. This compression/decompression routine was added to Flash to reduce the size of .swf files. It has nothing to do with the quality settings on your raster graphics or sounds (as discussed in Hours 3, "Importing Graphics into Flash," 10, "Including Sound in Animations," and 21, "Optimizing a Flash Site"). Basically, everything else, including your scripts, can be compressed (and then seamlessly decompressed on the user's machine). The Compress Movie option is available only when you publish as Flash 6 or later because older Flash players can't decompress these movies.

The default compression for the raster graphics and audio can be globally specified in the Flash tab of the Publish Settings dialog box (as discussed in Hours 21 and 10, respectively). You can override compression settings made for individual sounds if you check the Override Sound Settings option.

Finally, unlike most publishing settings, which are chosen as the last step, the choice of which version of Flash to export is one you should make early in a project. First of all, you can export Flash version 8, and your movie might play fine in the Flash 7 player; however, any new (previously unsupported) features will fail to execute and lead to unpredictable results. If you're not taking advantage of any Flash 8–only features, your movie will play fine. If you change this setting to, say, Flash 5 and simply use Test Movie, you'll see a report of any unsupported features you've included. This feature is nice because it enables you to fix these problems. However, instead of fixing problems after they're created, you can set the Flash Version option as the first step in a project. This way, as you build, all the unsupported actions will appear in yellow (refer to Figure 24.3).

Publishing HTML Files

Although the HTML tab of the Publish Settings dialog box has been discussed several times already, there's additional information in it that you'll find valuable (see Figure 24.5). First, realize that every setting in this tab (except for Device Fonts) affects only the HTML file. You can always open the HTML file in a text editor and make edits manually. If nothing else, the Publish Settings dialog box gives you a way to learn all the HTML settings that are available. To learn them, all you need to do is look at the corresponding HTML files created.

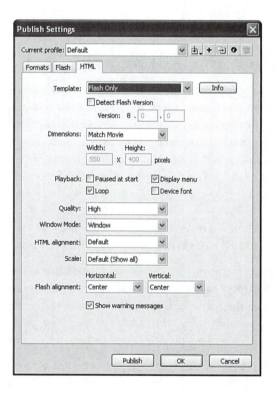

FIGURE 24.5
The HTML tab of the Publish Settings dialog box contains a number of options, including which HTML template you want to use.

Normally, users can right-click your movie to display a menu like the one shown in Figure 24.6 (on the Macintosh, they would use control+click). Only a minimized version of this menu will appear for users if you deselect Display Menu in the Playback section of the HTML tab. The menu isn't actually removed; it's just a lot shorter than usual. Keep in mind that the Debugger line appears only for users who happen to have Flash installed.

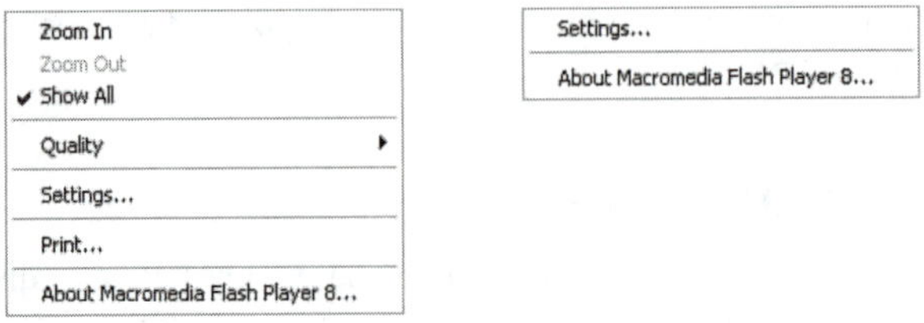

FIGURE 24.6
The menu that
appears when a
user right-clicks
your movie, as
shown on the
left, can be
reduced to the
version on the
right.

Zoom In	
Zoom Out	
✔ Show All	
Quality	▸
Settings...	
Print...	
About Macromedia Flash Player 8...	

| Settings... |
| About Macromedia Flash Player 8... |

The Windows Mode setting applies only to movies viewed in Windows and through Internet Explorer version 4 or later. Although this applies to a large audience, it is limited. Also, the other settings in this drop-down list—Opaque Windowless and Transparent Windowless—affect only HTML pages that have elements in layers. As if this weren't enough, the performance drops for these options. Feel free to explore these options, but I recommend leaving the default, Window.

Publishing GIF, JPG, and PNG Files

JPG and PNG are both static image formats. GIF has a sister format called *animated GIF* that is, in fact, an animation format. All three of these formats have their own unique attributes. GIF files always have 256 or fewer discrete colors and tend to be most appropriate for geometric images. JPG is best for photographic or continuous-tone images. JPG can also withstand significant compression with acceptable quality loss. PNG is a high-quality image format that allows for additional types of information to be included. For example, a PNG file created in Macromedia Fireworks has additional options, such as layers and shadow effects. Despite some discussion in the past, PNG hasn't become a web standard. However, when you want to export the best-quality image, PNG is a good choice—just don't expect a small file size.

When it comes to web delivery, your decision for static images is between JPG and GIF. Realize that the question about which static format to use arises only when you attempt to deliver an alternative image to users who don't have the Flash Player. For example, every Flash project I've worked on has provided no alternative. The users need the Flash Player; otherwise, they can't see the site—it's that simple.

When you want to provide an alternative to users who don't have the Flash Player (as you did in the task "Addressing Users Without Flash"), you need to decide between JPG and GIF. This decision is based on the nature of the image. Remember, though, that it's not the whole movie that's used; it's only one frame of the movie that you get to use for such static formats. Flash will, by default, use the first frame of your movie for any static image format. The movie's first frame, though, could be entirely black. In order to specify a different frame, you simply open the Frame panel and create a label in the chosen frame called #static. It's best to insert a new layer and then a keyframe exactly where you want this label, as shown in Figure 24.7, but this is a relatively simple way to tell Flash which frame to export.

Extra layer just for labels   Keyframe label

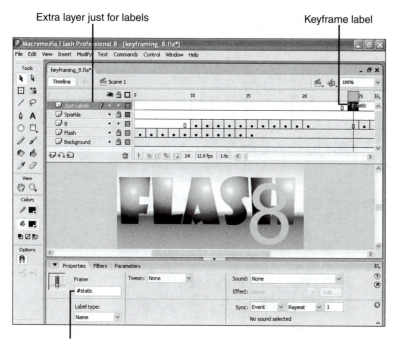

FIGURE 24.7
Labeling a frame with #static tells Flash you want this frame to be used (instead of Frame 1) when publishing a static image.

Keyframe label

After you decide which frame to use, you can decide (based on the contents of that frame) which format to use—GIF or JPG. Remember, photorealistic images are best in JPG format, and geometric shapes are best in GIF format.

PNG might seem like a useless format because the files are large and browsers don't really support them, but there is some value. Of course PNG is a great image format to import, as you saw in Hour 3, but here we're talking about exporting. If you want to export the highest quality possible, you should use PNG. There might be several reasons to do this. For instance, even though the options available for exporting a GIF file from Flash are extensive, previewing the effects of every slight change is a tedious process of trial and error. You have to make a change, publish, and then view the results. Frankly, there are better tools for creating GIF files (as well as JPG files, although this is not quite as obvious). Macromedia Fireworks, for example, lets you change all the output options for a GIF file while watching the image quality change (see Figure 24.8). This fact alone might make the extra steps you're about to learn worth the effort. For the most control over the GIF file you're creating, first use Flash to export a 24-bit PNG file (the export options for PNG are shown in

Figure 24.9). Then open that PNG file in another image-editing tool (such as Fireworks) and export the GIF file. You can still use Flash's Publish feature to create the GIF and HTML files—but you simply replace the GIF file Flash creates with one you create using a more suitable tool.

Preview of the exported image   JPG compression settings

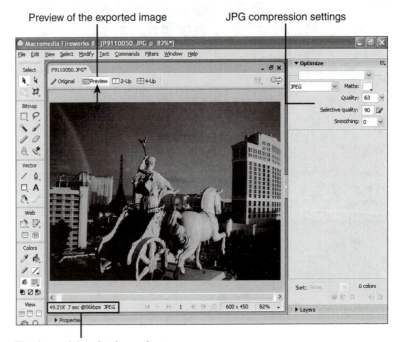

FIGURE 24.8
Fireworks is a much better tool than Flash for creating static graphics (such as JPGs).

File size and download speed

The choice between JPG and GIF might be moot if you want to supply animation to users who don't have the Flash Player. Only GIF has the Animated Playback option (see Figure 24.10). You have several options when creating an animated GIF. Most are self-explanatory. You won't notice, however, an option to specify the first and last frames—Flash will simply use the first and last frames of your movie. To override this, just label the frame you want to be used first as #first and the last frame as #last. Also, recall from a previous task that you can let Flash create the HTML image map to be used with your static (or animated) GIF. Flash will create that image map (with all the clickable areas) based on all the buttons that happen to be onscreen in the last frame of your movie. However, you might not have any buttons in the last frame. Just as you can specify which frame is used for static images, you can specify for which frame you want the onscreen buttons to be used in the creation of the image map. Simply label the frame #map. That's it.

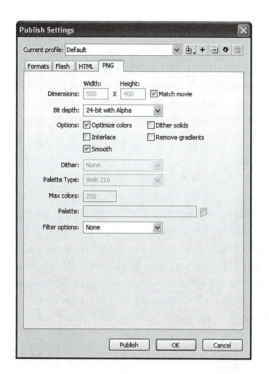

FIGURE 24.9
Exporting a PNG file gives you the best-quality static image.

FIGURE 24.10
Of all the traditionally static image formats, only GIF provides the Animated option.

Projectors

If you put your `.swf` file in a web page, users just need the Flash Player to view it. When you installed Flash, it installed the Flash Player, so you can simply double-click any `.swf` file on your computer and it will run. If you want to send this file to someone (that is, you don't want to publish it in a web page), you can. The only catch is that the user has to have the Flash Player installed.

Alternatively, you can create a projector, which is a standalone executable. Think of a projector as a modified version of the Flash Player that will play only the `.swf` file you specify. One way to make a standalone projector is to open a `.swf` file with the Flash Player (just double-click a `.swf` file on your computer). Select File, Create a Projector and then name the file you would like to create. That's all there is to it. One catch is that your `.swf` file grows by nearly 1MB when you convert it to a projector. That's the size of the Flash Player (which you're including in the projector). The other catch is that the projector you just made will run only on the platform you're using (Windows or Macintosh). `.swf` files work on any platform because the user already has the Flash Player unique to that platform installed. Because projectors have the platform-specific player built in, they can be played only on that platform.

To create a projector for whichever platform you're not using—Windows or Macintosh—you could repeat the steps just listed on a computer using the target platform. However, you don't have to do this. From the Formats tab of the Publish Settings dialog box, you can specify for which platforms you want the projector made (see Figure 24.11). The projector file that Flash creates can be sent to whomever you want. If you're sending a file from Windows to Macintosh, Flash saves the projector in a compressed and "bin-hexed" format. Bin-hexing is necessary to allow you to send the file to a Macintosh computer via email (or another method). The Macintosh user must decode the bin-hexed file by using software such as Aladdin System's freeware StuffIt Expander for Mac (available at www.aladdinsys.com).

Projectors provide a nice way to use Flash for standalone applications. For example, you might be making a presentation to an audience and want to use Flash to create the "slides." Obviously, you can add a lot of spice to your presentations. The action `fscommand` is designed for this purpose. The parameters for `fscommand` include `fullscreen`, `quit`, and many others. For example, you can put the action `fscommand ("fullscreen", "true")` in the very first frame to make your projector fill the screen. Then, in the last frame, you can place a button with the action `fscommand ("quit")` as a way to exit.

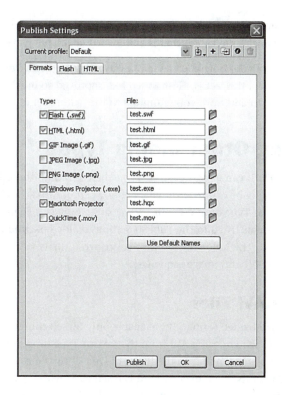

FIGURE 24.11
Standalone projectors can be exported when you publish for both Macintosh and Windows.

Although it is more difficult to distribute projectors than to simply post to a website, projectors work great for presentations. A lot of people create portfolios of their work that they distribute via CD-ROM. They can include lots of uncompressed audio and high-quality images, for example, and there are no download issues. Just remember that if you use the `fullscreen` option of `fscommand`, you need to give your users an obvious Quit button, too.

Better Projectors

If you're using a lot of projectors or just want some added features, you really ought to check out the various third-party projector-making tools listed in Appendix B, "Resources." You can add really powerful features above what Flash can do by itself.

By the Way

QuickTime

You can export a QuickTime video that includes Flash. Don't confuse this with how you imported QuickTime video in Hour 18, "Using Video." There you exported a

.swf (that just happened to include video). The Publish Settings QuickTime option lets you create a QuickTime video (that requires the QuickTime player).

Although it's kind of cool how you can add a Flash "layer" (including interactivity) to a QuickTime video, the fact is, Flash video has improved so much that there's little reason to do so. In addition, you're limited to the feature set of Flash 5 or earlier.

Exporting Other Media Types

Believe it or not, Flash can export even more media types than those listed in the Publish Settings dialog box. Just select File, Export, Export Movie, and you'll see a list under the Save as Type drop-down list that's quite long (see Figure 24.12). In addition to the formats listed in the Publish Settings dialog box, you might see others that interest you. The following sections cover two formats you might find particularly useful: AVI and image sequences.

Publishing AVI Files

AVI is another digital video format. It's available only by selecting File, Export, Export Movie and then choosing AVI from the Save as Type drop-down list in the Export Movie dialog box. Similar to the limits of QuickTime I'd avoid AVI. In fact, there are so many limits when exporting AVIs (such as Movie Clips don't play—only Graphic instances) that you'll often get better results simply doing a screen capture while your .swf plays. TechSmith's Camtasia software works great for this (www.camtasia.com).

Publishing Image Sequences

Image Sequences is another option that is available only in the Export Movie dialog box. A bitmap sequence, for example, will export a static BMP file of each frame in your movie. Several sequence formats are available (refer to Figure 24.12). They're all basically the same—only the file format varies. The process is the same for each format. You select File, Export, Export Movie, select the file format from the Export Movie dialog box, and then name the file. The name you give will be used only as the prefix. For example, if you name the file myMovie, the filename containing Frame 1 will be called myMovie0001.bmp (or whatever file extension matches the type you're exporting). After you name the file and click Save, you'll be shown a dialog box in which you can specify the details for the selected file type. It's sort of a mini version of the Publish tab. For bitmap sequences, you have to specify details for bitmaps, for example.

FIGURE 24.12
All the formats Flash can export (including those found in the Publish Settings dialog box) are listed in the Export Movie dialog box.

You might be intending to create an animation in another software package that can import sequences of static images. For example, if you have an animated GIF-creation tool, you could import a sequence of high-quality bitmaps that Flash exported. You could also use the static images from a QuickTime video inside Flash. Because you can't actually use QuickTime video in a .swf file, you could first import a QuickTime video into Flash, export a sequence of high-quality BMP files, and then delete the QuickTime video from your Flash file and import the BMP files into Flash. What's really convenient is that the numbered BMP files that Flash created upon export will be imported sequentially and placed in separate keyframes, thus saving you what would otherwise be a painstaking task of importing many individual frames.

Similarly to exporting AVI files, when you export image sequences, you can't use movie clips (they just don't animate). Obviously, audio won't have any effect either because you're exporting images only. This might seem like the least likely use for Flash; however, you should realize that any time you see something that *looks* like video in Flash, you're probably just watching a sequence of static images.

Summary

This hour discussed all the common ways to export Flash movies. Other, less traditional, applications, such as using projectors, static images, QuickTime video, and image sequences, were also discussed.

For the traditional .swf in HTML option, Publish gives you a nice interface to select options; then Flash actually creates the files for you. Templates can include code to optionally supply users with an alternative image. Also, other options in the Publish Settings dialog box let you specify how such an image will be exported.

Less-traditional applications, such as using projectors and QuickTime video, can give your Flash movies a life beyond the normal web page application. Some of these technologies are on the edge of innovation, and now you have a better idea where you can take Flash!

Q&A

Q *I'm working with people who have HTML experience, and we're including Flash within some very sophisticated HTML pages. Is it necessary for the HTML people to make customized templates for this project?*

A No. It's probably not worth creating a template unless you plan to use it a lot. You can simply export a .swf file and send it to your HTML people, and they can embed it into the web pages. You could even send them a sample HTML file that Flash's Publish feature created so they can dissect it. Quite often, the HTML will be worked out long before the Flash portion is done. The Flash movie you're making could already have a space waiting in a larger web page. Instead of using Publish (which could overwrite an HTML file), you can just use File, Export Movie and export the .swf file. Even faster, if you've set your publishing settings for Flash the way you want, you can just run Test Movie, and a .swf file will be exported.

Q *Now that I know how to publish, I know everything about Flash, right?*

A Not quite. I think it's fair to say that you have the foundation skills to use Flash effectively. This book isn't exhaustive, although you might be exhausted. You now need to go out and get your hands dirty. You can revisit this book if necessary, but this is the point where you *start* your Flash career, not retire from it.

Q *I feel like I've learned a lot in the last 24 one-hour chapters, but what if I have trouble with one of the topics? What's your phone number?*

A First, you're welcome to email me at flash8@phillipkerman.com. In fact, if you find a particular part of the book that was confusing or a task that didn't work, you're probably not the only one, so please do bring it to my attention. I will try to reply to your email and I'll be sure to tell you whether I find any of your requests beyond the call of duty. But, really, don't feel like you're imposing.

Workshop

The Workshop consists of quiz questions and answers to help you solidify your understanding of the material covered in this hour. You should try to answer the questions before checking the answers.

Quiz

1. What's the best image format for static images?

    A. JPG.

    B. GIF.

    C. It depends.

2. What happens to users who don't have the Flash Player when they visit your site?

    A. Their machine crashes.

    B. It depends on a variety of factors.

    C. The Flash Player is automatically installed and, with the exception of a short delay for downloading, users always experience the site as you intended.

3. Are all the formats that Flash can export visible under the Publish Settings dialog box's Formats tab?

    A. Yes. This is where you specify details for such exported files.

    B. No. Flash will export other types of files. However, you can't control the export details, so they're not listed here.

    C. No. Flash can export other file types than what's listed in the Export Movie dialog box (and from the Export Image dialog box, too).

Quiz Answers

1. C. The best quality and smallest file size depends on the nature of the image. Photographic images usually look best in JPG format, and geometric images are better in GIF format. The best way to compare is to test each (and compare file sizes as well).

2. B. Only if the user has a pretty new browser will he upgrade automatically (provided that you use the HTML contained in the appropriate template).

3. C. Other export file types are available. The ones in the Publish Settings dialog box are, generally, just the web formats.

Exercise

Publish your best work to date to your website. Send the link to me in an email message addressed to flash8@phillipkerman.com. I'll thank you for reading the book and provide you with some feedback.

PART V

Appendixes

APPENDIX A

Shapes You Can Make in Merge Drawing Mode

Flash 8 added a drawing mode called Object Drawing that you learned about earlier in the book. This appendix shows you how you can create several shapes by using the *other* draw mode called Merge. These are just a few examples of how you can sharpen your drawing skills. They are not necessarily the only ways to achieve the desired results.

When you're in Merge drawing mode (that is, not Object Drawing mode) Flash has some very unique drawing capabilities including selection (anything you can see, you can select), the Snap to Objects option, grouping, and shapes that eat away at one another because they're all in the same level. These are all discussed in Hour 2, "Drawing and Painting Original Art in Flash," and Hour 5, "Applied Layout Techniques." You'll now explore these capabilities further by using them in practice. Before you get started, be sure to have Snap to Objects turned on (via View, Snapping), Object Drawing turned off (unclick the button in the options area for any draw tool such as the Oval tool), and select a different color for fill than for stroke.

Semicircle

Follow these steps to make a semicircle:

1. Make sure that Snap to Objects is turned on and draw a circle. Also draw a vertical line that is much taller than the circle.

FIGURE A.1

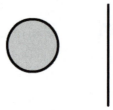

2. Double-click the center of the circle to select the line and the fill and then click and drag from the center of the circle so that you get the solid ring near your cursor. Snap the center of the circle to the line.

FIGURE A.2

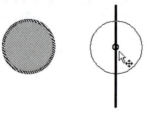

Your drawing should now look like the following figure:

FIGURE A.3

3. Click to select just the vertical line at the bottom. Using the arrow keys, nudge the vertical line up.

FIGURE A.4

4. Click away from the line to deselect it. With the Selection tool, bring your cursor near the top of the line you just moved until you see the cursor type that indicates you'll be dragging the end point. Click and start dragging.

FIGURE A.5

5. Don't snap the end point to the circle. Snap it to the end of the line, on top.

FIGURE A.6

6. Click one semicircle to select it. Then delete the fill.

FIGURE A.7

7. Click and delete the line portion that corresponds to the fill you just deleted.

FIGURE A.8

8. Click and delete the excess portions of the line.

FIGURE A.9

You now have a semicircle!

FIGURE A.10

Spokes on a Wheel

Follow these steps to make spokes on a wheel:

1. Follow the first five steps in the preceding section so you have a shape that looks like the following:

FIGURE A.11

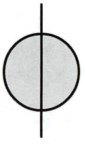

2. Click and delete the fills and the extraneous outside lines.

3. Select just the vertical line.

4. Open the Transform panel (by pressing Ctrl+T) and type **12** into the Rotate field.

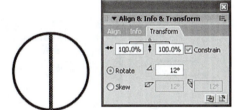

5. Press the "Copy and apply transform" button at the bottom right of the panel.

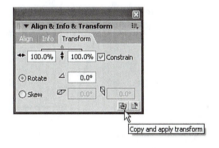

6. Continue to press that button as many times as needed to complete the circle.

Five-Pointed Star

Follow these steps to make a five-pointed star:

1. Draw a perfectly horizontal line. Then copy and paste it.

2. You'll first make a pentagon (which has five sides). To begin, with the duplicate line selected, use the Transform panel to rotate the line 72 degrees. You can figure the inside angle of any shape by dividing 360 (degrees) by the number of lines in the shape. In the case of a pentagon, each inside angle is 72 degrees because 360/5 = 72.

3. Select the line. Then click and drag the end of the line so that it snaps to the end of the first line.

4. Duplicate the new line.

5. Rotate the new duplicate line by 72 degrees and snap it as you did before.

6. Repeat steps 3–5 to make a pentagon.

7. Draw a line inside the pentagon that doesn't touch any edges.

8. Grab one end point of the new line and snap it to the bottom-left corner of the pentagon.

9. Grab the other end point and snap it to the top corner of the pentagon.

10. Draw another line in the larger area of the pentagon and connect it to the bottom-right and top corners of the pentagon.

FIGURE A.24

11. After you connect this new line, draw a small line in the space shown in the following figure and snap one end point to the bottom-right corner of the pentagon.

FIGURE A.25

12. In one motion, drag the other end point to the middle-left corner of the pentagon. If you drag this line partway and stop, it will break where it crosses the other line.

FIGURE A.26

13. Draw another line in the space shown in the following figure.

FIGURE A.27

14. Snap the ends of the new line to the middle-left and middle-right corners of the pentagon. As in step 12, if you drag the line partway and stop before snapping it to the corner, the line will break.

15. Draw the last line in the space shown in the following figure:

16. Snap this new line to the middle-right and bottom-left corners of the pentagon.

17. Remove excess lines.

Oblique Cube

Follow these steps to make an oblique cube:

1. Draw a square. Then delete the fill and duplicate the square.

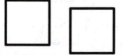

2. Move one box on top of the other, positioning it above and to the right of the other box.

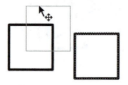

3. Draw four short lines that don't touch either box. If you find that Snap to Objects is making this step difficult, feel free to temporarily turn off this option. The lines are shown in the following figure:

4. Connect one end of one line to a corner of the rear square.

5. Connect the other end of that line to the corresponding corner of the front square.

6. Repeat steps 4–5 with the second, third, and fourth lines.

7. You can fill the panes of the cube with a gradient and use the Gradient Transform tool to fine tune the look.

Sine Waves

Follow these steps to make a sine wave:

1. Follow the first five steps in the semicircle exercise to create a circle with a line through it. This time, though, make it horizontal.

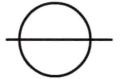

2. Click once to select the bottom half of the circle; then click and drag it away from the line.

FIGURE A.40

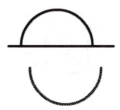

3. Remove the horizontal line.

FIGURE A.41

4. Click once to select the bottom image. Then click and drag from its left end point and snap it to the right end point of the top image.

FIGURE A.42

5. Copy and paste everything. Then select and drag to extend the cycle. Repeat this process to add as many waves as desired.

FIGURE A.43

6. When you're finished, you can scale the width or height of each wave however you want.

FIGURE A.44

3D Sphere

Follow these steps to make a 3D sphere:

1. This exercise is really easy—but the result looks cool. First, select the Oval tool (no line) and the built-in radial gradient.

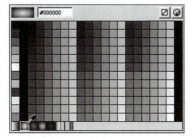

FIGURE A.45

2. Draw a circle.

FIGURE A.46

3. Select the Gradient Transform tool. If you pick up the circle handle in the center of the fill, you can move the center point of the fill up and to the left (where the imaginary light source is on your computer screen).

FIGURE A.47

4. Grab the square handle and move it to the left to change the shape of the radial gradient.

FIGURE A.48

5. Grab the bottom circle handle to rotate the shape of the gradient.

FIGURE A.49

6. Grab the circle handle that's between the rotating and shape handles to adjust the fall-off.

FIGURE A.50

7. Keep tweaking your image until you've turned the circle into a sphere. Notice that because of the arc in the fall-off, the circle has an equator.

Color Wheel

Follow these steps to make a color wheel:

1. You'll first triangle. To do this, draw a line and then duplicate it. Rotate the new line exactly 60 degrees and snap the ends of the two lines together. Now repeat this process with a third line to complete the triangle.

2. Select the entire triangle and choose Modify, Group so that it doesn't cut away from other shapes when you stack them.

3. Now, because I don't want the circles to eat away at each other yet, select the Oval tool and turn on Object Drawing. Draw a circle that's noticeably larger than the triangle.

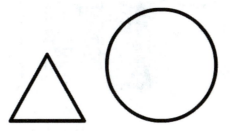

4. Use the Selection tool and select the circle; then make two copies.

5. Drag each circle by their centers and snap them to the three corners of the tri-angle.

FIGURE A.54

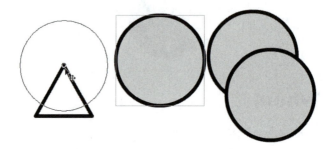

6. Select all three circles and via the Properties panel, change the fill to "no fill" (the diagonal red line).

FIGURE A.55

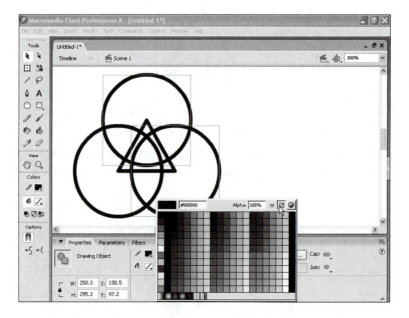

7. Next, delete the triangle. There are several ways to select the triangle so it's easy to delete: carefully click just the triangle; send all the circles to the back (Modify, Arrange, Send to Back); select all three circles and cut then paste them back after you delete the triangle; or, use the marquee technique to select just the triangle (though you may need to make sure Edit, Preferences, General "Contact-sensitive Selection and Lasso tools" is unchecked).

8. With the three circle outlines we need to turn them back into a shape to fill each segment. I prefer to just select all three and choose Modify, Break Apart. (Using Modify, Combine Shapes, Union is fine but then you'll need to enter the Drawing Object to fill each part with a unique color.)

FIGURE A.56

9. Now simply use the bucket tool and fill in the colors (Red, Green, Blue for the large parts; Cyan, Magenta, Yellow for the overlapping parts—or vice versa).

FIGURE A.57

APPENDIX B

Resources

Tutorials and Other Online Resources

You'll find that the sites listed here are great places to expand your knowledge. In addition, most have links to other similar sites.

Director Online User Group (DOUG)

www.director-online.com

Although this is targeted to the Director user, you'll find high-quality articles on many subjects, including many on Flash.

Macromedia

www.macromedia.com/support/flash/

You can't beat going straight to the source. Also, be sure to check out the Macromedia Exchange, where you can find more components (www.macromedia.com/exchange/flash) as well as the DevNet resource center (www.macromedia.com/devnet).

Moock.org

www.moock.org

Colin Moock's site includes great resources related to Flash.

Chattyfig

http://chattyfig.figleaf.com

You'll find several Flash related email listservs at this site. They're definitely the most active lists on Flash available.

Community MX

www.communitymx.com

This subscription-based educational site is dedicated to several Macromedia products.

OS Flash (Open Source Flash)

http://osflash.org

This site is rich with information on Flash including the FlashCoders Wiki.

Flash Kit

www.flashkit.com

This site offers downloadable tutorials so you can see the `.fla` source files as well as click through the tutorials. It offers sounds as well.

ActionScript.org

www.actionscript.org

This site offers lots of samples and news.

ActionScript.com

www.actionscript.com

This site has mostly news and discussion.

Flash Magazine

www.flashmagazine.com

This site provides articles and news about Flash.

FlashComponents.net

www.flashcomponents.net

This site offers tons of useful (and free) Flash components.

Studiowhiz.com

www.studiowhiz.com

This site includes more than just Flash information, and it includes general web forums.

We're Here

www.were-here.com

This is probably the most active web forum on Flash.

Ultrashock

www.ultrashock.com

This site has everything from tutorials to an active forum.

Content Sites

Generally, creating custom graphics and sounds will provide the closest match to the message you want to convey. However, plenty of sites contain clip media that you can use in your practice files.

Keep in mind that there really is "no free lunch." Some clip media that may appear free often aren't. Copyright laws are no joke either. If you are using any kind of art-work or sound in a movie that you make money creating, it's important that you pay for it. Often, the value an artist brings to a project will easily offset the cost. Sometimes the cheapest route is the one that appears most expensive.

Audio/Sound Sites

ACIDplanet.com

www.acidplanet.com

ACID is a loop-based music creation tool made by Sonic Foundry (www.sonicfoundry.com). It frequently has remix contests where you can compete by combining samples by a particular artist that Sonic Foundry provides.

Winamp

www.winamp.com

This is primarily a site with shareware software, and you'll also find clip sounds here.

Wavcentral

www.wavcentral.com

This site offers WAV files and much more. It's a good place to find sound (WAV only) as well as miscellaneous effects.

Images/Photos

Clip Art

www.clip-art.com

This site offers a variety of cartoon-style bitmap clip art. It also offers tutorials on image optimization as well as free downloads.

Clip Art Connection

www.clipartconnection.com

This is a site for free clip art.

GettyOne

www.gettyone.com

GettyOne is an umbrella site that offers a host of sites from high-end (expensive) to low-end (cheap) image options. It's a powerful resource, but you can't legally get free images. Images are divided into royalty-free and licensed images. Keep in mind that royalty-free is not actually free—it means that you pay only once; in contrast, with a licensed image, you have to pay every time you use it.

Photodisc

http://photodisc.com

A site that is accessible from GettyOne, Photodisc is a searchable site that offers low-cost, low-resolution files.

istockphoto

http://istockphoto.com

The prices on this site seem very reasonable, and it's a very easy site to use.

Fonts and Miscellaneous

Emigre

www.emigre.com

Emigre is a great source for fonts. Keep in mind that they're not free.

Miniml

www.miniml.com

Here you'll find bitmap fonts that look great at small sizes. Make sure that you follow the directions explicitly; otherwise, you'll get antialiased (blurry) looking text.

Fonts for Flash (FFF)

www.fontsforflash.com

This is another site where you'll find some great-looking small bitmap fonts.

Third-Party Products

It's unlikely that you can make a great Flash site using only Flash. Here are a few links to some of the most popular and powerful software tools that can enhance Flash. I've tested all these, but there are many others I haven't listed here.

ActionScript Viewer

http://buraks.com/asv/

ActionScript viewer lets you view and recover elements contained in a `.swf`. It's a great product that includes some invaluable plugins such as the Shared Object Viewer. You'll also find a Flash video captioning tool, Captionate, at buraks.com.

Swift 3D

www.swift3d.com

Swift 3D is a full-blown 3D modeling, animation, and rendering product. The primary focus is to let you create .swf stills and animations with 3D that you can import into Flash. This site also has supporting tools for some other popular 3D creation tools.

Toon Boom Studio

www.toonboomstudio.com

Toon Boom Studio has its roots in conventional cell animation. Unique features include color styles (where you can replace all uses of a particular color), rotating the Stage to help you draw (as in real life), and camera movements to simulate 3D. Plus, Flash can import source Toon Boom Studio work files.

Wildform

www.wildform.com

Wildform makes a really nice tool called Wild FX that helps you create sophisticated text animations automatically. It also has a Flash video encoder called Flix Pro that was sold to On2 (the makers of the new Flash video codec). See http://flix.on2.com/cart/store.php.

SWF Studio

www.northcode.com

This Windows-only product adds powerful functionality to standalone projectors created in Flash. For example, you can create files on the user's machine to save bookmarks.

Flash Studio Pro

www.multidmedia.com

This is another product that adds features to projectors. The company also makes other Flash tools, such as FlashCast for desktop recording.

Screenweaver

www.screenweaver.com

Screenweaver is similar to the other projector-making products. Its community site is very active.

Jugglor

www.flashjester.com

Similar to SWF Studio, this product adds features to projectors.

mProjector

www.screentime.com/software/mprojector/

This project works on Macintosh as well as Windows. Be sure to check out the Red Rubber Ball sample.

iceProjector

http://www.flashants.com

Yet another projector maker!

Zoomifyer

www.zoomify.com

There are several versions of this product, but you should definitely check out the demo. It lets you display super-high-resolution photos in a Flash movie.

Camtasia Studio

www.camtasia.com

This screen recorder (from TechSmith) outputs small and super-clear .swf movies.

Statistics

Although Flash is practically universal, it doesn't hurt to know exactly how popular it really is. This page on the Macromedia site gives a running census of how many people have the Flash and Shockwave players installed:

www.macromedia.com/software/player_census

This is especially useful if you need to report to a third party, such as a client, how compatible a Flash piece is with the general public.

Glossary

A

absolute address   An address that refers to a file or nested clip by including its full address (such as _root.clip.subclip). *See also* relative address.

ActionScript   The computer language Flash uses.

animated graphics   Moving images of any type. Often, Flash graphics and animated GIFs are image types seen on the Web.

artifact   An undesired side effect of a process such as compression.

.as file   A text file that contains just ActionScript code (used with #include or import).

AS2   Short for ActionScript 2.0; the latest version of ActionScript and the first fully object oriented programming such as class files.

aspect ratio   The ratio of height to width. Like a television or movie screen, the shape of a Flash animation remains the same, no matter its size.

authortime   The point in time when you edit a Flash movie. *See also* runtime.

B

behavior   A prewritten script that you can attach to a button, clip, or keyframe.

bitmapped graphic   *See* raster graphic.

blank keyframe   A keyframe that causes nothing to appear on the Stage. *See also* keyframe.

blend   A new feature in Flash Professional 8 that lets you apply compositing effects to symbol instances that control how much and what color of the objects underneath show through.

breakpoint A feature in the Actions panel that lets you identify a line of code that causes Flash to pause while debugging. This way you can step through your code and identify the cause of a bug.

brightness How much white is added to a color Brightness is one of the three ways to describe a color. *See also* saturation *and* hue.

button An item that a user can click to cause an action to occur.

button state A visual version of a button. For example, during clicking, the button is in its down state; when dormant, it is in its up state. When the mouse is hovered over the button, the button is in its over state.

Button symbol A symbol that is used to create interactive buttons that respond to mouse events. *See also* symbol.

C

codec Software used for turning raw video into small files. Codec is short for compressor/decompressor. That is, it compresses the video you embed into your .swf (or store as an .flv file) and then decompresses the video when the user watches it. Flash Player 8 supports On2's VP6 codec as well as the Sorenson Spark codec (which also works in Flash Player 7 and 6).

command A set of recorded steps that can be played back while you're editing a Flash file. It is similar to a macro.

component A movie clip with parameters unique to each instance. A component can include a custom user interface to populate the parameters.

concatenate To connect. ActionScript uses the plus symbol (+) to concatenate strings. If both operands surrounding the + are numbers, Flash performs addition.

coordinates Numbers signifying a place in a Cartesian plane, represented by (x,y). The top-left pixel in Flash, for instance, is (0,0) or (0x,0y).

D - E

down state A button state that occurs when the user clicks the button with the mouse.

event An occurrence for which you can trigger ActionScript. User events include `press` and `click`; more automatic events are `onLoad` and `onSoundComplete`.

export To move a file or an object from a Flash file. Often, the term is used to discuss the creation of distributable Flash files (.swf files).

expression A portion of ActionScript that can be evaluated but doesn't perform anything. For example, the expression `clip._alpha>50` has the value `true` or `false`, but it doesn't *do* anything by itself. *See also* statement.

F

.fla file   An editable Flash file.

.flv file   A Flash video file (already compressed).

Filters   A new feature in Flash Professional 8 that lets you add sophisticated visual effects (such as drop shadows) to text and symbol instances. These effects only moderately affect file size.

focus   The state of being active. Usually the last object clicked currently has focus. In Flash, a highlighted layer name indicates both which layer is active and that the Timeline has focus.

framerate   The rate, stated in frames per second (fps), at which the frames in an animation are played back for the user.

frame-by-frame animation   Animation that uses a series of keyframes, with no tweening, that creates a flipbook-like animation Flash file.

G

Graphic symbol   A type of symbol that is used for animated symbols that need to be previewed inside Flash.

grid   A system of vertical and horizontal rules that is used for precise placement of objects in a Flash file. *See also* ruler.

Guide layer   A special layer that does not export when you export a Flash file. This layer can be used to help with registration of various elements of a Flash file.

H

handles   Squares or circles that appear on objects when you transform them. For example, there's a handle to change an object's width.

hex   Short for Hexidecimal. A number system that, unlike the tradition base 10 with digits 0–9, it has 16 digits: 0–9, A,B,C,D,E,F. It's a way of describing color with only 6 digits: 2 each for RGB, as in #FF0000 for red. (Flash uses 0x instead of the standard # to indicate a hex value when it appears in ActionScript.)

hit state   The clickable area of a button.

HTML (Hypertext Markup Language) The language read by web browsers to present information on the Internet.

.html file   A Hypertext Markup Language text file, which is used to display text, graphics, and Flash movies in a web browser.

hue   The pure starting color. Hue is one of the three ways to describe a color. *See also* saturation *and* brightness.

hyperlink   Text or an object (such as an image) that can be clicked to take a user to related information, as used on the World Wide Web.

I - J

import   To bring a file or an object into a Flash file.

instance   An occurrence of a symbol on stage used from the Library. Although more than one instance can exist, only the master symbol must be saved; thus, instances help keep file sizes small. *See also* Library *and* symbol.

interface   The design with which users interact. Usually this is simply the screen the user sees.

K - L

keyframe   A frame in which you establish exactly what should appear on the Stage at a particular time.

layer   One of a stack of media in a Flash file Timeline. Layers are especially useful in animation because only one object can be tweened per layer when you're using motion tweening.

level   A stacking system for dynamically created or loaded elements. Levels only apply to graphics created with script. *See also* layer.

Library   A storage facility for all media elements used in a Flash file.

Library item   Each media element in a Library. *See also* symbol.

M

mapping   Matching a point in one frame with a point in another frame. The term *mapping* is applied to code hints in this book, but it's also a general term.

marquee   A selection technique using the Selection tool in which you start by clicking off any object and then dragging to encircle an object. The rectangle you create is sometimes called "marching ants."

Mask and Masked layers   Layer properties that always come in pairs: one for the mask and one that is masked (for example, Motion Guide and Guided). The graphical contents of the Mask layer determine which parts of the Masked layer will show through.

morph   A kind of animation that transitions one shape to another. *See also* shape tween.

Motion guide   A Guide layer that has an adjacent layer (below it) that is set to Guided. Tweened objects in the Guided layer will follow a path in the Guide layer.

motion tween   A utility to animate a single object from one frame to another, where the object's properties have changed over time. *See also* shape tween.

Movie Clip symbol A symbol that contains interactive controls, sounds, and even other movie clips. Movie clips can be placed in the Timeline of Button symbols to create animated buttons. Movie clips follow their own internal Timeline, which is independent of the main Timeline. *See also* symbol.

N - O

naming convention Any system you and your teammates use to name files and Library items consistently.

On2 VP6 The name for Flash Player 8's new codec. *See also* Sorenson Spark *and* codec.

Onion Skin tools Tools that enable you to edit one keyframe while viewing (dimly) frames that appear before or after the current frame.

over state A button state that occurs when the user passes the mouse over a button.

P

panel One of the dozen or so windows that let you set properties for a selected object onscreen. Examples include the Properties panel and the Align panel.

panning An effect that makes a sound seem to move from left to right (or right to left). Also refers to changing the camera's view, which you can simulate in Flash.

parameter Additional details that you provide when triggering certain ActionScript code. For example, stop() needs no parameters but gotoAndStop() needs to know which frame number you want to go to.

placeholder A temporary graphic that holds the place for the final artwork and that you use while waiting for the artwork to get created.

populate The process of filling data into a table.

property A characteristic that describes visual and other attributes at any give time. For example, a clip has an _alpha property, and a sound that's playing has a position property.

pseudo-code Instructions written in your own words. A good process is to start with pseudo code and then translate to real ActionScript.

Q

QuickTime A video format created by Apple. QuickTime is a common file format found on the Internet.

R

raster graphic   An image file format that contains the color information for each pixel. The file sizes of raster graphics are relatively large. Examples include `.jpg`, `.gif`, `.bmp`, `.pct`, and `.png`.

registration   The process of making sure that screen components are properly aligned (often from one frame to another). *See also* Guide layer.

relative address   An address that refers to a file or nested clip in a way that depends on the starting, or relative, location. *See also* absolute address.

rollover sound   A sound effect that plays any time a user places the cursor over a button.

ruler   A device that is used for precise measurement of objects in a Flash file. Rulers must be visible before you can create draggable guides. *See also* grid.

runtime   The point at which the user is watching a movie (as well as when you're testing the movie).

S

saturation   How deep or rich a color is. Saturation is one of the three ways to describe a color. *See also* brightness *and* hue.

scalable   The ability of an application to adapt well to more capacity.

scale   To resize as necessary.

scene   A component part of a Timeline in a Flash file.

scrub   A technique to preview an animation by dragging the red current-frame marker back and forth in the Timeline.

shape tween   A utility used to create a fluid motion between two shapes. *See also* motion tween.

Smart Clip   The old name for components. *See also* component.

Sorenson Spark   A proprietary codec technology included in earlier Flash Players (and still supported in 8). *See also* On2 VP6 *and* codec.

Stage   The large, white rectangle in the middle of the Flash workspace where a file is created. What is on the Stage is what the user will see when he or she plays your Flash file.

statement   A single line of code in a script. *See also* ActionScript *and* expression.

static graphic   A graphic with no animation or interactivity. A static graphic is the computer-image equivalent of a photograph or a painting.

.swd file   A file that is created when you select Control, Debug Movie and that can be used for remote debugging.

.swf file   A Flash file meant only for distribution. It can be watched but not edited.

symbol   A graphic, movie clip, or button that is stored in the Library. No matter how many instances of a symbol are used, it has to download only once, and changes made to the master symbol are immediately reflected in all instances already used. *See also* Button symbol; Graphic symbol; Library; Library item; *and* Movie Clip symbol.

sync   The timing between an animation and a corresponding sound. You choose sync settings in the Properties panel when a keyframe containing a sound is selected.

syntax   Rules for writing ActionScript that are rather unforgiving.

T

tile effect   A raster graphic used as the fill color in any shape you draw.

Timeline   An object on the Flash workspace that contains the sequence of frames, layers, and scenes that make up an animation.

Timeline effect   An animation effect that is produced through the application of ready-built scripts to change a movie.

trap   For a script to respond to a specific event.

tween   To have a change made between two objects. For example, you can tween to morph a solid circle into a doughnut. *See also* motion tween *and* shape tween.

U

up state   Normally, a button's default state, which occurs when the user has not clicked or passed over the button with the mouse.

URL (uniform resource locator)   A web address.

user   The person using a site or watching a movie.

V

variable   Something that stores numbers, strings, and other values so that you can access them later.

vector graphic   A graphic file that contains all the calculations to redraw an image onscreen. A vector graphic's file size remains small, and the image can be scaled to any size without any degradation to image quality. Drawings in Flash are saved as vector graphics.

W - X - Y - Z

web server   A computer that is both connected to the Internet and set up to serve pages when people type the proper address into a browser.

Index

SYMBOLS

A

How can we make this index more useful? Email us at indexes@samspublishing.com

Guide Layer (layer property), **245**
Guide Layers, **246, 255**
  off-limits areas, defining, 250-253
  registrations, 249-250
  text, placing, 253
Guides command (View menu), **253**

H

Hand tools, **11, 37-39**
hand-drawn masking transitions, **292-293**
handles, **66**
  side handles, cursor changes, 65
  square (at corners), cursor changes, 64-65
Hard Light blends, creating text highlights, **145**
Help button (Actions panel), **323**
Hex color systems, **133**
hiding
  docked panes, navigational pitfalls, 26
  layers, 246-248
  panels, 20
Hit frames, invisible buttons, **317**
Hit state of buttons, **305-307**
horizons, drawing mountains, **502**
horizontal (X) axis, **18**
house symbol, creating, **122**
HSB (hue, saturation, brightness), **115, 133**
HTML (Hypertext Markup Language), **416**
  A HREF tag, 420, 427
  and Flash, combining, 432-433

dynamic text, creating hyperlinks, 424
files
  hosting .swf file extension, 30-31
  opening in Notepad, 419
  publishing, 535-536
Flash Player updates, 526
Hex color systems, 133
OBJECT tag, 433
windows, 427-428
HTML tab (Publish Settings dialog), **523, 535**
hue (colors), **113**
hyperlinks
  creating, 341-342
    with dynamic text, 424
    with getURL Action, 420-423
  definition, 415
  movies, publishing, 420
  text, creating, 423
hypertext, Dreamweaver, **430**

I

iceProjector website, **573**
images
  bitmap images, grainy appearance, 89
  importing, 76, 79
  integrity, importing vector graphics, 79
  modular websites, 440-442
  natural-looking images via animations, 487
  points, mapping, 209
  sequences, 542-543
  websites, 570-571

implying motion (animation), **487-489**
Import command (File menu), **81-82, 88, 219, 392**
Import dialog, **75, 219**
importing
  audio, 76
  graphics
    raster graphics, 80-85, 88-91
    reasons to avoid, 74-75
    sizes, 80
    vector graphics, 75-79
  images, 76
  media, 466
  non-.jpg file extension, 85
  QuickTime videos, 392-395
  sounds to animations, 217-220
  video, supported formats, 390-392
indexHTML files, **416**
Info panel
  draggable objects, constraining, 355
  navigational pitfalls, 26-27
Ink Bottle tool, **49**
Ink Pencil Mode (Pencil tool), **42**
input text, **141-143, 461**
Insert Keyframe command (Insert menu), **168**
Insert Layer button, **243, 254**
Insert menu commands
  Convert to Symbol, 98, 123, 184, 266
  Frame, 177, 271
  Insert Keyframe, 168
  Keyframe, 159, 174, 177, 184, 230
  Layer, 22, 229, 243, 252
  New Symbol, 102, 270
  Scene, 475, 510

media
- compressing, 466
- exporting, 542
- importing, 466
- placeholders, 509
- publishing, 532

Merge Drawing mode
- 3D spheres, creating, 561-562
- color wheels, creating, 563-565
- five-pointed stars, creating, 554-557
- oblique cubes, creating, 558
- semicircles, creating, 550
- sine waves, creating, 559-560
- wheel spokes, creating, 552-553

Merge mode versus Object draw mode, 56

metadata, adding to movies, 530-531

methodologies (production), 507
- code-data separations, 509-512
- full-path reviews, 509
- project teamwork, 508
- roles, defining, 508
- system tests, 508

Miniml website, 571

Missing Font Warning dialogs, 140

Modify (never use), movie performance, 480

Modify command (Transform panel), 66

Modify menu commands
- Arrange, 123
- Break Apart, 281-284
- Convert to Symbol, 111, 124
- Curves, 207

Document, 156
Document Properties, 156
Layer, 248
Optimize, 472-474
Trace Bitmap, 89, 465

Modify Onion Markers, 174
- menu commands, 176, 472-473
- preset options, 175

modular websites, designing, 439
- external sounds, playing, 452-453
- movies/images, loading, 440-446
- shared library items, 446-451

Moock.Org website, 567

morphs, 203

motion blurs, creating, 288

Motion Guide (Path) layer and Guided (Ball) layer, 255

Motion Guide Layer (layer property), 246, 254-257

Motion Tweens
- animations, 192-194, 197
- automatically setting, 192
- blue tween frames, 207
- CCW (counterclockwise) rotation, 198
- Create Motion Tween, 190
- creating, 183-187
- CW (clockwise) rotation, 198
- fine-tuning, 192
- images, mapping points, 209
- instances, 187
  - changing properties, 189
  - Color tweening, 188-191
  - Position tweening, 188-191
  - Rotation tweening, 188-191
  - Scale tweening, 188-191

interpolated frames, 190-191, 207
keyframes, 192
- Custom Easing setting, 195-197
- Ease setting, 194
- editing, 190-191
- selecting, 199
Motion Guide Layers, 254
movie file sizes, 462
Name Tween layer, interpolated frames, 191
no-man's-land, 190
patterns, 191
red current frame markers, 190-191
rotating, 198-199
Shape Tween, 207-208
symbols, 187
Tint color style, 189
Yo-Yo animation, creating, 192-194

motion, implying (animations), 177-178, 487-489

mountains, drawing on horizons, 502

mouse events, button actions, 333

.mov files, 391

Move cursor (Gradient Transform tool), 138

Move Up/Down buttons (Behaviors panel), 340

move symbol (cursors), 60

movie clips, 99, 121
- actions, 336-339
- addressing, 343-346
- alpha settings, increasing/decreasing, 367
- animations, 265
- behavior, 266

N – O

X – Y – Z